Council Tax Handbook

15th edition

Alan Murdie

Child Poverty Action Group

Child Poverty Action Group works on behalf of the more than one in four children in the UK growing up in poverty. It does not have to be like this. We use our understanding of what causes poverty and the impact it has on children's lives to campaign for policies that will prevent and solve poverty – for good. We provide training, advice and information to make sure hard-up families get the financial support they need. We also carry out high-profile legal work to establish and protect families' rights. If you are not already supporting us, please consider making a donation, or ask for details of our membership schemes, training courses and publications.

Published by Child Poverty Action Group
30 Micawber Street, London N1 7TB
Tel: 020 7837 7979
staff@cpag.org.uk
www.cpag.org.uk

A CIP record for this book is available from the British Library

ISBN: 978 1 915324 26 9

Child Poverty Action Group is a charity registered in England and Wales (registration number 294841) and in Scotland (registration number SC039339), and is a company limited by guarantee, registered in England (registration number 1993854). VAT number: 690 808117.

Cover design by Colorido Studios
Internal design by Devious Designs
Content management system by Konnect Soft
Typeset by DLxml, a division of RefineCatch Limited, Bungay, Suffolk
Printed in the UK by CPI Group (UK) Ltd, Croydon CR0 4YY

The author

Alan Murdie LLB barrister has updated the *Council Tax Handbook* since 1998. He has a long-standing interest in local taxation and has been involved in many test cases. He is chairman of Nucleus Legal Advice in London.

Acknowledgements

Grateful thanks are due to Alexa Jenson, Daniel Norton and Rhys Stephens for checking the text of this edition, and to Martin Ward, author of the first two editions, on which this new edition is broadly based. Thanks for comments, observations and help received from staff and volunteers at Nucleus Legal Advice, various members of the Institute of Money Advisers and the staff of the library of the Honourable Society of Lincoln's Inn.

Many thanks to Nicola Johnston and CPAG's editorial team for editing and managing the production of the book, Katherine Dawson for compiling the index and to Kathleen Armstrong, Louise Heath and Claire Veryard for their careful proofreading.

The law described in this book was correct at 15 November 2025.

Contents

Abbreviations

AA	attendance allowance
ADP	adult disability payment
AFIP	armed forces independence payment
CDP	child disability payment
CTB	council tax benefit
CTR	council tax reduction
DAIP	debt advice and information package
DLA	disability living allowance
DWP	Department for Work and Pensions
ECB	Enforcement Conduct Board
ESA	employment and support allowance
FOI	freedom of information
HB	housing benefit
HMO	house in multiple occupation
HMRC	HM Revenue and Customs
ICO	Information Commissioner's Office
LGSCO	Local Government and Social Care Ombudsman
LPA	Law of Property Act 1925
LTC	Local Taxation Chamber of the First-tier Tribunal for Scotland
MHCLG	Ministry of Housing, Communities and Local Government
NI	national insurance
PADP	pension age disability payment
PC	pension credit
PHSO	Parliamentary and Health Service Ombudsman
PIP	personal independence payment
SADLA	Scottish adult disability living allowance
SMI	severely mentally impaired
SPSO	Scottish Public Services Ombudsman
SSP	statutory sick pay
UC	universal credit
VOA	Valuation Office Agency
VTE	Valuation Tribunal for England
VTW	Valuation Tribunal for Wales

Chapter 1

Overview

This chapter covers:

1. Introduction (below)
2. Administration (p2)
3. Legal background and references (p3)

1. Introduction

This *Handbook* explains council tax as it operates throughout England, Wales and Scotland. It will be helpful for taxpayers, advisers and administrators.

Council tax is a hybrid tax, combining elements of a property tax and a personal tax. It applies to domestic dwellings, which ordinarily means properties in which people live. Council tax is increasingly shaped by who lives in a dwelling and their circumstances. This *Handbook* provides a guide to the relevant rules.

Council tax was introduced on 1 April 1993 by the Local Government Finance Act 1992.[1] The scheme of the original 1992 Act was substantially altered by the Localism Act 2011 and Local Government Finance Act 2012.

The listing officer of the Valuation Office Agency or the assessor in Scotland is responsible for defining what is classed as a dwelling and assigning each one to a valuation band.[2] The valuation list includes each property's address, band and basic property information. A presumed valuation date of 1 April 1991 is used in England and Scotland for estimating bands. In Wales, the presumed date is 1 April 2003 – a revaluation is planned for 2028 and every five years after that.[3]

Council tax bills are normally calculated on the assumption that two adults live in a property. If only one adult lives there, a 25 per cent discount applies. Additional discounts may be available when other adult residents fall into specific disregarded categories – eg, they are students or severely mentally impaired. Such individuals are classed as 'disregarded for discount'.

Council tax statistics for England (September 2024)[4]

25.7 million dwellings in total

24.9 million liable for council tax

16 million pay full council tax (62.5 per cent of all dwellings)

8.8 million receive a discount, 8.4 million of these for single occupancy
120,000 pay a premium (up 57.8 per cent from 2023)
748,000 are exempt (2.9 per cent of all dwellings)
502,000 are empty
280,000 are registered as second homes

Council tax was originally designed with the expectation that the poorest households would receive full support through council tax benefit (CTB) covering up to 100 per cent of their liability. Between 1 April 1993 and 31 March 2013, central government funded a nationwide CTB system for those on low incomes or welfare benefits. On 1 April 2013, CTB was abolished and replaced by locally determined council tax reduction (CTR) schemes.

In England and Wales, each local authority sets its own CTR rules. As a result, two taxpayers with similar incomes may receive very different levels of support depending on where they live. In England, there are over 300 different support schemes, and 22 operate in Wales. All schemes must contain certain prescribed requirements, but local authorities have the flexibility to charge people under 60 a fixed percentage of the annual council tax regardless of their income. As a result, many who previously received 100 per cent CTB now pay part of their annual bill.

In Scotland, council tax support is more consistent due to nationwide regulations.

There are many differences in the way the council tax scheme operates in Scotland compared with England and Wales. Some chapters highlight variations as they arise; others provide separate sections for each jurisdiction. Domestic rates are still payable in Northern Ireland. This *Handbook* therefore does not apply to Northern Ireland.

2. Administration

In England and Wales, the responsibility for billing and collecting council tax lies with district councils, metropolitan districts, London boroughs, unitary authorities, combined authorities, the Common Council of the City of London and the Council of the Isles of Scilly. These bodies are known as billing authorities.[5] Each collects council tax on behalf of itself and other public bodies known as precepting authorities.

By law, councils must set their council tax levels between 1 and 11 March each year, but the tax is not invalid merely because it is set after that date.[6]

Since 2017, several councils have undergone structural changes, including mergers or shared service arrangements, often combining council tax collection and recovery functions. When such changes occur, powers to collect and recover tax, along with any existing tax liabilities, transfer to the new authority. Further council amalgamations are occurring under the Levelling Up and Regeneration Act 2023, and more are anticipated in England under plans contained in the *English Devolution White Paper* published in December 2024.[7]

In Scotland, local authorities are responsible for billing and levying council tax. They are also legally obliged to collect Scottish Water charges for household water and waste-water services, which are included in the annual council tax bill.[8]

Although local authorities are formally responsible for these functions, many contract out the day-to-day administration and collection to private companies. These companies may also be responsible for administering benefits and enforcing non-payment or undertaking certain types of enforcement. In England, they can also notify applicants about reductions, ascertain liability and collect penalties.[9]

3. Legal background and references

The legal framework for council tax is set out in the Local Government Finance Act 1992, as amended by the Local Government Act 2003, the Localism Act 2011, the Local Government Finance Act 2012 and, in Wales, the Local Government Finance (Wales) Act 2024.

The 1992 Act includes sections and Schedules that apply throughout England, Wales and Scotland, as well as certain provisions that apply only to specific jurisdictions.

These Acts enable the Secretary of State, the Welsh government or the Scottish government to create secondary legislation (statutory instruments) in the form of regulations which contain and amend the detailed rules of the council tax scheme. In practice, it is these regulations that govern the day-to-day operation of council tax. Some regulations are shared between England, Wales and Scotland, while others are distinct and have been implemented under the devolved powers of the governments in Wales and Scotland.

Most regulations have been amended or replaced since their original introduction. While the original texts can often be found at legislation.gov.uk, they may not always include the most recent amendments, so care should be taken to ensure you are consulting the latest version.

Each local authority is legally required to adopt a council tax reduction (CTR) scheme by 31 January each year, to take effect from the beginning of the financial year on 1 April. In England and Wales, the CTR scheme must comply with national regulations for pensioners and certain other prescribed categories. Beyond these requirements, each authority has discretion to design its own scheme for working-age residents. Consequently, there is significant variation in CTR entitlements across different local authority areas. Taxpayers must refer to their local scheme for specific details. These rules are legally binding on both the taxpayer and the local authority.

You will also find caselaw cited where relevant throughout this *Handbook*. These decisions interpret statutory provisions and may clarify how council tax rules are applied in specific circumstances.

Tax capping and referendums

Under the Local Government Finance Act 1992, the Secretary of State could originally limit the amount of council tax set by individual local authorities (known as 'capping'). The government could use this power to instruct councils to reduce their budget requirements – and, by extension, their council tax rates – if they were considered unreasonably high. When exercised, this often resulted in reduced council tax bills for residents. The Welsh government still has the power to cap council tax rises in Wales.

In England, the Localism Act 2011 replaced this power with a system of local referendums. Any local authority in England (including police and fire authorities) must hold a referendum if it proposes raising council tax above a threshold deemed excessive.[10] What constitutes 'excessive' is determined annually by the Secretary of State, through a set of principles.[11] Any amount which exceeds the relevant principle must be approved in a referendum of local voters.[12]

If a council proposes an excessive rise, it must also prepare substitute budget calculations based on a non-excessive increase, in case the referendum fails.[13]

Provision for a council tax referendum

If a local referendum is held and the majority of voters reject the proposed increase, the substitute calculations have effect for the financial year.[14]

The referendum can be scheduled at any time chosen by the authority, but it must be held no later than May, or by another deadline set by the Secretary of State.[15] The local authority must publish a statement of reasons for the council tax increase at least 28 days before the vote.[16] It must publish notice of the referendum no later than 25 days before the referendum date.[17]

The wording of the referendum question(s) must clearly state the percentage increase and explain the impact on council tax.[18]

The substitute calculations have effect if a local authority fails to hold a referendum on time.

A referendum may be challenged on a limited number of grounds in an election court or by judicial review.[19]

Practice notes and information letters

In addition to the legislation, the Ministry of Housing, Communities and Local Government (MHCLG) (in England), the Welsh government and the local authority associations have jointly produced and periodically update a series of practice notes. These provide guidance on interpreting the legislation and administrative arrangements, and promote good practice. There is no Scottish equivalent.

The MHCLG also produces council tax information letters, which update local authorities on the recent legislative changes, caselaw developments and procedural matters.

Although practice notes and information letters are not legally binding, local authorities are generally expected to take them into account when exercising discretionary powers.[20] This *Handbook* includes selected commentary and examples from those practice notes where they are useful.

Additionally, the Valuation Tribunal Service publishes a council tax guidance online newsletter, *Valuation in Practice,* and a range of guidance notes.

The Valuation Tribunal for England has issued a practice statement governing the conduct of hearings and appeal procedures. The Valuation Tribunal for Wales has issued its own best practice guidance. In Scotland, the Local Taxation Chamber sets out procedures for handling appeals. See p260 for more details.

The Ombudsman and the audit of local authorities

In addition to statutory and governmental regulation, the administrative performance of local authorities in England may also be reviewed by the Local Government and Social Care Ombudsman, who may investigate complaints. Separate Ombudsman schemes operate in Wales and Scotland.

The financial performance and conduct of local authorities is subject to independent scrutiny. This is undertaken by the District Auditor (in England), Audit Wales and Audit Scotland, under the relevant national legislation.[21]

Notes in the *Handbook*

Legal references are given in notes at the end of each chapter. Some notes begin with the letters E, W or S (or a combination) to indicate references to English, Welsh and/or Scottish law. See Appendix 3 for the abbreviations used in the notes.

Legal and other references

Local authorities are required to publish details of their local CTR schemes, which are usually available online.

The legislation governing council tax – statutes and regulations – is also available online, though not all versions are fully updated.

Comprehensive legal references can be found in:

- *Ryde on Rating and the Council Tax* (Butterworth's loose-leaf series) contains all relevant English and Welsh legislation, along with official practice notes. It is available in many large public reference libraries.
- CPAG's *Housing Benefit and Council Tax Reduction Legislation* consolidates CTR legislation across England, Wales and Scotland.

You can find detailed information on proceedings in the civil and criminal courts, which may involve council tax matters, in specialist works of law and procedure. Note that the rules of civil procedure, which apply in the county court and High Court, do not have an equivalent in council tax proceedings in magistrates' courts. The annual *Stone's Justices' Manual* also has details of appropriate procedures in the magistrates' court.

For caselaw and legal developments, *Rating and Valuation Reporter* covers changes to council tax and reports decisions of the courts in valuation and local taxation matters; judiciary.uk also contains some judgments.

The Valuation Office Agency and the Valuation Tribunal Service (VTS) websites provide information on valuation and appeals. The VTS website includes summaries of tribunal decisions. In Scotland, valuation appeals and decisions are available via the Local Taxation Chamber website.

You can find reports of Ombudsman decisions at the Ombudsman websites for England, Wales and Scotland.

See Appendix 1 for the relevant website addresses.

Notes

1. **Introduction**
 1 s1 LGFA 1992
 2 s17 LGFA 1992
 3 s20(1)(b) LGF(W)A 2024
 4 MHCLG, *Local Authority Council Taxbase in England: 2024 (revised)*, 7 March 2025

2. **Administration**
 5 **EW** s1 LGFA 1992
 6 s30(6) and 30(7) LGFA 1992
 7 MHCLG, *English Devolution White Paper*, December 2024
 8 Water and Sewerage Services to Dwellings (Collection of Unmetered Charges by Local Authority) (Scotland) Order 2023 No.52
 9 CTRS(DFE)(E) Regs

3. **Legal background and references**
 10 s52ZB(2) LGFA 1992; Schs 5 and 6 LA 2011; Local Authority (Conduct of Referendums) (Council Tax Increases) (England) Regulations 2012 No.444 as amended by SI 2023 No.1147
 11 s52ZC(1) LGFA 1992
 12 s4ZA LGFA 1992
 13 s52ZF LGFA 1992
 14 s52ZH LGFA 1992
 15 s52ZG LGFA 1992; The Local Authority (Referendums Relating to Council Tax Increases) (Date of Referendum) (England) Order 2013 No.2862
 16 Reg 11 LA(CR)(CTI)(E) Regs
 17 Sch 3 para 3 LA(CR)(CTI)(E) Regs
 18 Sch 1 LA(CR)(CTI)(E) Regs, as amended by the Local Authorities (Conduct of Referendums) (Council Tax Increases) (England) (Amendment) Regulations 2013 No.409
 19 Reg 20 LA(CR)(CTI)(E) Regs
 20 *British Oxygen v Minister of Technology* [1971] UKHL 4
 21 LGFA 1974; Public Audit (Wales) Act 2013

Chapter 2

Chargeable dwellings

This chapter covers:

1. Chargeable dwellings

Council tax is payable on all dwellings, unless they are exempt (see Chapter 4). Properties on which the tax must be paid are referred to as 'chargeable dwellings'.[1] The definition of a 'dwelling' in England and Wales differs from that which applies in Scotland. In most cases, however, the effect is the same.

Typical dwellings include houses, flats, bungalows, cottages and maisonettes used for domestic purposes. Sometimes, however, it may not be clear – eg, if one property consists of a number of dwellings or if a number of properties constitute one dwelling. Whether a property constitutes a dwelling is one of the grounds for making a proposal to alter the valuation list (see Chapter 3) and could be the subject of an appeal (see Chapter 11).

Reducing the amount of council tax payable

The amount of council tax payable for a dwelling may be reduced by:

- an alteration to the dwelling's valuation band (see Chapter 3);
- a fixed period or indefinite exemption (see Chapter 4);
- a disability reduction (see Chapter 6);
- a discount (see Chapter 7);
- council tax reduction (see Chapter 8);
- adopting certain payment arrangements, which may offer a discount (see Chapter 9);
- a discretionary reduction under section s13A Local Government Finance Act 1992 (see p135).

2. Dwellings in England and Wales

What counts as a dwelling

The legal definition of a dwelling for council tax purposes in England and Wales is not straightforward. The Local Government Finance Act 1992 defines a 'dwelling' as any property which:[2]

- would have been a hereditament (ie, a rateable unit – see below) for the purposes of section 115(1) of the General Rate Act 1967 if that Act had remained in force; *and*
- is not shown, or required to be shown, on a local or a central non-domestic rating list (see p16); *and*
- is not exempt from local non-domestic rating;[3] *or*
- is a composite hereditament – ie, mixed-use properties (see p16).

What is not a dwelling

Certain properties are specifically excluded from being dwellings, unless they constitute part of a larger property which is itself a dwelling. These are:[4]

- yards, gardens, outhouses or other land or buildings belonging to, or enjoyed with, property used wholly for the purposes of living accommodation; *or*
- private garages with either a floor area of 25 metres or less or used wholly or mainly to accommodate a private motor vehicle; *or*
- private storage premises used wholly or mainly to store domestic items.

These exclusions mean, for example, that a garage storing a private car that is not part of a larger property is not a dwelling and should not be included in any other dwelling's valuation. However, a concierge room in a block of flats may be included as domestic property as it serves the building and forms part of a collection of dwellings chargeable for council tax.[5]

In England, property used to generate electricity or heat by alternative energy sources (eg, biomass or wind) can be classed as domestic property. However, it is not a dwelling unless it forms part of a larger property which is itself a dwelling.[6]

Hereditaments

In 2015, the Supreme Court looked at the degree of connectedness between two offices of the same business operating on different floors of a building. It ruled that adjacent spaces would normally be considered connected and treated as one hereditament, but unity was not simply a matter of contiguity. If direct communication is possible between two occupied parts of a dwelling, by a door or a staircase, it is usually said that the occupier has created a new and larger hereditament in place of the two that previously existed.[7]

Where two spaces are geographically distinct, a functional test may still enable them to be treated as a single hereditament, but only where the use of the one section or unit is necessary to the effectual enjoyment of the other. This is normally decided by whether the two sections can be let separately.

Whether the use of one section is necessary for effective enjoyment of the other does not depend on the occupier's needs, but on the property's physical character and objectively ascertainable characteristics. The reasoning *Woolway v Mazars* has been adopted with council tax, even the Valuation Office Agency (VOA) seeks to distinguish this in other cases.[8] It led to the introduction of the legislation which provides that where two hereditaments are occupied or owned by the same person, and are in some way physically connected, they are to be treated as one hereditament and therefore subject to one rating. However, this only applied to non-domestic ratings, and not to council tax. The legal position is unclear if the heritaments are of mixed use (ie, business and residential). The VOA's position is that the provisions only apply to business premises.

Dwellings in a state of disrepair

In some cases, a property may be in such a state of disrepair that it cannot be classed as a dwelling. It could be so derelict that even with a reasonable amount of repairs, no one could be expected to live in it. Such a property ceases to be a hereditament and may be removed from the valuation list.

A High Court decision ruled that a hereditament ceases to exist for council tax purposes only if the property is 'truly derelict'. The fact that a property needs repair is not sufficient, even if those repairs are expensive or uneconomic.[9] A tribunal may find that the dwelling should be removed from the list if it is unreasonable to undertake repairs and no reasonable owner would attempt repairs.

Note: the actual intentions of the landlord or owner are not relevant. The tribunal considers the actions of a hypothetical reasonable owner – ie, someone who takes normal, sensible steps to maintain/repair a property and who would not overspend or undertake excessive work. Thus, an owner or landlord who is willing to spend more than what a reasonable person would to repair a property may still have the dwelling removed from the list for the uninhabitable period. For example, a valuation tribunal held that a dwelling with dangerous wiring and a missing gable wall should not appear in the valuation list while undergoing rebuilding.[10] The building was uninhabitable during the rebuild and failed to meet the definition of a rateable hereditament. If a dwelling can be repaired, it should remain on the valuation list and may be entitled to an empty dwelling exemption for 12 months while the repairs are carried out. For more information on exemptions, see Chapter 4.

Self-contained accommodation and annexes

If a dwelling is considered to be a single dwelling under the definition of a hereditament (see p8), but consists of more than one self-contained unit of living accommodation, the local authority will treat each self-contained unit of accommodation as a separate dwelling.[11]

A 'self-contained unit' is a building, or part of a building, which has been constructed or adapted for use as separate living accommodation.[12] Listing officers are advised to look for living and sleeping accommodation and at least minimal separate cooking and washing facilities before they decide that the property constitutes 'self-contained' living accommodation. For example, a property with more than one self-contained unit (eg, a large house adapted to provide a separate 'granny' annexe or separate staff accommodation) should be treated as two or more dwellings. The annexe may then be an exempt dwelling if unoccupied (see Chapter 4). Key factors considered include whether a self-contained unit or annexe has all the features necessary for independent living. The parties' actual intentions are not decisive and not as important as the physical characteristics.[13]

If a living unit does not have independent outside access, it does not necessarily mean it is part of a single dwelling.[14]

The view of the occupier (eg, if they say that the accommodation is used as a games room rather than living accommodation) will not prevent a listing officer from deciding that a separate dwelling exists.

Some clarification was found in *AF v Lucy Formela-Osborne (Listing Officer)*. This case considered an annexe that had previously been part of a holiday let near a farm, which was the main building.[15] The annexe was found to be 'reasonably suitable for use as separate living accommodation'. There was somewhere to live, sleep, wash and prepare food. Although the toilet facility was basic and shared, one was available. The tribunal acknowledged that if a shower had been absent, it might have been difficult to determine.[16]

Assessing whether a dwelling constitutes a self-contained unit takes place in stages. The listing officer must first determine that a hereditament exists and to what extent, and only then go on to consider whether the hereditament contains any self-contained units.[17]

Identifying self-contained units

The definition of a self-contained unit makes it clear there is a functional purpose (ie, that the unit was intended for use as accommodation), which allows a consistent approach to identifying these units.

Determining whether parts of a building are self-contained units includes the following considerations.[18]

- Is the part of the building identified reasonably suitable and fit for use as a self-contained dwelling?
- Are the physical characteristics of the dwelling, which may include services and fixtures, of reasonable suitability?

- What is the actual use of the self-contained part of the dwelling? While this may be relevant, it is not the key test and usually is not of significant weight in the assessment.
- What are the characteristics of the rest of the building and access?

A dwelling's size is also relevant, but the size of the areas in comparison to the rest of the building is not an issue.[19] Whether there is a door or a lock is not the only determinant,[20] but the existence of a door and its position may indicate that it has been constructed with a sufficient degree of privacy to be classed as self-contained.[21] *Council Tax Manual,* Practice Note 5 states:[22]

> A self-contained unit should have facilities for living, sleeping, preparation and cooking of food and bathing facilities such as a bath or shower, wash hand basin and lavatory. However in exceptional circumstances the lack of a facility does not prevent a unit from being self-contained, for example, a unit having shared bathing facilities – *Clement (LO) v Bryant and Others* (2003 RA 133).

However, as a general rule, the law also emphasises that a 'bricks and mortar' approach of objectivity is important, concentrating on physical features which are present. The High Court has emphasised the test is a physical one and failure of a valuation tribunal to identify its size and an absence of cooking facilities in its reasons meant that a finding of an annexe as separate living accommodation had to be quashed.[23]

If you are an interested person (see p38), you can make a proposal (see p40) to the listing officer not to show your home as a separate entry on the valuation list.

Buildings in multiple occupation

The listing officer has the discretion to treat a property which would otherwise be considered to be two or more separate dwellings as a single dwelling if it:[24]

- consists of a single self-contained unit, or such a unit together with or containing premises constructed or adapted for non-domestic purposes; *and*
- is occupied as more than one unit of separate living accommodation.

The decision whether to treat a number of domestic properties as one chargeable unit or dwelling is known as 'aggregation'. Similarly, the decision to treat a single property as a number of smaller individual units is 'disaggregation'.

Aggregation can occur, for example, to a property occupied by more than one household, but where the residents share facilities such as kitchens or bathrooms – eg, a group of bedsits, a hostel, a care home or refuge.

When a property has to be disaggregated, two (or more) 'new dwellings' legally come into existence for council tax purposes. When this happens, each of the new dwellings must be valued as they are physically on the date they are entered into the valuation list. When this happens, any physical alterations that have been made to the property must be included in the overall valuation.[25]

From 1 December 2023, new regulations for licensed houses in multiple occupation (HMOs) in England mean that the property is classed as a single dwelling with council tax liability falling on the owner.[26]

Specific provision has been made for care homes.[27] A care home must be registered in accordance with Part 1 of the Health and Social Care Act 2008 in England and Part 1 of the Regulation and Inspection of Social Care (Wales) Act 2016 in Wales.

A care home is treated as comprising the number of dwellings found by adding one to the number of self-contained units occupied or intended for occupation.

Any self-contained units identified within the care home are not treated as separate dwellings. Only the accommodation occupied by the care provider (ie, not the residents of the home) is disaggregated and counted separately.

The VOA will check the care certificate for the care home, which lists the number of registered people receiving care, the location of care-related accommodation and ancillary areas.

Sometimes, a care home may be situated on a site with sheltered accommodation where care is provided to people in their own homes. Any blocks where people occupy their own home inside a complex and who purchase a care package must be differentiated from the accommodation occupied by the number of registered persons on the care certificate.[28]

Decisions on disaggregation

To disaggregate a dwelling (split it into two or more), each unit must be capable of being lived in separately to be classed as a self-contained unit. The listing officer must exercise their discretion reasonably and should take into account all the circumstances, including the extent to which the parts of the property that are separately occupied have been structurally altered.

The listing officer's discretion regarding aggregation or disaggregation can only be challenged by judicial review.[29] However, the decision about what constitutes an individual self-contained unit within a dwelling can be challenged at the valuation tribunal; each separate unit has to be challenged individually as a separate appeal. This may mean starting multiple appeals in respect of a single dwelling when a disaggregation decision has been made (see Chapter 11).

The listing officer's decision that a property is, or should be treated as, only one dwelling rather than several may not only impact the single dwelling's valuation band. It may also impact liability and entitlement to discounts (also known as 'variations' in Scotland) or benefits and whether individual occupiers each receive bills, instead of the landlord. Decisions by the VOA or local authorities have often caused problems for tenants or occupiers sharing multiple-occupation dwellings who believe that the landlord should be liable to pay council tax on an HMO basis. In a case concerning general rates, it was held that a valuation officer should consider at least four factors when exercising their discretion – known as the 'bricks and mortar test'.[30] These are the degree:

- to which facilities, such as kitchens and bathrooms, are shared;
- of internal adaptations, such as entrance doors;
- of identifiably separate parts;
- of transience in the occupiers' residence.

In practice, a set of tests from a 1948 case have become the default position for the VOA in many cases to the exclusion of other cases. Since 2016, it has increasingly relied on the judgment in *John Laing and Son Ltd v Kingswood Assessment Area Committee and Others,* a case under the old rating system.[31] The *Laing* test sets down what are treated as the four conditions of rateability:

- actual occupation;
- exclusive use;
- value or benefit to the occupier;
- not too transient.

If the VOA considers that all four conditions are met, it often treats what it designates as a unit of property as a hereditament and a dwelling for council tax purposes. In practice, this moves the test of a hereditament and the existence of a dwelling onto the use of a dwelling, patterns of occupation and interpretation of the wording in letting agreements.

In contrast, the higher courts have confirmed the principles in the bricks and mortar test, focusing on what is physically constructed rather than the owner's intentions (see Chapter 5).[32] However, if two flats are converted to a single property, a new dwelling is created for council tax purposes.[33] The presence or absence of one characteristic is not normally determinative in itself, but an overall collection of features. A reasonable decision, looking at all the facts, should be made.[34]

A problem is that decisions may often be made in reference to selected cases rather than the overall position, it being recognised that there is a conflict of caselaw.[35]

In particular, between 2017 and 2023, the VOA adopted a system of desktop assessments, determining banding solely on tenancy agreements rather than multiple tests. This has resulted in a formulaic approach to cases. The VOA has also adopted a policy of omitting or excluding caselaw that does not conform to the *Laing* test and relies increasingly on copies of tenancy and letting agreements. One consequence is that if the VOA lacks information on tenancy agreements, a finding that a multiple property is a collection of separate self-contained dwellings may not be upheld.[36]

HMOs and other shared accommodation

The new rules adopt a definition of an HMO used by section 254 of the Housing Act 2004.[37] The change will ensure that where a unit (eg, a bedroom) within an

HMO relies on shared facilities and is included as part of the HMO, then the whole HMO property should be valued as one property.

To constitute a separate dwelling in shared accommodation, the unit must be suitable for use as a dwelling in the ordinary sense of the word. It must be suitable to be treated as a place where someone may live; it normally requires a place to sleep, facilities for hygiene, and some provision of facilities for cooking, eating and drinking. For example, the absence of cooking facilities indicates that a unit is not a self-contained dwelling, despite being en suite. This was followed in *Coll v Mooney*[38] where the court held the test is whether a unit is 'reasonably suitable' as separate living accommodation.

It must be constructed as a single dwelling and must have an element of separateness from other buildings or other parts of the same building. It must be capable of functioning as a dwelling in its own right and provide a form of privacy and security for the occupier. However, it appears from caselaw that there are no absolute rules as to how that separateness can be achieved. The High Court in 2001 found a lockable door was relevant.[39] However, later caselaw accepts that lockable access is not a necessary condition of a self-contained unit.[40]

Similarly, the fact that a separate unit would be difficult to sell or even unsaleable does not determine whether it can be classed as separate accommodation.[41]

In Wales, a refuge must be treated as a single dwelling for council tax purposes, even if it has more than one self-contained unit.[42]

A property is classed as a 'refuge' if it is:[43]

- operated on a not-for-profit basis; *and*
- used wholly or mainly for the temporary accommodation of people who have been subject to:
  - controlling, coercive or threatening behaviour; *or*
  - physical violence; *or*
  - abuse of any other description (whether physical or mental); *or*
  - threats of any such violence or abuse,

  from a partner with whom they are or were cohabiting.

A planning condition that affects the use or occupation of part of a property is a relevant factor but not the only one.[44] HMOs must be registered with the local authority (see Chapter 5) but a different definition applies regarding the number of people living in the property.

HMOs that were previously disaggregated are being proactively rebanded by the VOA into a single dwelling with the council tax paid by the landlord.

Is a HMO tenant still receiving council tax bills?

If you are a tenant or licensee in an HMO who continues to receive an individual council tax bill for a room you occupy for any date from 1 December 2023, you should challenge this with the VOA and local council.

If you are living in an HMO that is being rebanded, contact the VOA to ask about this process. You can also write to the council to request it remove you from liability to tax.

If you have been held liable for a bill on a disaggregated HMO dwelling before 1 December 2023, you may seek a discretionary reduction in addition to any other reduction that may apply (see p135).

Annexes and self-contained accommodation (ie, containing all facilities for independent cooking, washing and living) that do not form part of an HMO, as defined by the Housing Act 2004, will continue to be valued in the existing way.

Annexe property

A property that is extended or divided (eg, to create an annexe, studio or granny flat) can result in the creation of a new, separate dwelling for valuation purposes if it meets certain physical and functional criteria.

For example, when a property was extended and an annexe constructed creating a separate dwelling and a new entry on the list and then was merged back into the original dwelling, it was held a new dwelling for valuation purposes was created.[45] The valuation officer can alter the valuation band of the original property as well as valuing the extension separately if it constitutes a self-contained dwelling.[46] Cases in tax tribunals have followed a similar approach to annexes, treating physical characteristics, construction and reasonable suitableness as key tests.[47] In some cases, an annexe may attract an exemption from council tax (see Chapter 4).

Converted sheds and garages

In areas with high rents and a shortage of accommodation, some people have converted sheds and garages into places to rent. Converted sheds and garages may be excluded from the category of dwelling or may be part of the owner's dwelling. Even if they are treated as dwellings in their own right, in most cases, the owner will likely be held liable for the council tax (see Chapter 5).

Caravans and houseboats

A pitch for a caravan and a mooring for a houseboat are hereditaments (see p8). They can be considered dwellings for council tax purposes if they are occupied by a caravan or houseboat (including a boat which is no longer navigable[48]) which is someone's sole or main residence (see p84). Even if a pitch or mooring is empty, it may still be considered a dwelling if it is likely that its next use will be domestic – though it may qualify as an exempt dwelling (see Chapter 4). A mooring is classed as domestic property if it is occupied by a boat which is the sole or main residence of an individual.[49] Boats and caravans may be classed as hereditaments in their own right and treated as domestic dwellings. The key question is the degree of permanence in its position. A boat is only taxable if it is fixed or permanently moored.[50]

If a boat is moored at one spot or a caravan parked on the same pitch for a substantial period, its value may also be included in the council tax valuation of the mooring or pitch. Where this is for 12 months or more, the band value should include the value of the boat or caravan, even if it is temporarily removed for short periods (such as two to four weeks) as long as it returns to the same location.[51] The question is whether the occupation can be characterised as that of a 'settler' (long term and stable) or 'wayfarer' (transient and temporary). If the latter, then only the mooring or pitch should be valued.[52]

Properties on the non-domestic rating list

Property is domestic if it is used wholly for living accommodation. If it is not in use, it is still considered domestic if its next intended use will be domestic.

Most non-domestic property, such as business or industrial property, is shown on either the local or central non-domestic rating list. Such properties are not dwellings for council tax purposes and are liable for non-domestic rates.

Holiday caravans and beach huts

Holiday caravans and other caravans used for non-domestic purposes are subject to non-domestic rates. However, if you keep a caravan at home for use on holidays, you are not liable to pay non-domestic rates or council tax on it.

However, beach huts are liable to be listed as chargeable dwellings. The Upper Tribunal confirmed that a property does not need to fulfil all the purposes associated with living accommodation to be classed as domestic.[53]

Holiday lets and timeshare property

Properties let out as holiday lets (eg, cottages) may be subject to either council tax or business rates depending on how many days the accommodation is occupied each year. Holiday accommodation must be let for a minimum of 140 days in England and a minimum of 70 days in Wales to count as a non-domestic dwelling.[54]

Timeshare accommodation does not count as domestic property and is subject to non-domestic rates.

Composite hereditaments

A property is a composite hereditament if only part of it is used solely for domestic accommodation, while another part is used solely for non-domestic (business) purposes. Council tax is payable on the domestic portion and non-domestic rates are payable on the business portion.

You can appeal against a decision that a property is a composite hereditament, or against a decision on the proportion of a property used for domestic or non-domestic purposes. The key question is whether the character of a dwelling house has been lost due to business use.[55] For example, if a room or garage is predominantly used for business purposes, the property may be classed as a composite hereditament. However, working from home does not necessarily create a composite hereditament.

In *Tully v Jorgensen,* the appellant worked from home due to a disability that prevented regular commuting. The room used for work was not structurally adapted for business use and remained furnished as a domestic space. Outside of office hours, the room reverted to normal family use. No one visited for business purposes; if meetings were required, they took place elsewhere. Consequently, the room was part of the ordinary domestic accommodation and not a composite hereditament.[56]

When valuing a composite property, a listing officer is expected initially to value the property as a whole, and then apportion the relevant amount between domestic and non-domestic parts.[57]

When assessing only the domestic portion of a composite hereditament, the listing officer must consider the amount of the property that could reasonably be attributed to domestic use. The Court of Appeal has ruled that, provided the listing officer does so, they can value the domestic portion by any method they choose, and it is not necessary to value the whole composite hereditament first.[58]

Short-stay accommodation

Where a hotel or business provides accommodation for short periods to individuals whose sole or main residence is elsewhere, the part of the property which is wholly or mainly for that purpose is a non-domestic hereditament and is liable to non-domestic rates.[59] Property may be classed as 'wholly' used even if parts are vacant or unused. Property not in use is domestic property 'if it appears that when next in use it will be domestic'.[60] The accommodation must not be commercial self-contained, self-catering accommodation. The definition of a business includes a property run by a charity.[61]

However, small establishments such as guest houses are subject solely to council tax where:

- short-stay accommodation is offered for no more than six people at any one time; *and*
- the provider's sole or main residence is within the property; *and*
- the short-stay accommodation is subsidiary to the use of the property as a sole or main residence.

If you are placed in temporary bed and breakfast accommodation (eg, local authority homeless accommodation[62]), the owner of the dwelling is liable for council tax, not you (see Chapter 5).[63]

A building or a self-contained part of a building that is intended to be available for commercial letting as self-catering accommodation for short periods totalling

140 days or more in the coming year is not a domestic property and is not liable to council tax. In Wales, to avoid council tax liability, a property must also have been let as self-catering accommodation for at least 70 days during the previous year and have been available for letting for at least 140 days. Where such a property is let for less than 70 days over the previous year as part of a larger business with other lets at the same location or within very close proximity, in some circumstances, it may not be a domestic property chargeable to council tax.[64]

Property that is actually let for less than 70 days a year is likely to be deleted from the non-domestic rates (NDR) list and returned to the council tax list.

In England, during 2023/24, 10,710 self-catering holiday homes were removed from the NDR list. Of these, 9,280 were added back to the council tax list. In Wales, 1,240 such properties were removed from the NDR list, and 950 were added back to the council tax list. Others may have been excluded due to demolition or significant changes.[65]

Dwellings in different locations

The location of a dwelling is a major determining factor in how much council tax is payable and whether it should be treated as a single or multiple property. Two properties occupied by the same person or body and used for one purpose, but which are geographically separated (eg, by a road or public street) or if there is no common possession of the whole area concerned, should normally be treated as two separate hereditaments.[66]

If a dwelling (including a dwelling that is part of a larger single property) is within the area of two or more local authorities, or two or more parts of an authority's area, it should be treated as being in the area in which the greatest part of it is situated, or in terms of use, where the greater domestic value is situated.[67]

Where no part of a composite hereditament can reasonably be found to have a domestic use of greater value than any other part, the area within which the dwelling is treated as being situated is determined by agreement between the billing authorities. If they cannot agree, they draw lots to settle the matter.[68]

3. Dwellings in Scotland

In Scotland, a 'dwelling' means any land and 'heritages' – ie, rights that exist with the land, such as farming and fishing rights:[69]

- which consist of one or more dwelling houses with any garden, yard, garage, outhouse or other pertinent area belonging to and occupied with the dwelling house(s); *and*
- which would, but for the fact that it is a dwelling, be entered separately in the valuation roll.

The valuation roll only includes non-domestic and part-residential properties. Details of domestic dwellings are contained in the valuation lists.

A Scottish dwelling includes:

- the residential part of part-residential property (see p20); *and*
- part of any premises that was apportioned on 1 April 1989 as a dwelling house.

Caravans are only classified as dwellings if they are a person's sole or main residence.

Principles applicable for council tax in Scotland are similar to those in England, although not identical.[70]

What counts as a dwelling

Certain property types are explicitly included or excluded from the Scottish definition of a dwelling. The following properties are specifically included in the definition of a dwelling if, but for the fact that they are dwellings, they would be entered separately on the valuation roll:

- a garage, carport or car parking space used (or last used) wholly or mainly for private vehicles;[71]
- certain private storage premises used (or last used) wholly or mainly to store domestic articles (including cycles and other similar vehicles);[72]
- bed and breakfast accommodation run on a commercial basis by someone living there for letting to no more than six people a night;
- student halls of residence which include shared facilities;
- Ministry of Defence accommodation which is, or is likely to be, the sole or main residence of a member of the armed forces;
- school boarding accommodation;
- any part of a communal residential establishment (eg, hostel or care home) with shared facilities for residents, including those parts used wholly or mainly as the sole or main residence of a person employed there. **Note:** the parts occupied by residents are not dwellings, and are instead subject to non-domestic rates.

Note: some of the above dwellings are exempt from council tax (see Chapter 4).[73]

In determining what is a dwelling, a court or tribunal may consider both the physical characteristics *and* the use made of the property.[74]

Whether a property ceases to exist as a dwelling is an objective question of fact and degree. Usually, where the only reason a dwelling house cannot be lived in is that it is undergoing repairs or alterations, it does not mean that it ceases to be a dwelling house for council tax purposes. However, 'there may be cases where the works to a house are so extensive and require to be so prolonged, or where they involve the essential physical characteristics of a house being lost, that the proper conclusion is that the property has ceased to exist as a dwelling house while the works are carried out'.[75]

What is not a dwelling

Certain properties are specifically excluded from the Scottish definition of a dwelling, but may be subject to non-domestic rates. These are:

- certain huts, sheds and bothies that are no one's sole or main residence;
- certain self-catering holiday accommodation that is not someone's sole or main residence;
- women's refuges (except any part which is the sole or main residence of an employee of the voluntary organisation managing the refuge);[76]
- timeshare accommodation.[77]

If a dwelling is supplied by a combined heat and power station, the pipes, risers and other plant connected with the power station are not treated as part of the dwelling (and so are ignored for valuation purposes), except where they are within the solum (upper soil), garden, yard or garage of the dwelling.[78]

Thus, all pipes and risers for the transport of water between a power station and a block of flats (or tenement) are not treated as part of all the dwellings in the tenement, insofar as these pipes and risers are not located in or on tenement land. If the power station only benefits the tenement, it (and all the associated plant) counts as part of each dwelling. They are allocated equally between the dwellings they serve.

Buildings in multiple occupation (HMOs)

In Scotland, a house in multiple occupation (HMO) includes dwellings that are used as an HMO even if they were not originally constructed or subsequently adapted for such use and if they are sometimes occupied by just one person. All HMOs must be formally registered with the local authority.[79]

If requested by the assessor, the owner or landlord must provide evidence of letting, or of an intention to let, the property.[80]

Part-residential property

Certain properties with a mixed domestic and non-domestic use (eg, nursing homes and hospitals) are divided into their relevant parts. The non-domestic portion is listed on the valuation roll and the domestic portion is listed on the valuation list and is treated as a dwelling for council tax purposes.

Premises used for commercial or sporting purposes (known as 'part-residential subjects') are treated differently. The property is on the valuation roll, but an apportionment note indicates the net annual value and the rateable value based on the property's residential and non-residential uses.[81] The residential part counts as a dwelling for council tax purposes. **Note:** parts of a refuge, hostel or care home (see p127) used as accommodation for residents rather than employees are specifically excluded from the definition of part-residential subject.[82]

To be classed as self-catering holiday accommodation (and be included on the valuation roll, not the council tax list), a property must be let for a minimum of 70 days in any financial year. Any property included on the valuation roll as self-catering holiday accommodation at the end of a financial year will remain on the valuation roll at the start of the next financial year until the assessor reviews its status.

The 70 days of actual letting must be accompanied by at least a further 70 days of actual letting, or intention to let, or a combination of both.[83]

4. New and altered properties

A new dwelling may be created either by constructing a new building or by the structural alteration of an existing property. A new dwelling exists for council tax purposes from:[84]

- the date a completion notice is served; *or*
- from the completion date contained on the notice, if later. This applies when a dwelling is not completed, but the local authority believes it is substantially completed and it can be completed within three months from the date the notice is served.

A new or altered dwelling does not require a completion notice once someone starts to live there.

If a new or altered dwelling is unoccupied, it may be exempt from council tax for a period (see Chapter 4). When structural alterations create a new dwelling, the former dwelling(s) is considered to have ceased to exist on the completion date.

Completion notices

The local authority (in England and Wales) or assessor (in Scotland) may serve a completion notice on the owner of a building that has been completed or can reasonably be expected to be completed within three months.[85] This notice proposes a completion day for the building.

The proposed completion day becomes the actual completion day unless the owner appeals. While the appeal is pending, the proposed completion day is treated as the actual completion day.

In deciding whether a completion notice should be issued, the key test is whether the building is capable of occupation. The Lands Chamber of the Upper Tribunal has stated:[86]

> The building is only a hereditament if it is ready for occupation... If the building lacks features which will have to be provided before it can be occupied for that purpose and when provided will provide part of the hereditament and

form the basis of its valuation it does not constitute a hereditament and so does not fall to be shown in the Rating List. There is, in consequence, no scope for including in the List a building which is nearly, even very nearly, ready for occupation unless the completion notice procedure has been followed.

Therefore, a building that is nearly ready for occupation must not be entered in the list unless a proper completion notice has been issued.

Appealing against a completion notice

If you disagree with the date on a completion notice, you should first raise the issue with the local authority (in England and Wales) or the assessor (in Scotland).

In England and Wales, you should appeal directly to the Valuation Tribunal for England or the Valuation Tribunal for Wales within 28 days of the notice being sent (see p259).[87] Late appeal may be accepted if the delay was for reasons beyond your control.[88]

In Scotland, you must lodge an appeal with the Local Taxation Chamber within 21 days of receiving the completion notice.[89] You can download the form from localtaxationchamber.scot/apply.

Notes

1. **Chargeable dwellings**

1 **EW** s4(1) and (2) LGFA 1992
S s72(6) LGFA 1992

2. **Dwellings in England and Wales**

2 s3(1) LGFA 1992
3 s66(1A) and Sch 5 LGFA 1988
4 s3(4) LGFA 1992
5 *The Collection (Management) Ltd v Jackson* [2013] UKUT 166 (LC)
6 s3(4A) LGFA 1992, as defined in s66(1A) and s26(2) LGFA 1988; Climate Change and Sustainable Energy Act 2006
7 *Woolway v Mazars* [2015] UKSC 53
8 *Corkish (LO) v Berg* [2019] EWHC 2521 (Admin)
9 *Wilson v Coll (LO)* [2011] EWHC 2824 (Admin), reported as [2012] PTSR 1313
10 *Z Munter Farms Ltd v Pettitt* [2006] RVR 332
11 CT(CD)O
12 Art 2 CT(CD)O
13 *Re a Dwelling in London N2* [2015] RVR 157; *Corkish (LO) v Wright and Hart* [2014] EWHC 237 (Admin), para 5(5)
14 *Vaziri v Listing Officer* [2006] RVR 329
15 *AF v Lucy Formela-Osborne (LO)* [2025] VT00021059, 2 January 2025
16 *AF v Lucy Formela-Osborne (LO)* [2025] VT00021059, 2 January 2025, para 24
17 *Rawsthorne (LO) v Parr* [2009] EWHC 2002 (Admin)
18 *Corkish (LO) v Wright and Hart* [2014] EWHC 237 (Admin)
19 *Re a Dwelling in London N2* VTE Appeal 5090649355/084CAD [2015] RVR 157
20 *Jorgensen (LO) v Gomperts* [2006] RA 300
21 *Ramdhun v Coll (LO)* [2015] RVR 89
22 CTM, Practice Note 5, Appendix 1, Case Summaries Relating to Disaggregation, para 2.5

23 *Corkish (LO) v Wright and Hart* [2014] EWHC 237 (Admin), para 32
24 **E** Art 4 CT(CD)O, as amended by The Council Tax (Chargeable Dwellings, Exempt Dwellings and Discount Disregards) (Amendment) (England) Order 2003 No.3121
W Art 3A CT(CD)O
25 CTM, para 2.1, Logged CR10 Reports (Structural Alterations – Potential Increase in Band)
26 Council Tax (Chargeable Dwellings and Liability for Owners) (Amendment) (England) Regulations 2023 No.1175
27 **E** Art 3A CT(CD)O inserted by art 2 CT(CDEDDD)(A)(E) Regs
W The Council Tax (Chargeable Dwellings, Exempt Dwellings and Discount Disregards) (Amendment) (Wales) Order 2004 No.2921
28 CTM, Practice Note 5: Disaggregation of Dwellings, para 4.2
29 *Burtfield Estates Ltd v Dixon (LO)* [2016] VTE Appeal No.0655664341/254CAD; *Antopolski v VO* [2019] VTE Appeal Case 826184/084
30 *James v Williams* [1973] RA 305
31 *John Laing and Son Ltd v Kingswood Assessment Area Committee and Others* [1949] 1 All ER 224
32 *R v London South Eastern Valuation Tribunal and Neale ex parte Moore* [2001] RVR 94; *Baker (LO) v Gomperts* [2006] All ER(D) 1 July; *Listing Officer v Callear* [2012] EWHC 3697
33 *R v East Sussex Valuation Tribunal ex parte Silverstone* [1996] RVR 203
34 *Associated Provincial Picture Houses v Wednesbury Corporation* [1948] 1 KB 223
35 *Salisbury v Bunyan and Another* [2022] 4 WLR 16, para 36; *Stanuszek v Bunyan No.1* [2023] EWHC 3275; *Stanuszek v Bunyan No.1* [2023] EWHC 3275
36 *MD v Virk (Listing Officer)* [2023] VTE Appeal No.VT0010218
37 Art 2 CT(CD)O as amended by reg 2(2) Council Tax (Chargeable Dwellings and Liability for Owners) (Amendment) (England) Regulations 2023 No.1175
38 *Coll v Mooney* [2016] EWHC 485 (Admin)
39 *McColl v Sabacchi (LO)* [2001] EWHC 712 (Admin)
40 *Jorgensen (LO) v Gomperts* [2006] EWHC 1885 (Admin); *Ramdhun v Coll (LO)* [2014] EWHC 946 (Admin)
41 *Batty v Burfoot and Others* [1995] 2 EGLR 142
42 Art 3B CT(CD)O, inserted by art 3 The Council Tax (Chargeable Dwellings) (Amendment) (Wales) Order 2014 No.2653
43 Art 3 The Council Tax (Chargeable Dwellings) (Amendment) (Wales) Order 2014 No.2653
44 *Rodd v Ritchings* (1995) 2 EGLR 142
45 *Kelderman v Valuation Office Agency* [2014] EWHC 1592 (Admin)
46 *Corkish (LO) v Berg* [2019] EWHC 2521 (Admin)
47 *Fiander and Another v Revenue and Customs Commissioners* [2020] UKFTT 190 (TC)
48 *Nicholls v Wimbledon Valuation Officer* [1995] RVR 171
49 s66(4) LGFA 1988; *Stubbs v Hartnell* [1997] 6 WLUK 113
50 *Chelsea Yacht and Boat Co Ltd v Pope* [2001] 2 All ER 409
51 CTM, Practice Note 7: Application of Council Tax to Caravan Pitches and Moorings, para 6.2
52 *Reeves (LO) v Northrop (LO)* [2013] EWCA Civ 362
53 *Lewis v Christchurch BC; Lewis v Vivian* [1996] RA 229 per Jowitt J
54 **E** s66(B) LGFA 1988
W s66(2BB)(d)) LGFA 1988
See also *Gaer Ltd (trading as Gaer Cottages) v Williams (VO)* [2018] UKUT 327 (LC)
55 *Guthrie v Highland Region and Western Isles Assessor* [1995] RA 292
56 *Tully v Jorgensen (VO)* [2003] RA 233
57 *Listing Officer v Monmouth School* [2009] EWHC 2720 (Admin)
58 Reg 7 CT(SVD) Regs; *Atkinson and Others v Lord* [1997] RA 413
59 s66(2) LGFA 1988
60 s66(5) LGFA 1988; *Public Safety Charitable Trust v Milton Keynes Council* [2013] RA 275, per Sales J at para 37; *South Kesteven DC v Digital Pipeline Ltd* [2016] 1 WLR 2971, per Elias LJ at para 25
61 s66(8) LGFA 1988
62 Either under the Housing Act 1996 or the Children Act 1989
63 CT(LO) Regs
64 s66(2BB)(d) LGFA 1988
65 VOA, *Movement Between Non-domestic Rating and Council Tax Valuation Lists*, 17 December 2024
66 *Woolway v Mazars* [2015] UKSC 53

67 CT(SVD) Regs; see also VOA, CTM, Practice Note 10
68 Reg 3 CT(SVD) Regs, as amended by The Council Tax (Situation and Valuation of Dwellings) (Amendment) Regulations 1994 No.1747

3. **Dwellings in Scotland**

69 s72 LGFA 1992
70 *Assessor, Tayside Joint Valuation Board v Appellant* [2017] CSIH 64
71 Reg 2(2) CT(Dw)(S) Regs
72 Reg 2(3) CT(Dw)(S) Regs
73 CT(DPRS)(S) Regs
74 *The Old Course Ltd v Fife Council Assessor* [2016] CSIH 40 Lands Valuation Appeal Court, Court of Session
75 *Assessor for Tayside Joint Valuation Board v M* [2018] SC 106
76 Reg 3 CT(DPRS)(S) Regs
77 CT(Dw)(S) Regs
78 CT(Dw)(S) Regs 2010
79 Sch para 3 CT(LO)(S) Regs
80 Reg 5A CT(DPRS)(S) Regs, as amended by reg 3 The Council Tax (Dwellings and Part Residential Subjects) (Scotland) Amendment Regulations 2021 No.489
81 s72(8) and Sch 5 LGFA 1992
82 CT(D)(S) Regs
83 Regs 5A-D and Sch 2 para 2(b) CT(DPRS)(S) Regs, as amended by reg 2(3) and (4) The Council Tax (Dwellings and Part Residential Subjects) (Scotland) Amendment Regulations 2021 No.489

4. **New and altered properties**

84 **EW** s17 LGFA 1992; Sch 4A LGFA 1988
S s83(1) and Sch 6 LGFA 1992
85 **EW** s17 LGFA 1992; Sch 4A LGFA 1988
S s83(1) and Sch 6 LGFA 1992
86 *Porter v Trustees of Gladman Sipps* [2011] UKUT 204 (LC)
87 **E** Reg 21(5) VTE(CTRA)(P) Regs
W Reg 29(4) VTW Regs
88 **E** Reg 21(6) VTE(CTRA)(P) Regs
W Reg 29(5) VTW Regs
89 Sch 6 LGFA 1992

Chapter 3

Valuation

This chapter covers:

1. Who is responsible for valuations

England and Wales

At the time of writing, in England and Wales, the Valuation Office Agency (VOA), which is part of HMRC, is responsible for valuing dwellings for council tax purposes. The VOA employs a **listing officer** (also known as a valuation officer) for each local authority. The listing officer compiles and maintains the valuation list and is independent of the local authority.[1]

Note: from 1 April 2026, the government has announced that the VOA will be dissolved and its functions moved to HMRC.[2]

You can find details of your local Valuation Office and listing officer at gov.uk/government/organisations/valuation-office-agency or by calling 03000 501 501 (England) or 03000 505 505 (Wales).

Scotland

In Scotland, the **assessor** and any deputy assessor for each local authority decides which valuation band applies to each dwelling in the area.[3] The assessor is a professional valuer, employed by the local authority, who must comply with valuation directions from the HMRC commissioners.[4]

Details of the assessors are at saa.gov.uk.

Appointees

The commissioners via the VOA (in England and Wales) and the assessor (in Scotland) may appoint other people (eg, private surveyors) to carry out valuations.[5] Appointees can be given relevant information (eg, survey reports), but unauthorised disclosure of this data for non-valuation purposes is punishable by a fine or imprisonment.[6]

Complaints

If you are unhappy with a valuation decision and wish to appeal it, see p36 and Chapter 11.

Negotiating with the Valuation Office Agency

You can raise questions on the banding of your dwelling or other entries in the council tax list with the listing officer. This discussion may resolve the issues without the need for an appeal. Listing officers may agree on a band on the strength of evidence and representations. Listing officers should deal courteously with all queries and should not imply that it is not worthwhile for you to appeal.[7]

In 2023/24, the VOA received 1,350 complaints. Of these, 37 per cent were upheld.[8]

If you are dissatisfied with how a listing officer has handled your case, you can make a complaint for maladministration. However, note that the listing officer cannot substitute different bands than those set by parliament or alter the principles governing how council tax valuations are determined.

To complain about maladministration (eg, delays, bad service or misleading information) by any local listing officer, initially contact the office concerned. See p301 for more examples. If the response to your complaint is unsatisfactory, you can request a tier two review. If still dissatisfied, you can refer your case to the Adjudicator. The Adjudicator can recommend actions to rectify matters. This should normally be done within six months of the VOA's decision, unless there are exceptional circumstances. You can refer a complaint to the Adjudicator's Office in writing or by phone (see Appendix 1).

If you disagree with the Adjudicator's recommendations, you can complain to the Parliamentary and Health Service Ombudsman through your MP. This process can take time but can result in compensation if maladministration is found.

In Scotland, complaints should first be made to the Valuation Joint Board using the complaints form. If you remain dissatisfied, you can complain to the Scottish Public Services Ombudsman (SPSO) – the final stage for most complaints against public bodies (see p300).

Freedom of information and disclosure

The VOA is required to respond to requests for information under the Freedom of Information Act 2000. You can request details such as how your property's council tax band was decided and banding comparisons with similar properties.

If the VOA declines to provide the information, you can take the request to the Information Commissioner's Office (ICO). The ICO can order the VOA to disclose the information if it finds in your favour.

Where the ICO is satisfied on the balance of probabilities that the VOA no longer holds the information (eg, in connection with the compilation of the original valuation list for an area), it is not a breach of the duty to supply such information.[9]

The VOA may refuse requests for information about properties within a specific postcode if disclosure would identify, or enable identification of, an individual. This is permitted under the Freedom of Information Act – eg, section 44(1), which prohibits releasing information protected by other laws.[10] Requests may also be refused if the cost of providing the information is too high (section 12), or if the information is reasonably accessible by the taxpayer by other means (section 21).

However, information held by the VOA may be disclosed under the Act if it is required for civil proceedings and relates to a matter involving HMRC.[11]

In some cases, the information provided by the VOA may also be held by the council. If so, the council should make the information available if requested. It cannot use section 21 as a reason for its non-disclosure.[12]

Alternatively, you can seek an order for the disclosure of records from the valuation tribunal or the Local Taxation Chamber in Scotland (see Chapter 11) if you start an appeal with either tribunal.

2. The listing officer's and assessor's powers

The listing officer and assessor have powers to:

- enter dwellings; *and*
- obtain information from a past or present owner, occupier, the local authority and certain other people.

Desktop assessments

Most assessments are carried out as 'desktop' valuations, especially for standard residential properties. These are completed without a physical inspection, using Valuation Office Agency (VOA) records, existing entries on the list and publicly available data. Physical inspections are rare, typically used for larger premises or buildings containing multiple units.

However, desktop valuations can sometimes be inaccurate if:

- the property is newly built or has been structurally altered;

- the layout or structure is unusual;
- there are factual errors – eg, counting a cupboard as a bedroom.

If you believe that the listing officer lacks sufficient information to make an accurate assessment, you can ask for a physical inspection. However, there is no legal obligation for the VOA to do so unless directed by the valuation tribunal.

The VOA also uses internal guidance manuals to inform decisions. These manuals set out how the VOA interprets its powers and the law. Note, however, that they are not legally binding – only the legislation and caselaw define your rights.[13]

Powers of entry

A listing officer or any assistant with written authorisation from the listing officer (in Scotland, the local assessor or deputy assessor) may enter, survey and value a dwelling.[14] This can be done either at your request or if the listing officer exercises their statutory right of entry. You or the listing officer must give at least three clear days' written notice (excluding weekends and public holidays). In England, the officer must also obtain prior approval from the First-tier Tribunal to exercise this power.[15] This power is seldom, if ever, exercised. Usually, the officer will seek to agree on a convenient time for access and provide at least seven days' notice.

Listing officers carry identity cards and will ask your permission to take photographs during the visit.[16]

Intentionally delaying or obstructing the official may be a criminal offence. The penalty is a fine not exceeding level 1 on the standard scale.[17]

If there is a dispute over the facts and the VOA has refused to carry out an inspection, you may apply to the valuation tribunal or Local Taxation Chamber (LTC) to request an order directing the VOA to conduct an inspection.

Owner's and occupier's duty to provide information

The listing officer or assessor may require the current or former owner or occupier to provide information necessary for carrying out a valuation.[18] If the information is in the person's possession or control, they must supply it within 21 days of a written notice being served.

The initial notice must refer to section 27 of the Local Government Finance Act 1992. This should be a formal letter or email signed on behalf of the listing officer. A first reminder can be issued after 14 days, and a second notice should be sent 28 days after the initial request. This sets the 21-day response time.[19]

Failure to comply without a reasonable excuse may result in a fine of up to level 2 on the standard scale, although prosecutions are now rare.[20] Additionally, making a false statement in response to such a request can lead to a fine of up to £1,000.[21]

In Scotland, the assessor may issue an Assessor Information Notice requiring similar information to be provided.[22] A civil penalty may be imposed for failure to comply. Appeals against such penalties must be made to the LTC within 28 days of the civil penalty notice.

Local authority's duty to provide information

The listing officer or assessor may require the local authority to supply information about a property to assist with the valuation. In addition, if a local authority becomes aware of information that would assist the listing officer or assessor, it should proactively share that information, even if it has not been requested.[23] In practice, the local authority fulfils this duty by identifying newly constructed dwellings and referring existing ones that have been altered. However, this duty may extend further to include sharing any relevant information that would assist taxpayers and the authority – eg, by ensuring valuations are accurate and up to date.

Right to use other sources of information

Certain individuals and organisations must also supply information if the listing officer or assessor requests it.[24] A listing officer or assessor may also consider additional information available from other sources – eg, letting agents or utility companies. The owner or taxpayer should be informed of this information and its source.

Previously, there were instances where the VOA failed to notify owners or occupiers that council-supplied information was used when deciding to classify a shared house as separate dwellings (often referred to as houses in multiple occupation – HMOs) for council tax banding purposes. This issue has been largely resolved in England. As of 1 December 2023, all registered HMOs are now treated as a single dwelling for council tax purposes.

In Wales, however, properties may still be assessed as multiple dwellings.[25]

3. How dwellings are valued

Each dwelling is valued based on the price it could reasonably have been expected to sell for on the open market, subject to certain valuation assumptions, if sold on a specific date to a willing buyer.[26]

- In **England and Scotland**, the date is **1 April 1991**.
- In **Wales**, the date is **1 April 2003**. The Valuation Office Agency (VOA) will begin a revaluation of all properties in Wales starting May 2026, using property values as of 1 April 2023.

When valuing a property, the question posed is: 'What was this dwelling worth on the relevant date, assuming a willing buyer and applying the valuation assumptions?' (see below).

Theoretical and actual value

The valuation for council tax purposes represents a theoretical value of what the property was worth on the relevant date (see p29), not its actual market value. In Scotland, this is sometimes referred to as the 'statutory hypothesis'.[27]

This theoretical approach assumes the dwelling was in a reasonable state of repair, regardless of its real condition at the time.[28] Similarly, internal fixtures are ignored – eg, it makes no difference whether there is a modern kitchen installed or no kitchen fittings at all.

A council tax valuation must be made by applying all theoretical assumptions, even if they do not reflect the actual situation or condition today. Consequently, the actual sale price of the property in or since 1991 (2003 in Wales) is not automatically its council tax value, unless it happens to match the theoretical valuation. An actual sale price is only evidence towards the theoretical value, not definitive of it.

A dwelling built since 1991 has to be valued by imagining what it would have been worth had it existed in 1991, and then applying the valuation assumptions. The dwelling is allocated a valuation band from this theoretical valuation.

The valuation assumptions

To ensure that all properties are valued on a consistent basis, properties are not only assessed based on their market value on 1 April 1991 in England and Scotland (1 April 2003 in Wales), but also on a set of prescribed valuation assumptions.

Before applying the assumptions, the market value is assessed by considering various characteristics of the property including the number of rooms, its age, construction materials, whether there is a garden and the nature of the neighbouring environment. Once these have been considered, the following statutory valuation assumptions are applied.

Valuation assumptions

- The sale is with vacant possession.
- In England and Wales, a house is sold freehold and a flat (ie, part of a building divided horizontally to provide living units) is sold on a 99-year lease at a nominal rent.
- In England and Wales, the dwelling is sold free from any rent charge (ie, rare rental payments on freehold land usually associated with covenants) or other duty or obligation.
- In Scotland, the dwelling is sold free from any 'heritable security' – ie, any mortgage is paid off.

- The size, layout and character of the dwelling, and the physical state of its locality, are as they were on the valuation date.
- The dwelling is in reasonable repair.
- If there are common areas (eg, a shared hallway), these are in reasonable repair given the dwelling's age and characterand its locality. The buyer is liable for a reasonable share of maintenance costs.
- Any fixtures designed for a person with a physical disability which increase the value of the dwelling are ignored.
- The dwelling's use is permanently restricted to use as a private dwelling.
- The dwelling has no development value, except for development that does not require planning permission.

These assumptions are applied by the listing officer, whether or not they exist in fact.[29]

While rent charges are disregarded, other types of covenant that may affect a property can be considered when it is valued.[30]

In the case of shared ownership schemes, any reduction in value that arises due to the nature of shared ownership is disregarded, and they are treated as if granted for 99 years to a single owner.[31]

In areas such as national parks (eg, the Lake District), planning permissions may impose occupancy restrictions that limit who can live in the property – eg, requiring a local connection. These fall outside of the statutory presumption that a dwelling has no incumbrances. Therefore, such dwellings may sell for less on the open market because there are fewer potential buyers. As a result, they are generally placed in lower bands than properties without restrictions.[32]

For former council properties sold under right-to-buy legislation, the valuation figure used is not the actual (discounted) sale price. Instead, the pre-discount value and/or subsequent open market sales of comparable dwellings will be used.[33]

Reasonable repair and delisting

A dwelling is presumed to be in a reasonable state of repair, regardless of its actual condition.[34]

However, a distinction may be drawn between:

- a dwelling in need of repair and a dwelling in such a poor state that it should no longer be classified as a dwelling or hereditament (see p8), and should no longer be on the valuation list; *and*
- a dwelling is undergoing significant work and cannot be lived in during this time (see *Monk* below) and so it may be appropriate to adjust the valuation; *and*
- a dwelling requiring work but is capable of being lived in, therefore the presumption that it is in a reasonable state of repair.

There may come a point when property is so derelict it is incapable of repair.[35] A valuer or tribunal must avoid confusing the concept of the existence, or continued existence, of a hereditament on the one hand, from the separate question of the proper valuation of a hereditament on the other.

In the past, the VOA sometimes took a strict approach, whereby if a property could theoretically be repaired – regardless of the cost – it remained a hereditament. Because there is no economic test for council tax purposes, the cost of making the property habitable was considered irrelevant.

However, this approach has been rejected by the President of the Valuation Tribunal for England: 'Such a robust approach without giving proper consideration to whether a property is capable of occupation at the relevant date or whether it is reasonable for the owner to undertake such works to render it habitable is flawed, and fails to appreciate the reality of the situation, with respect in my opinion that approach is wrong.'[36] This decision clarified that habitability and reasonableness are essential considerations, and not just the theoretical possibility of repair.

A key case is *Newbigin (VO) v Monk,* in which the Supreme Court held that a dwelling undergoing major works or reconstruction, such that it could not be occupied or used beneficially, may warrant a nominal valuation or even removal from the valuation list. In this case, the property was assigned a nominal value of £1.[37] It established that 'radical alterations which render the hereditament unoccupiable, may justify a proposal to alter the rating list'.

The starting point in any valuation exercise is to establish if a dwelling exists in the first place, before the statutory valuation assumptions are applied. No hereditament may exist because a property is incapable of beneficial occupation. Although there is no economic test for the required repairs in council tax, the amount of repair works that are envisaged in reinstating a dwelling must be considered reasonable.[38] The test is not whether the property can be repaired whatever the cost, but whether it is reasonable to expect repairs to be undertaken, given the amount of work involved. Extensive works beyond what would reasonably be expected may result in an entirely new dwelling altogether.[39]

Listing officers are expected to ask: 'Having regard to the character of the property and a reasonable amount of repair works being undertaken, could the premises be occupied as a dwelling?'[40]

If the answer is no, the dwelling should be removed from the valuation list. If it is yes, it should be valued assuming it is in a reasonable state of repair. It is not possible to remove a property temporarily on grounds of disrepair; deletion is either permanent or not at all until the repair works are completed and a new dwelling capable of domestic occupation exists.[41] However, following *Monk,* a temporary band reduction may be granted where major works reduce a property's value during the work period. In effect, a property may lose its status as a dwelling while it is a building site.

Similarly, in Scotland, the view has been taken that 'it is not correct to treat them as if they are in a state of reasonable repair if, in fact, they are not. The assumption... does not apply at that stage. Rather, regard has to be had to the subjects' actual state and existing use.'[42]

A mere incapacity to be lived in temporarily while repairs or other alteration works are being carried out is not necessarily enough to cause a property to cease to be a dwelling.[43]

A tribunal may be expected to examine the timeline of damage and deterioration, and the point when remedial work commences. Typically, the earliest date where works actually commence will be considered the point where a dwelling may be delisted.[44]

Fixtures for a person with a disability

'Fixtures' are items permanently attached to a dwelling, such as a sink, toilet or lift. The value of fixtures should be ignored in the valuation if they:[45]

- are designed to make the dwelling suitable for use by a person with a physical disability; *and*
- increase the dwelling's value.

In such cases, the dwelling is valued as if those fixtures are not present. There is no requirement for someone with a disability to live in the dwelling. If such fixtures have been taken into account during the valuation process, the listing officer or assessor should be notified of this possible oversight.

However, the presence of fittings and adaptations may be relevant to obtaining a reduction in valuation from the council (see p37). There is also a separate disability reduction scheme (see Chapter 6).

Dwellings with mixed domestic and business use

In England and Wales, properties which include both a domestic and non-domestic component (known as 'composite hereditaments' – see p16) are valued on the proportion of the market value which might reasonably be attributed to the domestic use of the property. The valuation is based on the same rules and assumptions outlined above, except that the assumption that the property is permanently restricted for use as a private dwelling is ignored.

Scottish farmhouses, crofts and fish farms

In Scotland, dwellings such as farmhouses, cottages and croft houses connected with agriculture or fish farms are valued on the assumption that their availability is restricted to being used in that way. This lowers the property's value and may lead to it being placed in a lower valuation band. When valuing a dwelling for council tax, the listing officer or assessor must not ignore the effect of a planning condition restricting occupation to a person mainly employed on a farm.[46]

Proposals and appeals on valuations

The listing officer or assessor must apply the valuation assumptions in every case, whatever the condition of the dwelling (but see below if energy efficiency measures have been added). So, a valuation for council tax purposes may differ from a valuation for other purposes. The assumptions are applied in every case regardless of the actual circumstances on the relevant day (ie, 1 April 1991 for England and Scotland, and 1 April 2003 for Wales) and used by valuation tribunals and the Local Taxation Chamber, the High Court and the Court of Session when considering appeals against banding decisions.

A successful proposal must apply the assumptions described on p30 – failing to do so risks dismissal, even where real-world sale data appears compelling.

Energy efficiency measures

The installation of energy efficiency or renewable energy measures (eg, ground source heat pumps, insulation or solar panels) can affect the valuation of a dwelling for council tax purposes. If the property is sold and the measures have increased the value of the dwelling into the next council tax band level, it is possible to change the dwelling's valuation. However, in practice, only substantial improvements would likely move a property up a band on sale, and energy efficiency measures alone are unlikely to do so or will be disregarded.[47]

4. Compiling and maintaining valuation lists

The listing officer or assessor is responsible for compiling and maintaining each local authority's valuation list.[48]

Compiling the list

In **England and Scotland**, the valuation list in operation was compiled on 1 April 1993 and came into force on that day. In **Wales**, the current list came into force on 1 April 2005.

Any new lists must, as far as is reasonably practicable, be accurate on the date on which they are compiled. This means that properties must be revalued before publication, reflecting the relevant assumptions and any material changes that have occurred up to that date. As soon as is reasonably practicable after compiling the list, the listing officer or assessor should send a copy to the local authority. The local authority should deposit this at its principal office.[49]

Maintaining the list

The listing officer or assessor must accurately maintain the list for as long as it is used for council tax purposes.[50] They have an implied power to alter the list.[51] The listing officer or assessor notifies the local authority regularly of any alterations to the compiled list to take account of new dwellings, demolitions, successful appeals and other changes.

5. Inspecting the valuation list

Everyone has the right to inspect the valuation list, which must be made available free of charge at a reasonable time and place.[52]

Valuation lists can be inspected online at:

- gov.uk/government/organisations/valuation-office-agency (England and Wales);
- saa.gov.uk (Scotland).

You can make copies of the list. Alternatively, a copy can be requested from the local authority, listing officer or assessor. A reasonable charge can be made for this service.

If a person intentionally obstructs access to the valuation list, they may be liable on summary conviction to a fine not exceeding level 2 on the standard scale.[53]

What the valuation list shows

A valuation list must include the specific information below.[54] The list does not contain any personal information. The omission of any matter that should be included from a list does not render it invalid.[55]

The required contents of the valuation list

- Each dwelling in the local authority's area.
- Each dwelling's valuation band.
- A reference number for each dwelling.
- A marker indicating properties with mixed domestic and non-domestic use (England and Wales only).
- The effective date of any alteration.
- An indicator showing that an alteration has been made following an order of a valuation tribunal, the Local Taxation Chamber, the High Court or the Court of Session.
- Notes indicating that a dwelling is a private garage or domestic storage premises (Scotland only).

In addition, the online search shows whether the property has an 'improvement indicator', which indicates it will be revalued at the next sale.

There is no statutory format prescribed for presenting a valuation list. Listing officers and assessors typically order their lists alphabetically, by postal towns, then by streets within each town. Within each street, numbered addresses are shown first, then named-only addresses in alphabetical order. Addresses that cannot be allocated to a street appear at the end of the relevant postal town list under the heading 'within billing authority area'. Properties not allocated to a postal town appear at the end of the list.[56]

6. **Altering a valuation list**

The listing officer or assessor can alter a current valuation list following:

- the receipt of a proposal from an interested party or the local authority; *or*
- a successful appeal to the Valuation Tribunal for England (VTE), Valuation Tribunal for Wales (VTW), the Local Taxation Chamber (LTC) in Scotland, or to the High Court or Court of Session.

The Valuation Office Agency (VOA) may alter a dwelling's valuation band if the listing officer or assessor is satisfied that:[57]

- the valuation band is incorrect – eg, because of a clerical error; *or*
- the dwelling would have been placed in a different valuation band had the valuation been carried out correctly; *or*
- there has been a material increase (see below) in the dwelling's value and all, or part, of it has been sold or let on a lease for a term of seven years or more; *or*
- there has been a material reduction (see p37) in the dwelling's value; *or*
- part of the property has started to be used, or is no longer used, for business purposes, or the balance between business and domestic use has changed; *or*
- there has been a successful appeal against the current valuation band; *or*
- the listing officer made an earlier banding determination that is subsequently deemed incorrect, including a historical inaccuracy.[58]

The VOA should usually tell you within two months if it decides to alter the list.

A material increase in the dwelling's value

A 'material increase' in the value of a dwelling means any increase as a result of (in whole or in part) any building works or other physical alterations.[59] This includes works that increase the property's size or enhance its market value. However, the material increase does not affect the valuation until the dwelling (or any part of it) is sold. In England and Wales, this also applies if the dwelling is let on a lease for seven years or more. In England, certain energy efficiency and renewable energy installations are excluded from being treated as a material increase, under the Climate Change and Sustainable Energy Act 2006[60] – eg, where the majority of energy produced is used within the dwelling.

In England, any banding change due to a material increase takes effect from the date the alteration is entered on the list.[61] In Scotland and Wales, it takes effect from the date the sale or lease was completed.[62]

Even if a dwelling has not yet been sold or let, any future revaluation will take all material increases into account when setting the banding.

A material reduction in the dwelling's value

A 'material reduction' in the value of a dwelling should lead to an immediate revaluation and, where sufficiently significant, may lead to a rebanding of the dwelling. This only applies where the material reduction is caused (in whole or in part) by:[63]

- the demolition of any part of the dwelling (but not partial demolition during other building or engineering work); *or*
- any change in the physical state of the dwelling's locality; *or*
- any adaptation to make the dwelling suitable for someone with a physical disability.

Changes in the physical state of a locality give the greatest scope for proposals to lower a dwelling's valuation band. This is sometimes referred to as 'blighting'. Examples include a change in the character of the immediate environment because of a road-widening scheme, the deterioration of surrounding property or a change in the use of nearby business premises.

The reduction in value must occur after the entry of the dwelling on the valuation list.[64]

In *Chilton-Merryweather v Hunt & Ors*, the Court of Appeal clarified that while a mere increase in traffic may not qualify as a material change, different conclusions may be drawn where the character of the road changes or a quiet road becomes a 'rat-run'.[65] This distinction has been accepted at tribunal level, especially where surrounding property use has substantially changed – eg, a quiet community centre becoming a high-traffic venue.[66]

A material reduction takes effect from:

- in England and Wales, the day the material circumstances arose, if reasonably identifiable. If the exact date is unclear, from the date the proposal (see p38) was served on the listing officer or, in any other case, from the date it was entered on the list;[67]
- in Scotland, from either the date the property's value fell sufficiently to affect its banding, or the start of the financial year in which the proposal is made, whichever is later.[68]

How dwellings are revalued

The listing officer is under a duty to alter the valuation list where it is inaccurate.[69]

Where any of the prescribed conditions for changing a dwelling's valuation band are met, a revaluation must be carried out, applying the statutory valuation rules and assumptions on p30.

In England, this means that even when the dwelling's state has changed, the valuation must still reflect what the property would have sold for on the open market on 1 April 1991, applying the statutory assumptions.[70] If the change in value is only small, it might not be sufficient to justify a move from one valuation band to another.

When deciding whether to alter the valuation list, the listing officer may consider any relevant evidence showing what the accurate valuation of a dwelling was, regardless of when that evidence arises. This may include evidence of relevant sales post-dating 1 April 1991 and evidence of which arises after 1 April 1993.[71]

In Scotland and Wales, a material increase is assessed on the date the sale or transaction took place. In the case of a material increase in the value of the dwelling, the date of alteration takes effect from the date of the transaction, even if the increase is not identified for several years. The effective date of the alteration should be the day on which the first sale of the dwelling after the material increase is completed, not the date that you were informed or an assessor discovered it. If the change in value is only established some while after the first date of sale, the liable person may be faced with a backdated bill.[72]

If a dwelling ceases to be a composite hereditament, if there is a reduction in the domestic use of a dwelling, or if a new dwelling comes into existence, the relevant date is the date on which the relevant change to the property occurred. Where multiple changes have taken place affecting the valuation, the alteration to the list should reflect the date of the most recent change.[73]

Obtaining an alteration

If a list is inaccurate, you can make a proposal to the listing officer or assessor for an alteration to the list. In many cases, there are time limits for this (see p39).

Making a proposal is also the first stage in the appeal process (see Chapter 11).

Who can make a proposal

Any interested person can make a proposal to alter the list. An 'interested person' on any given day is:[74]

- the owner of the dwelling;
- anyone who is liable (solely or jointly) to pay council tax on the dwelling;
- in the case of an exempt dwelling or a dwelling where the council tax has been set at nil, the person who would otherwise be liable to pay the tax.

Local authorities in England can also make proposals to the listing officer.[75]

Getting council tax reduction (see Chapter 8) does not affect your ability to make a proposal as an interested person.

Time limits

You can make a proposal at any time if:

- a property should be added to or removed from the valuation list;[76]
- there has been a material increase (see p36) in the value of a dwelling and a relevant transaction;
- there has been a material reduction (see p37) in the value of a dwelling;
- there has been a change in use of part of a property from business to domestic (or vice versa), or a change in the balance between business and domestic use.[77]

However, there is a time limit in which to make a proposal in the following circumstances.[78]

- **Proposals about the original list**. Except in limited circumstances, the time limit to make a proposal has now expired.
- **Proposals by a new resident/owner or about a new property**. A proposal can be made within six months if:
  - you first become liable for the council tax on a particular dwelling; *or*
  - a new dwelling is added to the valuation list after 1 April 1993 (1 April 2005 in Wales).

  Such a proposal cannot be made, however, if:
  - it is based on the same facts that have already been considered and determined by the VTE, VTW or LTC, or by the High Court or Court of Session; *or*
  - the new taxpayer is a company which is a subsidiary of the preceding taxpayer; *or*
  - the preceding taxpayer is a company which is a subsidiary of the new taxpayer; *or*
  - the change of taxpayer is solely because of the formation of a new partnership involving someone from the previous partnership.
- **Appeal decisions concerning a comparable dwelling**. You can make a proposal within six months of an appeal decision relating to a comparable property, if that decision provides a reasonable basis to argue your property is wrongly banded.
- **Proposals after a VOA alteration.** If the listing officer or assessor alters the list for your dwelling, you can make a proposal within six months of the date the notice of the alteration was served.[79] Whether the notice was sent by first or second class post may be considered when calculating the time period.[80]

Otherwise, there are no discretionary powers to accept a proposal made after the permitted time limit, even if there are mitigating circumstances.[81]

In Wales, the listing officer may correct an inaccuracy in the original list if the band was too high. The alteration takes effect from the later of the date the list was compiled or six years prior to the date the alteration is entered in the list.[82]

Making a proposal

You must make the proposal in writing.[83] Use the official form (available from the listing officer or assessor), or write a letter including:[84]

- your full name and address;
- the capacity in which the proposal is being made – ie, whether you are the liable person or the owner of the dwelling;
- the dwelling address to which it relates;
- the date;
- the change you are proposing;
- why you believe the list is inaccurate and the relevant facts, dates and any supporting evidence.

Note: you are usually expected to pay council tax while your proposal is considered. However, if your proposal is that the dwelling should not be on the valuation list at all, and you are being billed for council tax, you should also inform the local authority that you are challenging liability to the tax.

Example

Max lives in a single room in a shared house in England. He proposes that the room should not be on the valuation list as a separate dwelling. He challenges both the listing and his liability, arguing the owner should be liable for council tax as it is part of a house in multiple occupation (HMO).

Max should also notify the local authority that he is challenging liability, and if he is summoned to court for non-payment, he should ask for an adjournment because of his active appeal.

You should address the proposal to the listing officer or assessor for your area and deliver or post it to the appropriate address. Keep a copy and get proof of postage, online confirmation or, if delivered by hand, a receipt.

Are you acting on behalf of someone else?

The VOA expects you to:

- provide a signed and dated authority to act from the taxpayer, which must be signed and dated by them within the last six months;
- confirm that you are entitled to make a valid proposal;
- submit relevant evidence questioning the current band;
- complete a property details questionnaire.

Evidence

You can use a wide range of evidence to establish value. Acceptable evidence includes:

- a plan of your property (floor plan or site layout);
- photographs of the property (inside and/or outside);
- sales data for up to two years either side of 1 April 1991 (England and Scotland) or 1 April 2003 (Wales) for your property or similar properties in your locality, and evidence that similarly sized properties are in a lower band. There must be no more than a 10 per cent difference in size between these properties and yours. Evidence of significantly larger properties within the locality in a lower band may also be accepted. Only the first five comparable properties are typically considered – keep your evidence focused and high quality. You may also provide evidence of the value of other properties with different characteristics (eg, a property with a lease of 125 years instead of 99), as the listing officer or the valuation tribunals should use their expertise to take into account such evidence and make adjustments when applying the valuation assumptions.[85]

Usually, a proposal can only deal with one dwelling. In England, however, you can make a multi-dwelling proposal if:[86]

- you make the proposal in the same capacity (eg, as the owner) and each of the dwellings is within the same building (or 'curtilage'); *or*
- a property is shown as a dwelling when it should not be or should be shown as a number of dwellings.

The tone of the list

The 'tone of the list' refers to a settled pattern or consensus of how similar properties in the same area are banded in the council tax valuation list. It acts as a benchmark or guide when deciding the correct banding for a dwelling.

The tone is established when a number of properties, similar in size, character, quality, detachment and location, were attributed the same level of assessment/band which, over time, has not been challenged. Assessments that have been challenged and subsequently agreed by parties or determined by a valuation tribunal may also be important in establishing the tone.

Best evidence

The best evidence on which to determine a banding is a sale on the appeal property or a comparable property which had completed at or around 1 April 1991.[87] If a property did not exist on 1 April 1991, the listing officer or assessor has regard to the sales completed on comparable properties in the locality around that date.[88]

Generally, house price calculators or indices are viewed as being unreliable for council tax purposes. This is because they are based on broad averages derived from wide geographical areas and including all property types and sizes.[89]

Response of the listing officer

In **England and Wales,** the listing officer should write within 28 days acknowledging receipt of the proposal, unless the proposal is considered to be invalid (see below). In **Scotland**, the assessor should acknowledge receipt of the proposal within 14 days. The acknowledgement should include details of the procedures that will be followed.[90]

Joint proposals in Scotland

In Scotland, other interested people (see p38) may write to the assessor indicating that they wish to support the proposal.[91] Provided the proposal has not been withdrawn or referred to the LTC, the original proposal should then be treated as a joint proposal.

Invalid proposals

Different procedures apply to invalid proposals in England, Wales and Scotland. If the listing officer or assessor fails to identify an invalid proposal at this stage, the point can still be raised at an appeal hearing.[92]

England

In England, if the listing officer considers that the proposal is invalid, they send you an 'invalidity notice'. They should do this within four weeks of receiving the proposal. This notice:[93]

- gives the reasons why the proposal is considered invalid; *and*
- provides you with a right to make a further proposal in relation to the same dwelling (see below) or to appeal to the VTE (see p44).

The listing officer can withdraw an invalidity notice at any time by informing you in writing. Unless an invalidity notice has been withdrawn, you can:

- make a further proposal, but only once and only if the original proposal was made within the appropriate time limit. If you make a further proposal, the earlier proposal, which resulted in the invalidity notice, is treated as withdrawn; *or*
- appeal to the VTE. You must send the tribunal a copy of the invalidity notice, together with a written statement. This should include the address of the dwelling and the reasons why you consider the proposal to be valid. Action on the original proposal is suspended until either the listing officer withdraws the invalidity notice or the VTE or High Court decides the validity of the proposal. If the listing officer withdraws an invalidity notice after an appeal has been started, they must inform the tribunal. See Chapter 11 for more details on tribunal hearings.

In some cases, a listing officer may apply to have a proposal treated as invalid at a tribunal even if no invalidity notice has been served.[94]

Wales

In Wales, if the listing officer believes that a proposal has not been validly made, they may serve an invalidity notice on you. They must do this within four weeks. The notice must explain the reasons for their decision and that you can either make a further proposal or appeal to the VTW. If you make a fresh proposal, the original is treated as withdrawn. You must make the fresh proposal within four weeks of the invalidity notice being served.

Scotland

In Scotland, a distinction is drawn between proposals that are considered invalid because:[95]

- you are not an appropriate person to make a proposal or because it is out of time; *and*
- you did not include the required information.

The assessor must write to you within six weeks of receiving the proposal, giving reasons for the decision, and describe your right to appeal to the assessor within four weeks. If no such appeal is made, the matter ends. If you did not include the required information, the letter must give reasons for the decision and identify the information that needs to be supplied. You may either:

- supply the information within four weeks; *or*
- appeal in writing to the assessor within four weeks.

If you do not supply the information or make an appeal within the four-week period, the assessor treats the proposal as invalidly made and that is the end of the matter.

If you make an appeal in either case but the assessor still considers the appeal invalid, they should inform the LTC in writing, within four weeks, that an appeal has been made. They should also give details of the proposal and their reasons for considering the proposal to be invalid.[96]

After a valid proposal has been made: England and Wales

Within six weeks of receiving a valid proposal, the listing officer should send a copy to anyone who appears liable for council tax on the dwelling. They should also send copies to the local authority if it has informed the listing officer in writing that it wishes to receive a copy of a class(es) of proposal, and your proposal falls within such a class. Each copy should be accompanied by a statement of the procedures to be followed.[97]

Following the receipt of a valid proposal:

- the listing officer may agree to the proposal (see p44);

- all interested parties may agree to a different alteration to the list (see below);
- an appeal may be made to the VTE/VTW (see below);
- the proposal may be withdrawn (see p45).

The listing officer agrees to the proposal

If the listing officer agrees to the proposal, they should notify you and the liable person (if different) that the valuation list will be altered accordingly. The listing officer should alter the valuation list within six weeks of the date of the letter.[98]

Agreeing to a different alteration

Before an appeal, the listing officer can agree an alteration to the list which is different from that proposed, but with which you agree. This requires the agreement of all interested parties. Negotiation can take place directly with the VOA. If an appeal has been lodged and a hearing date fixed, this can be postponed to allow more time for negotiations or the tribunal can issue further directions allowing for more time for settlement. If such an agreement is reached, the listing officer should alter the valuation list within six weeks of the date of the agreement and the original proposal may be treated as having been withdrawn.[99]

Appealing to the valuation tribunal

If the listing officer has issued a decision notice to the proposer, the taxpayer and any other competent person, any of these people can appeal to the VTE/VTW (see p259).

You make the appeal within three months. The tribunal's president can authorise a late appeal if the delay was due to circumstances beyond your control.

The appeal is started by serving the tribunal with a copy of the decision notice, together with the following information if this is not contained in the decision notice:

- the address of the dwelling;
- the reasons for the appeal;
- the name and address of:
  - the appellant;
  - the proposer (if different from the appellant);
  - the listing officer;
  - any other person who appears to be a taxpayer;
- any other interested person – ie, someone with a financial interest that may be affected by a change in the valuation.[100]

Where, after an appeal has been made to the VTE, the listing officer makes the proposed alteration to the list, they must notify the VTE. Once that notice is served, the appeal is treated as withdrawn on the date of service of the notice.[101]

In rare cases where neither the local authority nor the valuation office accepts responsibility for deciding whether a dwelling is on the list or should be taxed, or officials claim it is the responsibility of the other body, you should appeal both decision separately.

Time limits for appealing

Proposal	*Time limit*
Entry set out in the listing officer's notice is inaccurate	Within six months from date of notice
Becoming the taxpayer for the first time	Within six months of becoming the taxpayer
Dwelling should be deleted from the valuation list – eg, it is now used commercially or has been demolished	Any time
Dwelling should be included in the valuation list – eg, it is a new property or now used for domestic purposes	Any time
Dwelling should be shown in the valuation list as one entry – eg, the merger of an annexe with the main house	Any time
Dwelling should be shown in the valuation list as more than one entry – eg, a house split into flats	Any time
Material reduction in the value of the dwelling – eg, permanent, substantial physical changes in the area or other changes in the area such as adaptations for a disabled person	Any time
Material increase in the value of the dwelling – eg, it has been sold following an extension	Any time
Increase or decrease in the domestic use of the dwelling	Any time
Relevant local valuation tribunal or High Court case to be taken into account, giving details of judgment and address	Within six months of decision

Appeals are further described in Chapter 11.

Note: you cannot usually make another appeal on the same facts if a tribunal has already determined against you. The only situation where this may be allowed is where a tribunal has decided the matter in your absence,[102] but you can apply to a tribunal vice president to set aside a decision or make an application by judicial review.[103]

Withdrawing the proposal

You may withdraw the proposal:

- at any time before an appeal by writing to the tribunal; *or*
- orally at the hearing.

If you withdraw at the hearing, it only takes effect if the panel consents. All parties must be notified in writing of a withdrawal, and the date the proposal is withdrawn should be confirmed. Each party has the opportunity to begin a new appeal about the decision by serving a written notice. This must state that the new appellant wishes to proceed with an appeal and the reason for it.

Are you being pressured to withdraw?

Sometimes, VOA or local authority staff attempt to encourage people to withdraw their proposals and appeals. They may claim things such as 'A tribunal rejected a similar appeal' or 'You have no chance of winning'. Remember that a tribunal decision on any point is persuasive but not binding on subsequent tribunals. If you are subject to improper pressure over an appeal by an official either in the valuation office or from, or acting on behalf of, the local authority, you should make a formal complaint.

After a valid proposal has been made: Scotland

In Scotland, once a valid proposal has been received:

- the assessor may agree to the proposal (see below);
- an appeal may be made to the LTC (see below);
- the proposal may be withdrawn (see p47).

The assessor agrees to the proposal

If the assessor thinks the proposal is well founded, they should advise you (and any joint proposer) of this in writing. The assessor should alter the list within six weeks of the date of the letter.[104]

Appealing to the Local Taxation Chamber

If the assessor thinks the proposal is not well founded and it is not withdrawn, you should refer the disagreement to the LTC.

Within 28 days of the date the assessor issued you with the decision, you must apply to the LTC online at localtaxationchamber.scot or in writing or by email, to your local assessor.[105] See p271 for how to appeal to the LTC.

If the assessor has previously issued an invalidity notice on the grounds that:

- you are not an appropriate person to make the proposal or because the proposal is out of time, the 28-day period starts from the day the assessor withdrew the notice or you won the appeal against the notice; *or*
- the proposal does not include the required information, the 28-day period starts from the day that all the relevant information was supplied or the day you won the appeal against the notice.[106]

If you did not make your original proposal within six months of first becoming the taxpayer, under the Council Tax (Alteration of Lists and Appeals) (Scotland)

Regulations 1993, the tribunal has no discretion to waive the regulations to allow an appeal.[107]

Withdrawing the proposal

You can withdraw the proposal at any time by writing to the assessor.[108] If none of the proposers are currently liable for the tax on the dwelling, the assessor must write to at least one currently liable person telling them about the proposed withdrawal. An interested person (see p38) has six weeks from the date of the letter to advise the assessor that they wish to adopt the proposal. From that date, it is then treated as having been made by that person.

Notification of an alteration

Within six weeks of altering the list, the listing officer or assessor should write to the local authority stating the effect of the alteration. The local authority should alter its copy of the valuation list as soon as is reasonably practicable. Where new dwellings are created or split up (known as being disaggregated) or existing dwellings are combined (aggregated) into different dwellings or units, new account numbers for council tax must be created. This may mean that previous bills are extinguished where the change is retrospective.[109]

England and Wales

In England and Wales, when the listing officer alters the list, they should also write to the person who is currently liable for the tax on the dwelling within six weeks, advising them of the effect of the alteration and the process by which a proposal and appeal may be made.[110] This obligation to notify does not, however, apply if the alteration was made solely to correct a clerical error, or to reflect:

- a decision of the listing officer that a proposal is well founded; *or*
- an agreed alternative alteration; *or*
- a change in the address of the dwelling concerned; *or*
- a change in the area of the billing authority; *or*
- the decision of the VTE/VTW or the High Court in relation to the dwelling concerned.

Scotland

In Scotland, the assessor must notify a liable person within six weeks of the alteration being made. Where the alteration involves adding the dwelling to the list, the owner must also be notified within six weeks of the alteration. The notification should include a statement about the process by which a proposal may be made.

Additionally, the assessor must notify a liable person within six weeks of the alteration being made if:

- an alteration has been agreed, but the proposer is not a liable person at the time of the alteration; *or*

- an appeal decision has led to the alteration of the list but none of the parties to the appeal is a liable person on the date of the alteration.[111]

7. The valuation bands

The set amount of council tax and Scottish Water charges for each dwelling depends on the valuation band to which it is allocated. Different valuation bands apply in England,[112] Scotland[113] and Wales.[114] You can find out which band your property is in at gov.uk/council-tax-bands.

To determine which valuation band applies to a dwelling for any day, the situation at the end of the day is assumed to have existed throughout that day.[115]

England and Scotland

The original bands from the 1993 valuation list apply in England and Scotland, although the calculation ratio has changed (see p49).

Valuation bands in England

Valuation band	*Range of values*
A	Up to £40,000
B	£40,001 to £52,000
C	£52,001 to £68,000
D	£68,001 to £88,000
E	£88,001 to £120,000
F	£120,001 to £160,000
G	£160,001 to £320,000
H	£320,001 and over

Valuation bands in Scotland

Valuation band	*Range of values*
A	Up to £27,000
B	£27,001 to £35,000
C	£35,001 to £45,000
D	£45,001 to £58,000
E	£58,001 to £80,000
F	£80,001 to £106,000
G	£106,001 to £212,000
H	£212,001 and over

Wales

Since 1 April 2005, dwellings in Wales have fallen into one of the following bands, based on a theoretical valuation date of 1 April 2003.[116] These bands apply to all domestic dwellings from 1 April 2005.

Valuation bands in Wales from 1 April 2005 [117]

Valuation band	*Range of values*
A	Up to £44,000
B	£44,001 to £65,000
C	£65,001 to £91,000
D	£91,001 to £123,000
E	£123,001 to £162,000
F	£162,001 to £223,000
G	£223,001 to £324,000
H	£324,001 to £424,000
I	£424,001 and over

In the future, Welsh ministers may amend the council tax banding system.[118] Their powers include the ability to substitute existing bands, alter the ratios between bands and change the reference point used for the banding structure – eg, designating a band other than Band D as the baseline. They may also create new or revised descriptions of council tax bands.

How the amount of tax payable varies between bands

The council tax payable in any local authority depends on the valuation band assigned to the dwelling. The lower the value of the band, the lower the bill will be. Local authorities cannot alter the banding structure or the relative proportions between bands. The proportions between valuation bands are:

- **England: 6(A):7(B):8(C):9(D):11(E):13(F):15(G):18(H).**[119] This means, for example, that a Band H property is charged three times more than one in Band A and twice as much as one in Band D;[120]
- **Wales: 6(A):7(B):8(C):9(D):11(E):13(F):15(G):18(H):21(I).**[121] Meaning that households in the highest Band I pay around three and a half times as much council tax as those in Band A;
- **Scotland: 240(A):280(B):320(C):360(D):473(E):585(F):705(G):882(H).**[122] This reflects a different proportional structure set under Scottish legislation. The levels of tax payable for dwellings in the higher four bands (E to H) are greater, relative to those in the lower four bands.

In all three countries, the calculation of tax for different valuation bands in any financial year is worked out by the formula: **A x (N ÷ D)**. A is the average amount calculated (or last calculated) by the billing authority for each dwelling for that year, N is the number associated with the valuation band (as above) and D is the number associated with Band D.[123]

In 2025/26, the average council tax Band D payable:

- in England, is £2,280;[124]
- in Wales, is £2,170;[125]
- in Scotland, is £1,543.[126]

A high value council tax surcharge for England was announced in the November 2025 budget. From April 2028, this will apply to dwellings valued at £2 million or more. It will be calculated using updated valuations.

Notes

1. **Who is responsible for valuations**
   1 **EW** s20 LGFA 1992
   2 Treasury Statement by Minister James Murray, UIN HCWS607, 28 April 2025
   3 s84(1) LGFA 1992
   4 s86(5) and (10) LGFA 1992
   5 **EW** s21(3) LGFA 1992
   S s86(7) LGFA 1992
   6 **EW** s21 LGFA 1992
   S s86(8) and (9) LGFA 1992
   7 VOA, *Annual Report and Accounts 2015-2016*, 'Customer Charter', pp37-38
   8 VOA, *Annual Reports and Accounts 2023-2024*, HC 245 28 No 2024, pp30-31
   9 VOA Complaint Decision No.FS50412668, Freedom of Information Commissioner, 23 November 2011
   10 VOA Complaint Decision No.FS50563305, Freedom of Information Commissioner, 3 March 2015
   11 s18(1)(c) FOIA 2000
   12 VOA Complaint Decision No.Ref FS50599228, Freedom of Information Commissioner, 17 February 2015

2. **The listing officer's and assessor's powers**
   13 *Johnson v Revenue and Customs Commissioners* [2025] UKFTT(TC) 50
   14 **E** s25A LGFA 1992
   W s26 LGFA 1992
   S s89 LGFA 1992
   15 s25A LGFA 1992
   16 VOA charter, 8 February 2016
   17 **EW** s26 LGFA 1992
   S s89 LGFA 1992
   18 **EW** s27 LGFA 1992
   S s90 LGFA 1992
   19 CTM, Part 7: Requesting Information from Owners and Occupiers
   20 **EW** s27 LGFA 1992
   S s90 LGFA 1992
   21 **EW** s27 LGFA 1992; Sch 37 Part 9 Criminal Justice Act 2003
   S s90 LGFA 1992; The Criminal Justice Act 1991 (Commencement No.3) Order 1992 No.333
   22 ss26 and 30 Non-Domestic Rates (Scotland) Act 2020
   23 **EW** s27(6) LGFA 1992
   S s90 LGFA 1992
   24 **EW** s27 LGFA 1992
   S s90 LGFA 1992
   25 *R (on the application of Howard Gardens Manco Ltd) v Lucy Formela-Osborne* [2024] EWHC 1112 (Admin)

3. **How dwellings are valued**

26 **E** s21 LGFA 1992; CT(SVD) Regs
W s21 LGFA 1992; CT(SVD) Regs, as amended by CT(SVD)(W)(A) Regs
S s86(2) LGFA 1992 and CT(VD)(S) Regs

27 *Assessor for Lothian Valuation Joint Board (Appellant) v Mclaughlin* [2020] CSIH 16

28 *R v South Western Valuation Tribunal ex parte De Melo* [2000] RVR 73, CA

29 *R v East Sussex Valuation Tribunal ex parte Silverstone* [1996] RVR 203; *Clark v Bunyan* [2024] EWHC 486 (Admin)

30 *Coll (LO) v Walters* [2016] EWHC 831 (Admin)

31 *Call v Brannan; Call v Kozak and Another* [2015] All ER (D) 44 (Apr)

32 *Steels v Roberts (LO)* [2020] VTE Appeal No. M0855369; CTM, Practice Note 1; *Coll (LO) v Walters and Walters* [2016] EWHC 831 (Admin)

33 **EW** *Call v Brannan; Call v Kozak and Another* [2015] All ER (D) 44 (Apr)
S Reg 2(1) CT(VD)(S) Regs; *Assessor for Strathclyde v Rea* [1995] SC 577

34 *R v East Sussex Valuation Tribunal* [1996] RVR 203

35 *Wilson v Jo Coll (LO)* [2011] EWHC 2824 (Admin)

36 *Ward v Moore* [2021] VT00004192, 23 July 2021

37 *Newbigin (VO) v Monk* [2017] UKSC 14

38 *Wilson v Jo Coll (LO)* [2011] EWHC 2824 (Admin), para 40

39 *Sandeep Tewari v Virk* [2020] VTE Appeal No.M0826076

40 CTM, Practice Note 4

41 *Juggins v Dirk* [2020] VT00001060 para 17, 2 February 2021

42 *Assessor Tayside Joint Valuation Board v a Decision of the Valuation Appeal Committee for Perth and Kinross* [2017] CSIH 64, para 25

43 *Assessor Tayside Joint Valuation Board v a Decision of the Valuation Appeal Committee for Perth and Kinross* [2017] CSIH 64, para 25

44 *AB v Virk* [2022] VTE, 9 November 2022

45 **E** s21 LGFA 1992; CT(SVD) Regs
W s21 LGFA 1992; CT(SVD) Regs, as amended by CT(SVD)(W)(A) Regs
S s86(2) LGFA 1992; CT(VD)(S) Regs

46 Reg 3 CT(VD)(S) Regs; *The Appeal of Grampian Valuation Joint Board* [2003] RA 167 Sc

47 Parliamentary Answer by John Healy, Minister for Local Government, 13 December 2007; reg 3 CT(ALA)(E) Regs, as amended by reg 2(2)(c) CT(ALA)(E)(A) Regs

4. **Compiling and maintaining valuation lists**

48 **EW** ss22 and 22B LGFA 1992
S s84 LGFA 1992

49 **EW** ss22 and 22B LGFA 1992
S s85 LGFA 1992

50 **EW** s22 LGFA 1992
S s84 LGFA 1992

51 *National Car Parks Ltd v Baird (VO)* [2004] EWCA Civ 967; *BMC Properties and Management v Jackson (VO)* [2015] EWCA Civ 1306

5. **Inspecting the valuation list**

52 **EW** s28 LGFA 1992
S s91 LGFA 1992

53 **EW** s28 LGFA 1992
S s91 LGFA 1992

54 **EW** s23 LGFA 1992 and CT(CVL) Regs
S s84 LGFA 1992 and CT(CVL) Regs

55 **EW** s23 LGFA 1992
S s84 LGFA 1992

56 Valuation Tribunal Service, *Council Tax Guidance Manual*, para 3.4.1

6. **Altering a valuation list**

57 **E** Reg 3 CT(ALA)(E) Regs, as amended by reg 2 CT(ALA)(E)(A) Regs; VTE(CTRA)(P) Regs
W CT(ALA) Regs
S r4(1)(b)(i) CT(ALA)(S) Regs

58 *Adam v Listing Officer* [2014] EWHC 1110 (Admin)

59 **E** s24 LGFA 1992
S s87 LGFA 1992

60 Reg 3(2)(A) CT(ALA)(E) Regs, as amended by reg 2(2)(c) CT(ALA)(E)(A) Regs

61 Reg 9 CT(ALA)(E) Regs; *RG v Dawn Bunyan* [2022] VTE Appeal No.VT00007677

62 **W** Reg 14(2) CT(ALA) Regs, as amended by CT(ALA)(A)(W) Regs
S Reg 19 CT(ALA)(S) Regs; *Lothian Valuation Joint Board v Campbell and Campbell* [2011] CSIH 47

63 **E** s24 LGFA 1992
S s87(10) LGFA 1992; reg 31 First-tier Tribunal for Scotland Local Taxation Chamber (Rules of Procedure) Regulations 2022 No.364

64 *Tilly v Listing Officer for Tower Hamlets* [2001] RVR 250; *Greenwood & Greenwood v Corkish* [2021] VT00005491 & VT00005611 21 April 2021

65 *Chilton-Merryweather v Hunt & Ors* [2008] EWCA Civ 1025

66 *Klimiva v Corkish* [2021] VTE Appeal No.M0859608

67 **E** Reg 9 CT(ALA)(E) Regs
W Reg 14(5)(a) and (b) CT(ALA) Regs, as amended by CT(ALA)(A)(W) Regs
68 Reg 19(5) CT(ALA)(S) Regs
69 s22 LGFA 1992
70 **E** CT(SVD) Regs
W CT(SVD)(W)(A) Regs
S CT(VD)(S) Regs
71 Reg 3(1)(b)(i) CT(ALA)(E) Regs; *Listing Officer for Cornwall v Dannhauser* [2019] PTSR 743
72 *Lothian Valuation Joint Board v Campbell and Campbell* [2011] CSIH 47
73 **E** Reg 6 CT(SVD) Regs, as amended by CT(VALA)(E) Regs
S CT(VD)(S) Regs, as amended by CT(VD)(S)(A) Regs
74 **E** Reg 2 CT(ALA)(E) Regs
S Reg 3 CT(ALA)(S) Regs
75 Reg 4 CT(ALA)(E) Regs
76 **E** Reg 4 CT(ALA)(E) Regs
S Reg 5 CT(ALA)(S) Regs
77 **E** Reg 4 CT(ALA)(E) Regs
S Reg 5 CT(ALA)(S) Regs
78 **E** Reg 4 CT(ALA)(E) Regs
S Reg 5 CT(ALA)(S) Regs
79 **E** Reg 4(2) CT(ALA)(E) Regs
S Reg 5 CT(ALA)(S) Regs
80 *Rourke v Roberts (VO)* [2020] VTE Appeal No.VT00002325, paras 17-19
81 *Ashford v Listing Office* [2019] 4635837156/285CAD, 29 May 2019, para 19
82 s24 LGFA 1992; reg 2(2) CT(ALA)(A)(W) Regs, substituting reg 14 CT(ALA) Regs
83 **E** Reg 5 CT(ALA)(E) Regs
S Reg 6 CT(ALA)(S) Regs
84 **E** Reg 5 CT(ALA)(E) Regs
S Reg 6 CT(ALA)(S) Regs
85 *Pengelly v Listing Officer* [2014] EWHC 4142 (Admin)
86 Reg 5 CT(ALA)(E) Regs
87 *Domblides v Listing Officer* [2008] EWHC 3271 (Admin)
88 *Various Appellants v Moore (VO)* [2020] VTE Appeal No.M849753
89 *Domblides v Listing Officer* [2008] EWHC 3271 (Admin)
90 Reg 7 CT(ALA)(S) Regs
91 Reg 12 CT(ALA)(S) Regs
92 **E** CT(ALA)(E) Regs
W CT(ALA) Regs
S CT(ALA)(S) Regs
93 Reg 7 CT(ALA)(E) Regs
94 See reg 7(10) CT(ALA)(E) Regs
95 Regs 8 and 9 CT(ALA)(S) Regs
96 Reg 10 CT(ALA)(S) Regs
97 Reg 8 CT(ALA)(E) Regs
98 Reg 9(3) CT(ALA)(E) Regs
99 Reg 9(4) CT(ALA)(E) Regs
100 Reg 2 VTE(CTRA)(P) Regs
101 Reg 19(7) VTE(CTRA)(P) Regs
102 *Spitzer v Roberts LO* [2022] VT00006533, 3 February 2022
103 *Hakeem v VTS and LB Enfield* [2010] EWHC 152 (Admin); *Bailyelo v Corkish* [2017] VTE Appeal No.5690727898/084CAD
104 Reg 14 CT(ALA)(S) Regs
105 r35(3)(d) FTTSLTC(RP) Regs; see *Heeps v Assessor for Fife* [2023] Chamber Ref: FTS/LTC/CT/23/00034
106 r35(3)(d) FTTSLTC(RP) Regs
107 *Heeps v Assessor for Fife* [2023] Chamber Ref: FTS/LTC/CT/23/00034
108 Reg 11 CT(ALA)(S) Regs
109 **E** Reg 12(1) CT(ALA)(E) Regs
S Reg 16 CT(ALA)(S) Regs
110 Reg 12 CT(ALA)(E) Regs
111 Reg 16 CT(ALA)(S) Regs

7. **The valuation bands**

112 **E** s5(2) LGFA 1992
113 **S** s74(2) LGFA 1992
114 **W** s5(3) LGFA 1992
115 **EW** s2(2)(b) LGFA 1992; *BMC Properties and Management v Jackson (VO)* [2015] EWCA Civ 1306
S s71(2)(b) LGFA 1992
116 s5(3) LGFA 1992
117 Art 2(3) The Council Tax (Valuation Bands) (Wales) Order 2003 No.3046
118 s5 LGFA 1992 as amended by s17 LGF(W)A 2024
119 s5 LGFA 1992
120 s5 LGFA 1992
121 s5(1A) LGFA 1992
122 s74 LGFA 1992
123 s36 LGFA 1992
124 MHCLG, *Council Tax Levels Set by Local Authorities in England 2025 to 2026*, 25 April 2025
125 Statistics for Wales, *Council Tax Levels in Wales: April 2025 to March 2026*, 20 March 2025
126 Scottish Government, Dataset: Band D Council Tax 2025/26

Chapter 4

Exempt dwellings

This chapter covers:

No council tax is payable on a dwelling on any day when it falls into an exempt category. The local authority must establish each year which dwellings in its area are exempt. When determining whether a dwelling is exempt, the situation at the end of the day is assumed to have existed throughout that day.[1]

1. Exempt dwellings in England and Wales

An 'exempt dwelling' is one for which no council tax is payable for certain periods or indefinitely, provided it fits within one of the exemption Classes A to X. The classes of dwellings that are entitled to an exemption are set out in the Council Tax (Exempt Dwellings) Order 1992.[2]

***Exemption Classes B and D–X*[3]**

Class B	Unoccupied and owned by a charity (up to six months) and was last occupied for charitable purposes. See p55.
Class D	Unoccupied by someone detained or in prison. See p56.
Class E	Unoccupied by someone who has moved into a hospital, care home or certain hostels. See p57.
Class F	Unoccupied because someone has died. See p57.
Class G	Occupation is prohibited by law. See p58.
Class H	Unoccupied awaiting a minister of religion. See p59.
Class I	Unoccupied by someone receiving personal care elsewhere. See p60.
Class J	Unoccupied by someone providing care elsewhere. See p60.
Class K	Unoccupied owned by a student and last occupied by a student. See p61.

Class L	Repossessed dwelling. See p61.
Class M	Student halls of residence. See p62.
Class N	Occupied only by students or school/ college leavers. See p63.
Class O	Armed forces accommodation. See p64.
Class P	Visiting forces accommodation. See p64.
Class Q	Unoccupied dwelling held by a trustee in bankruptcy. See p64.
Class R	Empty caravan pitches or houseboat moorings. See p65.
Class S	Occupied only by people under 18. See p65.
Class T	Unoccupied annexes that cannot be let separately. See p65.
Class U	Occupied only by people who are severely mentally impaired (SMI). See p65.
Class V	Occupied by people with diplomatic, Commonwealth or consular privilege or immunity. See p66.
Class W	Annexes occupied by a dependent relative. See p66.
Class X	(Wales only) occupied by one or more care leavers, and every resident is either a care leaver, a relevant person under Class N (students etc) or a SMI person. See p66.

An exemption from council tax may be considered as a possession within the meaning of Article 1 Protocol 1 of the European Convention on Human Rights.[4]

In early 2025, there were 748,000 dwellings in England and 64,274 dwellings in Wales exempt from council tax.[5]

Vacant homes

In Wales, there are two classes of dwelling related to vacant homes – Classes A and C.

Exemption Classes A and C

Class A	For a 12-month period, a vacant dwelling requiring or undergoing major repair work or structural alteration or having undergone either if it is less than six months since the works were substantially completed.
Class C	A dwelling vacant for a six-month period or less – eg, following completion.

In England, these classes have been abolished or made discretionary.[6] Properties in England falling into these two categories no longer receive an automatic exemption and are liable for 100 per cent of the council tax. Any reduction is awarded as a discount only if your local authority decides that a discount should be given (see p131).

In some cases, you may still claim exemptions for previous years – eg, if you receive a new bill for a historic liability for a previous financial year. In this situation, you may also need to appeal the listing with the listing officer to remove the property from the valuation list.[7]

In addition, a local authority may exempt a class of dwelling by way of a discount that reduces the amount of council tax payable on a dwelling to zero (see Chapter 7).

The term 'vacant' refers to a dwelling which is both:[8]

- unoccupied; *and*
- substantially unfurnished.

The legislation does not define substantially unfurnished. In practice, many local authorities regard a dwelling as substantially unfurnished if there are insufficient furnishings to enable someone to live in the dwelling. However, the quantity of furniture present in the dwelling, in relation to its size, should be the determining factor, ignoring anything other than furniture – eg, a studio flat with a bed, sofa, table, two chairs and appliances would be substantially furnished, but the same items would not make a four-bedroom house substantially furnished.

The legislation defines an 'unoccupied dwelling' as one in which no one lives, and an 'occupied dwelling' as one where at least one person lives.[9] There is, however, a significant distinction between occupying a home and being solely or mainly resident in it (see p84). While the same person may occupy two or more dwellings at any one time, they can only be mainly resident in one. The local authority must consider each case on the particular facts.

Classes of exempt dwellings in England and Wales

Class B: unoccupied dwelling owned by a charitable body

An unoccupied dwelling owned by a body set up solely for charitable purposes is exempt for up to six months from the last day it was occupied. Almshouses and refuges are typical examples.

Four conditions must be met for the exemption to apply.[10]

- The dwelling must be owned by the charitable body.
- The body must be established for charitable purposes only.
- The dwelling must have been unoccupied for less than six months.
- The last occupation must have furthered the charity's objectives.

The charity must be the freeholder or hold the most inferior (ie, shortest) leasehold interest for a term of six months or more. The dwelling may be furnished or unfurnished. When deciding the day on which the dwelling was last occupied, any period of occupation of under six weeks is disregarded.[11]

It should normally be enough to have a short written statement from the charity, confirming that all four conditions are met and stating that the person making the statement believes the content is true.[12]

To show that the last occupation furthered the charity's objectives, the charity must provide information about the last occupier. It is not necessary that the property was exclusively occupied for charitable purposes.[13]

This may include details of the history of any letting and some details of the last occupier – eg, why they were receiving help from the charity and what benefits they received, where relevant. There should be sufficient evidence to show the charity's aims were being fulfilled.[14] Local authorities have been issued with a draft letter suitable for use by charities.[15]

Beyond this, where an unoccupied hereditament is not zero-rated and a billing authority decides that a discretionary relief should be available, then that authority sets the chargeable amount for the day, so you would need to check its policy.[16]

Class C: vacant dwellings in Wales

A vacant dwelling (one that is unoccupied and substantially unfurnished, or an unoccupied caravan or houseboat) is exempt for up to six months.[17] This exemption applies both to new and previously occupied dwellings. Any one period of not more than six weeks during which the dwelling is occupied is disregarded when deciding if the dwelling has been vacant.

Class D: dwelling unoccupied because the former resident is detained or in prison

An unoccupied dwelling is exempt indefinitely if the former resident is in prison or certain other forms of detention and the dwelling was previously their sole or main residence (see p84).[18] A person is considered detained if they would be regarded as such for a council tax discount (see p127).[19] The definition includes people detained under immigration or mental health powers, but not those in prison for non-payment of council tax. The exemption extends up until the dwelling is next occupied. Providing the dwelling continues to remain empty, the dwelling's owner is not liable while the last resident is in prison.[20]

This exemption includes not only former residents who were owners (ie, the freeholder or the leaseholder with the shortest lease of six months or more) but also former tenants, whether or not they are the person who is liable to pay council tax on the property.[21]

The dwelling is also exempt if the owner or tenant was previously the sole or main resident and, since the end of their imprisonment, has been in a hospital, care home, hostel or other accommodation where care is provided, or if they have been providing personal care to someone else.

In cases where the Parole Board has ordered that a person released from prison resides at an address other than their home, it has been held at tribunal level that such an individual may be 'a person in detention for the purposes of Class D, and in the terms of Schedule 1 to the Local Government Finance Act 1992 as being, "... detained in"... any other place by virtue of an order... of a court'. In such a situation, the 'any other place' may be a bail hostel and the 'order of a court' the Parole Board order.[22]

However, in a case where someone had been living extradited from abroad and placed under bail conditions that prevented their return to a property before later being sentenced to imprisonment, it was held that they were not entitled to the exemption, as the appeal property had not been their sole or main residence.[23]

Example

On leaving prison, Peter moves in with his elderly mother to look after her. Peter's former home remains exempt.

Class E: dwelling unoccupied because the former resident is in hospital or a care home

An unoccupied dwelling is exempt indefinitely if it was previously the sole or main residence (see p84) of an owner, tenant or licensee (or contract holder in Wales):[24]

- who would be disregarded for the purpose of a council tax discount because they are a patient in hospital, or are in a care home or certain hostels; *and*
- who, since they last occupied the dwelling, have either been in that type of accommodation, in detention, or receiving or providing care elsewhere.[25] The care must be required for old age, disability, mental or physical illness or past or present alcohol or drug dependence.

During temporary stays in hospital, you remain liable for council tax at your normal address. However, if your main residence is a hospital, your previous home is exempt from council tax, provided it is unoccupied.[26] It is not necessary that you were the last resident of the dwelling, only that you previously occupied it before going into permanent care in a hospital or a care home. This is because the exemption uses the word 'previously' rather than specifying the 'last' resident.[27]

Class F: unoccupied dwelling in which someone has died

A dwelling is exempt if it has been unoccupied since the former resident's death and the only person liable for council tax on the dwelling would be the deceased's personal representative, and no grant of probate or letters of administration has been made.[28] In the case of rented accommodation, the exemption is designed to discourage landlords, who would become liable for council tax following a tenant's death (or contract holder in Wales), from:

- pressing for the property to be cleared immediately to benefit from the six-month exemption for vacant dwellings; *or*
- seeking to pass on to the deceased's relatives or estate the council tax payable on the dwelling which is now unoccupied, but not vacant.

The exemption applies for each day for which the executor or administrator is liable for rent (there is no minimum period) and lasts up to six months after the grant of probate or letters of administration. For example, a delay of eight years in applying for probate will not restrict the exemption, even if the ultimate beneficiary is likely to be the same person as the executor.[29] The issue is not affected by whether the deceased left a will or not. The anticipation of inheritance does not create an actual material interest to render the Class F exemption invalid; provided there is no evidence of an entry in the Lands Registry to show a lease of six months or more has been granted, the exemption continues to apply.[30]

Any occupation of less than six weeks following the death is disregarded. Thus, the exemption is not ended if, for instance, a relative stays at the dwelling briefly to arrange the deceased's affairs or if carers who resided with the owner continue living in the property for more than a week.[31]

This exemption may not apply if the deceased left the dwelling to a beneficiary in their will who is a joint owner or who is already in occupation. In this case, the beneficiary becomes the taxpayer at the date of death, as they become the owner for council tax purposes on that date. This situation may arise at the death of a spouse or partner who was living apart, or if a relative living in the dwelling succeeds to the tenancy. However, there may be an argument for an exemption if the executor is given any discretion over the dwelling that might affect whether the beneficiary can occupy it. However, a valuation tribunal president has ruled that the exemption remains valid if the executor retains control, even where they are the named beneficiary, until legal title formally transfers.[32]

The Valuation Tribunal for England (VTE) has upheld a decision that members of a trust (as opposed to executors under a will) to whom a council tax payer had transferred her bungalow, to protect it from family business liabilities, were not entitled to claim the exemption following her death. Although the bungalow was treated as part of the estate for inheritance tax purposes, it belonged to the trustees.[33]

For information on the billing of executors, see p190.

If a dwelling is unoccupied and probate has not been granted, any existing class F exemption should remain in place. The duties of an executor[34] do not create liability or assist in determining liability where probate has not been obtained. The Local Government Finance Act 1992 is the primary legislation for council tax purposes and it does not impose liability on individuals who merely hold an equitable interest in the property. Had parliament intended such liability to arise, it would have stated so expressly.[35]

Class G: dwelling in which occupation is prohibited by law

A dwelling is exempt indefinitely if its occupation is prohibited by law. This means that either it is illegal to occupy the dwelling or it is kept unoccupied because of action under legal powers with a view to prohibiting occupation or acquiring the dwelling. This may include:

- a condition imposed by planning control under Part 3 of the Town and Country Planning Act 1990;[36]
- a planning enforcement notice;[37]
- property which is unoccupied because it is being acquired under a compulsory purchase order.

However, a dwelling on which a local authority has served a repair notice does not qualify for an exemption, even if the occupant has to move out temporarily.[38] Closely examine the planning conditions in the case of mixed business and residential use (eg, a public house) to see whether planning restrictions that limit the occupation are qualified and not absolute. If they only restrict occupation of the business portion and permit residential occupation, providing the use is ancillary to the building's use, the exemption will not be available.[39]

Where a dwelling is being converted or undergoing development under a planning permission that restricts occupancy, the development is deemed to commence from the point the works are commenced to trigger the exemption.[40] If the dwelling is actually occupied (eg, by squatters), it is not exempt from the charge. The squatters will normally be liable to pay the tax. See Chapter 5 for more information on liability.

Decisions under Class G have been narrowly interpreted to restrict its use. For example, potential breaches of the Occupiers' Liability Act 1957, the Defective Premises Act 1972 or section 11 of the Landlord and Tenant Act 1985, which might give rise to legal liability towards occupiers, are not sufficient to merit an exemption from council tax. The VTE vice president has applied equivalent principles to those in a business rates case where the High Court considered that a potential breach of health and safety legislation did not amount to either a prohibition in law on occupation or prevent an owner from entering premises to restore them.[41]

A toll house built on a bridge exempted from rating under still extant 18th-century statutes did not amount to an exemption from council tax under Class G, despite the billing authority previously assuming that the exemption applied.[42]

Class H: unoccupied dwelling held for a minister of religion

An unoccupied dwelling is exempt indefinitely if it is held to be available for occupation by a minister of any religious denomination and from where they will perform the duties of their office – eg, vicarages or manses.[43]

In determining the meaning of duties, tribunals have applied guidance originally issued to councils in 1994. Duties should include some of the following:

- conducting religious worship;
- providing pastoral care, especially to those who are sick, distressed or in need;
- conducting weddings, funerals or baptisms (or their equivalent);
- providing leadership to local members of their denomination;

- overseeing the ministry of others who perform these functions and providing support and pastoral care.

Administering an online forum and writing articles are not considered religious worship.[44]

The VTE refused to award an exemption where an appellant did not conduct weddings, funerals or baptisms or provide leadership to local members of his denomination. The members of the church to which he belonged consisted of approximately 25 people spread all over the world and were not considered by the panel to be a local congregation or community.[45] Similarly, a claim for a religious exemption, where there was no evidence of the appellant carrying out such duties from his home and the church to which he belonged was in Texas, was ruled not to be entitled.[46]

Class I: dwelling unoccupied because the former resident is receiving care elsewhere

An unoccupied dwelling is exempt indefinitely if it was the sole or main residence (see p84) of an owner, tenant or licensee who now has their sole or main residence elsewhere because they are receiving personal care (but not a hospital, care home or certain hostels).[47] The personal care must be required for old age, disability, physical or mental illness or past or present alcohol or drug dependence, and should be the primary reason for residing there.[48]

To qualify, the former resident must have been living in such accommodation, in prison or a detention centre, since the dwelling last ceased to be their residence.[49]

This exemption applies if the former resident was an owner and, in England, if they were a tenant or licensee, irrespective of whether they were liable for council tax on the dwelling. In Wales, this exemption extends to former tenants only if they were absent for the whole period since the dwelling last ceased to be their residence.

Class J: dwelling unoccupied because the former resident is providing care elsewhere

An unoccupied dwelling is exempt indefinitely if it was previously the sole or main residence (see p84) of an owner, tenant or licensee who is now solely or mainly resident elsewhere because they are providing personal care to someone.[50]

This exemption applies to former residents who were owners, as well as tenants or licensees, irrespective of whether they were liable for council tax on the dwelling.

The carer does not have to be disregarded for the purpose of a council tax discount. However, the person being cared for must require the care because of old age, disability, physical or mental illness or past or present alcohol or drug dependence.

The carer must have been absent from their own dwelling since it was last occupied because they have been providing such care. It has been held that a person cannot claim an exemption if they have never lived in the dwelling in question.[51]

A carer who acquires a property after starting caring for someone at another address may not be entitled to an exemption and may be at risk of a second home premium (see p137).[52]

Class K: dwelling left unoccupied by a student owner

An unoccupied dwelling is exempt indefinitely if it was last occupied as the sole or main residence (see p84) of its owner, who is now a student and they:[53]

- have been a student since they last occupied the dwelling; *or*
- have become a student within six weeks of leaving the dwelling.

'Student' has the same meaning as for council tax discount purposes (see p121). If there are joint owners of the unoccupied property, all of them must be students and at least one must have been solely or mainly resident there on the last day it was occupied, and the last one must have become a student within six weeks of the day it was last occupied as a sole or main residence.

Example

Ella owns a flat in York and lived there until she moved to London to start university. She left three weeks before her course started. Her flat in York is now unoccupied, apart from when she returns for short visits during vacations.

The flat in York is exempt because it is unoccupied and Ella became a student within six weeks of being solely resident there. It remains exempt when Ella returns in the vacations because, during these times, although it is occupied, the sole resident is a student.

If Ella decided to let the flat in York to a tenant, it would cease to be exempt because it would no longer be unoccupied. However, it would continue to be exempt if the new tenant were also a student.

Class L: unoccupied dwelling in the possession of a mortgage lender

An unoccupied dwelling is exempt indefinitely if a mortgagee (ie, a bank, building society or finance company) is in possession.[54] This usually arises following repossession due to mortgage arrears.

It is necessary to establish that the property is unoccupied and has been formally repossessed by the mortgage lender and/or that a Law of Property Act 1925 (LPA) receiver has been appointed by a mortgage company, as an alternative to formal repossession, and the LPA receiver acted for the mortgagor and not the mortgagee.

In terms of section 109 of the Law of Property Act 1925 and also Part 4, which covered the LPA receiver, the mortgagor and property tax:

where the mortgagee or LPA receiver is not in possession of an occupied property the tenant is liable for the payment of council tax or business rates. Where the property is unoccupied the mortgagor is liable for the payment of council tax or business rates. Where the mortgagor is in occupation and liable to pay the council tax or business rates, the LPA receiver has a statutory obligation as agent of the mortgagor to make that payment. The former owner should resist an attempt to place liability on them.

The payment or non-payment of council tax or business rates in such a case is between the mortgagor and their agent, the LPA receiver. The valuation tribunal will look at whether the title of the appeal property has been transferred to the lender when a property is formally repossessed.[55]

Class M: student halls of residence

A dwelling is exempt indefinitely if it is a hall of residence provided predominantly to accommodate students who would be disregarded for a discount (p121).[56] To qualify for the exemption, the hall must be either:

- owned or managed by a prescribed educational institution; *or*
- the subject of an agreement allowing a prescribed educational institution to nominate the majority of the people who are to occupy the accommodation.

This exemption also extends to halls of residence, mainly for the accommodation of students, owned or managed by a body set up solely for charitable purposes.[57] For example, a body set up by a university students' union to manage accommodation needs would fall within this definition. The term 'halls of residence' only applies to universities and similar institutions. It does not include boarding school houses for pupils and staff, as these are not 'halls of residence' and school children are not classed as 'students' for council tax purposes.[58]

A hall (or hostel) should be exempt even if some non-students (eg, wardens, tutors or family members) live there. This exemption does not cover any separate, self-contained flat or house provided for a non-student, such as a caretaker. If a hall of residence is used for more than 140 days a year for commercial purposes, such as conferences, it may be subject to non-domestic rates.

This exemption was considered straightforward until 2016 when Leicester City Council declined to award a Class M exemption to the majority of student rooms within three large blocks of purpose-built student accommodation operating as university halls of residence. Previously, the valuation office had banded each room as occupied by students.

In *Sulets v Leicester City Council*,[59] the VTE found that the en-suite rooms with cooking facilities that a single student occupied were each separate, self-contained flats and that 'in our view a separate flat for the accommodation of a single student (or, as may be, a couple sharing an intimate relationship) has no feature of a hall of residence...'. Consequently, each room attracted its own bill, except for what were termed 'cluster flats', whereby rooms occupied by one student received a designation of a hall of residence and a Class M exemption.

The VTE held that many rooms did not fall within the exemption. While the rooms were occupied, each room received a Class N exemption (see below) as being a dwelling occupied solely by a student. As a result, where the valuation office has elected to treat each room as a separate, chargeable dwelling, there may be a considerable administrative burden for both the billing authority and the bodies administering the student accommodation, with each formerly exempt hall of residence attracting multiple bills. In practice, different local authorities adopt different practices.

Class N: dwelling wholly occupied by students or 'relevant persons'

To be exempt, the dwelling must be either:[60]

- occupied by one or more residents, all of whom are 'relevant persons'; *or*
- occupied only by one or more 'relevant persons' as term-time accommodation.

There must be a distinction between 'residents' who live in the property permanently and 'occupants' who are students for part of a term.[61]

A 'relevant person' is a:[62]

- student disregarded for discount purposes (see p121); *or*
- student's spouse, civil partner or dependant who is not a British citizen and who is prevented by the terms of their leave to enter or remain in the UK from working or claiming benefits; *or*
- school or college leaver who is disregarded for discount purposes (see p120).

Nursing or midwifery students studying at university count as students.[63]

If the dwelling has more than one resident, they must all meet the qualifying conditions for the exemption to apply.

A dwelling occupied by a relevant person is regarded as term-time accommodation during any vacation in which they:

- hold a freehold or leasehold interest in, or licence to occupy, the whole or any part of the dwelling; *and*
- have previously used, or intend to use, the dwelling as term-time accommodation.

Example

Three students rent a house as joint tenants. It is exempt from council tax. The exemption ends when one of the students is dismissed from her course and no longer qualifies for a status discount. The three joint tenants are now jointly liable for the council tax on the dwelling. There are three residents, but two of them are disregarded for a discount. The bill is reduced by 25 per cent because there is only one adult resident who is not disregarded.

The exemption is only available to full-time students.[64]

However, the definition of a course as full time or part time by an educational institution is not conclusive; what counts is whether the course meets the statutory criteria of a minimum of 21 hours a week for at least 24 weeks a year.[65]

As a consequence of the decision in *Sulets v Leicester City Council* (see p62), during term time, the student accommodation should receive an exemption as a dwelling wholly occupied by a student. In periods between student lettings, the exemption will not apply even if the dwelling remains empty and liability will revert to the owner or the party with rights equivalent to an owner.[66]

A student is not precluded from claiming the exemption by working or being a company director.[67]

Class O: armed forces accommodation

An unoccupied or occupied dwelling is exempt indefinitely if it is owned by the Secretary of State for Defence and is used for armed forces accommodation.[68]

This includes, for example, armed forces barracks and married quarters. The Ministry of Defence pays contributions in place of council tax to local authorities. These contributions should broadly match the amount which would otherwise have been payable.[69]

In addition, a separate provision for members of the armed forces operates with the Military Covenant (see Chapter 7) and discounts where dwellings are empty while service personnel are accommodated elsewhere may be considered (see p134).

Class P: visiting forces accommodation

A dwelling is exempt indefinitely if at least one person who would be liable is a member (or dependant) of a visiting armed force and they are neither a British citizen nor ordinarily resident in the UK. The exemption applies even if not all the liable persons meet these criteria. For example, a dwelling in which the liable persons are a visiting serviceman and his British wife is exempt.[70]

Class Q: unoccupied dwelling held by a trustee in bankruptcy

An unoccupied dwelling is exempt indefinitely if the liable owner is a trustee in bankruptcy or the official receiver under the Insolvency Act 1986 or other bankruptcy legislation.[71] A 'trustee in bankruptcy' is the person appointed by a general meeting of a bankrupt person's creditors or the court, whose duty is to take over all their property, sell the property for cash and distribute the resulting funds among the creditors.

Bankruptcy starts with the making of the bankruptcy order.[72] The estate of the bankrupt will vest in the trustee or the official receiver from the date of appointment as a trustee.[73] If the person is discharged from bankruptcy but the property has not been repossessed, sold or revested, the Class Q exemption continues until the property legally returns to them.[74]

Class R: unoccupied pitch and mooring

A pitch or mooring not occupied by a caravan or boat is an exempt dwelling for council tax purposes.[75] In most cases, this is a question of fact about the actual ownership of an empty site and must also be distinguished from periods where a caravan is present and unoccupied.[76]

Class S: dwelling wholly occupied by someone under 18

A dwelling only occupied by one or more persons under 18 is exempt.[77]

Class T: unoccupied dwelling which cannot be let separately

A dwelling is exempt if it:

- is unoccupied; *and*
- forms part of a single property which includes another dwelling; *and*
- cannot be let separately from that other dwelling without breaching planning control.

An example of this exemption is an empty 'granny flat'.[78]

Class T exemption was considered in *BS v West Berkshire Council*.[79] The key question was whether the annexe could be let separately from the main dwelling without breaching planning control, within the meaning of section 171A of the Town and Country Planning Act 1990 and whether an appellant would also be liable to investigation for a breach of planning control should it be separately let. The tribunal found that absence of an explicit planning condition is not determinative. This is because to begin using a single dwelling as two or more dwellings is 'development' (being a change in use) under planning law.[80] In this case, a planning officer's email confirmed that separate letting might be breach of planning consent. The valuation tribunal found that conditions of the Class T exemption were met and the dwelling qualified for the Class T exemption and was not chargeable to council tax.

Class U: dwelling occupied by a severely mentally impaired person

A dwelling is exempt if it is only occupied by a SMI person(s) as defined for a council tax discount (see p124).[81]

A dwelling is also exempt if it is occupied by at least one SMI person and one or more students or relevant persons (see p121).[82] A property in which a number of SMI individuals reside and receive care services and which is not divided into separate units may not qualify for a Class U exemption but may be designated as a care home.[83] It is necessary to have a medical certificate from a practitioner confirming the impairment, otherwise any appeal is likely to be dismissed.[84]

An exemption under Class U may be backdated more than six years to the point of entitlement. In one case, the cause of action was from the point where the taxpayer became aware of the possible entitlement to relief. If the billing authority has taken no reasonable steps, the cause of action accrues from the date when the taxpayer becomes aware of their possible entitlement.[85]

Providing entitlement exists, relief can be awarded retrospectively to the date when the taxpayer first became entitled to relief. The six-year rule merely applies to the period within which they have to apply, not how far back the retrospective relief can go.[86] The Class U exemption is only available while the property is occupied and not after the taxpayer dies.[87]

Class V: people with diplomatic immunity

A dwelling is exempt if at least one liable person has diplomatic, Commonwealth or consular privilege or immunity and is not a permanent resident of the UK, or a British citizen, British subject or British protected person. This exemption does not apply if that person has another dwelling in the UK which is their main residence or if their main residence is in the UK.[88]

Class W: dwelling occupied by a dependent relative

This exemption applies to a dwelling, which is one of at least two dwellings in a single property, occupied by a dependent relative of a person living in another dwelling in the property.[89]

A relative is a dependant if they are 65 or over, SMI or substantially and permanently disabled by illness, injury, congenital deformity or otherwise.[90]

Relatives

A **'relative'** is a person's spouse, parent, child, grandparent, grandchild, sibling, uncle or aunt, nephew or niece (and also great-and great-great grandparent, grandchildren, uncle, aunt, nephew or niece). A relationship by marriage (or by living together as spouses or by civil partnership[91]) is treated as a relationship by birth and any stepchild of a person is treated as their child.

A Class W exemption may be backdated more than six years in some cases.[92]

Class X (Wales): dwelling occupied by a care leaver

This exemption applies in Wales where a dwelling is occupied by one or more care leavers and every resident is either a care leaver, a relevant person within the definition in Class N (ie, a student) or a SMI person.[93]

Who is a carer leaver?

A **'care leaver'** is someone who is 18 or over but has not yet reached 25 and was:

- previously looked after in the care system but is not currently being looked after by a local authority but would continue to be so if he or she were under the age of 18; *or*
- looked after by a local authority immediately before turning 18.

2. Exempt dwellings in Scotland

In Scotland, the Council Tax (Exempt Dwellings) (Scotland) Order 1997 sets out the classes of dwellings that are exempt from council tax.[94]

In September 2024, there were 47,779 unoccupied dwellings recorded as receiving exemptions in Scotland.[95]

Exempt unoccupied dwellings

Dwellings that are both unoccupied and unfurnished remain exempt from council tax liability for up to six months. After six months, a second claim for the exemption is possible after a property has been occupied for at least three months. The dwelling need not have been furnished in the three months.[96]

A property classed as an unoccupied dwelling is exempt if:[97]

- it is recently built and still unfurnished (see below);
- it is undergoing or has recently undergone major repair work or structural alteration (see p68);
- it was last occupied by a charity (see p68);
- it is unfurnished (see p68);
- it was last occupied by, and remains the sole liability of, someone in prison or someone living elsewhere to receive or provide care (see p68);
- it is owned by someone who has died (see p69);
- its occupation is prohibited by law (see p69);
- it is owned by a public sector housing authority pending demolition (see p69);
- it is being kept for occupation by a minister of religion (see p69);
- it was last occupied by a student (see p70);
- it has been repossessed following a mortgage default (see p70);
- it was last occupied together with certain agricultural lands (see p70);
- it is held by a trustee in bankruptcy (see p70);
- it is part of the same premises as, or situated within the same curtilage as, another dwelling and is difficult to let separately (see p70);
- it is the sole liable person is a student (see p70).

Unoccupied new dwelling

A dwelling that is unoccupied and unfurnished is exempt for up to six months if:[98]

- it has been less than six months since the effective date of the first entry on the valuation list; *and*
- there was no entry on the valuation list immediately before that effective date.

Unoccupied dwelling undergoing structural repair, improvement or reconstruction

An unoccupied dwelling is exempt if it cannot be lived in because, since the last occupation date, it has been undergoing, or has undergone, structural alteration or major repair work to make it habitable.[99]

The lack of occupation must be because of the work being carried out. If someone occupies the dwelling, it is not exempt. The exemption may last for 12 months after the dwelling was last occupied, or (if sooner) for six months after the major repair work or alteration was substantially completed. The property may remain furnished.

The test is one of fact and the existence of an exemption will not normally justify removing a dwelling from the valuation roll. However, decision makers have recognised the possibility of cases 'in which the works are so extensive and so prolonged or where the essential physical characteristics of a house were lost' resulting in the property ceasing to exist as a dwelling house 'while the works are carried out' (see Chapters 2 and 3).[100] A property undergoing repairs will not ordinarily be regarded as having ceased to be a dwelling house. Much depends on the nature of the works, their duration, and whether the property retains the basic physical characteristics of a dwelling house during the course of them.

Unoccupied dwelling last occupied by a charity

An unoccupied dwelling last occupied by a charitable body is exempt for up to six months if it was last occupied to further the charity's objectives.[101] 'Charitable' has the same meaning as in income tax law. Any period of occupation for less than six weeks is disregarded.[102] The property may remain furnished.

Unoccupied and unfurnished dwelling

Unoccupied and unfurnished dwellings are exempt for up to six months from the end of the last period of six weeks or more during which the dwelling was occupied or furnished.[103]

Dwelling last occupied by someone in prison, or living elsewhere to receive or provide care

An unoccupied dwelling is exempt indefinitely if it was last occupied as the sole or main residence (see p84) of someone who continues to be liable for council tax, and since the last day of occupation they are:

- disregarded for the purpose of a council tax discount because they are in prison or detention, or are in a hospital, care home or certain care hostels in Scotland, England or Wales (see Chapter 7); *or*
- receiving personal care elsewhere because of their old age, disability, physical or mental illness or past or present alcohol or drug dependence; *or*

- providing personal care elsewhere to someone who needs it because of old age, disablement, illness, past or present alcohol or drug dependence, or past or present mental illness or disorder.[104]

Any period of occupation of less than six weeks since the last day of occupation is disregarded. The property may remain furnished.

No exemption was available to a former prisoner released from detention but forced to live in emergency accommodation because of concerns for his safety and the resulting conditions of his licence. Neither reason qualified as a situation where occupation was 'prohibited by law' or prevented by 'reason of action taken under the powers conferred by an Act of Parliament'. The reasons the appellant could not occupy his property concerned him, not the property.[105]

A care home service is one covered by Schedule 12 of the Public Services Reform (Scotland) Act 2010.[106]

Dwelling owned by someone who has died

To be exempt, the dwelling must be no one's sole or main residence (see p84). Additionally, the deceased person's estate must be liable to pay the council tax.[107] In such cases, the dwelling is exempt:

- indefinitely if no grant of confirmation to the estate of that person has been made; *or*
- for up to six months from the date such a grant is made.

The property may remain furnished.

Dwelling in which occupation is prohibited

If it is prohibited by law to occupy a dwelling, that dwelling is exempt indefinitely.[108] The property may remain furnished. The fact that such a property is actually occupied should not make it ineligible for the exemption.

It is also exempt if it is kept unoccupied because legal action is underway to prohibit its occupation or to acquire it under a compulsory purchase order. In these circumstances, if the dwelling is actually occupied, it is not exempt. It may remain furnished.

Unoccupied dwelling owned by a housing body pending demolition

A dwelling owned by a local authority or registered social landlord, which is unoccupied pending demolition, is exempt.[109] It may remain furnished.

Dwelling held for a minister of religion

A dwelling, such as a manse, which is no one's sole or main residence (see p84) is exempt indefinitely if it is being held by, or on behalf of, any religious body to be available for a minister of religion to occupy as a residence from which to perform the duties of their office.[110] The property may remain furnished.

Student's unoccupied dwelling

An unoccupied dwelling which is a student's main residence and which was last occupied by a student(s) is exempt for up to four months from the last day it was occupied for six weeks or more.[111] This applies, for example, to the student's term-time accommodation during vacations if the accommodation remains unoccupied. The property may remain furnished.

Dwelling repossessed by a mortgage lender

A dwelling which is no one's sole or main residence (see p84) is exempt indefinitely if a mortgage lender has repossessed it.[112] The property may remain furnished.

Dwelling last occupied with agricultural lands

An unoccupied and unfurnished dwelling is exempt indefinitely if it was last used and occupied with the land on which it is situated. The land must be:[113]

- agricultural or pastoral; *or*
- woodlands, market gardens, orchards, allotments or allotment gardens; *or*
- used for poultry farming and exceeding one-tenth of a hectare.

Dwelling held by a trustee in bankruptcy

A dwelling which is no one's sole or main residence (see p84) is exempt indefinitely if the only person who would be liable is a bankruptcy trustee.[114]

Unoccupied dwelling that is difficult to let separately

An unoccupied dwelling, such as an empty 'granny flat' or staff accommodation, is exempt indefinitely if:[115]

- it forms part of premises which include another dwelling; *or*
- it is situated within the 'curtilage' of another dwelling; *and*
- it is difficult to let separately from that other dwelling; *and*
- the person who would be liable for it has their sole or main residence in that other dwelling.

The property may remain furnished.

Unoccupied dwelling for which the sole liable person is a student

A dwelling which is no one's sole or main residence (see p84) is exempt indefinitely if the person who would be liable is a student for the purpose of a council tax discount (see p121).

If there are joint owners/joint tenants, they must all be students.[116] The property may remain furnished.

Exempt occupied dwellings

An occupied dwelling is exempt if it:[117]

- is only occupied by one or more students, school or college leavers or under-18-year-olds (see below);
- is occupied by a student or a student's spouse (see below);
- is a housing association 'trial' property for older people or disabled people (see below);
- is a students' hall of residence (see below);
- is armed forces accommodation (see p72);
- is visiting forces accommodation (see p72);
- includes garages, carports and storage sheds (see p72);
- is occupied by a severely mentally impaired (SMI) person (see p72);
- is occupied by a care leaver (see p72);
- is 'prescribed housing support accommodation' (see p72);
- is occupied by a person under the Homes for Ukraine scheme or another approved scheme for displaced people from abroad (see p73).

Dwelling occupied only by students or under-18-year-olds

A dwelling is exempt indefinitely if it is not the sole or main residence (see p84) of anyone other than a student for the purpose of a council tax discount (see p121) or a person under 18, and at least one such person occupies it.[118] Also included is a student's spouse or dependant who is not a British citizen and who is prevented by the Immigration Rules from either claiming benefits or working in the UK.[119]

Temporary dwelling for older or disabled people owned by a registered housing association

A dwelling owned by a registered housing association is exempt indefinitely if:

- it is not the sole or main residence (see p84) of any person; *and*
- it is for people over pension age or with a disability who are likely in the future to have their sole or main residences in other dwellings the housing association provides.

This provides an exemption for trial dwellings for older or disabled people who are likely to live in other property owned by the association in the future. In practice, most local authorities do not charge council tax for the trial period while the person is still liable elsewhere.

Halls of residence

A dwelling is exempt if it is, or is part of, a hall of residence provided predominantly to accommodate students and which:[120]

- is owned and managed by a prescribed educational institution for the purpose of a council tax discount; *or*

- is the subject of an agreement allowing a prescribed educational institution to nominate the majority of the people who are to occupy the accommodation.

The fact that a student hall of residence may be used for commercial lettings between terms does not affect entitlement to an exemption, providing its predominant purpose remains the accommodation of students.[121] The decision in *Sulets v Leicester City Council* (see p62) has yet to be tested in Scotland. Student halls may also be classified differently under the category 'university buildings'.

Armed forces accommodation

An occupied or unoccupied dwelling is exempt indefinitely if it is owned by the Secretary of State for Defence for armed forces accommodation.[122]

The local authority receives compensating payments for these dwellings.

Visiting forces accommodation

A dwelling is exempt indefinitely if a member of a visiting armed force or their dependant (but not a dependant who is a British citizen or is ordinarily resident in the UK) would be liable.[123]

Garages, carports and storage sheds

Certain garages, carports, parking spaces and premises used for storing domestic items, including cycles and similar vehicles, are considered dwellings (see p15). They are exempt indefinitely from council tax.[124]

Dwelling occupied by a severely mentally impaired person

A dwelling is exempt if it is only occupied by a SMI person(s), as defined for the purposes of a council tax discount (see p124).[125]

A dwelling is also exempt if it is occupied by at least one SMI person and one or more students or relevant persons (see p121).[126]

Dwelling occupied by a care leaver

A dwelling is exempt if it is occupied exclusively by one or more care leavers.[127] You are a care leaver if you are at least 18 but not yet 26 years old and were previously in the care of a local authority (at age 16 or subsequently). Dwellings jointly occupied by one or more care leavers and other specified persons (including students and persons under 18) are also exempt.[128]

Prescribed housing support accommodation

A dwelling is exempt if it falls into the 'prescribed housing support accommodation' category.[129] To be exempt:

- the dwelling must be the residence of at least one person who is a tenant, sub-tenant or who has a licence to occupy the dwelling; *and*
- at least one licensee, tenant or sub-tenant of the dwelling must use a registered prescribed housing support service; *and*

- all the residents must share the use of a kitchen, bathroom, shower room or toilet room, and these must also be shared with at least one other person who is not resident in the dwelling.

A dwelling is not exempt if each resident has exclusive use of a kitchen and a bathroom/shower room (either containing a toilet or if there is a separate toilet which all the residents can use).[130]

Dwelling occupied by people from abroad under certain settlement schemes

A dwelling which is the sole or main residence of at least one person who has entered the UK under a scheme and is being provided as accommodation without payment in return is exempt. The dwelling must not be occupied by a person other than someone who can be disregarded based on their circumstances – eg, a student. The schemes and arrangements are:[131]

- the Homes for Ukraine scheme – from 2025, this also includes a close family member;[132]
- the Afghan Citizens Resettlement Scheme;
- the Afghan Relocations and Assistance Policy;
- the Community Sponsorship Scheme;
- the UK Resettlement Scheme;
- the Vulnerable Children's Resettlement Scheme;
- the Vulnerable Persons Resettlement Scheme.

3. How exempt dwellings are identified

Local authorities must take reasonable steps each financial year to establish whether any dwellings in their area are exempt from council tax for any period during the year.[133] Most are likely to do periodic postal surveys and use other sources of information, such as the electoral roll and benefit records. Most local authorities also carry out regular visits to unoccupied exempt dwellings.

If the local authority has no reason to believe that a dwelling will be, or was, exempt, it will assume it is a chargeable dwelling for council tax billing purposes.[134] Alternatively, if it has reason to believe that a dwelling will be, or was, exempt for a period during the year, it must make that assumption for council tax billing purposes.[135]

4. Notification of exemption

If the local authority assumes that a dwelling is exempt, it must write to the person who would otherwise be liable.[136] It must do this as soon as is reasonably practicable.[137] The requirement does not apply in Scotland if:[138]

- the liable person is a housing body; *or*
- the dwelling is a separate garage, carport or storage shed.

The local authority should also supply a statement that:[139]

- shows the valuation band for the dwelling;
- summarises how to make a proposal for altering the valuation list;
- in Scotland, shows the amounts set as council tax and Scottish Water charges;
- in England and Wales, specifies the estimate or actual amount of council tax (before any disability reduction, discount, transitional relief (in Wales) or council tax reduction);
- summarises the most common classes of dwelling which are exempt;[140]
- in Scotland, summarises your obligation to correct any incorrect assumptions the local authority may have made in awarding the exemption, and includes the penalty which may be imposed if this obligation is not met.

The authority need not give the above information if it was provided when the scheme was introduced or on any bill (demand notice).[141] If more than one person could be liable, the local authority only needs to write to one of them.[142]

In England and Wales, where a taxpayer believes their dwelling is exempt (based on what the local authority told them) and the local authority subsequently removes the exemption (either without justification or due to an error), then the taxpayer may be able to resist repayment using the legal concept of 'estoppel'. This means the council may be legally prevented from going back on its earlier assurances, as the taxpayer relied on those assurances in good faith. Seek professional advice in this situation.[143]

In Scotland, the Local Taxation Chamber has held that when a local authority wrongly awards an exemption due to official error and the taxpayer acts in good faith, the local authority cannot remove the exemption for previous years, only for the current year.[144]

In Scotland, even if a dwelling is exempt from council tax, the occupant remains liable to pay water and sewage charges.[145]

The duty to correct false assumptions

If you have been notified that the dwelling is or will be exempt, you have a duty to tell the local authority if there is reason to believe that this is not the case. You should notify the local authority in writing within 21 days.[146]

If two or more people are jointly liable, they all have a duty to notify the local authority. Only one of them, however, has to supply the information for this obligation to be met.[147]

5. Penalties

The local authority has the discretion to impose a penalty of £70 (in England) or £50 (in Wales and Scotland) on a liable person who fails to notify it that their dwelling is no longer exempt. There are higher penalties for failing to supply information requested by the local authority for council tax purposes.[148]

Such penalties are not criminal convictions, but if unpaid, they can be recovered through the magistrates' court (sheriff court in Scotland) in the same way as unpaid council tax.

Each time the local authority repeats the request and the person fails to supply the information, the authority can impose a further penalty of £280 (in England) or £200 (in Wales and Scotland).[149]

You can appeal against a penalty,[150] although English and Welsh local authorities have the discretion to quash the penalty beforehand.[151] In England and Wales, you appeal directly to the valuation tribunal (see p266).

In Scotland, a local authority may revoke the penalty if you have a reasonable excuse.[152] If it does not, you can appeal to the Local Taxation Chamber within two months of receiving the penalty notice.

In practice, penalties are rarely used as they cannot be recovered through the courts while an appeal against the penalty is outstanding. As a result, few local authorities consider enforcing penalties worth the time and effort.

A local authority may also impose a larger penalty as an alternative to prosecution for a criminal offence of falsely supplying information.[153]

6. Appealing an exemption decision

If the local authority decides that the dwelling is not exempt, you can appeal in writing to the local authority if you are an aggrieved person.[154] There is no time limit for making such appeals. You are an 'aggrieved person' if you would be liable to pay the tax if the dwelling were not exempt, or you are the owner (if different). The appeal letter should state clearly why the dwelling should be exempt. The local authority has two months to reply.[155]

If granted, exemptions can be backdated to the date the exemption conditions were first met, the start of the scheme or when the particular exemption was first introduced, whichever is the latest. There is no requirement to show good cause for the backdating.

In **England and Wales**, you can make a further appeal by writing directly to the Valuation Tribunal for England or the Valuation Tribunal for Wales. You should normally do this within two months of the date the local authority notified you of its decision, or within four months of the date you made the initial written representation if the local authority has not responded. The tribunal president has the power to allow an out-of-time appeal if you have failed to meet the appropriate time limit because of reasons beyond your control.

In **Scotland**, you can further appeal by writing to the local authority. If the authority refuses the appeal, you may appeal to the Local Taxation Chamber. You can download the form at localtaxationchamber.scot/apply. You must appeal within four months of the date on which you first raised the grievance with the local authority in writing. If you make the appeal out of time, you must give reasons for the delay.

In theory, the local authority may start enforcing payment of the original bill while the appeal is pending, but once a formal appeal has begun, it should suspend recovery and a court may also order a stay on proceedings (see p277).

In an increasing number of cases, billing authorities have removed an exemption which they have previously awarded and recognised for more than one financial year. If you are in this situation, appeal to the tribunal.

See Chapter 11 for more information about appeals.

Notes

1 **EW** s2(2)(a) LGFA 1992
S s71(2)(a) LGFA 1992

1. **Exempt dwellings in England and Wales**

2 As amended from 1 April 2013 by CT(ED)(E)(A)O 2012
3 CT(ED)O
4 *Burnip v Birmingham City Council* [2013] PTSR 117; *R (Hardy) v Sandwell MBC* [2015] PTSR 1292
5 **E** MHCLG, *Council Taxbase* 2024 in England, 7 March 2025
W Welsh government, *Council Tax Dwellings April 2025 – March 2026*, 21 January 2025
6 Art 2 CT(ED)(E)(A)O 2012; s11A LGFA 1992
7 *Olanike Baiyelo v Corkish (LO)* [2017] VTE Appeal No.5690727898/084CAD
8 Art 2(2) CT(ED)O, as amended by CT(ED)(A)O
9 Art 2(2) CT(ED)O, as amended by CT(ED)(A)(E)O
10 *Ealing LB and Others v Notting Hill Housing Trust and Another* [2015] All ER (D) (Feb)
11 Class B CT(ED)O, as amended by art 4(a) CT(ED)(A)O
12 *Ealing LB and Others v Notting Hill Housing Trust and Another* [2015] All ER (D) (Feb)
13 *Royal London Mutual Insurance Society Ltd v Hendon Corpn* [1958] 56 LGR 285
14 *Ealing LB and Others v Notting Hill Housing Trust and Another* [2015] All ER (D) (Feb) per Mostyn, J
15 Department for Communities and Local Government, Appendix 1 'Class B: Council Tax Exemptions', *Council Tax Information Newsletter*, 19 March 2015, at gov.uk/government/publications/council-tax-information-letter-class-b-council-tax-exemptions
16 Added by Sch 1 para 2 Rating (Empty Properties) Act 2007
17 Class C CT(ED)O, as amended by CT(ED)(E)(A)O 2012
18 Class D CT(ED)O

19 s6 LGFA 1992
20 *Mr & Mrs Essex (Appellants) v Kirklees BC* [2021] VTE Appeal No.VT00003672
21 CT(ED)O, as amended by art 4(b) CT(ED)(A)O
22 VTE Appeal No.2935M155193/254C [2015], reported in Valuation Tribunal Service, *Valuation in Practice,* No.38, October 2015
23 *Clemence v Denbighshire DC* [2025] VTW Appeal No.6830M571/CTL/2
24 Class E CT(ED)O, as amended for Wales by Sch 1 The Renting Homes (Wales) Act 2016 (Consequential Amendments to Secondary Legislation) Regulations 2022 No.907 from 12 August 2022
25 Class E CT(ED)O
26 Parliamentary Answer given by Dr Alan Whitehead, Under-Secretary of State for Transport, Local Government and the Regions, 24 January 2002
27 VTE Appeal No.3315M96513/176C [2013], reported in Valuation Tribunal Service, *Valuation in Practice,* No.29, July/August 2013
28 Class F CT(ED)O, as amended by art 4(d) CT(ED)(A)O; reg 2 Sch 1 para 12(b) iii 2022 No.907
29 *Tew v Lewisham LBC* [2018] VTE Appeal No.5690M202173084C/4
30 *N R v Maldon DC* [2019] Appeal No.1545M251794/282C, 19 July 2019
31 *Executor for W Anderson v West Berkshire Council* [2019] VTE Appeal No.0340M254315/281C
32 *AH v City of Bradford DC* [2022] VT00005807, 28 November 2022
33 Noted in Valuation Tribunal Service, *Valuation in Practice,* No.19, November 2010; see also *Trustees of Mrs R's Trust v Northumberland CC* [2018] VTE Appeal No.935M232094/280C
34 ss25-43 Administration of Estates Act 1925
35 *Pratten v Bath and North East Somerset Council* [2019] VTE Appeal No.0114M258275/283C; *Tew v Lewisham LBC* [2018] VTE Appeal No.5690M202173084C/4
36 Class G CT(ED)O
E as amended by art 2(2) CT(ED)(A)(E)O
37 *The Owner v Lewisham LBC* [2014] VTE Appeal Nos.5690M118693/084C and 5690M118694/084C
38 *Watson v Rhondda Cynon Taff BC* [2001] EWHC 913 (Admin)
39 *Appellant v Ipswich BC* [2018] VTE Appeal No.M0227773
40 *Codling v Norwich City Council* [2020] Appeal No.VT00000261, 24 February 2020
41 *JF v Hyndburn BC* [2015] VTE Appeal No.2330M122093/254C, citing *Pall Mall Investments (London) Ltd v Gloucester City Council* [2014] EWHC 2247 (Admin)
42 *Taylor v The County of Herefordshire DC* [2013] VTE Appeal No.1850M84073/221C
43 Class H CT(ED)O
44 *DC v Waveney DC* [2018] VTE Appeal No.3535M215822/037C
45 *DC v Waveney DC* [2018] VTE Appeal No.3535M215822/037C
46 *Appellant v Waverley BC (Billing Authority)* [2019] VTE Appeal No.3650M247075/281C
47 Class I CT(ED)O
48 See *Price v Walsall MBC* [2021] VT M0261496, 5 November 2021, para 32
49 Art 3 Council Tax (Chargeable Dwellings, Exempt Dwellings and Discount Disregards) (Amendment) Order 2004 No.2921
50 Class J CT(ED)O
51 *A v Trafford MBC* [2014] VTE Appeal No.4245M125453/254C
52 *Bedford v Flintshire CC* [2019] VTW App No.6835M11/CTL/1, 20 May 2019
53 Class K CT(ED)O
54 Class L CT(ED)O
55 *R v Scarborough BC* [2018] VTE 2730M202816/254C
56 Class M CT(ED)O
57 Class M CT(ED)O
58 *Stowe School Ltd v Aylesbury Vale DC* [2012] RA 111
59 *Sulets v Leicester City Council* [2017] VTE Appeal No.2465M197400/037C
60 Class N CT(ED)O
61 *Kingsley v Barnet Magistrates Court and Another* [2009] EWHC 464 (Admin)
62 Class N CT(ED)O
63 CTM Practice Note 2, para 28
64 *Jagoo v Bristol City Council* [2017] EWHC 926 (Admin)
65 *Michaelides v Liverpool Council* [2020] VT00000387, 26 February 2020
66 *A v Eastbourne BC* [2014] VTE Appeal No.M0130075
67 *Clews v Sheffield City Council* [2019] VTE Appeal No.4420M255934/282C
68 Class O CT(ED)O
69 CTM Practice Note 2, para 30
70 Class P CT(ED)O

71 Class Q CT(ED)O, as amended by The Council Tax (Exempt Dwellings) (Amendment) Order 1993 No.150
72 s278 IA 1986
73 s306 IA 1986
74 *Tanna v Nottingham City Council* [2021] VTE VT00002765 and VT00002766, 20 July 2021
75 Class R CT(ED)O
76 *Best Holdings (UK) Ltd v Bath and East Somerset DC* [2020] VT00007385 and VT00007386, 9 March 1992
77 Class S CT(ED)O
78 Class T CT(ED)O
79 VTE Decision VT00014823, 17 December 2024, judgment of Mr F J Steward, vice president
80 s55(1) and (3)(a) The Town and Country Planning Act 1990
81 Class U CT(ED)O
82 CT(ED)O
83 *Appellant v Hounslow LBC* [2015] VTE Appeal No.M0093133
84 *Andrew v Blackpool BC* [2020] VTE Appeal No.M0251474
85 *Quaglieri v South Ribble BC* [2021] VTE Appeal No.VT00003854
86 *Quaglieri v South Ribble BC* [2021] VTE Appeal No.VT00003854
87 *CS v Walsall BC* [2019] VTE Appeal No.4630M244934/283C
88 Class V CT(ED)O
89 Class W CT(ED)O
90 CT(ED)O
91 Class W art 5(b) CT(ED)O, amended for Wales by Council Tax (Chargeable Dwellings, Exempt Dwellings and Discount Disregards) Amendment Order 1997 No.556 and for England by CT(ED)(A)(E)O 2005
92 *Patman v Medway Council* [2021] VTE Appeal No.VT00002063
93 Art 3 CT(ED)O amended for Wales by art 2 Council Tax (Exempt Dwellings) (Amendment) (Wales) Order 2019 No.432

2. **Exempt dwellings in Scotland**

94 CT(ED)(S)O 1997, as amended by CT(ED)(S)(A)O 2012, CT(ED)(S)(A)O 2018, CT(ED)(S)(A)O 2023 and CT(ED)(S)(A)O
95 Scottish government, *Second Homes and Empty Properties in September 2024*, 17 December 2024
96 Art 2 CT(ED)(S)(A)O 2012
97 CT(ED)(S)O 1997
98 Sch 1 para 1 CT(ED)(S)O 1997
99 Sch 1 para 2 CT(ED)(S)O 1997, as amended by The Council Tax (Exempt Dwellings) (Scotland) Amendment (No.2) Order 1999 No.140
100 *Assessor Tayside Joint Valuation Board v Decision by the Valuation Appeal Committee for Perth and Kinross* [2018] SCLR 316
101 Sch 1 para 3 CT(ED)(S)O 1997
102 Art 2 CT(ED)(S)O 1997
103 Sch 1 para 4 CT(ED)(S)O 1997
104 Sch 1 para 5 CT(ED)(S)O 1997
105 *Okonski v East Dunbartonshire Council* [2024] FTS/LTC/CT/24/00001, 25 June 2024
106 Class E CT(ED)O, as amended by art 2 and Sch 2 para 17(a) The Public Services Reform (Scotland) Act 2010 (Consequential Modifications of Enactments) Order 2011 No.2581
107 Sch 1 para 6 CT(ED)(S)O 1997
108 Sch 1 para 7 CT(ED)(S)O 1997
109 Sch 1 para 8 CT(ED)(S)O 1997
110 Sch 1 para 9 CT(ED)(S)O 1997
111 Sch 1 para 11 CT(ED)(S)O 1997
112 Sch 1 para 13 CT(ED)(S)O 1997
113 Sch 1 para 14 CT(ED)(S)O 1997
114 Sch 1 para 21 CT(ED)(S)O 1997
115 Sch 1 para 19 CT(ED)(S)O 1997
116 Sch 1 para 12 CT(ED)(S)O 1997
117 CT(ED)(S)(A)O
118 Sch 1 para 10(a)(iii) and (iv) CT(ED)(S)O 1997; see also the Education (Graduate Endowment and Student Support) (Scotland) Act 2001
119 Sch 1 para 10(a)(ii) CT(ED)(S)O 1997
120 Sch 1 para 16 CT(ED)(S)O 1997
121 *Assessor for Lothian Region v Heriot-Watt University* [1998] SC 736
122 Sch 1 para 17 CT(ED)(S)O 1997
123 Sch 1 para 22 CT(ED)(S)O 1997
124 Sch 1 para 20 CT(ED)(S)O 1997
125 Class U CT(ED)(S)O 1997
126 CT(ED)O
127 Sch 1 para 10(a)(iii) CT(ED)(S)O, as amended by art 2 CT(ED)(S)(A)O 2018
128 Policy note to CT(ED)(S)(A)O 2018

129 CT(ED)(S)O 1997 was amended by CT(ED)(S)(A)O 2006. Such a dwelling has the same meaning as accommodation defined by s91(8) the Housing (Scotland) Act 2001 and The Housing (Scotland) Act 2001 (Housing Support Services) Regulations 2002 No.444, registered by the Scottish Commission for the regulation of care as a prescribed housing support service under the Regulation of Care (Scotland) Act 2001.
130 Sch 1 para 25 (1)-(3) CT(ED)(S)O 1997, as amended by art 2 CT(ED)(S)O 2007
131 Sch 1 para 26 CT(ED)(S)O 1992; CT(ED)(S)O 1997, as amended by para 2 CT(ED)(S)(A)O 2022 and CT(ED)(S)(A)O 2023
132 Art 2(2) CT(ED)(S)(A)O 2025

3. **How exempt dwellings are identified**
133 **EW** Reg 8 CT(AE) Regs
S Reg 7 CT(AE)(S) Regs
134 **EW** Reg 9(1) CT(AE) Regs
S Reg 7 CT(AE)(S) Regs
135 **EW** Reg 9(2) CT(AE) Regs
S Reg 8 CT(AE)(S) Regs

4. **Notification of exemption**
136 **EW** Reg 10(1) CT(AE) Regs
137 **EW** Reg 10(2) CT(AE) Regs
S Reg 9 CT(AE)(S) Regs
138 **EW** Reg 10 CT(AE) Regs
S Reg 9 CT(AE)(S) Regs
139 **EW** Reg 10 CT(AE) Regs
S Reg 9 CT(AE)(S) Regs
140 **EW** Reg 10(3) CT(AE) Regs
S Reg 9 CT(AE)(S) Regs
141 **EW** Reg 10 CT(AE) Regs
S Reg 9 CT(AE)(S) Regs
142 **EW** Reg 10 CT(AE) Regs
S Reg 9 CT(AE)(S) Regs
143 See *Ellis v Lambeth LBC* [1999] EWCA Civ 1807; *Tallington Lakes Ltd* [2007] EWHC 1955 (Ch)
144 *Susan Louden v City of Edinburgh* [2023] FTS/LTC/CT/23/41252, 20 December 2023
145 s36(1)(b) Water Industry (Scotland) Act 2002
146 **EW** Reg 11 CT(AE) Regs
147 **EW** Reg 11 CT(AE) Regs
S Reg 10 CT(AE)(S) Regs

5. **Penalties**
148 LGFE(SP)O
149 **EW** Sch 3 LGFA 1992; LGFE(SP)O
S s97(4) and Sch 3 LGFA 1992
150 **EW** s14(2) and Sch 3 LGFA 1992
S s97(4) and Sch 3 LGFA 1992
151 **EW** Sch 3 para 1 LGFA 1992
152 s97(4) and Sch 3 LGFA 1992
153 **EW** s14 LGFA 2012

6. **Appealing an exemption decision**
154 **EW** s16 LGFA 1992
S s81 LGFA 1992
155 **EW** s16 LGFA 1992
S s81 LGFA 1992

Chapter 5

Liability

This chapter covers:

1. Who is liable

Council tax is payable on any dwelling which is not exempt. See Chapter 4 for information on exemptions. Normally, the person liable to pay council tax is an adult resident of the dwelling. To be liable, the person must have their sole or main residence in the dwelling and have a right to occupy it.[1]

A hierarchy of liability determines who is liable to pay council tax.[2] This lists different categories of occupier, based on security of occupancy, including owners, tenants, licensees and squatters. Normally, the person(s) whose sole or main residence is in a dwelling and who has the most secure interest in it will be the liable taxpayer(s) and the person to whom the council tax bill will be sent.

Hierarchy of liability in England and Wales

1. A resident with a freehold interest in the whole or any part of the dwelling.
2. A resident with a leasehold interest (including an assured tenancy or assured shorthold tenancy) in the whole or any part of the dwelling which is not inferior to (shorter than) another such interest held by another resident.
3. A resident statutory tenant,[3] secure tenant[4] or introductory[5] tenant of the whole or any part of the dwelling.[6]
4. A resident with a contractual licence to occupy the whole or any part of the dwelling.
5. A resident (including a squatter).

6. A person who is a mortgagee in possession of the owner's interest in the dwelling. In the case of secure or introductory tenants, and a mortgagee in possession, a date for these to come into force has yet to be appointed.[7]
7. A non-resident owner – ie, the person who has the inferior (shortest) lease granted for a term of six months or more of the whole, or any part, of the dwelling. If there is no such leaseholder, the freeholder is the owner.[8] An owner of a hereditament is further defined as the person entitled to possession of it under the Local Government Finance Act 1988.[9]

Hierarchy of liability in Scotland[10]

1. A resident owner of the whole or any part of the dwelling.
2. A resident tenant of the whole or any part of the dwelling.
3. A resident statutory tenant,[11] resident statutory assured tenant[12] or resident secure tenant[13] of the whole or any part of the dwelling.[14]
4. A resident sub-tenant of the whole or any part of the dwelling.
5. A resident of the dwelling or:
   - a sub-tenant of the whole or any part of the dwelling under a sub-lease granted for a term of six months or more;
   - a tenant, under a lease granted for a term of six months or more, of any part of the dwelling which is not subject to a sub-lease granted for a term of six months or more;
   - an owner of any part of the dwelling which is not subject to a lease granted for a term of six months or more.

Working down the list, as soon as a description is reached which applies to someone in respect of the dwelling in question, that person is the liable person.[15] If more than one person fits that description, they are usually jointly liable (see p95). This will normally be an owner-occupier or a council, housing association or private tenant. However, a tenant is not liable if the landlord lives in the same dwelling. If no one is solely or mainly resident (see p84) in the dwelling, the non-resident owner is liable. In certain instances, however, the owner is always liable (see p91).

A contractual arrangement between a landlord and tenant is a private matter between them and does not alter who is liable for the council tax under section 6 of the 1992 Act.[16]

To determine the liable person on any day, the situation at the end of the day is assumed to have existed throughout that day (see p84).[17]

In certain cases, the liable person may also be a person who is disregarded for the purpose of a discount (see Chapter 7). The rules on discounts are separate and do not affect liability, except in some cases where they affect severely mentally impaired people and students who would otherwise be held jointly liable (see p97).

When the owner dies and the property is unoccupied, the deceased's representative may become liable in their capacity as owner of the estate, but the dwelling is likely to be exempt until probate or letters of administration are obtained. See Chapter 4 for more information.

A taxpayer who is made bankrupt and vacates a property is no longer liable to pay council tax on any property they formerly owned, having ceased to be the owner or occupier of the property. The liability changes on the date the trustee is appointed or when the official receiver becomes trustee. As a result, the trustee becomes liable for council tax when no one occupies the property or is a tenant or sub-tenant.[18] However, the trustee in bankruptcy will be exempt from paying council tax under Class Q.[19] If the mortgagee (such as a bank) takes possession, it could become liable to pay council tax at the property. In the case of repossessed property, the liable person would be the person who is a mortgagee in possession of the owner's interest in the dwelling. A mortgagee in possession is exempt from paying if claiming an exemption under Class L only where a mortgagee is in place.[20]

A person is not liable if they are only a beneficial owner – eg, if they took possession of a property through a county court order to settle a debt, but they do not have a material interest in the property and so do not fulfil the council tax definition of an owner.[21]

Note: you do not have to pay council tax unless a bill has been sent with your name on it or you have been served with a bill, if your name is unknown, addressed to the 'council taxpayer' (see p190). In Scotland, you may be liable if you are unnamed but you are jointly liable with someone who has been billed.

In *R v D*, the billing authority argued that a trial judge was wrong in law to rule that the defendant was under no obligation to inform it of the fact that she resided at a particular address. The defendant phoned the council to say she had moved out of the property she owned (leaving a tenant there who was granted the single occupier discount). The council contended that the defendant had remained at the property and made a false statement to escape liability for council tax, stating that notifying residency was implied in the legislation. The Court of Appeal ruled that it was wrong to equate a liability to pay with a liability to notify. There was no provision in the Local Government Finance Act 1992 or any statutory instrument which imposed a liability to notify the billing authority of residency. The court also disagreed that there was any implied obligation to notify. There was 'no common law relationship between the council and the defendant that could give rise to any such duty of notification; nor was there any relevant fiduciary duty or equitable obligation in this regard'.[22]

Consequently, there is no duty prescribed in the council tax regulations relating to billing to report yourself to a billing authority if you do not receive a council tax demand, nor is one implied. It has been held at tribunal level that there is no requirement for a resident to notify the billing authority of changes to the liable person (moving in or out); only to notify a change of circumstances for liability purposes if in receipt of a discount or exemption which they would cease to qualify for as a result of the change. As no discount or exemption was in place on the account, the panel found that the appellant should not be subject to a penalty and allowed the appeal.[23]

In Scotland, in addition to council tax, Scottish Water charges are payable for any dwelling which is not exempt, except if:

- Scottish Water does not provide a supply of water to the dwelling; *or*
- the water is supplied by meter; *or*
- Scottish Water is under an obligation to provide a supply free of charge.

Caravans and boats in England and Wales

A caravan or houseboat owner is liable for council tax except for the days when someone other than the owner is resident.[24] The normal council tax definitions of 'resident' (see p84) and 'owner' apply in the case of residential caravans or boats, but the definition of 'owner' is extended to include:[25]

- the person who has possession under any hire purchase or conditional sale agreement; *or*
- the person entitled to the property apart from any mortgage or bill of sale which applies to it.[26] In *Hyett v Wakefield Council*, the court held that even when a receiver (appointed under the Law of Property Act 1925) is managing the property for a mortgagee (lender), that does not make the mortgagee 'in possession' for council tax purposes. Consequently, the landlord remained liable for the council tax once the tenant had moved out, even where the receivers were a company connected with the mortgagee and were charging fees over a long period.[27]

Moveable structures such as transportable caravans (not statics) and houseboats may be relocated during the course of a year and questions may be raised as to whether they should be classed as hereditaments and be chargeable for council tax (see Chapter 2). For both caravans and houseboats, examining the degree of permanence at any location may be necessary. Guidance states:[28]

> A formal pitch or formal mooring constructed or laid out, perhaps with the provision for services, will constitute a hereditament. This should be distinguished from a temporary wayfarer's pitch, eg roadside or a mooring on a mud flat or natural river bank, which would have to be occupied for a sufficient length of time for it to constitute a hereditament.

A key issue is the length of time that a caravan or houseboat may remain in any one location. Under the old rates system (from which the concept of the hereditament is derived), rateable occupation and liability to pay did not arise for a resident who was only occupying for a matter of days, weeks or even months.[29]

A houseboat moored for two years was found to have sufficient permanence to be classed as a dwelling.[30]

In contrast, the Valuation Tribunal for England found that a motorboat was a chattel rather than a dwelling where no agreement or mooring licence had been granted, and it did not have an exclusive right to occupy any specific part of the riverbank.[31] The boat was not fixed to any one position and it moved regularly, at least every three weeks, due to collisions with rowers and the eroding riverbank. The panel decided the appellant was of no fixed abode and the boat was deleted from the valuation list.

Daily liability

Liability to pay council tax arises daily. The situation at the end of the day is assumed to have existed throughout the day.[32] The amount payable for the day is the annual amount set by the local authority for that year for dwellings in the relevant valuation band, divided by the number of days in the financial year (365 or 366).

2. Who is a resident

Council tax is usually payable by someone who is resident in the dwelling. If no one is resident, the non-resident owner is liable. To count as resident, you must:

- be aged 18 or over; *and*
- be solely or mainly resident in the dwelling (see below).[33]

If everyone living in the dwelling is aged under 18, the dwelling is exempt from council tax.

Sole or main residence

If a potentially liable person has more than one home, the local authority must decide which is their main residence. The concept of 'sole or main residence' is not defined in legislation, but has been considered by the courts.

Where the taxpayer lives (England and Wales)

The Court of Appeal decision in *R (Williams) v Horsham District Council* clarifies the approach to take.[34] The starting point for deciding sole or main residence is section 6(5) of the Local Government Finance Act 1992, where 'sole or main residence' refers to premises where the taxpayer actually resides. The court introduced the 'reasonable onlooker' test: with knowledge of the facts, would a reasonable onlooker regard a particular dwelling as the person's home? This test helps establish objectivity and ensures that local authorities do not rely solely on procedural or bureaucratic indicators.

Following this case, it is clear that the starting point for any appeal is section 6 and the question of who actually lives in the dwelling.

Factors that may establish a home may be wide-ranging and can vary with the facts. In addition to the taxpayer's evidence and the fact that they may have paid rent for (and moved belongings into) a property for a period, relevant factors can include:

- personal circumstances – eg, age, nationality, the presence of family members, employment, income (including benefits);
- time spent at a property during the period of residence and whether there at weekends or for other periods;
- presence during Christmas and other holiday periods;
- whether a person has a home elsewhere.

A tribunal should be aware that facts may be consistent with a number of different life stories.

By emphasising section 6, the Court of Appeal confirmed that resident tenants, licensees and even trespassers should normally be placed ahead of non-resident owners in terms of liability for council tax. Valuation tribunals have often used factors such as voter registration and registration for medical treatment to determine sole or main residence. However, the key question following the *Williams* case is: 'Where does the taxpayer actually live?' Hypothetical questions, such as where a person might move or remain in the event of job loss or serious illness or where they might live were tenants to move out, do not, in themselves, determine the answer to this question.

The vice president of the Valuation Tribunal for England has stated:

> There would be nothing wrong in any council tax payer who owns a number of dwellings so ordering his affairs as to minimise liability for council tax provided, for the purposes of this discount in issue, there was a genuine change of sole or main residence as part of that process... Billing authorities and the Tribunal have to bear in mind the apparent motivation of the council taxpayer in such circumstances and the burden of proof to establish a change of sole or main residence remains with that taxpayer.[35]

The judgment in *Williams* is particularly important if you have let your principal home to tenants or to someone who normally lives or works abroad. In *Parry v Derbyshire Dales District Council*,[36] the taxpayer lived in Spain and let his UK cottage to tenants. The High Court held that the taxpayer was resident in Spain for local tax purposes and the fact that the tenant left did not mean that Mr Parry ceased to reside in Spain. The court followed the approach of the Court of Appeal in the *Williams* case: setting out a hierarchy of liability based on who is actually resident in the dwelling rather than security of tenure is crucial to determining the liable person for council tax purposes. In some cases, it would follow that a person's home may be different to their sole or main residence. 'Home' has been judicially considered the place where a person has a degree of physical and emotional attachment. The test as to whether a person occupied premises as their home is both qualitative and quantitative, and a decision maker must weigh all the relevant facts reasonably.[37]

Following the *Williams* case, a person letting a dwelling to tenants should ensure that bill calculation relates to when the tenants actually move out of a dwelling, not necessarily when they move in.

Example

Ted and Kelly live with their 17-year-old daughter. Kelly is the joint property owner with her sister, who often comes to stay and has her own bedroom, but who has her main home elsewhere. The non-resident joint owner is not liable.

If the couple separate and Ted moves out, Kelly would be liable by herself, but Ted would remain jointly liable for any charges that arose while living as a couple.

If Kelly also leaves the dwelling, leaving their daughter as the only person living there, the dwelling may be exempt, as it is the sole residence of someone under 18. On the daughter's 18th birthday, she would become the sole liable person as the only resident of the dwelling.

Kelly's sister remains not liable as her main residence is elsewhere.

The fact that people may have, for whatever reason, used a dwelling to provide a residential postal address does not, in itself, mean that such persons were actually residing there.[38]

Local authorities sometimes treat tenants as still liable if they move out of a property before the end of their tenancy.[39]

If you reside abroad, it is helpful to give a breakdown of the number of days you spend in the UK compared to the time you spend overseas, together with any documentation establishing what you do abroad, employment history while abroad and documents issued in another country confirming residency or settlement arrangements. You can show proof of a letting to tenants by contracts, rental payments and receipts, and credit checks.[40]

Periodic tenancies

Some confusion has arisen in decisions about whether 'presumed periodic tenancies', arising under statute or by contract, may constitute qualifying leasehold tenancies of more than six months and are therefore classed as 'surviving' when residents move out (and also in respect of entitlement to housing benefit on a property that is no longer occupied).[41] One judgment held that vacating a property did not terminate a tenant's liability to pay council tax which was otherwise due. In *Leeds City Council v Broadley*,[42] the court held the tenancy agreement in question created the equivalent of a single leasehold interest 'granted for a term of six months or more', albeit that the interest was initially fixed for a term of years. The fact that it changed to a periodic tenancy afterwards did not affect this. It was only the termination of the tenant's interest in the property which ended liability. This has been followed at tribunal level.[43]

Under the Renter's Rights Act 2025, in England, all assured shorthold tenancies will automatically convert into assured periodic tenancies – ie, rolling tenancies without a fixed end date. The government has stated that clause 27 of the bill, when it comes into law, is intended to ensure that assured tenants remain liable for council tax until the end of their tenancy agreement. This will include where the tenant has served notice to end the tenancy but leaves the property before the notice period has ended. In that instance, the liability will not fall to the landlord until the tenancy has ended.[44]

However, no decisions to date have fully considered the issue in the context of sole or main residence and how it is determined by asking where a person actually lives, as in *Williams*.

In *Branwell v Valuation Office Agency*, the High Court stated: 'The hierarchy in section 6 shows that Parliament decided that liability should depend on residence in, and rights to reside in, a dwelling. That is an intelligible and rational legislative choice. It connects liability with actual enjoyment of the dwelling, or if no one is living in it, with the right to occupy it.'

The key proviso is the words 'if no one is living in it'. Following the *Williams* case, if the former tenant no longer lives in the dwelling and begins living elsewhere and actually has their sole or main residence elsewhere, they can no longer be said to reside in the dwelling and cease to be considered liable under section 6. Once the right to occupy the dwelling is terminated, whether by giving notice and moving out, by abandonment or eviction, and the person begins living elsewhere and establishes another sole or main residence in another dwelling, any liability for council tax at the former home should cease.

Thus, if a tenant vacates a property without proper notice and is settled elsewhere, the landlord becomes liable to pay the council tax during this period of non-occupancy, because the landlord has the remaining material interest and the ultimate right in law to use and occupy the home, and not the former tenant or occupier.

When the tenant gives no formal written notice, notice can be inferred from conduct. Examples include returning and accepting keys, a refusal to agree to the new tenancy, patterns of rental payment and their cessation.[45] The date a landlord receives the keys may be treated as the effective end of the tenancy, along with the details of any communications – eg, by text messages.[46]

The question of sole or main residence may also be indicated by asking where a person normally sleeps either most or all of the time. In *Sumeghova v McMahon*,[47] the Court of Appeal ruled that the place where a person sleeps was of great importance in determining where their principal or only home was; while it might not be decisive, it would influence any court considerably. Even though it is normally the case that a person's main residence will be at the matrimonial or family home,[48] there may be exceptions – eg, where a married couple live in separate dwellings.[49]

Example

Sam is the tenant of a flat on an assured tenancy beginning on 1 September and pays council tax from 1 September. He gives notice and moves out after Christmas. He moves in with his partner, Zoe, at her address in the same billing authority area.

The landlord does not let Sam's flat immediately and it stands empty. Applying the hierarchy under section 6, as Sam no longer has residence in the flat, he ceases to have any liability. Instead, Sam becomes jointly liable to pay council tax with Zoe at the address where they live together. The liability for council tax at Sam's former address falls upon the landlord unless a new tenant or occupier moves in.

If a person has never lived in a dwelling, they cannot be considered to be resident in it, even if they are the owner of the dwelling or have no fixed abode. Material drawn from social media showing persons such as ex-partners together is not necessarily proof of joint residence as individuals remain in touch but may not be resident together.[50]

Where the taxpayer lives (Scotland)

The same approach to residence taken in the *Williams* case (see p84) has been applied in Scotland. A taxpayer lived during the week, and some weekends, in a dwelling closer to his job rather than in the dwelling where his wife and family resided.[51] The Court of Session ruled that the Valuation Appeal Committee (VAC) was entitled to find that the weekday dwelling was his sole or main residence.

In cases where liability may fall upon the landlord, it is essential that the Local Taxation Chamber (LTC), which incorporates what was the VAC, establishes whether a property has been truly abandoned or is merely temporarily unoccupied, and can identify the situation from evidence.[52]

Council tax discounts and reductions

The question of sole or main residence is important when calculating discounts and disability reductions. Where more than oneadult lives in a property, this can affect the amount of council tax support available and discount entitlement if only one adult remains. The local authority must be notified within 21 days when a person moves in or out of the property, if a change in sole or main residence (based upon the test in *Williams* – see p84) has arisen.

Simply using a property as a postal address to receive mail or store belongings there does not count as residence for council tax purposes.

Example

Joan is a pensioner with an adult son, Paul, who is homeles. Although Paul visits occassionally and receives post at Joan's address, he usually stays in hostels or with friends. Paul does not have sole or main residence with Joan for council tax purposes, so she is entitled to a single occupier discount.

Establishing sole or main residence

Sometimes, the local authority does not accept a taxpayer's evidence that a person resides at a particular dwelling. If this is the case, the taxpayer can use various types of evidence – eg, bank statements, utility bills, extracts from official registers, forms of identification and statements from neighbours and professionals who know the situation. Bank statements showing transactions for living costs carried out in a particular area might support a statement that a person is living there.[53]

A local authority is expected to act reasonably when assessing evidence. For example, if proof of a tenancy agreement is supported by signatures and addresses of witnesses which are in doubt, the local authority should investigate the details and try to contact the witnesses, not merely ignore or dismiss the evidence as insufficient or untrustworthy.[54]

If the local authority does not accept the evidence provided, you should make an appeal to the valuation tribunal in England or Wales or to the LTC in Scotland.

You can set out the facts of your case, including any evidence you have in a witness statement. A witness statement must include your name and address, and state the relevant facts. A local authority that refuses to accept evidence in a witness statement may be liable for breach of statutory duty in civil law.

A lands registry entry may not be conclusive to prove ownership of a dwelling if it can be rebutted by other evidence. You should not be held liable where evidence clearly shows that the ownership of the property had changed hands, despite the lands registry showing otherwise.[55]

The fact that a billing authority cannot find copies or records of documents does not mean it has not received these. Different forms of proof can be used as evidence such as tenancy agreements and related documents (eg, reference-related documents) and utility bills; and electricity usage patterns may be a fact from which occupation can be inferred. Photographs and receipts for deliveries of goods may also be used.

The tribunal may find that receipts and stamps are evidence that the documents have been received and acknowledged.[56]

Residence in more than one place

A person can have both a sole or main residence and also a residence in another dwelling for discount and other council tax purposes. This has been accepted in an appeal against the imposition of an empty property discount under section 11B of the Local Government Finance Act 1992.[57]

A billing authority can increase the council tax on any dwelling in England continuously empty for two or more years, for which the dwelling's owner is liable.[58]

In one tribunal case, the owner who was appealing had occupied the property from time to time for renovation and, to a limited extent, had lived inside it. Supporting evidence included a gas bill, a bank statement, a home insurance policy letter, photographs and other documents, including an electoral roll form, and was supported by a witness statement. Non-occupation should not be inferred simply because the appellant had other addresses for his bank accounts and did not show up on credit checks at the appeal property, or because of a date inconsistency in correspondence. The tribunal accepted that the legislation also uses the word 'resident' in other contexts, and from its inception, the possibility that a person may own one or more properties and pay council tax in respect of both has been a basic feature. The panel identified that the correct test to be an empty property was 'simply whether the appeal property was unoccupied and unfurnished'.[59]

Further recognition of the principle that a person may have two different residences simultaneously is found in other branches of taxation law. In *Frost v Feltham*, it was ruled: 'If someone lives in two houses the question, which does he use as the principal or more important one, cannot be determined solely by reference to the way in which he divides his time between the two.'[60]

When it comes to determining what is your main residence when you have a choice of two, the approach is to identify which is the 'principal' or 'most important' one.[61]

It has also been recognised that there are 'an infinity of variations of circumstances to take into account in deciding which was a man's main home. Each case would differ from the other; there might be cases where it was very difficult to decide the question.'[62]

A resident is distinguishable from a mere visitor to a property.[63] Merely because a couple are married, and one is treated as having a sole main residence at one location, is not sufficient reason in itself to conclude that both spouses share the same sole or main residence.[64]

The period of time is not in itself conclusive.

Homeless accommodation

The position is more complicated with accommodation for homeless people if the properties are self-contained flats leased by a council to provide accommodation for homeless people. In such cases, the homeless person occupying the property may be held liable as a resident by a tribunal, notwithstanding that they are homeless and in temporary accommodation. In *App v London Borough of Hammersmith and Fulham*,[65] the valuation tribunal ruled that homeless people placed in short-term accommodation were liable for council tax. Although they were homeless in legal terms, the flats were their actual place of residence and the only place they had to live. Each flat therefore became that person's sole residence for the period in which they were in occupation. The tribunal found the non-secure tenancy agreements to amount to a licence to occupy, sufficient to impose liability on the occupiers, notwithstanding they were being treated as homeless. However, it may still be possible to argue non-liability if occupation is too transient or if the accommodation is arranged through a managing agent.[66]

3. When the owner is always liable

If there are no residents in the dwelling, the non-resident owner is liable. Additionally, the Secretary of State or Welsh or Scottish ministers have power to specify circumstances in which, even if there are residents, the owner is always liable.[67] The owner (not the residents) is liable for the council tax on:

- care homes and certain hostels providing care and support (see below);
- houses in multiple occupation (HMOs) (see below);
- second homes with domestic staff (see p94);
- houses of religious communities (see p94);
- residences of ministers of religion (see p94);
- school boarding accommodation in Scotland (see p95);
- accommodation provided to an asylum seeker (see p95).

Care homes and hostels

An owner is liable to pay council tax on care homes and certain hostels providing care and support that are registered in England under the Care Standards Act 2000 and under Part 1 of the Health and Social Care Act 2008.[68]

In Wales, the definition of an owner who is liable to pay council tax on a care home specifies that it is any home within the meaning of the Regulation and Inspection of Social Care (Wales) Act 2016 *or* under section 18 or 19 of the Care Act 2014 or section 35 or 36 of the Social Services and Well-being (Wales) Act 2014 *or* a hostel within the meaning of paragraph 7 of Schedule 1 of the Act.[69]

In Scotland, the owner is liable for council tax for any building in which a care home service provides accommodation, or a private hospital which is not used wholly or mainly as the sole or main residence of a person.[70]

Houses in multiple occupation

The owner of an HMO is liable even if they have no beneficial interest in the property.[71] A dwelling is classed as an HMO if:[72]

- it was originally constructed or later adapted for occupation by more than one household; *or*
- each person who lives in part of it is either:
  - a tenant or licensee able to occupy only part of the dwelling; *or*
  - a licensee liable to pay rent or a licence fee on only part of the dwelling; *or*
- in England as Wales, it is defined as a HMO under the Housing Act 2004 (see p92).

Examples include some bedsits, hostels, nurses' homes and long-stay hospital wards classed as dwellings. In England and Wales, even if only one person lives in the dwelling, it could still be classed as an HMO if it was built or adapted for multiple households.

The High Court has held: 'the focus must be not upon the state of the premises and not upon the intention of the landlord in letting them, underlying these provisions is a distinction between those houses which are genuinely in shared accommodation by those who have a link between them so as to constitute a single household, as contrasted with those who have no real link between them, as for instance in the example of... effectively a hostel for the homeless.'[73]

The term 'tenant' includes a secure tenant or a statutory tenant. In England and Wales, the normal definition of an owner applies for an HMO, except if someone has a leasehold interest. In this case, it must be an interest in the whole dwelling. Otherwise, the person who has a freehold interest in the whole or any part of the dwelling is liable.[74]

The Housing Act 2004 defines a dwelling as an HMO if:[75]

- it consists of one or more units of living accommodation that are not self-contained flat(s);
- the living accommodation is occupied by people who do not form a single household, as their only or main residence (or it is treated as such);
- there is no other use of the accommodation – eg, in the case of a student hall of residence or work-related accommodation;
- at least one person occupying the accommodation pays rent;
- two or more of the households share one or more basic amenities (ie, a kitchen, toilet or bathroom) or the living accommodation does not have one of those amenities.

The Housing Act 2004 also states a building will count as an HMO if it was converted into flats and does not meet the required building standards. However, this is not an HMO for council tax purposes. The Housing Act 2004 also includes exemptions to a building counting as a HMO if it is managed or controlled by certain landords, but again that rule does not apply for council tax purposes.[76]

The definitions of an HMO for council tax differ from the definitions used for licensing, though there is significant overlap. For council tax, a multi-occupation dwelling merely requires there be two or more tenants or licence holders occupying the premises.[77] This is so even though in other legislation a house is not registerable as an HMO unless three people are living in it at the same time. Courts and tribunals must always follow the definition that appears in the council tax regulations.[78]

An HMO for council tax purposes could, therefore, be a self-contained flat occupied by people who do not form a single household, or a converted building containing one or more self-contained units, occupied by people who do not form a single household. The High Court held that the correct test to apply when addressing whether a building had been constructed or adapted for use as separate living accommodation was an objective 'bricks and mortar' test which looked at the reality of what had been constructed and/or how it had been adapted.[79] This was an objective, not a subjective, test and therefore the intention of use, whether actual or prospective, was irrelevant to the determination.

The tribunal will look for evidence of adaptation – eg, if separate locks have been fitted to the rooms of residents and they have their own keys and facilities.

Exclusive possession

When deciding residents' status and the degree of exclusive possession (ie, whether they only occupy part of the dwelling), tribunals can look beyond the tenancy or licence agreement and examine the actual facts.[80] This is crucial where the evidence and the accuracy of documents produced at the hearing are challenged – eg, parties may have used standard pre-printed tenancy forms which do not reflect the actual legal position between them. However, documents alone should not decide that a property is an HMO simply because there are a number of tenants in the dwelling and the owner retains the use of one room – eg, for storing furniture which the tenants do not wish to use.

The High Court ruled in one case that the test to apply is whether the rent paid gives the tenants the right to occupy the entire dwelling or only part of it.[81] The key issue was whether, ultimately, the tenants had exclusive possession of the whole house. In this case, the owner's furniture was kept locked in the conservatory, which meant the tenants could not use the conservatory. It was decided that this fact was not sufficient, since the statutory test that had to be applied was whether a tenant was a 'tenant of part only of the dwelling'. They remained tenants of the conservatory even though, in fact, they were unable to use or readily gain access to it. The only items of furniture stored in the conservatory were those that the tenants were paying rent for and, since the terms of the tenancy had not been varied, they were entitled to ask for the key at any time and, if they chose to do so, they could exclude the landlord from the conservatory and also exclude her furniture from that area so long as they stored or used the furniture in another location. They were, therefore, tenants of the whole dwelling, including the conservatory.

In another case, a key issue was whether the tenants were responsible for paying rent on the dwelling as a whole.[82] The tribunal had erred in finding that they were not, contrary to what was written in the lease.

The question of what the lease or tenancy agreement says is important, but it is not conclusive in determining exclusive possession and may not be considered binding on an individual if they have not signed it. The lease need not be in writing to be binding, but if a written lease has not been signed, then a valuation tribunal is entitled to consider all the relevant evidence and conclude that the property constitutes an HMO.[83] An important question may be whether the occupiers made the agreement together with the landlord or made separate arrangements. If it was the latter, the house is more likely to qualify as an HMO. What a lease or rental agreement says about liability to pay council tax on a dwelling is an important factor, but does not always determine the issue. Exceptions are recognised[84] and a valuation tribunal should not just accept the view of one side on the question of a multiple occupation dwelling – eg, just the opinion of a local authority inspector.[85]

Where residents of an HMO are wrongly held liable, evidence from the residents themselves may be crucial. In one case, the Valuation Tribunal for England (VTE) accepted a witness statement from a tenant as to his whereabouts over a disputed period of liability and his evidence that he never signed any tenancy agreement with other occupiers of a property or lived with them as part of the same household.[86] The tribunal rejected as evidence a purported rent book which contained serious discrepancies and was branded as false by the tenant who had actually been living in a different borough for two of the four years in the period of liability in dispute. The VTE accepted the tenant's oral evidence and witness statement as consistent and arising from a direct knowledge of the facts and the situation of the dwelling during the disputed period.

Similar principles apply to evidence submitted to the Local Taxation Chamber in Scotland. Any tribunal which applies the wrong tests and makes errors of fact and law may have its decision overturned by the Court of Session on appeal.[87]

Second homes with domestic staff

A dwelling fits into this category if:[88]

- the employer, who does not live in it as their main residence, occupies it from time to time; *and*
- all the residents are either employed in domestic service in the dwelling or are the employer's family members.

Religious communities

For the owner to be liable, a religious community must live in the dwelling whose main occupation consists of prayer, contemplation, education, the relief of suffering or any combination of these.[89] Monasteries and convents come within this description. Members of such communities may qualify to be disregarded for a council tax discount (see p128).

Accommodation for ministers of religion

A minister of religion (of any faith) must live in the dwelling as a residence from where they perform their duties of office. If the minister owns the dwelling, they are liable for council tax. There are exceptions to this rule for English or Welsh dwellings that a minister of the Church of England/Wales owns, who is in receipt of a stipend. In such a case, the Diocesan Board of Finance becomes liable. In Scotland, the body liable for paying the minister is liable for council tax.[90]

School boarding accommodation

In Scotland, the owner of school boarding accommodation which is specifically included in the definition of a dwelling (see p19) is liable for the council tax.[91]

Accommodation occupied by asylum seekers

Asylum seekers occupying accommodation under section 95 of the Immigration and Asylum Act 1999 are not liable for council tax. The owner is liable.[92]

4. Joint liability

If two or more people fall into the liable category (eg, joint owners, joint tenants or simply joint residents), they are jointly and severally liable, except if one is severely mentally impaired or a student (see p97).[93] Naming more than one person on a council tax demand does not make each person liable for a set percentage of the total sum due; all of the named people are liable for the whole amount.[94]

Where people live together who have different interests in the property, the person who comes higher up on the hierarchy of liability is the liable person. For example, the property owner will be liable if the other person living at the property is a tenant or licensee.

Additionally, a liable person's partner is jointly liable if they are:[95]

- married to or in a civil partnership with the liable person; *or*
- living with their partner as a married couple or as if in a civil partnership; *and*
- a resident of the dwelling.

This applies whether or not the partner has a legal interest in the dwelling. The definition of a couple used to establish joint liability for council tax is similar to that applied with many social security benefits (see CPAG's *Welfare Benefits Handbook*). To be a couple under the social security rules, however, both partners must reside in the same *household*. For council tax, it is only necessary to show that they reside in the same *dwelling*. As it is possible for a single dwelling to contain more than one household, there will be some situations when the two definitions do not coincide. For instance, if a married couple are estranged but continue to live in the same house and have separate households, they are still classed as a jointly liable couple for council tax purposes as they remain married and continue to reside in the same dwelling. In *Routhan v Arun* (decided under the old rates law), it was held that spouses living together can be jointly liable for rates, regardless of who holds the title. If one spouse leaves, they may still be considered in occupation unless they show the separation is complete. Liability depends on the facts, and the duty to support a spouse or children does not automatically make someone liable.[96]

However, those residing in the same property as part of different households are not a couple for council tax reduction (CTR) purposes because they reside in different households. This means that both partners are jointly liable, but each can make a separate claim for reductions based on an apportioned (50 per cent) share of council tax liability and their own individual circumstances. See Chapter 8 for more information on CTR.

In terms of joint and several liability for council tax, the meaning of provisions can be difficult to interpret as 'husband', 'wife' and 'married' are not defined in previous council tax law other than by reference to gender. There is a substantial body of social security caselaw on the various criteria that must be considered and, arguably, this will be persuasive in establishing a relationship in council tax cases. Simply because two people share accommodation, a local authority should not presume that they are sharing as the equivalent of a married couple or a couple living together as spouses, resulting in joint and several liability. Examples where the council may make erroneous inferences include cases where siblings live together and situations where two people of the same sex (whether related or not) live at, or use, the same address but on different terms.

It is difficult to see how the local authority could conclude that two unmarried people are living together as spouses unless they are members of the same household (as opposed to merely being resident in the same dwelling) without details of a sexual relationship and the roles assumed in the household. Although there is no established 'right to privacy' in domestic law, you may take legal action[97] for breach of confidence or harassment where your private information is released, misused or improperly demanded. More generally, the local authority's power to demand such information is limited in light of Article 8 of the European Convention on Human Rights, enshrining a right to privacy, and the limits placed in law as to what information may be sought.

If the questions the local authority asks you are unreasonable, you should make a formal complaint. It is a good idea to involve your Member of Parliament. You can also complain to the local authority's monitoring officer and to the Local Government and Social Care Ombudsman. You may be able to take action through a tribunal or the civil courts in extreme cases where confidentiality is broken or improper information requested. You can challenge an erroneous decision on joint and several liability (see p101) – eg, by complaining.

You cannot have joint and several liability where the facts show that you do not have sole or main residence in a dwelling with another person. A finding that you do not have sole or main residence in a dwelling removes you from any liability for council tax altogether from the effective date you ceased to reside. In polygamous marriages, all partners resident in the dwelling are jointly liable[98] and the regulations make specific provision for CTR schemes (see Chapter 8).

In Wales, care leavers aged 24 or under who fall within and meet the conditions prescribed within the regulations are not jointly or severally liable, even if they are married or in a civil partnership.[99]

The significance of joint liability

Even though multiple people may be jointly liable, a council tax bill does not need to name all of them. In Scotland, someone who is jointly liable with the person(s) named on the bill, but whose name is not included, is still liable to make the required payments. See Chapter 9 for more details. In England and Wales, a liable person is not required to pay until they have been billed. If the local authority wants to recover the council tax from someone who is jointly liable but not named on the original bill, it must issue a fresh bill (a joint taxpayers' notice).[100] In practice, local authorities tend to pursue the first two named persons on a bill.

To be eligible for CTR, you must be liable for council tax. If someone other than your partner is jointly liable, any CTR is worked out on your apportioned share, even though the local authority may be seeking to recover all of the council tax due from one person. If you receive CTR, the late identification of retrospective joint liability may mean you have been overpaid, and could raise the possibility of the newly identified jointly liable person making a late claim for a reduction. In England and Wales, if the local authority refuses to exercise its discretion to reduce a bill in a case of late billing, you should apply for a discretionary reduction in council tax under section 13A(1) of the Local Government Finance Act 2012 (see p135) and you have a right to appeal to a valuation tribunal (see Chapter 11). For more information on CTR, see Chapter 8.

Joint liability and severe mental impairment

A person who is disregarded for discount purposes because of a severe mental impairment (see p124) is not held jointly liable if there is someone else with the same status and legal interest in the property who is not severely mentally impaired (SMI).[101] However, a SMI person is liable for the tax if:

- they are the only liable person; *or*
- they are the only owner, tenant or contractual licensee, even if their partner is not SMI; *or*
- all the jointly liable people are SMI.

Dwellings in which all the occupants are SMI are exempt (see p65).[102]

Example

Oliver and Fred are a couple and are joint owners. Oliver is SMI and is disregarded for discount purposes. Normally, the couple (as joint owners and residents) would be liable, but as Oliver is SMI, Fred is liable. If he were to no longer reside in the dwelling, it would become exempt.

Where a SMI person owns their own home and resides there, it is important to determine whether their care in a hospital or care home should be treated as permanent. Billing authorities should be careful to distinguish between categories of care and not assume that a person has lost their sole or main residence and will never return home. If someone permanently goes into a care home, nursing home or hospital, a ruling from the Court of Protection may be required if they do not have the mental capacity to choose their place of residence. The billing authority cannot determine this.

Students

A student who is disregarded for discount purposes (see p121) is not held jointly liable if there is someone else with the same status and legal interest in the property who is not a student.

5. Change of circumstances

A change of circumstances may change council tax liability during the year – eg, a liable owner may sell the dwelling or a liable tenant may move to live elsewhere. Liability for council tax arises on a daily basis and the situation at the end of the day is assumed to have lasted all that day.[103] Consequently, the liable person is liable for the first day of residence in the dwelling and also the last if on an assured shorthold tenancy they are being treated as the equivalent of the owner under the hierarchy of liability.[104]

If a liable person dies, there is no liability for any part of the day on which they die. The registrar of births and deaths must notify the billing authority within seven days of registering the death of any person aged 18 or over with the deceased's name, usual address and the date of their death.[105]

Situations involving domestic abuse

Councils may grant a discount on a second home where domestic abuse has led a liable person to live there. In such cases, check the local authority council tax discount policy. If a discount is available, an application in writing is usually needed, unless the council can confirm entitlement from existing evidence or information already provided.

When you leave a dwelling because of domestic abuse, your council tax liability will end if you no longer hold a material interest in that dwelling. 'Material interest' means 'a freehold interest or a leasehold interest which was granted for a term of six months or more'.[106]

Anyone permanently leaving rented accommodation should give notice that they are ending their tenancy or otherwise terminating their right to occupy premises. In one case, a valuation tribunal held that where a person left their home due to domestic abuse and a former assured shorthold tenancy had become a monthly periodic tenancy, they no longer had a material interest in the property.[107] **Note:** following the commencement of the Renter's Rights Act 2025, tenancies in England will all be monthly periodic.

Where possible, you should provide evidence to confirm the abuse or that you are seeking help in relation to it.

You may also apply for a discretionary reduction under section 13A(1) of the Local Government Finance Act 2012 (see p135) if you are having difficulty paying council tax as a result of having to move.

6. Backdating liability

Liability may be backdated to previous years. Council tax liability is based on the date you became liable (ie, had your sole or main residence in the dwelling), not the date the local authority notifies you.[108] The local authority may serve a demand for a dwelling you lived in up to six years ago – even if you have moved out. However, if a local authority delays serving a demand notice, it may render the notice invalid if it causes prejudice by seeking to enforce it through the magistrates' or sheriff court. See Chapters 9 and 10 for more details.

Backdating under the council tax reduction schemes varies between local authorities in England and Wales, but you may apply for a discretionary reduction under section 13A(1)(c) of the Local Government Finance Act 2012 (see p135). You may seek a discretionary reduction regardless of when the alleged liability arose.

You can appeal if you want to challenge the local authority (see Chapter 11). It may also be worth making a complaint for delay where a local authority suddenly seeks to impose a backdated liability for previous years, and to establish why a local authority has failed to establish liability earlier or reversed an earlier decision. The former president of the Valuation Tribunal for England Professor Graham Zellick ruled that the Limitation Act 1980 set a limit on when proceedings must be initiated but did not set a limit on the number of years in the past in respect of which sums may be recovered.[109]

The Ombudsman has indicated that extensive delay in informing a person of liability may amount to maladministration. In such a case, you can start a court claim for judicial review.[110]

7. How the liable person is identified

To establish liability, the local authority has a variety of powers that require people and organisations to provide information. It can also use its own information obtained for other purposes. If the local authority cannot identify a liable person by name, it may serve a bill on the 'council taxpayer'. The residents of the dwelling will then need to decide who has to pay the tax.

The local authority's own information

A local authority may use information obtained under any other enactment in England and Wales, provided that it was not obtained in its role as a police authority and, in Scotland, that it is not information obtained through social work activities, unless it consists solely of names and addresses.[111]

Information from residents, owners or managing agents

The local authority has the power to write to anyone who appears to be a resident, owner or managing agent of a particular dwelling, requesting information it requires to identify the liable person or the person who would be liable if the dwelling were not exempt.[112] The rules may place a burden on officials of housing associations and those who manage accommodation for vulnerable individuals. A 'managing agent' means any person authorised to arrange lettings of the dwelling concerned. If you receive a written enquiry, you must supply the required information within 21 days if it is in your possession or control.

Information from other public bodies

The local authority has the power to request information from:[113]
- any billing authority;
- any levying authority;
- the electoral registration officer for any area in Great Britain.

In Scotland, information may also be requested from the assessor.

The local authority may also obtain information from HMRC to:[114]
- make a council tax reduction (CTR) scheme;
- determine entitlement or continued entitlement to CTR;
- prevent, detect or secure evidence of, or prosecute the commission of, a council tax offence;
- use in valuation tribunal proceedings.

Penalties

A local authority in England can impose a fine of £70 on anyone who fails to respond to a request for information needed to identify the liable person.[115] In Wales and Scotland, the penalty is £50. An English or Welsh authority may quash such a penalty. A Scottish authority may revoke a penalty if you have a reasonable excuse for failing to supply the information.[116] Each time the local authority repeats the request and you fail to supply the information, it can impose another £280 penalty (£200 in Wales and Scotland).[117]

In Scotland, additional penalties of up to £500 help to police claims related to the variable charges on long-term empty homes.[118]

Additionally, the power to impose penalties has been extended in an attempt to bring the law in line with provisions in social security benefits, even though local taxation law is essentially different from social security law. These regulations affect not only taxpayers but also individuals providing information on behalf of vulnerable people, including owners of houses in multiple occupation, managers of hostels and accommodation, and lawyers and advisers acting on behalf of taxpayers.

Billing authorities may authorise officers and third parties to delegate these functions to individuals with proper authority. These officers can collect information for 'detecting and securing evidence of the commission' of offences connected with an application for an award of a reduction of council tax, including access to electronic records.[119]

It is a criminal offence to:

- intentionally delay or obstruct an authorised officer requesting information;[120]
- refuse or fail (without reasonable excuse) to give access to electronic records, or to fail to provide information when required to do so;[121]
- knowingly provide false information to get CTR;
- provide a false document, or cause one to be provided, which is materially incorrect.[122] It must actually affect the issue of whether you receive a reduction or not, and not simply be any error or mistake.

A time limit of three months from the date the authority considered evidence justifying a prosecution, or 12 months from the commission of the offence, is placed on bringing proceedings, whichever period expires last.[123]

You may appeal against a penalty.[124]

8. Appealing a liability decision

You can appeal a decision on liability by writing to the local authority.[125] There is no time limit for making an appeal. To appeal, you must be an 'aggrieved person' – ie, the person considered liable to pay the tax or the owner (if different). In the appeal letter clearly state why you believe the decision is wrong. It is advisable to reference your right to take an appeal to the Valuation Tribunal for England (VTE), the Valuation Tribunal for Wales (VTW) or the Local Taxation Chamber (LTC) in Scotland if the local authority does not accept the appeal. The local authority has two months to answer.[126]

If the local authority refuses to alter its decision or fails to answer within two months, you can make a further appeal.[127] In England or Wales, you write to the VTE/VTW. In Scotland, you make a further appeal by writing again to the local authority and it should pass the appeal to the LTC. It is also advised to send a copy of your appeal to the LTC in case your letter to the local authority is delayed or lost. For more information about appeals, see Chapter 11.

The local authority can enforce payment of the original bill while the appeal is pending, but if recovery proceedings have started in the magistrates' court (or sheriff court in Scotland), you should request an adjournment of the hearing, pending the appeal outcome.[128]

Notes

1. **Who is liable**
1 s6(5) LGFA 1992
2 **EW** s6 LGFA 1992
S s75 LGFA 1992
3 Within the meaning of the Rent Act 1977 or the Rent (Agriculture) Act 1976
4 Within the meaning of Part IV of the Housing Act 1985
5 Within the meaning of Chapter I of Part V of the Housing Act 1996
6 **EW** s6(6) LGFA 1992
7 **EW** s6(5) LGFA 1992
8 **EW** s6(5) LGFA 1992
9 s65 LGFA 1988
10 s75(2) LGFA 1992
11 Within the meaning of the Rent (Scotland) Act 1984
12 Within the meaning of the Housing (Scotland) Act 1988
13 Within the meaning of Part III of the Housing (Scotland) Act 1987
14 s75(5) LGFA 1992
15 **EW** s6(2) LGFA 1992; *DV-W v Cheshire West & Cheshire Council* [2022] VTE Appeal No.00009795, reported in Valuation Tribunal Service, *Valuation in Practice*, No.66, November 2022
S s75(2) LGFA 1992
16 *Broderick v Coventry City Council* [2020] EWHC 2083 (Admin)
17 **EW** s2(2)(c) LGFA 1992
S s71(2)(c) LGFA 1992
18 s6 LGFA 1992
19 Class Q CT(ED)O
20 CT(ED)O; *Fairhurst v Roberts (LO)* [2021] VT 00002227, 17 March 2021
21 s6(6) LGFA 1992; *Fairhurst v Roberts (LO)* [2021] VT 00002227, 17 March 2021
22 *R v D* [2019] EWCA Crim 209; reported as [2019] 2 Cr App R 15
23 *Aricioglu v Harlow DC* [2019] VTE Appeal No.1540M251814/282C, reported in Valuation Tribunal Service, *Valuation in Practice*, No.54, October 2019; *R v D* [2019] EWCA Crim 209; reported as [2019] 2 Cr App R 15
24 **EW** ss6-7 LGFA 1992
25 **EW** ss6-7 LGFA 1992
26 See s6(2)(ea) LGFA 1992
27 *Hyett v Wakefield* [2018] EWHC 337 (Admin)
28 CTM, Practice Note 7: Application of Council Tax to Caravan Pitches and Moorings
29 *R v St Pancras Assessment Committee* [1877] 2 QBD 581 per Lush, J
30 *Reeves v Northrop* [2013] EWCA Civ 362, reported as [2013] PTSR 1256
31 *EL v Moore (LO)* [2022] VTE Appeal No.M0867093
32 **EW** s2 LGFA 1992
S s71 LGFA 1992

2. **Who is a resident**
33 **EW** s6(5) LGFA 1992
S s99(1) LGFA 1992
34 *R (Williams) v Horsham DC* [2004] EWCA Civ 39
35 *A v South Oxfordshire DC* [2015] VTE Appeal No.3115M81253/22s, para 29
36 *Parry v Derbyshire Dales DC* [2006] RA 25
37 *R (on the application of Walford) v Worcestershire CC* [2014] 3 All ER 128

38 See VTE Appeal No.5900M109133/084C [2013]
39 **EW** see *CT v Horsham DC (HB)* [2013] UKUT 617 (AAC) and *MacAttram v LB Camden* [2012] EWHC 1033 (Admin)
40 See *Abbasi v Bury MBC* [2020] VTE Appeal No.VT00000258
41 *Trustees Berwick Settlement v Shropshire Council* [2014] VTE Appeal No.3245M131738/176C, contrasting *CT v Horsham DC (HB)* [2013] UKUT 617 (AAC)
42 *Leeds City Council v Broadley* [2016] 4 WLR 137
43 *Oyston v Leeds City Council* [2011] VTE Appeal No.4720M6769/244C
44 Statement by Matthew Pennycock, Minister for Housing and Planning, Renters' Rights Bill Third Sitting, *Hansard*, 29 October 2024, col 97
45 *Stephen Stubbs v Northumberland CC* [2021] VTE Appeal No.VT00004594
46 *Proctor v Durham CC* [2021] VTE Appeal No.VT00004507
47 *Sumeghova v McMahon* [2002] All ER (D) 371 (Oct), reported as [2003] RVR 8
48 See *Codner v Wiltshire Valuation and Community Charge Tribunal* [1994] RVR 169; *Doncaster BC v Stark and Stark* [1998] RVR 80
49 *Newton v Kirklees Council* [2019] VTE Appeal No.4715M262995/282C
50 VTE Appeal No:5810M186253/084C 2016, reported in Valuation Tribunal Service, *Valuation in Practice*, No.42, October 2016
51 *Highland Council v Highland and Western Isles Region Valuation Committee* [2008] RA 311 Sc20; *Dundee Council v Dundee Valuation Assessment Committee and Fleming Hansen* [2011] CSIH 73
52 See VTE Appeal No.0738M144734/254C [2015]
53 *Marshall v Bath and North East Somerset Council* [2024] EWHC 2551 (Admin), para 25: reviewing VTE decision No.VT00016508, 19 April 2024
54 See VTE Appeal No.0738M144734/254C [2015]
55 *LB v Cheshire East Council* [2024] VTE 00022216, 10 September 2024, para 28
56 *Ali v Oldham Council* [2020] VTE Appeal No.M0244474, para 17
57 *Khan v Burnley BC* [2017] VTE Appeal No.2315M198655/254C/S
58 s11A(4A) LGFA 2012
59 *Khan v Burnley BC*, VTE Appeal No.2315M198655/254C/S, para 17
60 *Frost v Feltham* [1981] STC 115
61 *Frost v Feltham* n.56 at 455 and approved in *R (Williams) v Horsham DC* [2004] and *Marshall v Bath and North East Somerset Council* [2024] EWHC 2551 (Admin)
62 *Byrne v Rowbotham* (1969) 210, *Estates Gazette*, p823
63 *Appellant Taxpayer v Birmingham City Council* [2017] VTE Appeal No.4605M183073/176C
64 VTE Appeal No.0405M119713/037C [2014]
65 VTE Appeal No.M0247401 [2019]
66 *Reeves v Northrop Note* 21; *John Laing & Sons v Kingswood Area Assessment Committee* [1949] 1 All ER 224

3. **When the owner is always liable**

67 **EW** s8(1) LGFA 1992
S s76(1) LGFA 1992
68 **E** CT(LO)(A)(E) Regs as amended by 2023 SI 1175; Sch 1 para 7 Care Act 2014 (Consequential Amendments) (Secondary Legislation) Order 2015 No.643
W CT(LO)(A)(W) Regs
69 Reg 2(aa) CT(LO) Regs, as amended by The Regulation and Inspection of Social Care (Wales) Act 2016 (Consequential Amendments to Secondary Legislation) Regulations 2018 No.48 (W15)
70 Sch 1 para 1 CT(LO)(S) Regs
71 *Soor and Another v Mayor & Burgesses LB Redbridge* [2013] EWHC 1239 (Admin)
72 **EW** CT(LO) Regs
S CT(LO)(S) Regs
73 *Watts v Preston City Council* [2009] EWHC (Admin) 2179, para 23
74 **EW** CT(LO) Regs
75 Part 2 and ss257-260 Housing Act 2004
76 Reg 1(2) CT(LO) Regs 1992
77 *Shah v Croydon LBC* [2013] EWHC 3657 (Admin)
78 *Shah v Croydon LBC* [2013] EWHC 3657 (Admin), para 43
79 *Baker (LO) v Gomperts* [2006] All ER (D) 01 (Jul)
80 *Norris and Norris v Birmingham City Council* [2001] RVR 89
81 *R (on the application of Goremsandu) v Harrow LBC* [2010] EWHC 1873 (Admin)
82 *Watts v Preston City Council* [2009] EWHC 2179 (Admin)

83 *Walsh v Lonsdale* [1882] 21 Ch 9; *Soor v Mayor Burgesses of the LB of Redbridge* [2013] EWHC 1239 (Admin)
84 *The UHU Property Trust v Lincoln City Council* [2000] unreported, per Sullivan J, cited in *Shah v Croydon LBC* [2013] EWHC 3657 (Admin), para 22
85 *Naz v LB Redbridge* [2013] EWHC 1268 (Admin), reported as [2013] All ER (D) 13
86 *O'Shaughnessy v LB Hackney* [2013] VTE Appeal No.5360M70010/052C/1
87 *Dundee City Council v Dundee Valuation Appeal Committee and another* [2011] CSIH 73
88 **EW** CT(LO) Regs
S CT(LO)(S) Regs
89 **EW** CT(LO) Regs
S CT(LO)(S) Regs
90 **EW** CT(LO) Regs
S CT(LO)(S) Regs
91 **S** CT(LO)(S) Regs
92 *R v Hackney LBC ex parte Adebiri and other appeals* [1997] *The Times*, 4 November 1997
EW Reg 2 CT(LO) Regs
S CT(LO)(S) Regs

4. **Joint liability**
93 **EW** s6(3)-(4) LGFA 1992
S s75(3)-(4) LGFA 1992
94 *Trustees of Mrs R's Testamentary Trust v Northumberland CC* [2018] VTE Appeal No.2935M232094/280C
95 **EW** s9 LGFA 1992
S s77 LGFA 1992
96 *Routhan v Arun* [1982] QB 502 per Lord Everleigh at 517B; *Moore v Durham City Council* [1987] Lexis Citation 9 May 1987 May LJ, Simon Brown, J
97 *Wainwright v The Home Office* [2003] UKHL 53; European Court of Human Rights [2006] Application No.12350/04, 26 September 2006
98 Department of the Environment, *Council Tax Practice Note No.2: Liability, Discounts and Exemptions*, 1993
99 Reg 5(7) CT(APDD) Regs; s6(4A) and (4B) LGFA 1992
100 **EW** Reg 28 CT(AE) Regs
101 **EW** ss6(4) and 9(2) LGFA 1992
S ss75(4) and 77(2) LGFA 1992
102 **EW** CT(ED)O

5. **Change of circumstances**
103 **EW** s2 LGFA 1992
S s71 LGFA 1992
104 *Appellants v Bedford Unitary Authority* [2018] VTE Appeal No.0235M233864/282C
105 **EW** Reg 5(1) CT(AE) Regs
106 s6 LGFA 1992
107 *Smith v Darlington Borough Council* [2020] VTE Appeal No.VT00000271

6. **Backdating liability**
108 *Hammersmith and Fulham Billing Authority v Butler* [2001] RVR 197
109 *Holdsworth v Bradford City Council* [2015] RA 215; VTE Appeal No.4705M141113/254C
110 *R v Lambeth LBC ex parte Ahijah-Sterling* [1986] RVR 27

7. **How the liable person is identified**
111 **EW** Reg 6 CT(AE) Regs
S Reg 5 CT(AE)(S) Regs
112 **EW** Regs 3 and 12 CT(AE) Regs
S Reg 2 CT(AE)(S) Regs
113 **EW** Reg 3 CT(AE) Regs
S Council Tax (Administration and Enforcement) (Scotland) Amendment Regulations 2012 No.338
114 Sch 2 para 15A(1)-(4) LGFA 1992
115 **EW** s14(2) and Sch 3 LGFA 1992
S s97(4) and Sch 3 LGFA 1992
116 **EW** s14(2) and Sch 3 LGFA 1992
S s97(4) and Sch 3 LGFA 1992
117 **EW** s14(2) and Sch 3 LGFA 1992
S s97(4) and Sch 3 LGFA 1992
118 Sch 3 para 2(1A) LGFA 1992; s3(1)(5)(a) Local Government Finance (Unoccupied Properties etc.) (Scotland) Act 2012
119 **E** Regs 4 and 5 CTRS(DFE)(E) Regs
W Reg 5 CTRS(DFE)(W) Regs
120 **E** Reg 6 CTRS(DFE)(E) Regs
W Reg 6 CTRS(DFE)(W) Regs
121 **E** Regs 4, 5 and 6 CTRS(DFE)(E) Regs
W Reg 6(1)(b) CTRS(DFE)(W) Regs
122 **E** Reg 7 CTRS(DFE)(E) Regs
W Reg 9(1) CTRS(DFE)(W) Regs
123 **E** Reg 10 CTRS(DFE)(E) Regs
W Reg 12 CTRS(DFE)(W) Regs
124 **EW** s14(2) and Sch 3 LGFA 1992
S s97(4) and Sch 3 LGFA 1992

8. **Appealing a liability decision**

125 **EW** s16 LGFA 1992
S s81 LGFA 1992

126 **EW** s16 LGFA 1992
S s81 LGFA 1992

127 **EW** s16 LGFA 1992
S s81 LGFA 1992

128 *R v Ealing Justices ex parte Coatsworth* [1980] 126, *Solicitors Journal* 128

Chapter 6

Disability reductions

This chapter covers:

1. What is a disability reduction

Disability reduction schemes apply in England and Wales,[1] and in Scotland.[2] A disability reduction aims to relieve an eligible person of what would otherwise be an increase in their council tax liability when they need an additional room in their dwelling.[3] The basic amount of council tax and, in Scotland, Scottish Water charges,[4] may be reduced if:

- a disabled person (of any age) lives in the dwelling; *and*
- the dwelling has certain features that are essential or of major importance to the disabled person because of their disability; *or*
- the disabled person uses a wheelchair in the home.

A disability reduction reduces your council tax to the amount payable for a home in the valuation band below yours (or by one-sixth if you are in Band A) – see p113. The reduction can be applied to residential care or nursing homes, as well as to any other dwelling. **Note:** disability reductions are distinct from the severe mental impairment exemption (see p97).

In addition to the disability reduction scheme, if you have added adaptations (eg, a lift or adapted kitchen units), the value of these fixtures should have been ignored in the valuation of the dwelling if they added to its value (see p33) or counted towards lowering the band if they reduced the value of the dwelling.[5]

An award of disability reduction can be backdated for up to six years or more (see p112). This can significantly reduce arrears or debts, particularly if enforcement action is already underway. So you should apply for a disability reduction if you think you are entitled to one.

2. When a disability reduction can be made

The disabled person

The dwelling must be the sole or main residence (see p84) of at least one disabled child or adult. They need not be the person liable to pay council tax on the dwelling. No additional reduction is made if more than one disabled person lives there.

To count as disabled for the purpose of the reduction, a person must be substantially and permanently disabled, whether by congenital disorder from birth, illness, injury or otherwise. There is no general test of substantially and permanently disabled. This means that someone with a learning disability, impairment or a mental health problem could qualify, as well as someone with a physical impairment.

Social services departments in England and Wales and social work departments in Scotland have the discretion to maintain a register of, and provide various services to, people who are substantially and permanently disabled. They have considerably more experience in assessing disability than council tax staff. If you are on the disabled person's register, this should be accepted as sufficient evidence that you meet the criterion of substantially and permanently disabled. However, if you are not on the register, this does not necessarily mean you are not substantially and permanently disabled, as registering is not compulsory (apart from for disabled children[6]).

The dwelling

The dwelling must have at least one of the following features:

- a room (but not a sole bathroom, a kitchen or a lavatory) predominantly used by the disabled person – eg, a room used for dialysis equipment; *or*
- an additional bathroom or kitchen that is necessary to meet the needs of the disabled person; *or*
- sufficient floor space for wheelchair use.

The feature must be essential or of major importance to the disabled person's wellbeing because of the nature of their impairment.[7] The High Court has ruled that there must be an 'appropriate causative link' between the impairment and the use or need for the additional feature.[8] One additional room is enough, but an application may not succeed if it is not possible to clearly distinguish features in the room that make it different to any other room, and it cannot be demonstrated to relate to the wellbeing of the person.[9]

The local authority should consider the following questions.

- Would the disabled person find it physically impossible or extremely difficult to live in the property without the feature?
- Would their health deteriorate or disability worsen without it?

- Is there a clear difference in how the room is used compared to similar rooms in other dwellings?

A sole bathroom or kitchen, even if specially adapted, is not sufficient to qualify, as everyone needs a bathroom or kitchen.[10]

Simply having the disabled person's equipment in a room used for other purposes or used merely for storing their equipment will not fulfil the requirement of the room being additional.[11] In an appeal in 2015,[12] the appellant lived in a one-bedroom flat and had to use a kidney dialysis machine for several hours every day. Due to limited space, the dialysis machine was kept in the living room, which was used every day and night, along with chairs, a sofa and a television. The application for a disability reduction failed because the room itself was not exclusively or predominantly used for meeting disability-related needs. It was not a distinct additional room and so did not fulfil the conditions for a disability reduction set out in the regulations.

Evidence to support a claim for a disability reduction

- Medical evidence – eg, GP letters, specialist reports, occupational therapy assessments.
- Carer or support worker statements confirming usage and necessity of the room/space.
- Photos or layout plans showing adaptations or how the space is used.
- Details of equipment or assistive technology used in the room or dwelling.
- Statements from household members explaining the impact of the disability on daily living and space needs.

Adaptation of an existing room

A case decided that there is no requirement in the regulations that prevents an existing room from being the extra room.[13] The room may qualify if it has been specially adapted or constructed. *Crowley v Rutland District Council* [2021] found that the adaptation of an existing bathroom to enable a disabled person to shower may qualify. It found that being able to shower would meet the test of the bathroom being of major importance to his wellbeing and, as the appellant could not use the bath in the family bathroom, would also meet the test of it being 'by reason of the nature and extent of his disability'.

A local authority or valuation tribunal could award a reduction if it concludes that, without the room, it would be extremely difficult or impossible for the person to live an independent life in the dwelling.[14] For example, the Valuation Tribunal for England (VTE) ruled a room used for storing a nebuliser, an oxygen concentrator and other breathing apparatus needed by a disabled resident fulfilled that requirement.[15] The tribunal rejected the billing authority's view that, as the room used to store the equipment was the appellant's spare bedroom, it did not alter its potential use as a bedroom, because it was impractical for the appellant to have the oxygen concentrator in the same bedroom as she slept because of its size and the noise it made when operating. There was a causative link, as the room was essential or of major importance to her wellbeing because, without it, she would be unable to sleep properly or reside in the dwelling.[16]

Similarly, the VTE held in a 2022 case that in properties with two bathrooms, no physical adaptation was required by the regulations.[17] It was sufficient that an existing ground-floor bathroom was being used predominantly by a disabled person with limited mobility who found showering easier than taking a bath. The key question was whether the room was essential or of major importance to his wellbeing due to the nature and extent of his disability. Without the ground-floor bathroom, the appellant might have been confined to the upper floor or required to climb the stairs without assistance during the day, which was potentially unsafe.

Creation of an extra bedroom

The creation of an extra bedroom to meet the disability needs may also attract a reduction. In a 2015 appeal,[18] the tribunal held that a ground-floor bedroom added to meet the specific needs of a disabled resident did qualify. The appellant had a bedroom upstairs, but the additional bedroom was created specifically because the nature and extent of the appellant's impairment necessitated provision on the ground floor. It did not matter that his wife sometimes shared the bedroom with him.

Similarly, in another case, a couple occupied a two-bedroom flat instead of a single-bedroom property (exceeding what would ordinarily have been needed) because the disabled partner's medical condition required him to sleep in a separate room. A reduction was granted. A causative link was established as a separate bedroom was necessary for his condition.[19]

A reduction for sufficient additional floor space may be available if a disabled person uses a non-standard wheelchair or even a wheeled frame.[20]

Major importance

The use of the room has to be of major importance to the disabled person, and a question to ask is whether the room would be being used in a particular way if the disabled person were not present.

Two High Court rulings concerning three appeals during 2006 clarified the law on rooms attracting a reduction and the meaning of major importance.[21]

In the case of *Titley*, the profoundly deaf taxpayer lived alone in a two-bedroom house. His living room was fitted with a hearing loop box enabling him to hear the television and communicate with visitors. In the case of *Clothier*, there were two bedrooms occupied by two adults with Down's syndrome who were being looked after by their parents. Both bedrooms were used for therapy and periods of relaxation, which enabled the adult children to cope with their condition. The High Court ruled that a disability reduction should not be awarded in either case.

The court held that it was necessary to consider whether a room was specifically required to meet the needs of a disabled person.

The court stressed that having a disabled resident in a property was not enough. To get the reduction, the dwelling must have a room that would not be required if the disabled person were not present.

In both these cases, the rooms were not considered additional, since they would be essential or of major importance to almost any household. In the case of *Titley*, the taxpayer would have been using the living room if he were not deaf. Similarly, in *Clothier*, the rooms were not additional; the two adult children would still have required a bedroom if they did not have Down's syndrome. Difficulties may also arise if a room is used only for storing equipment, as well as for other uses, such as a spare room.[22] A room occupied by a live-in carer may qualify (see p111).

However, in the *Hanson* case, the appellant succeeded. She was a disabled woman, registered as partially sighted. She had a bedroom converted into an en-suite bathroom in 1996, a few months after she moved into the property, and 19 months before she was registered as blind. In 2004, she became aware of the right to a disability reduction for council tax but was refused. This decision was upheld by a valuation tribunal, which rejected her appeal on the basis that the bathroom was not essential to her needs.

The High Court, however, upheld her appeal, concluding that the adaptation was of *major importance* to her because of her specific impairment, as it reduced the risk of tripping or slipping.

This case was followed in a 2022 VTE decision. The appellant, because of health problems, was unable to share a bedroom with her partner and different bedrooms were needed to maintain a quality of life. The property had two bedrooms and two bathrooms. Considering the legislation, the tribunal found it was not a requirement that rooms needed to be adapted for a qualifying individual to meet the criteria for a reduction, only that the room was required for that person's needs, which the tribunal found had been demonstrated by the appellant. Thus, the emphasis is on the needs of the disabled person, not simply physical adaptation of a dwelling.[23]

Social needs of the disabled person

A room that fulfils the social needs of a disabled person (not only their physical or mental needs) may also qualify for a disability reduction. A valuation tribunal vice president addressed this in a 2014 decision.[24] The room concerned contained specialist electronic and computerised equipment for the disabled person's use. It was installed to assist and allow them to pursue leisure interests, work as a volunteer for the RNIB, continue with social science research and enjoy many of the pastimes that a sighted person would take for granted.

The vice president rejected arguments that the room was merely a home office, and that the equipment was portable and could be moved to another room. The room was of major importance to the appellant's wellbeing and quality of life. It provided something extra that was necessary to meet the needs of a disabled person. The equipment was sensitive and expensive and it would be impractical for it to be moved.

Therapy rooms for behavioural problems

An additional room used specifically for therapy to treat a disabled child's behavioural issues was found to qualify, as the therapy could only take place in that dedicated space.[25] The room was primarily used by the child to meet their specific needs and was considered of major importance to the child's wellbeing.

The benefit also extends to the family, provided the needs of the disabled person are being met. For example, one case recognised that a family would struggle to care for their disabled son in a home with only one bathroom.[26] Due to his behavioural issues, he refused to use the shared family bathroom, making an additional bathroom essential for his psychological wellbeing. This need was supported by clear evidence of his behavioural and neurodivergent difficulties.

Bedroom used by a live-in carer

A bedroom used by a live-in carer who provides care for the disabled person may qualify for the reduction. The High Court ruled that such a bedroom qualified as a room meeting the needs of a disabled person.[27]

3. Getting a disability reduction

Who can get a reduction

The person liable to pay council tax on the dwelling is entitled to apply for a disability reduction. They may be solely or jointly liable. If there is joint liability, an application made by one of the liable people is treated as having been made on behalf of all of them. None of the liable people need to be disabled.

The local authority may also award a disability reduction to someone who will become liable for council tax on the dwelling – eg, following work on it to meet the needs of a disabled person.

Applications

A written application is required for each financial year (April to March) from the liable person or someone acting on their behalf. If you are applying on behalf of someone, the local authority normally requires written authorisation or a copy of a power of attorney. There is no prescribed form, but most local authorities have a standard application form.

Once a written application has been made, a repeat application is required each financial year. Local authorities should ideally send a repeat application form and a reminder at the appropriate time each year, but they are not required to do so. Local authorities should not generally require a full application in a second or subsequent year; it will often be sufficient to seek the liable person's confirmation that the circumstances have not changed.

Backdating and repeat applications

You can apply for a disability reduction for previous years – not just the current one – provided that the qualifying conditions were met during those years – ie, backdated to when the qualifying conditions were met. The year(s) in question should be identified on the application. You do not need to apply separately for each year of backdating; one letter with all the relevant information is enough.

Following the decisions in *Arca v Carlisle City Council*[28] and *HS v Leicester City Council*,[29] a disability reduction can be backdated for up to six years from the date of making an application. However, it is currently unclear whether it may be extended further, as can be done with discounts.

In the *Arca* case, the tribunal ruled that a taxpayer who applied for a disability reduction on 3 November 2011 was entitled to a reduction dating back to 2 November 2005, six years before the written application was made. The president of the Valuation Tribunal for England (VTE) held that an application was permissible as a proceeding within the Limitation Act 1980, which places a six-year time limit upon civil law claims reaching the tribunal. While this is a decision of the VTE and not of the High Court, the president stated that 'until the matter is settled by a higher court... billing authorities would be well advised not only to regard this decision as representing a correct statement of the law but also as the interpretation almost certainly to be applied by this tribunal in any future appeal raising the same issue unless fresh arguments can be made'.[30] However, in the case of discounts, in *HS v Leicester City Council*,[31] it was held that reductions by way of discount could be backdated more than six years, which conflicts with the position in *Arca*. In a future case, it seems possible that a tribunal or higher court might reach a different decision if the ruling in *HS v Leicester City Council* is also considered.

Also, the Limitation Act 1980 restriction may not apply if evidence has not been available before due to fraud, concealment or mistake.[32] For example, if a disabled person was previously given wrong advice by the local authority, the Limitation Act 1980 may not apply.

In Scotland, the limitation period is 20 years.[33]

Applying for backdating

- Be clear about the dates from which you believe you qualify.
- Explain any delays in applying.
- Provide supporting evidence – eg, medical reports, care plans and dates of adaptations.

– Ask the council to consider backdating beyond six years, citing *HS v Leicester* and any relevant circumstances.

Information required by the local authority

The local authority may require a supporting letter from a doctor, occupational therapist or social worker, confirming that the disabled person needs the specific qualifying feature of the dwelling due to their disability. There is no statutory requirement to provide such evidence, however, and local authorities should consider on a case-by-case basis whether verification is necessary.

Some local authorities send an officer to visit the dwelling and interview residents or carers.

Note: imposing excessive demands for evidence or bureaucracy could breach equality law, particularly under the Equality Act 2010.

When considering whether the reduction applies, a local authority in England or Wales may make a written request for information it reasonably requires at any time and to anyone.[34] It may also require you to respond within a specified period, but must give you at least 21 days to answer.

4. How the reduction is made

If a disability reduction is awarded, the liable person's council tax bill is reduced to the amount for the valuation band immediately below the dwelling's actual band – eg, from Band D to Band C.

The reduction applies for each day that the qualifying conditions are met.

The amount payable on a dwelling that qualifies for a disability reduction in Band A is reduced by the same proportion of the bill as dwellings in valuation Bands B, C and D, being equivalent to five-ninths of Band D.[35]

Example

Huw's dwelling is in Band C on the valuation list. Following the award of a disability reduction, his council tax amount payable is the same as that of a Band B dwelling.

The disability reduction does not alter the actual valuation of the dwelling or its banding on the valuation list. Huw's bill should show both the dwelling's actual band and the reduction.

The effect of the reduction on other forms of help

If you are entitled to a disability reduction, the following are calculated based on the reduced bill, not the original higher amount:

- any discount – eg, single person or student discount; *or*

- council tax reduction (CTR). **Note:** a retrospective award of a disability reduction may cause an overpayment of CTR. Get advice if this applies to you.

5. Change of circumstances

If there is a change in circumstances (eg, if the disabled person moves to alternative accommodation), the liable person may no longer be entitled to a disability reduction. If the liable person believes they have ceased to be eligible for the reduction, they must notify the local authority. If they do not, the remaining liable taxpayer may face recovery action for an underpayment of council tax for the period after the dwelling ceases to be occupied by the qualifying disabled person.

This obligation extends to all those who are jointly liable for the tax on the dwelling in question.

6. Appealing a disability reduction decision

If the local authority refuses to award a disability reduction, you can appeal in writing to the local authority.[36] You can appeal if you are liable to pay the tax or if you are the owner of the property (if different). In the appeal letter, clearly state why you believe the decision is wrong. The local authority has two months to answer.[37]

If no reduction is awarded, or if the local authority fails to answer within two months, you can make a further appeal.[38] In England or Wales, you write to the Valuation Tribunal for England or the Valuation Tribunal for Wales. In Scotland, you make a further appeal by writing again to the local authority and it should pass the appeal to the Local Taxation Chamber (LTC). It is also advised to send a copy of your appeal to the LTC in case your letter to the local authority is delayed or lost. For more information about appeals, see Chapter 11.

While an appeal is pending, the local authority can still enforce payment of the original bill, unless it agrees to suspend recovery until the appeal is resolved. Alternatively, the magistrates' court (sheriff court in Scotland) may agree to an adjournment of any proceedings which may be issued if an agreement to suspend recovery is not reached and an appeal against the decision has been lodged.[39]

Notes

1. What is a disability reduction

1 s13 LGFA 1992; CT(RD) Regs; CT(RDTA)(W)(A) Regs
2 s80(1)-(4) and (6)-(7) LGFA 1992; CT(RD)(S) Regs
3 *Luton BC v Ball HC* [2001] RVR 198
4 CT(RD)(S) Regs
5 **EW** Reg 6 CT(SVD) Regs
S Reg 2 CT(VD)(S) Regs

2. When a disability reduction can be made

6 s2(1) Children Act 1989
7 *Sandwell MBC v Perks* [2003] EWHC 1749 (Admin), reported as [2003] RVR 317
8 *R (Sandwell MBC) v Perks* [2003] EWHC 1749 per Silber, J
9 *MSP v Blackburn and Darwen* [2024] VT00019836, 4 September 2024, reported in Valuation Tribunal Service, *Valuation in Practice*, No.76, May 2025
10 **EW** Reg 6 CT(SVD) Regs
S Reg 2 CT(VD)(S) Regs
11 *Howell Williams v Wirral MBC* [1981] RA 189 CA
12 VTE Appeal No.3810M143554/084C [2015]
13 *Crowley v Rutland DC* [2021] VT00004036, 2 September 2021
14 VTE Appeal No.2235M10253/084C [2013]
15 *Bector v Wolverhampton City Council* [2019] VTE Appeal No.4635M259959/283C
16 *Bector v Wolverhampton City Council* [2019] VTE Appeal No.4635M259959/283C
17 *SM v Huntingdonshire DC* [2022] VT00010280, 24 August 2022
18 VTE Appeal No.5480M138614/084C [2015]
19 VTE Appeal No.2820M165193/037C [2016]
20 VTE Appeal No.5060M73251/053C [2011], para 25
21 *South Gloucestershire Council v Titley and Another* [2006] EWHC 3117 (Admin); *Hanson v Middlesbrough Council* [2006] RA 320 (HC)
22 *M v Fenland DC* [2018] VTE Appeal No.0515M234834/282C
23 *DW v South Ribble BC* [2022] VTE Appeal No.00007002
24 VTE Appeal No.2710M130673/254C [2014]
25 *Dr R Deb v St Albans City and District Council* [2021] VT 00005147, 6 October 2021
26 *FA v Luton BC* [2023] VT 00008157, 9 January 2023
27 *Tyburn Film Productions Ltd v Royal Borough of Windsor and Maidenhead* [2020] EWHC 913 (Admin)

3. Getting a disability reduction

28 *Arca v Carlisle City Council* [2013] RA 248; VTE Appeal No.0915M85513/254C, per President Professor Zellick
29 *HS v Leicester City Council* [2015] VTE Appeal No.2465M142876/037C
30 *Arca v Carlisle City Council* [2013] RA 248; VTE Appeal No.0915M85513/254C, per President Professor Zellick
31 *HS v Leicester City Council* [2015] VTE Appeal No.2465M142876/037C
32 s32 Limitation Act 1980
33 s7 Prescription and Limitation (Scotland) Act 1973
34 Reg 5 CT(RD) Regs

4. How the reduction is made

35 Reg 3A(b) CT(RD) Regs

6. Appealing a disability reduction decision

36 **EW** s16 LGFA 1992
S s81 LGFA 1992
37 **EW** s16 LGFA 1992
S s81 LGFA 1992
38 **EW** s16 LGFA 1992
S s81 LGFA 1992
39 *Wiltshire Council v Piggin* [2014] EWHC 4386 (Admin), reported as [2015] RVR 45

Chapter 7

Discounts and premiums

This chapter covers:

1. Single person (25 per cent) discount

Council tax (and Scottish Water charges in Scotland) is initially based on the assumption that at least two adults live in a dwelling. As council tax is essentially a land-based tax, the bill does not increase if more than two adults live in a property, but it should be reduced by 25 per cent if only one person is the sole or main resident. See p84 for what counts as sole or main residence.

Local authorities ignore or disregard certain people, however, when deciding how many people are solely or mainly resident in the dwelling (see p117). Effectively, they are not counted as living in the dwelling for council tax purposes.

To decide whether the single person discount applies for any day, the situation at the end of that day is assumed to have existed throughout that day.[1] Details of the discount are listed on the annual council tax bill. If the number or type of residents changes during the year, the discount is recalculated and adjusted for the relevant days.

Scottish Water charges

In Scotland, the water charge element may also qualify for a 25 per cent discount in relation to a dwelling and, in some cases, a discount of 35 per cent.[2]

It is important to note that council tax and water charges are treated separately and distinctly from water and sewerage charges, each each governed by its own legislation and subject to different rules for discounts and exemptions. Consequently, the single person discount is 25 per cent for the council tax element and, where applicable, up to 35 per cent for the water charge element. These discounts are independent of each other and cannot be combined into a single overall reduction on the total bill.[3]

It is important to notify the local authority if your circumstances change – eg, if someone over 18 moves in, a child turns 18 or the property is no longer your main residence. You can usually update your details via your council's website.

Discounts and other forms of help

You can get a single person discount in addition to any disability reduction, transitional relief on a bill for an earlier year or council tax reduction (CTR). Local authorities must take reasonable steps to find out whether a bill should include a discount or premium. If, after doing so, the local authority finds no reason to believe a discount or premium applies, it is entitled to issue a bill based for the full chargeable amount.

Discounts are applied after a disability reduction, but before calculating main CTR.

Example

Murray lives alone. The council tax liability for his property is £1,000. He gets a CTR award of 85 per cent.

The single person discount is applied before his CTR is calculated. 25 per cent of £1,000 = £250. His liability after discount = £750

Murray's CTR is applied to the discounted liability of £750: 85 per cent of £750 = £637.50 (the amount covered by CTR)

Murray must pay the remaining amount = £112.50 (£750 – £637.50)

The billing authority works out alternative maximum CTR (known as 'second adult rebate' – see p175) based on your full council tax liability, ignoring any discount granted. This rebate is intended to compensate you if additional adults living with you cannot afford to meet the cost of losing this discount.

2. Who counts for discount purposes

Billing by local authorities assumes there are two adult residents both aged over 18 occupying each dwelling. However, only adults solely or mainly resident in the dwelling are counted when determining whether a discount applies. People under 18 and those solely or mainly resident elsewhere are ignored.[4]

Example

Eve lives with her 15-year-old daughter. A 25 per cent single person discount is granted as only one person over 18 resides in the dwelling.

Eve's friend, Lola, comes to stay but keeps a home elsewhere. If the local authority decides that Lola is mainly resident elsewhere, the discount should continue. If it decides that Lola is now mainly resident in Eve's home, the discount no longer applies from the day she moved in.

Local authorities can request specific information from residents to verify discount entitlement or to correct discount assumptions.[5]

3. **Who is disregarded for discount purposes**

In addition to those who are ignored for the purposes of a single person discount (see p116), certain categories of people are disregarded.[6] They are sometimes described as 'having a status discount' or being 'invisible'. They do not affect the level of tax on the dwelling. The categories are listed below.

Note: being disregarded does not automatically reduce the tax bill. A discount is applied only if there is one adult or no adults counted as residents after disregarding those listed below. A liable person may be disregarded for the purpose of a discount, but is still liable for the council tax – except if they are students or are considered severely mentally impaired. See Chapter 5 for more details.

The discount applied is:[7]

- **25 per cent** if there is only one resident in the property who is not a disregarded person;
- **50 per cent** if all the residents in the property are disregarded;
- **full exemption** if:
  - all the residents in the property are students (see p121) or 'relevant persons';
  - all the residents in the property are severely mentally impaired (SMI) (see p124).

People disregarded for discount purposes

Young people – ie:

– people aged under 18, or people aged 18 or 19 for whom child benefit is payable (or would be payable if they were not in local authority care) (see p120);

– education leavers who are under 20 (see p120);

- care leavers aged 18–25 in Scotland and aged 18–24 in Wales (see p120);
- youth trainees (see p120);
- students under 20 studying up to A level, Scottish Advanced Higher or equivalent (see p121).

Full-time students in higher education (see p122).
Foreign language assistants who are classed as students (see p123).
People with diplomatic, Commonwealth or consular privilege or immunity.
Spouses or dependants of foreign students (see p123).
Student nurses (see p124).
Apprentices (see p124).
People in prison and other forms of detention (see p127).
People who are severely mentally impaired (see p124).
Certain carers (see p125).
Hospital patients (see p127).
People in care homes, private hospitals and hostels (see p127).
Members of international headquarters and defence organisations and their dependants (see p128).
Members of visiting forces (see p128).
Members of religious communities (see p128).
Residents in certain hostels and night shelters and other accommodation for those with no fixed abode (England and Wales only) (see p127).
People under the Homes for Ukraine scheme (see p129).

Examples

Sarah and Kay are joint owner-occupiers. Sarah is a full-time student and therefore disregarded for a discount. Kay is in full-time work and is not disregarded. As there are only two residents and Sarah is disregarded, a 25 per cent discount should be granted. Although they are both joint resident owners, only Kay is liable for the reduced amount of council tax.

Ross and Sasha are joint owner-occupiers. Their daughter, Ruby (20), lives with them. She is a full-time student. Their son, Cole (17), also lives with them. He is in full-time work. Ruby, as a full-time student, is disregarded for discount purposes, and Cole, being under 18, is ignored. Nevertheless, no discount is awarded because two adults (the joint owner-occupiers) live in the house and are not ignored or discounted.

Jiya and Dev are liable joint tenants. No one else lives with them. Dev has Alzheimer's disease and receives the daily living component of personal independence payment (PIP). He is considered severely mentally impaired. In these circumstances, a 25 per cent status discount is awarded because there are only two people solely or mainly resident in the dwelling and one is disregarded for discount purposes. In this instance, only Jiya is liable for council tax.

Sam, a carer, comes to live with Jiya and Dev, who provide him with free accommodation plus £50 a week. In these circumstances, Jiya and Dev lose their discount as two adults are now living in the dwelling who are not disregarded for discount purposes. If Sam is paid £44 a week or less (see p125 and p126), however, the discount would continue, as there would still be only one adult living in the dwelling who was not disregarded.

Young people

If you fall into one of the following groups, you are disregarded for discount purposes.

- **18- and 19-year-olds[8] for whom child benefit is payable** (or would be if you were not in local authority care).[9] The conditions of entitlement to child benefit are described in CPAG's *Welfare Benefits Handbook*.
- **Education leavers under 20.** If you are under 20, and have left school or college on or after 1 May in any year after undertaking a qualifying course of education (ie, up to A level, Scottish Advanced Higher or equivalent) or additionally, in England and Wales, full-time education, you should be disregarded to work out a discount between 1 May and 31 October in the same year.[10] You continue to be disregarded if you go on to another form of further or higher education.
- **Youth trainees** who are under 25 and have an approved individual training plan.[11] You are regarded as undertaking training from the day the course or programme begins until you complete, abandon or are dismissed from it.
- **Apprentices** (see p124).
- **Young people leaving care in Scotland.**[12] You can get a discount if you:[13]
  - are over 18 but under 26; *and*
  - were looked after by a local authority[14] on or after your 16th birthday; *and*
  - are no longer looked after by a local authority. 'Looked after' has the meaning given in the Children (Scotland) Act 1995.[15]
- **Young people leaving care in Wales.** You can get a discount if you:[16]
  - are over 18 but under 25; *and*
  - are a category 3 young person under section 104 of the Social Services and Well-being (Wales) Act 2014; *and*
  - are no longer looked after by a local authority.
- **Under 20 in non-advanced education.** Usually, you are regarded as a student if your course is for more than 12 hours a week (see p121).
- **Under 20 in higher education.** The rules are the same as for those aged 20 or over (see p122).

Note: if you are under 18, you are ignored for council tax purposes (see p117).

Students

Dwellings wholly occupied by students are exempt from council tax (see p63). If you are living with a non-student over 18, you are disregarded for discount purposes if you are a student.[17]

If you are aged under 20, whether you count as a student for council tax purposes can depend on whether you are on an advanced or non-advanced course. For older students, one rule applies whatever the level of your course.

Under 20 in non-advanced education

You are regarded as a 'student' for council tax purposes if you are aged under 20 and on a non-advanced course of more than 12 hours a week.[18] From September 2025, it may be possible for the hours to be less than 12 if you are ill or have a physical or mental disability.[19] Rules can vary slightly by council, so check with your local authority.

Non-advanced course

A **'non-advanced course'** is one below the level of a foundation degree, honours degree, HNC, HND or NVQ/SVQ level 4. It includes A levels, Scottish Advanced Highers, national diplomas and national certificates. The course must last more than three months. It does not include evening classes, correspondence courses, or courses taken due to your office or occupation.[20]

Only hours required by the course count, rather than those you actually do, if they differ. To work out your hours, average out over term times the hours required under the course for tuition, supervised study, exams, and supervised exercises, experiments, projects and practical work.

You are treated as a student each day from the day you start the course until the day you complete it, abandon it or are dismissed from it.[21] So you count as a student during term times, during short vacations at Christmas and Easter, and during the summer if your course continues after the summer. If your course ends in the summer and you begin a different one in the autumn, you do not count as a student in the summer between courses. However, you might be able to get a discount. In Scotland, you are treated as a student if you have completed a HNC or HND and have received an offer of a place entering on the second or third year respectively of a full-time first degree course. That first degree course must start within six months of the completed course.[22]

Example

Vikram is 18 and taking three A levels at college. Including his classes, exams and supervised study, his course hours are 18 a week. He is a student for council tax purposes.

Under 20 in higher education

The rules are the same as for those aged 20 or over (see below).

20 or over in non-advanced or higher education

You are regarded as a 'student' for council tax purposes if the course requires you to undertake periods of study, tuition or work experience for at least 21 hours a week in at least 24 weeks each academic year.[23]

If you are on a sandwich course, required periods of work experience are included.

To count as a student, you must be enrolled on a course with an educational institution based in a relevant territory (defined as England, Wales, Scotland, Northern Ireland or a European Economic Area member state).

You are a student from the day you begin the course until the day you complete it, abandon it or are no longer permitted by the educational institution to undertake it.[24]

If you take time out and are no longer enrolled on the course during that period, you do not count as a student for council tax purposes and you may become liable for council tax. If this is the case, check whether you are eligible for council tax reduction (CTR).

If you take time out but are still enrolled on the course, you continue to count as a student, provided you have not abandoned it completely and the institution has not said you can no longer undertake the course. A temporary suspension or leave of absence may not disqualify you, as the law implies a final dismissal is required to lose student status.

Note: a valuation tribunal decision[25] indicates that students repeating a full-time course on a part-time basis may not meet the definition of full-time student, even if their normal attendance is on a full-time basis. It is therefore important to get in writing the institution's expectations of the hours.

Your college or university determines the number of hours of your course. You may need evidence from it to prove to the local authority that you count as a student. Institutions must provide you with a certificate if you ask for one while you are a student or for up to a year after you leave the course.[26] After that, they may still give you a certificate, but are not legally required to do so. There is no prescribed format for such certificates in the legislation; only the content and that any information provided can be verified by contacting the college directly. The certificate must contain:[27]

- the name and address of the institution; *and*
- your full name; *and*
- your term-time address and home address (if the institution knows this); *and*
- a statement confirming you are (or were) a student; *and*
- the start and end dates of your course.

Postgraduate students

Full-time postgraduate students are treated as students for council tax purposes in the same way as other full-time higher education students.

The requirement is to 'undertake' the course for the prescribed periods as opposed to 'attend' it, as was previously required. This should make it easier for postgraduate students to show they meet the requirements for council tax exemption, including through their periods of 'study, tuition or work experience', and that their research counts as 'study'.[28]

Some postgraduate students face problems during the thesis writing-up period after the formal teaching or research ends. While some local authorities accept that the student remains enrolled and exempt, others refuse exemption, arguing that the person is no longer 'within the period of their course'. A High Court ruling reinforced this stricter view, though that specific case involved a writing-up period lasting more than two years.[29] The case has been used by some local authorities to suggest that PhD students are ineligible for exemption even during the formal period of the course, but this should be challenged as the ruling related only to a writing-up period.

If this affects you, check the official course dates as confirmed by your university and get advice from your students' union or institution's advice centre.

Note: if you have completed an undergraduate course and intend to start a postgraduate course in the next academic year, you are not a student as you are not within the period of either course. Depending on your circumstances, however, you may be eligible for CTR or a discount on the bill.

Foreign language assistants

You are classed as a student, and so disregarded for discount purposes, if you registered with the British Council and hold a current appointment as a foreign language assistant at a school or other educational institution in Great Britain.[30]

Spouse, civil partner or dependant of foreign students

A foreign student's spouse, civil partner or dependant who is prevented from working or claiming benefit must be disregarded for discount purposes or may be exempt.[31] To qualify, they must not be a British citizen and must be prevented from working in the UK or claiming benefits under the immigration rules. Importantly, only one of the two conditions (barred from working or barred from claiming benefits) needs to be met to qualify.

The decision in *Harrow London Borough Council v Ayiku*[32] clarified that the non-British spouse of a student was a 'relevant person' and exempt from liability to pay council tax, even though she was allowed to work in the UK. A student's spouse who has limited leave to enter the UK is prevented, as a condition of their leave to remain in the UK, from claiming benefits or CTR (see Chapter 8).

Student nurses

Although the council tax legislation includes references to 'student nurses',[33] the definition refers to traditional hospital-based courses phased out in the 1990s, and so is now redundant. However, students currently studying nursing in higher education are treated as students under definition that applies to other full-time students, as made clear in amendments to the council tax regulations in 1994.[34] If an authority seeks proof of student nurse status, direct it to these regulations.

Apprentices

An apprentice is someone, of any age, who is:

- employed to learn a trade, business, profession, office, employment or vocation; *and*
- undertaking training leading to an accredited qualification; *and*
- receiving a salary or allowance (or both) of no more than £195 a week before any deductions for income tax and national insurance.[35] Guidance to local authorities advises that when calculating earnings, any overtime or bonuses should be ignored.

The training must lead to an accredited qualification.[36] Most councils ask for evidence (eg,a copy of the apprenticeship agreement or a signed agreement between the apprentice and the employer) along with recent wage slips.

In some cases, eligibility may be disputed where a course includes an industry placement. For example, in *LE v North Yorkshire*,[37] the appellant was on a level 6 BSc (Honours) Professional Policing Practice degree, delivered jointly by the Open University and North Yorkshire Police. The Open University described this as an apprenticeship. The appellant was required to work 40 hours a week for the police, with 20 hours dedicated to off-the-job training as part of the qualification. The tribunal found this did not meet the statutory definition of either a student or an apprenticeship, and so no discount was allowed.

Severely mentally impaired people

For council tax purposes, you are considered severely mentally impaired (SMI) if you have a severe impairment of intelligence and social functioning (however caused) that appears to be permanent.[38] You must have a certificate of confirmation from a registered medical practitioner. Doctors must issue certificates free of charge.[39]

Conditions commonly associated with SMI include Alzheimer's disease, other forms of dementia, Parkinson's disease, severe learning difficulties or a stroke, but many others may apply. Having one of these conditions does not in itself mean that you will be diagnosed as SMI by a doctor.

To qualify for the discount, you must be entitled to one of the following:[40]

- universal credit (the limited capability for work/limited capability for work and work-related activity element must be included);
- employment and support allowance (in Scotland);
- attendance allowance (AA) or pension age disability payment (PADP);
- the standard or enhanced rate of the daily living component of PIP or adult disability payment (ADP);
- the middle or highest rate care component of disability living allowance (DLA), Scottish adult disability living allowance (SADLA) or child disability payment (CDP);
- armed forces independence payment (AFIP);
- incapacity benefit or severe disablement allowance;
- an increase in disablement pension for constant attendance;
- unemployability supplement (this was abolished in 1987 but existing claimants remain entitled);
- constant attendance allowance or unemployability allowance payable under the industrial injuries or war pension schemes.

If you would have been entitled to one of the above benefits except for the fact that you have reached pension age, you still qualify for the discount.[41]

Note: the government is proposing changing the title and definition of SMI to improve access to support.[42]

Carers

You are disregarded for discount purposes as a carer if you are providing care or support (or both):[43]

- to someone in receipt of certain benefits (see below); *or*
- to another person on behalf of a local authority or charitable body (see p126); *or*
- to another person, are employed by them and were introduced by a charitable body (see p126).

Caring for someone in receipt of certain benefits

You must:

- be resident in the same dwelling as the person being cared for; *and*
- provide care for at least 35 hours a week on average; *and*
- not be the partner of the person being cared for, or, if caring for a child under 18, not be the child's parent; *and*
- be caring for someone entitled to:[44]
  - lower or higher rate AA (only the higher rate in Scotland); *or*
  - the higher rate of PADP in Scotland; *or*
  - the middle or highest rate care component of DLA (only the highest rate in Scotland); *or*
  - the highest rate of the care component of CDP/SADLA in Scotland; *or*

- the standard or enhanced rate of the daily living component of PIP (only the enhanced rate in Scotland)/ADP;
- AFIP; *or*
- an increase in constant attendance allowance under the industrial injuries or war pensions scheme; *or*
- the highest rate of constant attendance allowance payable on top of full-rate disablement benefit paid for an industrial injury.

More than one person living in the same dwelling can count as a carer. You do not have to claim carer's allowance, carer support payment or the carer's element in UC to qualify for this disregard, and your income and savings will not affect your eligibility.

Example

Owen and Lisa care for Lisa's mother, Jean, who lives with them. Jean has dementia and receives AA. Owen and Lisa provide at least 35 hours of care and are disregarded, along with Jean. The household receives a 50 per cent discount on their council tax bill. All three occupiers are disregarded, but cannot claim an exemption.

A dwelling left empty by a carer is exempt, whether or not you meet any of the above criteria. A dwelling left empty by someone who has moved to receive care elsewhere is also exempt (see p60).

For more information on carers and council tax, see carersuk.org.

Carers providing care on behalf of a local authority or charitable body

You must:

- be providing the care or support on behalf of a charitable body, government department, local authority, the Court of Common Council of the City of London or the Council of the Isles of Scilly, and be resident in premises provided by, or on behalf of, that organisation, so that the best care can be provided; *and*
- be engaged or employed for at least 24 hours a week; *and*
- be paid no more than £44 a week.

Carers introduced by a charitable body

You must:

- be employed to provide care or support by the person who needs the care for at least 24 hours a week; *and*
- be earning no more than £44 a week from this employment; *and*
- have been introduced to the person by a charitable body; *and*
- be resident in premises provided by, or on behalf of, the person being cared for to enable the best care to be provided.

People in hospital, care homes and hostels

If you have a short stay in **hospital**, it does not affect council tax liability or the amount of tax that must be paid. If you have been, or are likely to be, in a hospital for so long that you can no longer be considered solely or even mainly resident in your home, you should be ignored for the purpose of a discount. A dwelling left empty because you are solely or mainly resident in hospital is exempt from council tax (see p57).

You do not lose sole or main residence by being in hospital or respite care if the intention is to return to your home.[45]

Most hospitals are subject to non-domestic rates, but some long-stay hospitals can be considered dwellings for council tax purposes. Patients solely or mainly resident in such a hospital are disregarded for discount purposes.[46] In this context, and for the purpose of exemptions, a 'hospital' means:[47]

- an NHS hospital; *and*
- a military, air force or naval unit or establishment in which medical or surgical treatment is provided within the meaning of the Armed Forces Act 2006.

Note that people who are detained in a psychiatric hospital or a care home as a result of a sentence or order of a criminal court are classed as in detention rather than as being in care or in hospital.

The owners, rather than the residents, of **care homes, independent hospitals and hostels** are liable for the council tax (see p91). The owners may be eligible for a disability reduction (see p107). If you are solely or mainly resident in such accommodation, you are disregarded for discount purposes if you are receiving care or treatment (or both) in the home, hospital or hostel.[48] If you have left your own home empty, it may be exempt from the council tax. See p57 for details.

You are also disregarded if you live in a **hostel for homeless people**[49] – eg, run by the Salvation Army. Most of the accommodation must be communal (ie, not divided into self-contained units) and most agreements to occupy the accommodation must be under licences that do not constitute tenancies. The disregard applies to resident staff as well as residents, provided the accommodation is predominantly for those with no fixed abode on the terms and conditions specified.

People in prison or other forms of detention

In many cases, if you are in prison or another form of detention, you are no longer considered solely or mainly resident in your dwelling and should therefore be ignored for discount purposes. Dwellings left empty by people in detention are exempt from council tax (see p56). However, if the detention is for a short period, you may still be considered as mainly occupying the dwelling.

A disregard for discount purposes applies if you are:[50]

- detained in a prison, hospital or any other place by a British court; *or*

- detained under the deportation provisions of the Immigration Act 1971; *or*
- detained under the Mental Health Act 1983 or the Mental Health (Care and Treatment) (Scotland) Act 2003 or the Criminal Procedure (Scotland) Act 1995;[51] *or*
- imprisoned, detained or in custody for more than 48 hours under the Armed Forces Act 2006.[52]

You are not considered detained if you are in police custody before your first court appearance, or are detained for non-payment of council tax in England or Wales, or non-payment of a fine in England, Wales or Scotland.[53]

If you are on temporary release, you are treated as being detained.

Members of religious communities

You are a member of a religious community if:[54]

- the principal occupation of the community consists of prayer, contemplation, education, the relief of suffering, or any combination of these; *and*
- you have no income or capital of your own and are dependent on the community to provide for your material needs.

For the disregard to be applied, you must be able to show that you are fully supported by the community for your daily living needs – eg, bed and board.[55]

In considering whether you have any income, the local authority should disregard any pensions from former employment. Claiming to have no income or capital may be rebutted by proof that you have obtained credit and sold property.[56]

In *Appellants v Watford BC*, all residents at the appeal property were members of the Society of African Missions. They received no salary or payment for work carried out through the Society. Each member depended on the Society for bed, board, food and all living and working expenses, and none of them owned any other property. The valuation tribunal allowed the appeal that the criteria for a 50 per cent discount were met.[57]

The owner, not the residents, is liable for the tax on a dwelling occupied by a religious community (see p94).

Members of visiting international headquarters and defence organisations

A member (or dependant) of certain international headquarters or defence organisations listed in section 1 of the International Headquarters and Defence Organisations Act 1964 is disregarded for discount purposes.[58]

Members of visiting forces

Members of visiting forces and any of their dependants who are neither British citizens nor ordinarily resident in the UK are disregarded for the purposes of a discount.[59] A dwelling is exempt from council tax if one of the liable people has a relevant association with a visiting force. See p64 for more details on exemptions. Therefore, this disregard only applies if none of the liable people have a relevant association. This would be the case, for example, if a member of a visiting force lodges with a British citizen.

People under the Homes for Ukraine scheme

Households do not lose council tax discounts if they host anyone under the Homes for Ukraine scheme.[60] This applies to Ukrainians admitted to the UK under the Immigration Rules staying with a sponsor family or household.[61] This protects the host's single person discount and the 50 per cent discount received by households where all the occupants are already disregarded. It also ensures that there is no loss of a council tax exemption.

4. Getting a discount

Before calculating the council tax chargeable on a dwelling, a local authority should take reasonable steps to actively establish whether any discount should be granted.[62] Failure to do so may be raised in appeals about failure to award discounts, backdated claims for discounts or a refusal by billing authorities to repay any overpaid tax where a discount was not awarded.[63]

Scottish local authorities are specifically obliged to actively seek confirmation on the use of properties as second homes and long-term empty properties. This is important now that the discounts or charges on these properties can be increased or decreased depending on their status (see p132).

If the local authority has reason to believe that a discount applies, it should assume this when calculating the council tax liability for the dwelling,[64] even if it does not have conclusive evidence.

Applications

If the local authority has not granted a discount, a liable person may request one in writing. Most local authorities have online and paper claim forms for council tax discounts. You should include any relevant evidence supporting the request. In the case of a student, a student's certificate may prove useful, but is not necessary. In the case of someone who is severely mentally impaired, a medical certificate is required.

Backdating discounts

There is no time limit on backdating discounts, so authorities must grant discounts for a past period if the appropriate conditions were met. Unlike the provisions for backdating most social security benefits, there is no requirement to show good cause before a discount is backdated, or any other restriction in the legislation.

There is no time limit on how much backdating you can apply for (ie, you can apply for a discount to be backdated further than the six years imposed by the Limitation Act 1980), but in some cases the local authority may raise the decision in *Arca v Carlisle City Council*[65] and suggest that backdating can only be allowed for six years. However, in recent decisions, the President of the Valuation Tribunal for England clarified that the six-year period only relates to the right to bring an appeal against a decision, rather than to legal proceedings, such as starting an appeal to the valuation tribunal. This is known as the 'cause of action'.[66] In particular, a local authority must make enquiries about discount (and premiums) before calculating the council tax bill. If it has not taken such steps, that strengthens your case for backdating once you are aware you are eligible.[67]

Examples from caselaw

In *Randhawa v Hounslow*, the valuation tribunal upheld an appeal for the backdating of council tax discount from 2021 to 2010.[68] The resident provided several documents to demonstrate that she was the sole resident at the appeal property from 2010, including bank statements from January 2010, utility bills from January and February 2014 and a statement from the water supplier confirming the account was established in 2009.

In *AM v LB Bromley*, the taxpayer was not aware of the right to claim a discount until September 2022.[69] The valuation tribunal ruled that the limitation period began from that date, giving the taxpayer six years in which to begin the appeal. The taxpayer was able to obtain backdating to 2013, the date he had moved in as a single resident. A number of other tribunal rulings support this position.

Other exceptions exist to the six-year limit – eg, under section 32 of the Limitation Act 1980, where relevant evidence has been concealed, fraud has been committed or there has been a mistake.

If a discount should not have been granted for a past period, it may be withdrawn and you may have to appeal to the valuation tribunal.

Not only are the restrictions imposed on backdating by *Arca* much more limited than some councils suggest, but this decision is only persuasive in Wales and Scotland. Moreover, the Limitation Act does not apply in Scotland where the equivalent legislation (Prescription and Limitation (Scotland) Act 1973) sets a 20-year limit.

Have you discovered you should have received a discount?

If you have recently discovered you should have received a discount, write to your local authority requesting the discount to be applied and the discount to be backdated to the earliest date you were eligible. Include any supporting evidence for your eligibility.

The duty to correct false assumptions

If a discount is awarded, the local authority must inform the liable person in writing, normally via tax bill. If that person, or any jointly liable person, has reason to believe that the discount should not have been awarded or that a smaller discount should be in place, they should notify the local authority in writing within 21 days of becoming aware that the discount was incorrect.[70] This duty only applies if your awareness of the error arises before the end of the financial year after the one the discount relates to.[71]

Penalties

The local authority has the discretion to impose a penalty of £70 (in England) and £50 (in Wales or Scotland) on a liable person who fails to notify it that a discount should not have been granted.[72] The penalty may be imposed on someone who, through negligence, fails to promptly notify the billing authority of a relevant change in circumstances or who makes an incorrect statement. An English or Welsh authority may quash such a penalty. A Scottish local authority may revoke the imposition of such a penalty if there is a reasonable excuse for the failure.[73] Each time the local authority repeats the request and the person continues to fail to supply the information, a further £280 penalty in England, or a further £200 penalty in Wales and £500 in Scotland, can be imposed.[74]

In Scotland, the maximum fine is £500 for providing false or misleading information to obtain a reduction that is not due or to avoid a punitive 100 per cent increase if it truly is a long-term empty property.[75]

You can appeal against a penalty (see Chapter 11).[76] If you appeal, you do not need to pay the penalty before the appeal has been decided.

The billing authority may offer civil penalties as an alternative to a criminal prosecution (see Chapter 9).

5. **Unoccupied dwellings discounts**

An unoccupied dwelling is one in which no person lives as their sole or main residence. Local authorities have the discretion to award discounts for certain classes of unoccupied dwellings. The discount can be reduced ('varied' in Scotland) as the local authority sees fit.[77]

English billing authorities may decide to replace the double discount where the dwelling has no resident. Each council can change the amount of allowable discount (which originally allowed two discounts of 25 per cent)[78] to a lower discount (with a minimum discount of 10 per cent).

See p137 for information about long-term empty and periodically occupied dwellings (second homes).

England and Wales

Many authorities offer no discount for such properties, while others offer a short period of exemption (eg, one month) followed by full liability – or a short period of exemption, followed by a longer period of discount, followed by full liability. Contact your local authority to find out what discount, if any, it allows. After one year in Wales or two years in England, the rules for long-term empty properties apply (see p137).

Dwellings where discount cannot be changed

Local authorities cannot reduce the amount of discount applicable to some properties. These dwellings receive a discount of 50 per cent. This includes properties that consist of a pitch occupied by a caravan, a mooring occupied by a boat, job-related dwellings, and unoccupied dwellings left empty because a person is required to occupy another dwelling because of their job (see p133).

Scotland

Scottish local authorities can apply a variable discretionary reduction to empty dwellings and dwellings that are second homes.[79]

Unoccupied dwellings and second homes[80]

An **'unoccupied dwelling'** is a dwelling which is no one's sole or main residence but is not a second home.

A **'second home'** is a furnished dwelling which is no one's sole or main residence but the liable person can produce evidence to establish that it is lived in, other than as a sole or main residence, for at least 25 days during any period of 12 months.

The premium does not apply where the property is undergoing repairs or where the taxpayer has bought the property within the last six months, or a longer period if agreed by the local authority.

The local authority must be able to establish that a premium is in place if challenged on appeal at a tribunal. The evidential burden is on the council to show that it has changed the default 50 per cent scheme. If the authority cannot provide evidence of the change, the tribunal could decide the authority has not calculated the taxpayer's liability correctly. The default position for a dwelling which is no one's sole or main residence or residence is a 50 per cent discount under section 11 of the Local Government Finance Act 1992.[81]

The taxpayer can supply evidence to support their case that the property has not been occupied for more than 25 days.[82] The discount is 50 per cent for every day where there is no resident in the dwelling.[83] However, the local authority may reduce the discount to any percentage not less than 10 per cent.

Where the property has been unoccupied as a sole or main residence for a continuous period exceeding 12 months, the local authority can:[84]

- apply no discount; *or*
- increase the amount of council tax payable by up to 100 per cent.

The local authority may also modify the discount for different cases, or different classes of case, including for different areas.

If the dwelling is a periodically occupied property (a second home), the authority cannot make a modification to increase council tax liability, and:[85]

- the discount percentage may not be greater than 50 per cent;
- the discount percentage may not be less than 10 per cent;
- the modification can impose no variation in council tax liability.

Unoccupied properties for sale or let are protected from variation where they are continuously unoccupied for less than two years *and* are being marketed on fair terms and at a fair price, and the owner would accept a reasonable offer.[86]

Note if someone moves in for less than three months (within any 12-month period), the property is still considered continuously unoccupied. This rule closes a loophole where someone might briefly occupy a property to restart the 'empty clock'.

Purpose-built holiday homes and job-related dwellings (see below) are subject to the 50 per cent discount and cannot be varied.[87]

Unoccupied dwellings that are uninhabitable due to major repair work or structural alteration are protected from variation for six months from the date the liable person purchased the property.[88]

The council cannot discriminate between private people and social landlords solely on the grounds of ownership.

Job-related dwellings and discounts

A 'job-related dwelling' is one that your employer provides to you or your partner because of your or their employment and which:[89]

- is necessary to perform the job properly; *or*
- improves how duties are performed and where it is customary for employers to provide accommodation to employees or under contract; *or*
- is part of special security arrangements.

Job-related dwellings include any accommodation provided as a second home as part of your employment (eg, a live-in caretaker), and property owned as a second home if your employment requires you to occupy another dwelling – eg, you are a publican who is required to live in other licensed premises as a tenant of a brewery. Armed forces accommodation provided by the Ministry of Defence may also qualify as an employment-related dwelling for a member of the armed forces.[90]

If you also have a second home in England on which council tax is payable, the local authority in which the second home is situated is prevented from reducing the 50 per cent discount.

In Scotland, to be job-related, the dwelling must be owned or tenanted by someone whose sole or main residence is a different dwelling.[91]

Company directors and partnerships

If a company provides the dwelling and you are either a director[92] of it or of an associated company, the local authority may reduce the discount unless:[93]

- you are employed as a full-time director; *or*
- the company is non-profit making; *or*
- the company is established for charitable purposes.

It is also crucial that you actually reside in the dwelling; a few nights each week will not be sufficient.[94]

Ministers of religion

Ministers of any religious denomination who are required to live in accommodation as part of their role are entitled to a discount. This discount also applies to the minister's spouse or partner.[95] This protection extends to a second home as well.[96]

6. **Miscellaneous discounts**

Local authorities have the power to give discretionary discounts.[97] Examples include hard-to-sell property, single occupiers called up for 28 days or more as members of the reserve forces, and occupied and unoccupied property without mains services – eg, beach chalets.[98] You should check with your local authority whether additional discounts are available.

7. Discretionary reductions

Discretionary decision under s13A Local Government Finance Act 1992

Local authorities in **England and Wales** have the power to reduce someone's council tax under section 13A of the Local Government Finance Act 1992 for any reason, including financial need or other personal circumstances.[99] It includes the power to reduce a bill to zero.[100] Discretionary reductions are not available in Scotland.

Discretionary relief, while it is included in the wider statutory council tax reduction (CTR) scheme, is separate from CTR. Each local authority in **England** must specify the reductions it will apply to council tax payable by people whom it considers to be in financial need.[101] In **Wales**, local authorities set their schemes according to regulations made by Welsh Ministers to help people in financial hardship.[102]

Meaning of financial need

The term 'financial need' is not defined, but should be interpreted broadly and flexibly, guided by caselaw.

The courts have held: 'To need is not the same as want. "Need" is a lack of what is essential for the ordinary business of living.'[103] Financial need is distinct from hardship and poverty – it has a lower threshold or and may also include people who are, or will be, in debt unless support is given. This means people struggling to meet ordinary bills or expenses may qualify. Note that 'financial need' does not require a person to be without any money or assets; certain amounts and types of savings are allowed.

A council may award a reduction to cover any liability regardless of when the liability arose, so a discretionary reduction can be used to clear arrears of council tax from an earlier year or years – ie, at any time before the CTR schemes came into force.[104]

Local authorities can reduce sums payable in individual cases and in groups of people[105] – eg, to victims of flooding or people receiving particular benefits or in particular circumstances such as pregnancy. Authorities can also apply discretionary reductions for long-term empty and second homes (see p142).

The power under section 13A(2)(b) does not include a residency requirement on the class of person eligible for a discretionary reduction. Imposing a residency requirement or imposing a restriction may amount to unlawful indirect discrimination, especially if imposed without necessary consultation or the council having due regard to its public sector equality duties.[106]

Applications

Each local authority's CTR scheme must explain how to apply for a discretionary reduction.[107] Generally, you must apply to the council in writing or call the council tax department. There is no standard application form, but when applying, it is advisable to include:

- a full income and expenditure breakdown for your household;
- supporting evidence, such as bank statements, benefit letters or medical documents (where relevant).

It has been held at valuation tribunal level that the burden rests on the taxpayer to provide sufficient evidence in any appeal to confirm that their expenditure exceeds their income and that they cannot afford the council tax payments.[108]

Possession of a capital asset might not disentitle you from claiming a discretionary reduction – eg, where your only source of income is from property rental.[109]

Note: you do not have to get CTR to apply for a discretionary reduction. Even if you are entitled to CTR under your local authority's CTR scheme, it can still award you a discretionary reduction.

Discretionary decisions

Although a local authority is likely to have a written policy explaining how it decides applications for discretionary reductions, it is still expected to consider each case on its individual merits. The council must also act reasonably when deciding whether to grant a reduction.

There is nothing in law preventing a council from awarding discretionary relief automatically, even without a formal application.

An important decision clarifying the scope and factors a local authority should take into account when considering a discretionary reduction is *SC and CW v East Riding of Yorkshire Council* (see p267).[110]

The local authority should consider an application for a reduction for hardship in light of the practice statement issued by the valuation tribunal.[111]

Challenging a decision

If you disagree with the council's decision on your application for a discretionary reduction, you can appeal against it (see p267).

For a tribunal to consider an application for relief, it is important that an application is first made to the billing authority.[112]

Energy efficiency discount schemes in Scotland

All Scottish billing authorities must operate an energy efficiency discount scheme. These offer council tax discounts where certain energy efficiency improvements have been made to a dwelling.[113] The local authority has discretion over which energy efficiency measures qualify, the type of dwellings included, the level of reduction and the application process.[114]

To be eligible:[115]

- you must be liable to pay council tax for the dwelling; *and*
- energy efficiency improvements must have been made to that dwelling (whether by you or not); *and*
- the improvements were made in the same financial year in which you are liable to pay council tax; *and*
- the dwelling must not have previously received a reduction under the energy efficiency scheme for that financial year.

Energy efficiency schemes may typically provide a one-off discount for introducing certain measures to a dwelling – eg, loft and cavity wall insulation works carried out with a cost to the householder. The work must have been done within the past 12 months and you must provide proof of payment.

The amount of discount depends on the number of improvements and the cost to the householder.

The minimum reduction that must be granted is:[116]

- at least £50 where the annual council tax bill is £50 or more; *or*
- the full amount of liability if the bill is under £50.

A billing authority may reduce a bill to nil.[117]

8. Premiums

Long-term empty and second homes

To help tackle housing shortages, local authorities have the discretion to charge a council tax premium (an additional charge) on:

- long-term empty properties; *or*
- periodically occupied properties (commonly known as 'second homes').

Definition of long-term empty property

A 'long-term empty property' is one that has been unoccupied for:[118]

– at least one year in Wales and Scotland;

– at least two years in England.

This includes periods when the property is empty and is undergoing major structural repair or alteration work, or is unoccupied and unfurnished, such as newly built properties. Whether a property is furnished or unfurnished is a question of fact for the valuation tribunal.[119] Photographic evidence can be important to determine whether a property is furnished or unfurnished at any particular time.[120]

Properties vacant for shorter periods may be exempt (see Chapter 4) or have a discount applied (see p131). Local authorities can also apply discretionary reductions in cases where homes are empty due to special circumstances – eg, hardship, flooding or fire. You can still claim exemptions for previous years in some cases.

Note:

- It may be necessary to closely examine the wording of the determination by the billing authority to identify the criteria being applied.
- The authority must not assume non-occupation simply because the householder had other addresses for their bank accounts and does not show up on credit checks at the appeal property, or an inconsistency with the dating in correspondence.
- Statements from the householder and supporting documents are generally considered stronger evidence than assumptions made by the local authority. To challenge a claim that a property has been continuously empty for two years, you need to show that it was occupied during that period, however briefly.[121]

England

Long-term empty properties

Local authorities can charge a council tax premium.[122] In England, a dwelling is 'long-term empty' if it has been continuously empty and substantially unfurnished for over two years. Some exceptions apply (see p141). Local authorities have discretion on whether to apply a premium, and the exact rates to be charged, which consider local housing needs and policy priorities.

Maximum premium amounts[123]

	Maximum premium
From 1 April 2013	50 per cent
From 1 April 2019	100 per cent
From 1 April 2020	100 per cent (property empty for less than five years)
	200 per cent (property empty for over five years)
From 1 April 2021	100 per cent (property empty for less than five years)
	200 per cent (property empty for between five and 10 years)
	300 per cent (property empty for over 10 years)

Example

Mia and Ben bought a property three years ago. They are majorly renovating it in their spare time. The property has remained unoccupied and substantially unfurnished. The local authority applies the full premium of 100 per cent. The monthly council tax due is £400, made up of the full charge (£200) plus a premium of 100 per cent (£200).

Second homes

From 1 April 2025, local authorities in England can impose a premium on certain properties.[124]

This is an additional council tax charge on dwellings that:

- have no resident living there as their sole or main home; *and*
- are substantially furnished.

These are typically second homes, holiday homes or periodically occupied dwellings.

The billing authority can determine that, for any financial year, a premium may apply to a dwelling where the original 50 per cent empty property does not apply. The council must not have already increased the council tax by more than 100 per cent under other provisions – ie, the premium cannot push the tax above double the standard charge.

Before applying a second home premium, a billing authority must decide to apply the premium at least one year before the financial year it will take effect – eg, to apply the premium from 1 April 2026, the determination must be made by 31 March 2025. It must publish this in at least one local newspaper, at least 21 days before the decision.[125]

It must consider any guidance issued by the Secretary of State.[126] Failure to publish a notice will not invalidate the determination or resolution,[127] but failure to consider government guidance may make a determination legally challengeable.[128]

A council can revoke or vary a second home premium determination, but only before the start of the financial year in which it would apply.[129]

Wales

Long-term empty properties

Local authorities in Wales have wide discretion to reduce or remove council tax discounts on a dwelling where no one is resident.[130]

Since April 2023, they also have discretion to charge a premium of up to 300 per cent on long-term empty homes[131] – ie, the council tax bill can be up to four times the standard rate. Some exceptions apply (see p141).

In Wales, a long-term empty dwelling is a dwelling which is both unoccupied and substantially unfurnished for a continuous period of at least one year.[132] Periods of furnishing or occupying a dwelling lasting six weeks or less do not affect the one-year limit – ie, brief use or staging the property does not prevent it being classed as a long-term empty dwelling.[133]

From 1 April 2017, local authorities in Wales may specify different percentages up to 100 per cent and, from 1 April 2023, a maximum premium of up to 300 per cent for different dwellings based on the length of time for which they have been empty, with the aim of applying stepped incremental increases over time.[134]

What factors should the local authority consider when using discretion to charge a premium?

Welsh government guidance lists the following factors[135] (it is not an exhaustive list):

- numbers and percentages of long-term empty homes or second homes in the area;
- distribution of long-term empty homes or second homes and other housing throughout the authority and an assessment of their impact on property values in particular areas;
- potential impact on local economies and the tourism industry;
- patterns of demand for, and availability of, affordable homes;
- potential impact on local public services;
- potential impact on the local community;
- other measures that are available to increase housing supply;
- other measures that are available to help bring empty properties back into use.

Second homes

Local authorities in Wales have discretion to charge second home owners an additional council tax premium, up to a maximum of 100 per cent – ie, up to doubling the amount payable.[136] A second home is a dwelling which is not your sole or main home and is substantially furnished.

For a second home premium to apply, a billing authority must make a determination under section 12B of the Local Government Finance Act 1992 at least one year before the beginning of the financial year to which the premium relates – ie, for a premium to apply from 1 April 2026, a billing authority must make a determination before 1 April 2025. A billing authority may decide to charge a higher rate.

There are seven main categories of properties exempt from the second home premium:

- properties for sale – they must be marketed at a reasonable price (freehold or with a lease of more than seven years);[137]
- properties for rent – they must be marketed at a reasonable rent;
- job-related dwellings;
- seasonal holiday homes where year-round occupancy is prohibited;
- occupied caravan pitches and boat moorings;
- recently marketed properties for rent or sale (for up to one year);
- dwellings and annexes which would be occupied if the occupier was not serving with the armed forces.

Also included as exceptions are single dwellings within a property which is divided into several dwellings and one or more of the other dwellings is occupied or is a sole or main residence.[138]

From 1 April 2023, additional planning-related exceptions apply where a planning condition restricts occupation:[139]

- specifying that the dwelling can only be used for holiday let; *or*

- preventing occupancy as a person's sole or main residence; *or*
- preventing occupancy for at least 28 consecutive days in any one-year period.

Scotland

Scottish local authorities have the discretion to charge a premium of up to 100 per cent on long-term empty properties. Some exemptions apply (see below).[140] The premium only applies to the council tax proportion of the council tax bill, not the water and sewerage charge.

A premium may be applied if a property has been unoccupied for one year or more. An 'unoccupied dwelling' is any dwelling which is not someone's sole or main residence, but does not fall within the definition of a second home (see p132 for the definition). An unoccupied dwelling may be either furnished or unfurnished, but is either not lived in at all or is lived in for fewer than 25 days in any 12-month period. If your property was not lived in for at least 25 days in the last 12 months, it must be classified as an unoccupied property rather than as a second home. Local authorities in Scotland can also choose to remove any discount for second homes altogether.[141]

You can appeal if the local authority classes your second home as an empty property and applies a premium. It is for you to prove that your property is a genuine second home and you may need to provide evidence such as utility bills.

When a premium cannot be applied

There are exceptions where the premium will not apply. This means you will pay the normal rate for an unoccupied property, but the extra charge (premium) will not be added to your bill. The following table summarises situations where the premium may not be applied.

Class of dwelling	*Applicarion*	*Definition*
Class H	Long-term empty homes and second homes	Dwellings being actively marketed for let (12 months limit)
Class I	Long-term empty homes and second homes	Unoccupied dwellings which fell within exempt Class F and where probate has recently been granted (12 months from grant of probate/letters of administration)
Class J	Second homes only	Job-related dwellings
Class K	Second homes only	Occupied caravan pitches and boat moorings

Class L	Second homes only	Seasonal homes where year-round, permanent occupation is prohibited, specified for use as holiday accommodation or planning condition preventing occupancy for more than 28 days continuously
Class M	Long-term empty home only	Empty properties requiring or undergoing major repairs or structural alterations (12 months limit)

A dwelling is exempt from the premium if it:[142]

- would be someone's sole or main residence if they were not residing in armed forces accommodation;
- is an annexe that forms part ofthe main dwelling or is treated as part of it;
- is genuinely being marketed for sale or for rent. In England and Wales, the exemption lasts for up to one year from the date it was placed on the market. In Scotland, the time limit is two years;[143]
- used as a residence, even if not a sole or main residence.[144]

Support for owners of empty property

To help bring empty properties back into use, most local authorities have empty homes or urban renewal teams. Support available may include:

- loans for central heating installation, boiler replacement and heating efficiency measures;
- an empty homes grant to help with the costs of refurbishment;
- a matching service which matches empty homes with possible buyers;
- providing a letter to support VAT reduction for renovation work.

Contact your local authority to find out what is available in your area. Your local authority's council tax reduction scheme may also include help for certain types of empty dwellings.

Discretionary reductions for long-term empty and second homes

In England and Wales, local authorities have discretionary powers under section 13A of the Local Government Finance Act 1992 to reduce council tax liability – including any premium charged on long-term empty properties or second homes (see p135). You can apply for a discretionary reduction if there are good reasons why the property cannot be lived in, sold or let, or if paying the premium is causing you hardship (see p135).

Some local authorities have stated that they may refuse section 13A reductions to people who have invested in the property market and are now facing declining property values.[145] However, a blanket policy refusing all such applications could be unlawful.[146]

While valuation tribunals cannot change the local policy itself (as section 66 of the Act restricts this to judicial review),[147] they can intervene if a local authority's policy unlawfully fetters its discretion.[148]

9. Appealing a discount/premium decision

If the local authority refuses to grant a discount or if you disagree about your liability to pay a premium, you can appeal in writing if you are an aggrieved person.[149] There is no time limit for making such an appeal and you can ask for backdating. You are an 'aggrieved person' if you are liable to pay the council tax or you are the owner (if different).

The appeal letter should clearly explain why the discount should be granted or a premium removed. The local authority has two months to respond.[150] If the local authority refuses your request, or fails to respond within two months of receiving the appeal, you can further appeal to the Valuation Tribunal for England or the Valuation Tribunal for Wales (VTW).

In Wales, guidance states that you should initially contact the local authority to resolve the problem. If you remain dissatisfied after a discussion, you can appeal to the local authority. If you disagree with the outcome of the local authority appeals process or if the local authority does not respond within eight weeks, you can appeal to the VTW (see Chapter 11).[151]

In Scotland, a further appeal is made by writing again to the local authority. The local authority should pass the appeal to the secretary of the Local Taxation Chamber. See Chapter 11 for further details.[152]

The local authority may enforce payment of the original bill while the appeal is pending (see Chapter 10). The local authority may be prepared to agree to suspend recovery action while awaiting the outcome of the appeal. Alternatively, you can seek an adjournment from the magistrates' court or sheriff court if recovery proceedings are commenced while a formal appeal is underway.[153]

Notes

1. **Single person (25 per cent) discount**
   1 **EW** s2(2)(d) LGFA 1992
   S s71(2)(d) LGFA 1992
   2 Reg 4 The Water and Sewerage Charges (Exemption and Reduction) (Scotland) Regulations 2006 No.72; Water Services Charges (Billing and Collection) (Scotland) Order 2010 No.10
   3 *Mitchell v Renfrewshire Council* [2024] LTC Ref: FTS/LTC/CT/23/00019, 20 May 2024

2. **Who counts for discount purposes**
   4 **EW** s6 LGFA 1992
   S s99(1) LGFA 1992
   5 Regs 3 and 16 CT(A&E) Regs

3. **Who is disregarded for discount purposes**
   6 **EW** s11 and Sch 1 LGFA 1992; CT(DD)O; CT(APDD) Regs
   S CT(D)(S)CAO; CT(D)(S) Regs; The Council Tax (Discounts) (Scotland) Amendment Regulations 2018 No.39
   7 s11 LGFA 1992
   8 Department for Communities and Local Government, Council Tax Information Letter 2/2006 stated: 'It is our view that, under Schedule 7 to the Local Government Finance Act 1992, (these) 19 year olds will fall to be disregarded for CT purposes.'
   9 Sch 1 para 3 LGFA 1992
   10 **EW** CT(APDD) Regs
   S CT(D)(S)CAO
   11 **E** CT(DD)O
   EW Reg 3 CT(EDDD)(A)O
   S Art 8 CT(D)(S)CAO
   12 The Council Tax (Discounts) (Scotland) Amendment Regulations 2018 No.39
   13 Sch 1 para 6 CT(D)(S) Regs
   14 Within the meaning of ss17(6) and 29(7) Children (Scotland) Act 1995
   15 Sch 6 para 5 CT(D)(S) Regs amended by reg 3 SSI 2018 No.39
   16 The Council Tax (Additional Provisions for Discount Disregards) (Amendment) (Wales) Regulations 2019 No.431
   17 Sch 1 para 4 LGFA 1992
   18 **EW** Sch 1 para 5(1) CT(DD)O
   S Art 6(1)(b) and Sch 1 para 1(a) CT(D)(S)CAO
   19 The Child Benefit (Miscellaneous Amendments) Regulations 2025 No.818
   20 **EW** Sch 1 para 6(1) CT(DD)O
   S Sch 1 para 2 CT(D)(S)CAO
   21 **EW** Sch 1 para 3 CT(DD)O
   S Art 2 CT(D)(S)CAO
   22 The Council Tax (Discounts) (Scotland) Amendment Order 2014 No.37
   23 **EW** Sch 1 para 4(1) CT(DD)O
   S Art 6(4)(c) CT(D)(S)CAO
   24 **EW** Sch 1 para 3 CT(DD)O, as amended by reg 2(1) and (2)(a) The Local Government (Miscellaneous Amendments) (EU Exit) Regulations 2018 No.1386
   S Arts 2 and 6(4)(e) CT(D)(S)CAO
   25 *The Appellant v the Billing Authority* [2012] VTE Appeal Nos.1765M88934/176C and 1765M88933/176C
   26 Sch 1 para 5 LGFA 1992
   27 Art 5 CT(DD)O
   28 Successfully challenged in *Feller v Cambridge City Council* [2011] EWHC 1252 (Admin)
   29 *Fayad v Lewisham LB* [2008] EWHC 2531 (Admin)
   30 Art 4 and Sch 1 para 2 CT(DD)O
   31 CT(DDED)(A)O, as amended. See also CT(ED)(S)(A)O 1995 and CT(D)(S)(A) Regs
   32 *Harrow LBC v Ayiku* [2012] EWHC 1200
   33 Sch 1 para 7 CT(DD)O
   34 The Council Tax (Discount Disregards) (Amendment) Order 1994 No.543
   35 **E** Amended by art 2(2) CT(DD)(A)(E)O
   W Amended by CT(DD)(A)(W)O
   S CT(D)(S)CAO
   36 **EW** Art 4(b)(i) and b(ii) CT(DD)O, as amended W SI 2010 No.2448; art 2(3) and Sch 3 The Deregulation Act 2015 (Consequential Amendments) Order 2015 No.971
   37 VTE VT00020788, 8 July 2024
   38 Sch 1 para 2 LGFA 1992

39 **EW** Reg 22 and Sch 2 The National Health Service (General Medical Services Contracts) Regulations 2015 No.1862
S Reg 25 and Sch 4 The National Health Service (General Medical Services Contracts) (Scotland) Regulations 2018 No.66
40 **EW** Art 3 CT(DD)O
S Art 4(2) CT(S)(D)CAO; The Council Tax (Discounts) (Scotland) Amendment Order 2023 No.25
41 **EW** CT(DD)O
S Art 4(3) CT(D)(S)CAO
42 MHCLG, *Modernising and Improving the Administration of Council Tax*, 20 June 2025
43 **E** CT(APDD) Regs, as amended by The Council Tax and Non-Domestic Rating (Amendment) (England) Regulations 2006 No.3395
W The Council Tax (Additional Provisions for Discount Disregards) (Amendment) (Wales) Regulations 2007 No.581
S Reg 2 CT(D)(S) Regs 1992
44 **EW** Art 3(2)(b) and (h) CT(DD)O
S Reg 2 CT(D)(S) Regs
45 See *Ahir v LB Hillingdon Council* [2023] VTE Appeal No.VT00011715
46 Sch 1 para 6 LGFA 1992
47 Sch 1 para 6 LGFA 1992; National Health Service Act 2006; National Health Service (Wales) Act 2006; s108 National Health Service (Scotland) Act 1978
48 Sch 1 paras 7-8 LGFA 1992
49 Sch 1 para 10 LGFA 1992
50 Sch 1 para 1 LGFA 1992
EW CT(DD)O
S Reg 3 CT(D)(S)CAO
51 Sch 1 para 1(c)-(d) LGFA 1992
52 s300 Armed Forces Act 2006
53 Sch 1 para 1 LGFA 1992; art 9 The Health and Social Care Act 2008 (Consequential Amendments No.2) Order 2010 No.813
EW CT(DD)O
54 **E** CT(APDD) Regs
W CT(APDD) Regs, as amended by reg 2 The Council Tax (Additional Provisions for Discount Disregards) (Amendment) (Wales) Regulations 2019 No.431
S CT(D)(S) Regs
55 *Betul Cann v LB Ealing* [2021] VTE Appeal No.VT00001699
56 *Betul Cann v LB Ealing* [2021] VTE Appeal No.VT00001699
57 *Appellants v Watford BC* [2017] VTE Appeal No.1945M212874/037C
58 Sch 1 para 11 LGFA 1992; The European Union Military Staff (Immunities and Privileges) Order 2009 No.887; The International Organisations (Immunities and Privileges) (Scotland) Order 2009 No.44
59 **EW** CT(APDD) Amdt Regs
S CT(D)(S)(A) Regs
See also The Visiting Forces and International Headquarters (Application of Law) (Amendment) Order 2009 No.705 and The European Union Military Staff (Immunities and Privileges) Order 2009 No.887
60 **E** Reg 3(1) CT(APDD) Regs, as amended by reg 2 The Council Tax (Discount Disregards and Exempt Dwellings) (Amendment) (England) Regulations 2022 No.439
W Reg 5(8) CT(APDD) Regs, inserted by The Council Tax (Amendments Relating to Discount Disregards and Exempt Dwellings) (Wales) Regulations 2022 No.722 and amended by reg 2 The Council Tax (Additional Provisions for Discount Disregards) (Amendment) (Wales) Regulations 2023 No.154
S Sch 1 para 7(1)(a) and (b) and 7(2) CT(D)(S) Regs, as amended by reg 2 The Council Tax Reduction and Council Tax (Discounts) (Miscellaneous Amendment) (Scotland) Regulations 2025 No.55
61 See gov.uk/guidance/immigration-rules/immigration-rules-appendix-ukraine-scheme

4. **Getting a discount**

62 **EW** Reg 14 CT(AE) Regs
S Reg 12 CT(AE)(S) Regs
63 *Singh v Leicester City Council* [2015] VTE Appeal No.2465M142876/037C
64 **EW** Reg 15 CT(AE) Regs
S Reg 13 CT(AE)(S) Regs
65 *Arca v Carlisle City Council* [2013] RA 248; VTE Appeal No.0915M85513/254C
66 s9 Limitation Act 1980
67 *HS v Leicester City Council* [2015] VTE Appeal No.2465M142876/037C; *Holdsworth et al v City of Bradford MDC* [2015] VTE Appeal No.2465M142876/037C; *AM v LB Bromley* [2024] 00014406 5 August
68 *Randhawa v Hounslow* [2021] VTE Appeal No.VT00004432

69 *AM v LB Bromley* [2024] 00014406 5 August, para 9
70 **EW** Reg 16 CT(AE) Regs
S Reg 15 CT(AE)(S) Regs
71 **EW** Reg 16 CT(AE) Regs
S Reg 15 CT(AE)(S) Regs
72 **EW** s14(2) and Sch 3 LGFA 1992
S s97(4) and Sch 3 LGFA 1992
73 **EW** s14(2) and Sch 3 LGFA 1992
S s97(4) and Sch 3 LGFA 1992
74 **EW** s14(2) and Sch 3 LGFA 1992
S s97(4) and Sch 3 LGFA 1992
75 Sch 3 para 2(1A) LGFA 1992
76 **EW** s14(2) and Sch 3 LGFA 1992
S s97(4) and Sch 3 LGFA 1992

5. **Unoccupied dwellings discounts**

77 **E** s11A LGFA 1992
W s12 LGFA 1992
S Schs 1 and 2 CT(VUD)(S) Regs
78 s11(2)(a) LGFA 1992
79 CT(VUD)(S) Regs
80 Reg 2 CT(VUD)(S) Regs
81 *MM v Kirklees Council* [2023] VT 00012005, 5 January 2023
82 *Bell v East Lothian Council* [2024] FTS/LTC/CT/24/00200, 9 June 2024
83 Reg 3 CT(VUD)(S) Regs
84 Regs 4-6 CT(VUD)(S) Regs
85 Reg 6(1A) CT(VUD)(S) Regs
86 Sch 2 CT(VUD)(S) Regs
87 Sch 1 CT(VUD)(S) Regs
88 Reg 5 CT(VUD)(S) Regs
89 **E** Sch 1 CT(PCD)(E) Regs
W Reg 6 Sch 1 The Council Tax (Prescribed Classes of Dwellings) (Wales) Regulations 1998 No.105
S Sch 1 para 2 CT(VUD)(S) Regs
90 Regs 5 and 6(2)(b) The Council Tax (Prescribed Classes of Dwellings) (England) (Amendment) Regulations 2012 No.2964; *Westdijk v Birmingham City Council* [2022] VTE Appeal No.VT00007141
91 Sch 1 paras 2(1) CT(VUD)(S) Regs
92 As defined by ss67 and 69 of the Income Tax (Earnings and Pensions) Act 2003
93 **E** Sch 1 paras 2 and 3 CT(PCD)(E) Regs
W Reg 6 and Sch 1 The Council Tax (Prescribed Classes of Dwellings) (Wales) Regulations 1998 No.105
S Sch 1 paras 2(6)-(7) CT(VUD)(S) Regs
94 *Lever v Southwark LB* [2009] EWHC 536 (Admin), CO/9305/2008
95 **E** Sch 1 CT(PCD)(E) Regs
W Sch 1 para 3 CT(PCD)(W) Regs
S Sch 1 paras 2(5)-(7) CT(VUD)(S) Regs
96 **E** Regs 2 and 6 CT(PCD)(E) Regs
W Reg 10 and Sch CT(EHA)(W) Regs
S Reg 5 and Sch 1 CT(VUD)(S) Regs

6. **Miscellaneous discounts**

97 s13A LGFA 1992
98 Parliamentary Answer given in the House of Commons by John Healy, Minister for Local Government, 2 February 2009

7. **Discretionary reductions**

99 This power was originally introduced under LGFA 1992 and re-enacted by s10(1) LGFA 2012
100 s13A(1)(c) LGFA 1992
101 s13A(2)(a) and (b) LGFA 1992
102 s13A(4) LGFA 1992
103 *R v Gloucestershire CC and another ex parte Barry* [1997] 2 All ER 1 (HL)
104 *Morgan v Warwick* DC [2015] RVR 224
105 s13A(7) LGFA 1992
106 *R (Winder and others) v Sandwell MBC* and the Equality and Human Rights Commission (intervening) [2014] EWHC 2617
107 Sch 1A para 2(7) and 1B para 5(1)(c) LGFA 1992
108 *Appellants v LB Southwark* [2017] VTE Appeal No.5840M205253/084C
109 *AHR v Sheffield City Council* [2023] VTE Appeal No.VT00012067
110 *SC and CW v East Riding of Yorkshire Council* [2014] VTE Appeal Nos.2001M113393/CTR and 2001M117053/CTR
111 Valuation Tribunal Service, Practice Statement PS 10, pp32-33, 1 April 2020
112 *DG v Liverpool City Council*, Appeal No.4310M140277/CTR cited in *MM v Kirklees Council* [2023] VTE Appeal No.00012005
113 s80A LGFA 1992
114 s80A(3) LGFA 1992
115 s80A(5) LGFA 1992
116 s80A(7) LGFA 1992
117 s80A(8) LGFA 1992

8. **Premiums**

118 **E** s11B(1)(b) LGFA 1992
W ss112A and 112B LGFA 1992, as inserted by s139 Housing (Wales) Act 2014
S Reg 6 CT(VUD)(S) Regs
119 *Heslop v Sefton Council* [2017] EWHC 3041

120 See *Smith v Wolverhampton City Council* [2020] VTE Appeal No.M0264735
121 *Khan v Preston BC* [2017] VTE Appeal No.2315M198655/254C/S
122 s11B(1)(b) LGFA 1992
123 s11B(1A)-(1C) LGFA 1992
124 s11C LGFA 1992
125 s11C(1) LGFA 1992
126 s11C(4) LGFA 1992; MHCLG, *Guidance on the Implementation of the Council Tax Premiums on Long-term Empty Homes and Second Homes*, November 2024
127 s11C((9) LGFA 1992
128 *British Oxygen Ltd v Minister of Technology* [1971] AC 610
129 s11C(6) LGFA 1992
130 The Council Tax (Prescribed Classes of Dwellings) (Wales) Regulations 1998 No.105
131 ss12A and 12B LGFA 1992
132 Welsh Government, *Guidance on the Implementation of the Council Tax Premiums on Long-term Empty Homes and Second Homes in Wales*, January 2016
133 s11B(9) LGFA 1992
134 Welsh Government, *Exemptions to the Council Tax Premium on Long-term Empty Homes in Wales*, 13 March 2015; ss12A and 12B LGFA 1992; CT(EHA)(W) Regs, as amended by reg 2 The Council Tax (Exceptions to Higher Amounts) (Wales) (Amendment) Regulations 2023 No.253
135 s12A(11) LGFA 1992; Welsh Government, *Guidance on the Implementation of the Council Tax Premiums on Long-Term Empty Homes and Second Homes in Wales*, January 2016
136 s112B LGFA 1992
137 Reg 4 CT(EHA)(W) Regs
138 Reg 6 CT(EHA)(W) Regs
139 Reg 9 CT(EHA)(W) Regs, as amended by reg 2 The Council Tax (Exceptions to Higher Amounts) (Wales) (Amendment) Regulations 2023 No.253
140 Reg 6 CT(VUD)(S) Regs
141 The Council Tax (Variation for Unoccupied Dwellings) (Scotland) Regulations 2013 No.45, as amended by reg 3 The Council Tax (Variation for Unoccupied Dwellings) (Scotland) Amendment Regulations 2016 No.369
142 **E** CT(PCD)(E) Regs
W CT(EHA)(W) Regs
S Sch 2 para 2 CT(VUD)(S) Regs
143 Sch 2 para 1 CT(VUD)(S) Regs
144 *A v Ipswich BC* [2018] VTE Appeal No.M0234114
145 Oxford City Council Discretionary Discount Policy 2020, para 3
146 *Padfield v Minister of Agriculture* [1968] AC 997
147 *K and SL v Hereford Council* [2022] VTE Appeal No.00010569, para 21
148 *City of Bradford MDC v Kazi* [2024] EWCA Civ 1037; see also *British Oxygen Co Ltd v Minister of Technology* [1971] AC 610

9. Appealing a discount/premium decision

149 **EW** s16 LGFA 1992
S s81 LGFA 1992
150 **EW** s16 LGFA 1992
S s81 LGFA 1992
151 Welsh Government, *Council Tax on Empty and Second Homes*, 9 March 2023
152 **EW** s16 LGFA 1992
S s81 LGFA 1992
153 *Wiltshire CC v Piggin* [2014] EWHC 4386 (Admin)

8

Chapter 8

Council tax reduction schemes

This chapter covers:

1. What is council tax reduction

If you have a low income, you may qualify for council tax reduction (CTR) to help with your council tax bill. Eligibility and the amount you receive depend on your age, income, savings, who lives with you and, importantly, where you live as different rules apply in England, Wales and Scotland (see p151). CTR is sometimes called council tax support or rebate, depending on the local authority.

CTR schemes must include provision for individuals or groups of people who are in financial need.[1] Schemes must state which classes of people are entitled to a reduction, based on factors such as income, capital, number of dependants and whether an application for CTR has been made.[2]

In England and Wales, you also can apply for discretionary council tax reduction if you have difficulty affording your council tax, even if you do not meet the usual criteria (see p135).

Definitions

The following definitions are used throughout this chapter.

A **'child'** is anyone under the age of 16.

A **'young person'** is someone aged 16 or over but under 20, and who counts as a 'qualifying young person' for child benefit purposes. This does not include a young person who is getting universal credit or employment and support allowance. It also does not include young people excluded from benefits under section 6 of the Children (Leaving Care) Act 2000.[3] For more about the definition of qualifying young person, see CPAG's *Welfare Benefits Handbook.*

A **'couple'** means:[4]

- two people who are married or in a civil partnership and are members of the same household; *or*
- two people who are not married or in a civil partnership but are living together as if they were.

There is a substantial body of benefits caselaw on what it means to live together 'as if married or civil partners'. Local authorities making CTR decisions should apply the same principles. See CPAG's *Welfare Benefits Handbook* for details.

Regulations also include provisions for applicants in polygamous marriages. Seek advice if this applies to you.[5]

Requirements for council tax reduction schemes

Prescribed requirements and default schemes

CTR schemes differ in England, Wales and Scotland. In each country, there are two sets of rules: working-age rules and pension-age rules. This chapter refers to people the pension-age rules apply to as 'pension-age' applicants and everyone else as 'working-age' applicants, regardless of actual age.

In some circumstances, the working-age rules may apply even if you are over pension age (see p155).

In Scotland, the working-age rules are the same across all local authorities. In England and Wales, these rules vary by local authority, so the help you get may depend on where you live.

The pension-age rules for CTR are broadly the same across England, Wales and Scotland. It is a requirement that if you qualify for CTR as a pension-age applicant and your income is low enough, your CTR covers all of your council tax (unless a deduction is made due to a non-dependant living with you (see p159)).[6]

In England and Wales, certain aspects of CTR schemes are set by national 'prescribed requirements' regulations, which all local authorities must follow.[7]

Provided these requirements are met, local authorities can design their own CTR schemes. In Wales, if a local authority does not produce its own scheme, a default scheme prepared by the Welsh government automatically applies.

England

In England, each local authority must have its own CTR scheme, which must adhere to the prescribed requirements. These set out minimum legal requirements for pension-age applicants, including who should qualify and how much CTR they should get.

Local authorities have a great deal of discretion to set their own rules for working-age applicants.

If the pension-age rules apply	You can get CTR on up to 100 per cent of your bill, depending on your circumstances. See sections 2, 3 and 5.
	You can get CTR on up to 25 per cent of your bill, based on the income of a second adult. See sections 2, 3 and 6.
If the working-age rules apply	You can get CTR on a percentage of your bill, subject to a means test. See sections 2 and 4.
	You may get CTR on a percentage of your bill, based on the income of a second adult in some local authority areas. See sections 2, 4 and 6.

Wales

In Wales, each local authority must either create its own CTR scheme that meets the minimum prescribed requirements or adopt the default scheme (see p149).

The prescribed requirements set out who qualifies for CTR and how much they receive. This includes specific rules for pension-age applicants, as well as minimum standards for working-age applicants.

If the pension-age rules apply	You can get CTR on up to 100 per cent of your bill, depending on your circumstances. See sections 2, 3 and 5.
If the working-age rules apply	You can get CTR on up to 100 per cent of your bill, subject to a means test. See sections 2, 4 and 5.

Scotland

In Scotland, a national CTR scheme is administered by local authorities. It has separate rules for pension-age and working-age applicants, ensuring consistent support across Scotland while allowing local councils to manage applications.

If the pension-age rules apply	You can get CTR on up to 100 per cent of your bill, depending on your circumstances. See sections 2, 3 and 5. You can get CTR on up to 25 per cent of your bill, based on the income of a second adult. See sections 2 , 3 and 6.
If the working-age rules apply	You can get CTR on up to 100 per cent of your bill, depending on your circumstances. See sections 2, 4 and 5. You can get CTR on up to 25 per cent of your bill, based on the income of a second adult. See sections 2, 4 and 6.

Consultation on schemes

Each financial year, local authorities in England and Wales must decide whether to revise or replace their CTR schemes.[8] Before making changes, they must consult with those likely to be affected – eg, council taxpayers.

If a council reduces or removes CTR, it must put in place transitional provisions to protect affected claimants from sudden losses.

If you believe your local authority's CTR scheme is flawed or the correct procedures were not followed when adopting or revising it, the only way to challenge it is through judicial review.[9] For information on judicial reviews, see p318.

Types of council tax reduction

If you meet the qualifying conditions, you may qualify for one of the following types of CTR. If you qualify for more than one, you receive the one that gives you the largest reduction.

- **Main CTR** (England, Wales and Scotland) is the most common type of CTR. Your entitlement depends on the amount of your council tax, your family's circumstances and your (your partner's) income and savings (see p157).
- **Alternative maximum CTR** (England and Scotland) is also known as **'second adult rebate'**. You may qualify if another adult lives with you who is not part of your family and has a low income. This type of CTR is based on the other adult's income, not your own needs or resources (see p175).

- **Band E–H CTR** (Scotland only) provides support if your home is in council tax band E, F, G, or H. Entitlement depends on the amount of your council tax and your income and savings (see p178).

In England or Wales, if you cannot afford your council tax, you can apply for discretionary CTR even if you do not qualify for other types of CTR (see p135).

2. **Eligibility conditions**

The following basic conditions apply to all council tax reduction (CTR) schemes in England, Wales and Scotland for both pension-age and working-age applicants. To qualify for CTR, you must:[10]

- be liable for council tax for the dwelling (see p80); *and*
- satisfy the right to reside test and the habitual residence test (see p154); *and*
- not be subject to immigration control (there are some exceptions); *and*
- provide required information in your application (see p180).

If you do not meet these conditions, you are not eligible for CTR.

Additionally, in Scotland and Wales, and in England for pension-age applicants, you must:

- be living in the property as your sole or main residence (see p153); *and*
- not be absent from the dwelling (some temporary absences can be ignored – see p153).

For working-age applicants in England, local authorities have more discretion over how these rules apply. See p156 and check your local authority's CTR scheme.

Extra eligibility rules apply for the different types of CTR. For:

- **main CTR**, see p157; *and*
- alternative maximum CTR (**second adult rebate**), see p175; *and*
- **band E–H CTR**, see p178.

Online calculators

Many councils provide online calculators to help you estimate eligibility. If you have a low income or you are struggling to pay your council tax bill, it is always worth seeing whether you qualify.

Liability to pay council tax

Unless a dwelling is exempt, someone is liable to pay council tax on it. You are a 'resident' of a dwelling if it is your sole or main residence. If you are under 18, you are not liable for council tax on any dwelling in which you live. Other residents aged 18 or over are liable instead. If there are no residents, the dwelling may be exempt. See Chapter 5 for more about liability.

Where you are resident

You are resident in the home where you live – ie, your normal sole or main residence (see p84).[11] A property can still count as your sole or main residence even if you spend substantial time away from it, if it remains the main place where you live. However, if you are absent from the property, you do not usually qualify for CTR unless your absence is temporary and can be ignored.

If you are not yet liable for the council tax on the property (eg, because you have not yet moved in) but are likely to be eligible for CTR when you become liable, you can apply in advance (see p181).

In some circumstances, you can argue that you are resident in a property even if you have not stayed there – eg, you moved your furniture and belongings in but then had to go into hospital.[12] However, if your main residence is elsewhere, you are not entitled to CTR for a dwelling – ie, second homes do not qualify.

Temporary absence from home

In Wales and Scotland, and for pension-age applicants in England, you cannot qualify for CTR if you are absent from home. However, the following temporary absence can be ignored. This is also likely to apply to working-age applicants in England, but check your local scheme. Note that if you get universal credit (UC), absences from home are treated differently for CTR than UC.

You can still get CTR for your normal home while you are away for:

- **up to 13 weeks**, for any reason, provided you have not let or sublet your dwelling to someone else.[13] You must be unlikely to be away for longer than this;
- **up to 52 weeks** if you intend to return to the dwelling (normally within 52 weeks), have not let or sublet it and fulfil certain conditions. The circumstances in which you can remain eligible for up to 52 weeks include:[14]
  - you are on remand in custody awaiting trial or sentencing;
  - you are on bail and required to live in a bail hostel or approved premises;
  - you are a patient in a hospital or similar institution;
  - you, your partner or a dependent child under 16 is receiving medical treatment or convalescence (in the UK or abroad), not in residential accommodation;
  - you are on a training course (in the UK or abroad) to help you secure work;
  - you are providing medically approved care for someone else (in the UK or abroad);
  - you are caring for a child whose parent or guardian is temporarily away for medically approved care or medical treatment;

- you receiving non-residential, medically approved care (in the UK or abroad);
- you are a student;
- you are away due to fear of violence;
- you are in residential accommodation on a trial basis, intending to return home if it is unsuitable. CTR is limited to 13 weeks per trial period, and all trial periods must not exceed 52 weeks total.

In **England**, the above absence-from-home rules only apply if you are still in Great Britain. If you are outside Great Britain, you can get CTR for up to four weeks, provided your absence is unlikely to last longer than this. In limited cases, this can be extended to eight weeks. You can be absent from Great Britain for up to 26 weeks if your absence is for one of the reasons which would allow a 52-week absence under the Welsh or Scottish rules above. If you are working age in England, your council can set its own rules. These are unlikely to be more generous than those for pension-age applicants, but may be more restrictive.

Right to reside and the habitual residence tests

To be entitled to CTR, you must satisfy both parts of the habitual residence test: you must be habitually resident in fact and have a non-excluded right to reside in the common travel area (the UK, Ireland, Channel Islands and Isle of Man). See CPAG's *Benefits for Migrants Handbook* for more information on these tests.

Not be subject to immigration control

You are not usually entitled to CTR if you are defined as a person subject to immigration control.[15] However, in Scotland, you are not excluded from CTR due to being a person subject to immigration control if you meet certain conditions.[16] See CPAG's *Benefits for Migrants Handbook* for more information.

3. Pension-age rules

The pension-age rules for council tax reduction (CTR) are similar in England, Wales and Scotland. If the pension-age rules apply to you, you may qualify for:

- main CTR, if you or your partner get the guarantee credit of pension credit (PC) or if your income (and your partner's income, if you have one) is low enough and you (and your partner) have no more than £16,000 capital. For how main CTR is calculated, see p157; *or*
- alternative maximum CTR (second adult rebate) if you live in England or Scotland and you meet the conditions on p175; *or*
- band E–H CTR if you live in Scotland and meet the conditions on p178.

If you qualify for more than one type of CTR, you receive whichever gives you the largest reduction in your council tax liability.

Note: if you or your partner get the guarantee credit of PC, all of your income and capital are disregarded. If you are pension age and your income is low enough, your CTR must cover all of your council tax (unless you have a 'non-dependant') (for the definition of non-dependant, see p159).[17]

When the pension-age rules apply

The pension-age rules apply to you if:[18]

- you are at least pension age. Pension age is 66 and will reach 67 between 2026 and 2028. To check your pension age, see gov.uk/state-pension-age; *and*
- you or your partner do not get universal credit (UC – but see below) or income-related employment and support allowance (ESA).

Note: in England, the pension-age rules apply from the date you reach pension age or, if you have a partner, the date you both reach pension age. However, if either of you gets UC or income-related ESA (because one of you is under pension age), the working-age rules apply. Any UC paid after you both reach pension age (ie, your final payment) is ignored. If neither of you gets UC or income-related ESA, the pension-age rules apply – these are often more generous. If you are a mixed-age couple (one of you is under pension age), you can only make a new claim for PC in limited cases. Usually, you are expected to claim UC instead.

From 2025/26, pension age applicants who migrated to UC from working tax credit do not lose their entitlement to pension age support.

4. Working-age rules

The working-age rules apply if:[19]

- you are under pension age (and, in Scotland, so is your partner); *or*
- you are pension age or over and you or your partner get universal credit (UC – but see below) or income-related employment and support allowance (ESA).

In England, the pension-age rules apply once you (or both you and your partner) reach pension age – even if you are still getting a final UC payment during the last assessment period before switching to pension-age income (see above).

Are you in a mixed-age couple?

In Scotland, if you are under pension age but your partner is not (ie, you are a 'mixed-age couple'), the working-age rules cannot apply unless one of you gets UC or income-related ESA. In this case, your partner must make the application and the pension-age rules apply. In England and Wales, if neither of you gets UC or income-related ESA, whether the working-age rules or pension-age rules apply depends on who makes the council tax reduction (CTR) application. Usually, the pension-age rules are more generous. Working-age schemes are set by local authorities. Some councils protect certain groups of working-age applicants from the restrictions mentioned below, so it is always worth checking your local authority's CTR scheme on its website.

Working-age rules in England

Each English local authority sets its own CTR scheme for working-age applicants. While all schemes must be based on financial need, the amount of help you get can vary significantly depending on where you live.[20]

You cannot qualify for working-age CTR unless you satisfy the general conditions for all CTR schemes on p152. In addition, each council sets additional rules.

Generally, local authorities calculate main CTR for working-age applicants by setting a capital limit (ie, an amount of capital beyond which you do not qualify), and by comparing your income to your applicable amount, in the same way entitlement to main CTR is decided for pension-age applicants (see p158). However, many local authorities vary aspects of the calculations to require that all working-age applicants pay a minimum amount (sometimes up to 50 per cent of the annual bill), even those on very low incomes.

How local authorities may limit CTR for working-age applicants

Property band capping – your CTR may be capped at the level you would receive if you lived in a lower-band property, even if your actual home is in a higher council tax band.

Minimum entitlement threshold – some authorities will not pay CTR unless your entitlement exceeds a minimum weekly amount – eg, £2, £4 or £5 a week.

Minimum payments – many schemes require you to pay a portion of your council tax, regardless of income – eg, by basing CTR on a percentage of your bill, such as 75 per cent of your liability.

Lower capital limits – some councils set the working-age capital limit as low as £6,000.

Higher income taper rates – under the pension-age rules, CTR reduces by 20p for every £1 of income above your applicable amount. Some councils increase this taper to 25p or 30p for working-age applicants, reducing your entitlement more steeply.

Different treatment of income – some schemes vary the amount of or type of income that is disregarded when calculating CTR entitlement for working-age applicants or for certain groups of working-age applicants.

Reducing or removing second adult rebate – some councils reduce or remove this option entirely for working-age applicants.

Changing non-dependant deductions – some local authorities apply higher deductions or vary them based on income or relationship.

Working-age rules in Wales

Welsh local authorities can devise their own CTR schemes, but the schemes must adhere to the prescribed requirements set by the Welsh government (see p149). The prescribed requirements detail the classes of working-age applicants who must be entitled to main CTR and how their entitlement should be calculated.

There is no alternative maximum CTR scheme ('second adult rebate') in Wales. This means that both pension-age and working-age applicants can only qualify for CTR based on financial circumstances of their own household.

Working-age rules in Scotland

Scotland has a national CTR scheme, with separate regulations for people of working age and pension age.

You may be entitled to main CTR, alternative maximum CTR (second adult rebate – see p175) or band E–H CTR, if your home is in council tax band E, F, G or H (see p178). If you meet the conditions for more than one type, you get the type that gives you the highest reduction.

5. Main council tax reduction

Your entitlement to main council tax reduction (CTR) depends on your family circumstances, your income and capital and, if you are a member of a couple, the income and capital of your partner. If there are other adults living with you who are not jointly liable for council tax with you (other than your partner), a non-dependant deduction may be made on the basis that they are expected to contribute to the council tax bill.

You qualify for main CTR if:

- you live in Wales or Scotland, or in England and the pension-age rules apply to you (see p155) (if you live in England and the working-age rules apply too); *and*
- you meet the general conditions on p152 which apply to all CTR schemes; *and*
- you do not have capital of more than £16,000, unless you or your partner get the guarantee credit of pension credit (PC); *and*
- your income is low enough; *and*
- if you live in England or Scotland, the amount of main CTR is more than the amount you would get under second adult rebate or, in Scotland, band E–H CTR (otherwise you get the other type of CTR instead).

Are you a student?

In Wales and Scotland (for working-age applicants), you cannot qualify for main CTR as a student unless you fall into one of the exceptions (eg, being a lone parent).[21] The exceptions are similar to those for housing benefit (HB). See CPAG's *Welfare Benefit Handbook* for details.

In England, the rules for students vary by local authority, so it is important to check your local authority's scheme.

If *you* are not eligible for CTR but your partner is not a student, they may be able to claim instead.

How much main CTR you get may depend on:

- whether you live in England, Wales or Scotland; *and*
- whether the pension-age or working-age rules apply (see p155); *and*
- your maximum CTR (see below); *and*
- your applicable amount (see p162); *and*
- your (and your partner's) income and capital (see p166 and p172); *and*
- how many people live with you in the dwelling, their circumstances and income.

How to calculate main council tax reduction

Your entitlement to main CTR is worked out as follows.

Step 1: calculate your maximum CTR (see below). If you or your partner gets the guarantee credit of PC and meet the qualifying conditions, you are entitled to your maximum CTR and do not need to follow any further steps. If neither of you gets the guarantee credit, follow the remaining steps.

Step 2: calculate your applicable amount (see p162).

Step 3: calculate your and your partner's income (see p166).

Step 4: calculate your and your partner's capital (see p172). If it is over £16,000, you do not qualify for CTR.

Note: in England, the working-age rules vary considerably (see p156). Check the rules in your area. In Wales, local authorities may vary some, very limited, aspects of the calculation.

Maximum council tax reduction

If you live in Wales or Scotland, or if the pension-age rules apply to you in England, your maximum CTR is the council tax for the property, minus any council tax discount (see Chapter 7) or disability reduction (see Chapter 6) to which you are entitled. Any non-dependant deductions (see p159) are then made from the maximum CTR amount.[22]

If you are jointly liable for council tax with others (not including your partner), your net liability (after discounts and reductions) is divided equally by the number of liable people. Students who are not eligible for CTR are ignored when calculating your share.[23] Your maximum CTR is based on your share of the council tax.

If you live in England and the working-age rules apply, your maximum CTR may be worked out differently. For example, it may be based on a percentage of your council tax liability or based on the rate for a lower-band property than the one you live in. Check your council's scheme for details.

Example

Rio (37) lives alone in a band B property in England and gets a 25 per cent single occupier discount. His weekly council tax bill is £22.89 after the discount. His council requires working-age applicants to pay at least 22 per cent of their council tax. So, Rio's maximum CTR is 78 per cent of £22.89 = £17.85 a week. He must pay the remaining £5.04 per week himself.

Non-dependant deductions

If someone lives with you who is not part of your family and is not liable for council tax, they may reduce how much CTR you get. They are called 'non-dependants'. Examples include adult sons or daughters, friends or relatives. A non-dependant deduction may be taken from your CTR, based on the assumption that the non-dependant contributes towards the council tax, whether or not they do. You may therefore need to ask them to contribute.

Someone is not usually considered to live with you if they have not been there long enough for it to be considered their normal home. They can only be treated as living with you if they share some accommodation with you.

Definitions

For CTR, your **'family'** includes your partner (ie, someone you live with as a couple) and any children or young people you or your partner are responsible for, who are members of your household (see below).[24] You are treated as responsible for a child or young person if they normally live with you. If care is split equally between two households, or it is unclear which household they live in, they are treated as living with the person who receives child benefit for them.[25]

The term **'household'** is not defined in the regulations, so it should be given its ordinary meaning. A temporary absence of your partner, a child or young person does not affect their position as part of your household.[26]

Some people do not count as non-dependants, meaning no non-dependant deduction is made from your CTR. These include:[27]

- a member of your family;
- a child or young person living with you who is not a member of your household;
- in most cases, someone who pays rent to you or your partner on a commercial basis (the rent may still count as income);

- certain live-in carers;
- a person granted leave to enter or remain in the UK under or outside the immigration rules made under section 3(2) of the Immigration Act 1971. Some schemes specifically exclude people from being treated as non-dependants, such as those who have left Ukraine, Afghanistan, Sudan, Israel, Palestine or Lebanon); *and*
- in most cases, someone who is jointly and severally liable for council tax with you.

Exceptions to non-dependant deductions rules

Even if a non-dependant lives with you, no deduction is made in certain circumstances. This is the case in Scotland or Wales or if the pension-age rules apply to you in England. If the working-age rules apply to you in England, your local authority has discretion to vary the rules.

No non-dependant deduction is made if you or (in England and Scotland) your partner are:[28]

- getting attendance allowance (AA) or pension age disability payment (PADP);
- getting the care component of disability living allowance (DLA), Scottish adult disability living allowance (SADLA) or child disability payment (CDP);
- getting the daily living component of personal independence payment (PIP) or adult disability payment (ADP);
- getting armed forces independence payment (AFIP);
- blind, severely sight impaired, partially sighted, or treated as such (this also applies in Wales if your partner meets this condition).

Note: in Wales, if only your partner gets one of the above benefits, get advice about whether you would be better off if your partner is the CTR applicant.

No deduction is made for a non-dependant who:[29]

- lives with you but has their normal home elsewhere (see p84 and p153); *or*
- is on universal credit (UC) and does not have any earned income; *or*
- is on PC or income-related employment and support allowance (ESA) (in Wales this only applies if they are not in the work-related activity group); *or*
- is receiving a training allowance for youth training; *or*
- is a full-time student; *or*
- has been in hospital for more than 52 weeks (separate stays which are not more than 28 days apart are added together when calculating the 52 weeks); *or*
- is a member of the armed forces or reserve forces and is absent on operations (this only applies in England and Scotland); *or*
- is disregarded for a council tax discount (see p118).

Amount of non-dependant deduction

The amount of the non-dependant deduction is set by regulations. In England, local authorities can set different deduction amounts in their working-age CTR schemes.[30]

England	Deduction 2025/26
If the non-dependant is:	
Working 16 hours a week or more with an average weekly gross income of:	
Below £266.00	£5.00
£266.00 to £462.99	£10.20
£463.00 to £576.99	£12.80
£577.00 or above	£15.35
Not working or working less than 16 hours a week	£5.00
Wales	
If the non-dependant is:	
Working 16 hours a week or more with an average weekly gross income of:	
Below £266.00	£6.25
£266.00 to £462.99	£12.45
£463.00 to £576.99	£15.65
£577.00 or above	£18.70
Not working or working less than 16 hours a week	£6.25
Scotland	
If the non-dependant is:	
Working 16 hours a week or more with an average weekly gross income of:	
Below £273	£5.35
£273 to £473.99	£10.55
£474.00 to £585.99	£13.40
£586.00 or above	£15.95
Not working or working less than 16 hours a week	£5.35

Certain amounts may be disregarded when calculating a non-dependant's weekly gross income – eg, disability benefits and certain charitable funds such as those to compensate for medical injuries and acts of terrorism.[31]

If a non-dependant couple lives with you, only one deduction is made for them both. It is based on their combined income and the partner whose circumstances result in the highest deduction.

If are jointly liable for council tax with someone who is not your partner, the deduction is divided equally between you.

Example

Alice (70) lives alone in a band D property in England and gets the guarantee credit of PC Her son, James, comes to live with her. He works 30 hours a week and has a gross income of £410 a week. Her CTR for 2025/26 is calculated as:

Before James moves in:	
Weekly council tax	£28.88
Minus 25 per cent single occupier discount	£7.22
Net liability	£21.66
Weekly CTR	£21.66
Alice does not have to pay any council tax.	
After James moves in:	
Weekly council tax	£28.88
No single occupier discount so:	
Net liability	£28.88
Minus non-dependant deduction	£12.80
Maximum CTR	£16.08
Alice is now required to pay £12.80 council tax.	

Shortly after James moves in, Alice is awarded AA. As a result, the non-dependant deduction stops. She then gets full CTR on the weekly liability of £28.88.

Applicable amounts

Your applicable amount is a weekly amount the government says you need to live on each week, based on your circumstances.

Main CTR is usually calculated by comparing your income to your applicable amount. This is always the case in Scotland and Wales, and for pension-age applicants in England. In England, if you are of working-age, check your council's scheme – most use an applicable amount, but they do not have to.

If you get UC, see below, if you get PC, see p164, and if you still get income-related ESA, see p165. If you have a low income, but do not get a means-tested benefit, see p165.

If you get universal credit

In Scotland and Wales, if you or your partner get UC, your applicable amount is your 'maximum UC amount' set by the DWP (before any deductions such as sanctions or repayment of advances) multiplied by 12 and the result divided by 52 to give a weekly figure.[32]

(Maximum UC amount x 12) ÷ 52 = weekly applicable amount

You can find your maximum UC amount in your UC online journal. It is made up of the total of:

- a standard allowance (depending on your age and whether you are single or in a couple);
- a child element for each child, subject to a 'two-child limit' (exceptions may apply), with an increase for a disabled or severely disabled child;
- an element for an adult assessed as having limited capability for work (LCW) and limited capability for work-related activity (LCWRA). A separate element, abolished for new claimants, for someone assessed as just having LCW can still be paid in some cases;
- a carer element for someone caring for a severely disabled person;
- a childcare costs element;
- a housing costs element for help with your rent or any service charges that you pay;
- a transitional element if you have transferred to UC under the managed migration process and would otherwise be worse off than on legacy benefits. If you have transferred to UC under the natural migration process (or under the managed migration process but are not entitled to a transitional element) and you are entitled to a transitional SDP element as a result, this is treated as if it is part of your maximum amount. The DWP refers to both of these elements as 'transitional protection'.

Standard allowance rates 2025/26	*per month*
Single claimant	
Under 25	£316.98
25 or over	£400.14
Joint claimants	
Both under 25	£497.55
One or both 25 or over	£628.10

Element rates 2025/26	*per month*
First child born before 6 April 2017	£339.00
Second child/all children born on or after 6 April 2017	£292.81
Disabled child addition	
Lower rate	£158.76
Higher rate	£495.87
Limited capability for work	£158.76
Limited capability for work-related activity	£423.27
Carer	£201.68

Childcare costs		
One child		up to £1,031.88
Two or more children		up to £1,768.94

See CPAG's *Welfare Benefits Handbook* for the housing costs element and transitional element.

Even if your actual UC payment is low (or zero) because of deductions like advance payments or sanctions, your CTR should be based on the full, pre-deduction amount.

Because your UC amount can change monthly (eg, due to earnings or childcare), your CTR may also change frequently (this is called 'frequent reassessment'). Your local authority should get updates from the DWP via data sharing. It is also important to report changes in your circumstances.

If you get pension credit

If you get PC, your applicable amount is made up of:[33]

- a personal allowance based on whether you are single or in a couple; *and*
- additional amounts for at least the first two dependent children you are responsible for; *and*
- any premiums you or members of your family (see p159) qualify for, based on your circumstances or the benefits you receive.

See CPAG's *Welfare Benefits Handbook* for more information about applicable amounts. The rules for calculating applicable amounts for CTR are usually the same as those used in calculating HB.

Pension-age applicable amounts for 2025/26[34]

Personal allowances		***England****	***Wales***	***Scotland***
Single	Reached pension age	–	£244.40	£244.40
	(England only) reached pension age before 1 April 2021	£244.40	–	–
	(England only) reached pension age after 1 April 2021	£227.10	–	–
Couple	One or both pension age or over	–	£366.00	£366.00
	(England only) one or both pension age or over before 1 April 2021	£366.00	–	–
	Reached pension age after 1 April 2021	£346.60	–	–
Addtional amounts				
Dependent child/ young person*	Under 20	£84.66	£84.66	£105.85

Premiums				
Carer		£46.40	£46.40	£46.40
Disability	Single	–	£43.20	£43.20
	Couple	–	£61.65	£61.65
Disabled child		£81.37	£81.37	£81.37
Enhanced disability	Single	–	£21.20	£32.75
	Couple	–	£30.25	£30.25
	Child	£32.75	£32.75	£32.75
Severe disability	Someone is getting a carer benefit**	£82.90	£82.90	£82.90
	No one getting a carer payment	£165.80	£165.80	£165.80
Family***	Ordinary rate	£19.48	£19.48	£19.48

* In England, there is no 'two-child limit' for pension-age schemes from 1 April 2025.[35] In Wales and Scotland, there is no 'two-child limit'. Your applicable amount includes an allowance for each child or young person who is a member of your family.

** Carer's benefits are carer's allowance, carer support payment or UC which includes the carer element.

*** In England and Scotland, a family premium is not included in new applications from 1 May 2016.

If you get income-related employment and support allowance

Note: income-related ESA is in the process of being replaced by UC. The DWP plans to end income-related ESA by April 2026.

In Wales and Scotland, you do not need to work out your applicable amount if you are entitled to income-related ESA, as it 'passports' you to maximum CTR (see p158), providing you meet the eligibility conditions on p152. Any other income you have is ignored. Your maximum CTR may still have a deduction made for any non-dependant who lives with you (see p159). **Note**: if you get new-style contributory ESA, this does not passport you to maximum CTR.

If you do not get a means-tested benefit

If you have a low income but you do not get a means-tested benefit like UC or PC, your applicable amount is usually calculated using the same rules as for HB. See CPAG's *Welfare Benefits Handbook* for the amounts. Check with your council for specific guidance.

Income less than or equal to your applicable amount

In Scotland or Wales, or under the pension-age rules in England, you are entitled to full CTR (ie, your maximum CTR) if your weekly income is equal to, or less than, your applicable amount, and you meet the other qualifying conditions for main CTR (see p157).

If you or your partner get the guarantee credit of PC, all your income and capital are disregarded. This means your income is automatically treated as less than your applicable amount, so you get full CTR.

If you get income-related ESA, all of your income is disregarded.[36]

If you live in England and the working-age rules apply to you, how your main CTR is calculated depends on your local authority's CTR scheme. In many areas, you may get your maximum CTR if your income is equal to or less than your applicable amount, but note that maximum CTR might not cover your full council tax liability (see p156).

If CTR does not cover your full council tax liability and your remaining income is below your applicable amount, this cannot be appealed to the tribunal.[37]

Income greater than your applicable amount

In Scotland or Wales, or for the pension-age rules in England, if your income is greater than your applicable amount, work out the difference between the two amounts. Your weekly entitlement is reduced by 20p for each £1 of excess weekly income, until entitlement is withdrawn – this is known as the taper.

For the working-age rules in England, how main CTR is calculated depends on your local authority's CTR scheme. In many areas, a higher taper is applied. However, English local authorities may also set a lower taper, and some do.

Income

Your income is calculated on a weekly basis.[38] The local authority includes earned and unearned income which you and your partner have. This includes:

- wages from employment; *and*
- earnings from self-employment; *and*
- some social security benefits; *and*
- payments from a trust or a charity.

Tariff income is also included. This is the income you are assumed to have from savings or other capital assets. Your actual income from these sources is ignored (see p174).

If the pension-age rules apply to you (see p155), the regulations specify what counts as income. Any monies not listed in the regulations are ignored when calculating your income. Some income is fully or partially disregarded.[39]

If the working-age rules apply to you and you live in Wales or Scotland, all of your and your partner's income is taken into account unless it is specifically disregarded. Most English local authorities calculate the income of working-age applicants in this way too. If you get UC and the DWP shares your information with the local authority, then in general, the same amount of earned income used to calculate your UC award can be used to assess your CTR. It is converted into a weekly figure rather than a monthly one.

The rules for calculating income are complex and only an overview is given in this chapter (see p170). See CPAG's *Welfare Benefits Handbook* for further information. The rules for CTR often mirror those for HB.

Income rules for pension-age council tax reduction

If you get pension credit

If you or your partner get the **guarantee credit** element of PC, all of your income and capital is disregarded and you qualify for main CTR equal to your maximum CTR (see p158).[40]

If you or your partner get the **savings credit** element of PC but not the guarantee credit, the local authority calculates your income for CTR by using the DWP's assessment of your income for the savings credit of PC and adding the amount of the savings credit awarded. However, if you have earnings, the local authority deducts any childcare disregard you qualify for and it may disregard more of your earned income under the rules on p171.

If you do not get pension credit

If the pension-age rules apply to you but neither you nor your partner gets PC, your income is assessed by the local authority.

The following are defined as income for CTR, but some income may be disregarded when calculating your entitlement:[41]

- earnings from employment or self-employment (see p170 for how this is calculated and p171 for how much is disregarded). **Note**: statutory sick pay (SSP) and statutory maternity/adoption/paternity/shared parental/parental bereavement/neonatal care pay are treated as earnings;
- retirement pensions;
- income from annuities (the capital value of the annuity is ignored);
- war pensions. Any disability increases are disregarded in full; £10 of the war pension itself is also disregarded. In Wales, local authorities are given discretion to increase this disregard.[42] In England and Wales, check your council's policy;
- widow's pension and widowed parent's allowance (however, the first £15 of the latter is disregarded);
- certain other payments.

Some benefits are not counted as income. These include:

- HB;
- AA/PADP, DLA/SADLA/CDP, PIP/ADP and AFIP;
- child benefit and guardian's allowance;
- Scottish child payment;
- bereavement support payment;
- social fund payments and, in Scotland, funeral support payment;

- Christmas bonus;
- carer's allowance supplement (Scotland only);
- early years assistance.

Certain other income is disregarded, including the following.[43]

- £15 of any maintenance payments paid to you or your partner by a current or former spouse or civil partner. In Wales, this only applies if a family premium is included in your applicable amount. All maintenance paid for a child or young person is fully disregarded.
- Income from an annuity purchased with a loan secured on your home (a home income plan) if it is used to pay the interest on that loan.
- Certain contributions paid to your son or daughter aged under 25 while they are in education.
- Payments from a discretionary trust. However, if these are used to pay essential bills, there is a weekly limit on the amount that can be disregard.
- Compensation for personal injury – in some cases, including accidents or disease.
- The first £20 a week of income from a tenant or boarder who lives in your home is always disregarded. If you provide board and lodgings, 50 per cent of the remaining income is also disregarded.

Note: the disregards for maintenance and contributions to students listed above are subject to an overall limit of £20.

Income rules for working-age applicants

In Wales and Scotland, all of your income is counted, unless it is specifically disregarded. If you still get income-related ESA, all of your income and capital are disregarded and you are entitled to your maximum CTR (see p158).

In Wales and Scotland if you get UC (on your own or jointly with a partner), your local authority usually uses the DWP's income and capital assessment, and adds your UC entitlement to calculate your CTR. Any other income is disregarded.[44]

In Scotland, your local authority can estimate an average where your income fluctuates from week to week.[45]

In all other cases, the local authority makes its own assessment of your income. See p170 for how earned income is calculated, and p169 for the rules about income other than earnings. The rules set out below apply throughout Scotland and, with minor differences, in Wales. Local authorities in England have much more discretion when deciding how to assess income for working-age applicants. Most local authorities follow similar rules to those in Wales and Scotland, but they are not required to.

Benefits

Some benefits are not counted as income.[46] These include AA/PADP, DLA/SADLA/CDP, PIP/ADP, child benefit and Scottish child payment. Some benefits are partially disregarded – eg, the first £15 a week of widowed parent's allowance. Check your local scheme for a full list of disregards.

Other income

Other types of unearned income are disregarded.[47] Common examples include the following.

- Maintenance payments for children included in your family are fully disregarded, provided they are made by a liable relative – eg, the child's parent or step-parent.
- £15 a week of maintenance payments paid for you or your partner by a former partner can be disregarded. In Wales, this applies only if you qualify for a family premium.[48]
- Compensation for personal injury. In some cases, this includes for accidents or disease.
- The first £20 a week of income from a tenant or boarder who lives in your home is always disregarded. If you provide board and lodgings, 50 per cent of the remaining income is also disregarded.
- If you let property other than your own home:
  - if the capital value is disregarded, any rent used to pay the mortgage payments, council tax and water charges on the property are disregarded for the period covered by the rent. Any remaining rent counts as income, whether or not you have any other letting costs;
  - if the capital value is *not* disregarded, all letting costs can be deducted and the net rent counts as capital, not as income.[49] However, you are assumed to have 'tariff income' from the capital value of the property. The capital value is the property's market or surrender value minus 10 per cent if there would be costs involved in the sale, and minus any debts secured on it, such as a mortgage.[50] In most cases, if the property's capital value exceeds £16,000 (or a lower local limit), you are not likely to qualify for CTR. In some circumstances (eg, if you have a sitting tenant or there is 'planning blight'), you may be able to argue that the likely resale value is low.
- Any regular voluntary payments from charities or individuals (such as friends and family) are disregarded. One-off or irregular payments count as capital.
- Certain payments from public bodies, including local authority welfare provision, discretionary housing payments, social services payments and payments from government trusts are also disregarded.

For more details, see CPAG's *Welfare Benefits Handbook* (the rules for CTR usually mirror the HB rules).

Earned income

The rules below apply to pension-age applicants in England, Wales and Scotland and to working-age applicants in Wales and Scotland. English local authorities can set their own rules for working-age applicants, but they are often very similar.

Earnings are income from employment, self-employment or any office or position you hold. This includes all bonuses and commissions, payments in lieu of notice, holiday pay and retainers. If you live in Scotland or if the working-age rules apply to you and you live in Wales, holiday pay, which is paid more than four weeks after your employment ends, is not counted as earnings. SSP and statutory parental payments (eg, statutory maternity pay) are also treated as earnings.[51]

Weekly earnings from self-employment for pension-age applicants are averaged over a year (if your business is established) or over a shorter period if the business is new. If the pattern of the business changes, the period can be adjusted to best reflect your current income. If the working-age rules apply and you live in Scotland or Wales, your earnings from self-employment are calculated over a period that gives an accurate reflection of your weekly income, but the assessment period must not exceed 52 weeks.[52]

Expenses counted as earnings

Any expenses you receive that are not wholly incurred for doing your job, including travelling expenses between your home and place of employment, count as income.

Amounts not included as earnings from employment

The following are *not* included as income from employment for CTR purposes:[53]

- payments in kind – eg, free meals;
- reimbursed expenses that are wholly, exclusively and necessarily incurred in the performance of your job or employment;
- redundancy payments;
- occupational pensions;
- lump-sum payment made under the Iron and Steel Employees Re-adaptation Benefits Scheme (pension-age applicants only);
- compensation awarded by an employment tribunal for unfair dismissal or unlawful discrimination (pension-age applicants only; may count as earnings for working-age applicants in Scotland or Wales);
- payments for involvement with service user groups – eg, those consulted by public bodies or health boards;
- some non-cash vouchers.

Earnings are assessed net of tax and national insurance (NI).

Sums disregarded from earnings

An amount may be disregarded from your earnings – ie, some of your earnings are ignored. The amount depends on your circumstances. The main disregards are:[54]

- £5 a week for a single person; *or*
- £10 a week for a couple; *or*
- £20 a week if you get the disability premium, severe disability premium, carer premium or a component in your applicable amount, or you have an award of UC and have LCW or LCWRA; *or*
- £25 a week for a lone parent.

Only the highest disregard that applied to you is used, *plus* an additional £17.10 a week disregard if:[55]

- you or your partner:
  - are 25 or over and work at least 30 hours a week; *or*
  - work at least 16 hours a week and your applicable amount includes a child premium; *or*
  - work at least 16 hours a week and qualify for the disability premium or a component in your applicable amount; *or*
- you are a lone parent working at least 16 hours a week.

Note: in Scotland, the £17.10 disregard does not apply if you get UC.

If you and your partner both work, the disregard normally applies to your combined earnings. The disregards apply to pension-age applicants in England, Wales and Scotland. They also apply to working-age applicants in Wales and Scotland. Local authorities in England have discretion to use higher or lower disregards for working-age applicants or not to apply a disregard at all.

You may qualify for an earnings disregard in some other circumstances – eg, if you are treated as not having LCW, you are doing exempt or permitted work, or you are a part-time firefighter. Get advice if these apply to you.

Childcare costs disregarded

In some circumstances, the amount you pay for childcare can also be disregarded from your earnings, subject to a weekly maximum.

In England, Wales or Scotland, if the pension-age rules apply to you, or if you are a working-age applicant in Wales or Scotland, the full amount of your eligible childcare costs can be disregarded up to the following weekly maximums:[56]

- £175 for one child (in Scotland, £280 if you get UC);
- £300 for two or more children (in Scotland, £479 if you get UC).

If you are a working-age applicant in England, there is no requirement for your local authority to disregard any amount for childcare costs.

Eligible childcare costs are those you pay to a registered childcare provider, after school club or other approved provider specified in the regulations. The child must be part of your CTR family (see p159).[57] To be eligible, you must be:

- a lone parent working 16 hours or more a week; *or*
- part of a couple, both working 16 hours a week or more; *or*
- part of a couple, one working 16 hours a week or more, provided that the other partner is:
  - incapacitated – eg, they qualify for the disability premium or a component in your applicable amount, or get a disability benefit or main phase ESA, or certain other benefits; *or*
  - in hospital or similar institution; *or*
  - in prison.

In some cases, you can be treated as working 16 hours a week – eg, for up to 28 weeks if you are getting SSP or ESA and were working at least 16 hours a week immediately before.

You can get a childcare disregard until the Sunday before the first Monday in September after the child's 15th birthday, or after their 16th birthday if the child is disabled. A child is considered disabled if they get the care component of DLA/CDP (in Scotland, either component counts), the daily living component of PIP/ADP (in Scotland, either component counts) or are registered severely sight impaired or blind.

Capital

If the pension-age rules apply to you, you cannot qualify for main CTR if you (and your partner) have capital over £16,000, unless you or your partner receive the guarantee credit of PC. In Scotland, this also applies to band E–H CTR.

The £16,000 capital limit also applies to working-age applicants in Wales and Scotland.[58] Local authorities in England can set a different capital limit for working-age applicants.

Some types of capital are ignored permanently or temporarily. All of your capital is ignored if:[59]

- you (or your partner) get the guarantee credit of PC (see p158); *or*
- in Wales or Scotland, you (or your partner) get income-related ESA. In England, this depends on the working-age rules in your area.

In Wales and Scotland, if you get UC (or you jointly get UC with your partner), your local authority must use the DWP's capital figure – ie, the one used to calculate your UC.[60]

If you do not provide enough information, the council may estimate your capital.

What counts as capital

The term 'capital' is not defined. In general, it means lump-sum or one-off payments rather than a series of payments – eg, it includes savings, property and statutory redundancy payments.

If you have two accounts with the same bank, and one is in credit while the other is overdrawn, the overdraft can be offset against the account in credit to calculate your net capital.[61]

If you jointly own a capital asset with someone else under a joint tenancy arrangement, you and the other owner(s) are treated as owning it in equal shares; if you own it as tenants in common, it is the value of your actual share that is counted.[62] See CPAG's *Welfare Benefits Handbook* for further information on the treatment of jointly owned capital. The rules are similar to those for HB.

Disregarded capital

Some capital is disregarded for a fixed period, some indefinitely. Disregarded capital includes:[63]

- the value of any personal possessions;
- the value of the home you live in (but not more than one home);
- insurance policy payouts for loss or damage to your home or personal possessions, for one year;
- assets from a former business if you are in the process of disposing of them;
- premises acquired that you intend to live in within 26 weeks of the date of acquisition (or longer if reasonable);
- premises needing essential repairs or alterations before you can live there you intend live in, for a period of 26 weeks from the date you first take steps to carry out the repairs, or as long as is needed for them to be completed;
- premises occupied in whole or in part by a relative who is over pension age (see p155) or is incapacitated;
- premises occupied by a former partner as their home, in specified circumstances;
- any case where you are taking reasonable steps to dispose of an interest in capital – eg, selling your home to pay for care costs or entering sheltered accommodation, for 26 weeks or longer if reasonable;
- certain business assets.

Rules differentiate between capital in the UK and outside it. See CPAG's *Welfare Benefits Handbook* for more information.

Notional capital

In certain circumstances, you may be treated as having capital that you do not actually have. You are treated as still having capital you have deliberately disposed of – usually to qualify for CTR or increase the amount of CTR you receive.[64] Some local authorities have been known to decide that applicants have done this simply because their savings have been reduced prior to an application. However, for this rule to apply the local authority has to prove, on the balance of probabilities, that you deliberately intended to reduce your capital to get or increase your CTR.

The regulations specify for pension-age applicants (and you can argue it should also apply to working-age applicants) that you should not be treated as depriving yourself of capital, if you dispose of it to:[65]

- reduce or pay debts – eg, credit cards, loans or rent arrears; *or*
- purchase goods or services, if the expenditure is reasonable – eg, paying for essential dental work or buying a second-hand car if you need it for work.

These are not seen as deliberate deprivation even if they reduce your capital below the £16,000 threshold.

If you are treated as having notional capital, the amount of it reduces over time as though you were spending it to meet your living costs. This is called the 'diminishing notional capital rule'.[66] The notional capital figure drops weekly/monthly, reducing its impact on your CTR over time. Eventually, it disappears entirely, and you are no longer affected.

In England, the working-age rules on notional capital and diminishing notional capital depend on your local authority's CTR scheme.

Tariff income from capital

When calculating your income, the local authority includes a notional (assumed) figure for the income you are 'deemed' to derive from any capital you and your partner have that is not ignored. This 'tariff income' is worked out in the following way.[67]

- If you are a pensioner: the first £10,000 of your capital is ignored and you are assumed to earn £1 from each £500 of capital or part of £500 you have above £10,000.
- If you are a working-age applicant in Wales or Scotland, the first £6,000 of your capital is ignored and you are assumed to earn £1 for each £250 of capital or part of £250 you have above £6,000. In England, any capital limits and tariff income rules are set by your local authority.

In England for working-age applicants, different capital limits apply – eg, in some cases if your capital is over £6,000 you will not qualify for CTR. Check your local authority's capital rules.

Example

Elis (37) lives in Wales. He has capital of £7,100. This is £1,100 over the £6,000 limit.

£1,100 ÷ £250 = 4.4. This is rounded up to five.

Elis is deemed to receive £5 a week in tariff income.

Calculating weekly income

All income for CTR is calculated on a weekly basis. If your earnings and other income are paid in any other frequency, they have to be converted into a weekly amount.[68]

Payment frequency	*How to convert to weekly income*
Calendar month	Multiply the amount by 12, then divide by 52
Every three months	Multiply the amount by four, then divide by 52
Annually (one a year)	Divide the amount by 52
Any other period	Divide the payment amount by the number of days it covers, then multiply the result by seven

6. Alternative maximum council tax reduction (second adult rebate)

In **England and Scotland**, alternative maximum council tax reduction (also known as 'second adult rebate') is a form of council tax reduction (CTR) designed to help if:[69]

- you are liable to pay council tax; *and*
- you share your home with one or more adults (the 'second adults'). A second adult is someone who:
  - lives in your household; *and*
  - is not your partner; *and*
  - is not jointly liable for council tax; *and*
  - does not pay you rent; *and*
- the second adult is on a low income.

There is no second adult rebate in Wales.

Examples include an adult son or daughter, a friend or relative staying with you.

Second adult rebate can be received instead of, but not as well as, main CTR (or, in Scotland, band E–H CTR). When you apply for CTR, the local authority must assess your entitlement to each type and award whichever is the higher – sometimes referred to as the 'best buy'.[70]

You qualify for a second adult rebate if:[71]

- you live in Scotland or, if the pension-age rules apply to you (see 155), you live in England; *and*
- you meet the general rules which apply to all types of CTR, described on p152; *and*

- you are the only person liable for the council tax on the home (with certain exceptions – see p80); *and*
- no one living in your home is liable to pay you rent; *and*
- you have one or more second adults living with you on a low income (see p177).

In England, if the working-age rules apply to you, whether you can get second adult rebate depends on your local authority's CTR scheme.

Note: second adult rebate is based on the second adult's circumstances, not *your* income and capital. Therefore, you can usually get second adult rebate even if you have a high income and/or capital over £16,000, or if you are a student who is liable to pay council tax.

Example

Priya owns her own home and earns £40,000 a year. She is liable for council tax of £1,125 a year after her 25 per cent single occupier discount. Her income is too high for her to qualify for main CTR. When her adult son, Zac, who is on a low income, moves in with her, Priya loses her single occupier discount. Her council tax liability is now £1,500. Because Zac is a second adult and not financially dependent on her, Priya is eligible for a second adult rebate.

Who does not count as a second adult

Someone living with you does not count as a second adult if they are:[72]

- aged under 18; *or*
- disregarded for council tax purposes (see p118); *or*
- your partner with whom you are jointly liable for council tax; *or*
- jointly liable to pay the council tax with you – eg, they are a joint tenant or joint owner. Although you cannot get second adult rebate for them, they may be able to claim main CTR for their own share of the bill.

Examples

Connor owns his home. His mother lives with him and gets the guarantee credit of pension credit (PC). Connor is liable for council tax and can apply for second adult rebate, as his mother is not liable for council tax and does not pay rent.

Emma lives with her partner, who is a full-time student and is disregarded for council tax. Emma's two adult children live with them. The daughter (20) is unemployed and gets universal credit (UC). The son (25) is in low-paid employment. Emma is the only one liable for council tax and may qualify for the second adult rebate, as the adult daughter and son are second adults.

Calculating second adult rebate

The amount of second adult rebate you get is a percentage of your council tax liability, after any disability reduction has been deducted. The percentage is based on the gross income of the second adult. If there is more than one second adult, their combined gross income is used. Any PC, income-related employment and support allowance (ESA) or, in Scotland, UC with no earned income a second adult gets is not counted when calculating their income. You can get a 100 per cent rebate if the second adult gets one of these benefits and everyone else (including you) is a student.

Amount of second adult rebate 2025/26 [73]

Income of second adult(s)	***Second adult rebate***
Second adult(s) on PC or income-related ESA	25 per cent
Second adult(s) on UC and has no earned income (Scotland)	25 per cent
In Scotland, if the pension-age rules apply, second adult(s) on UC	25 per cent
Second adult(s) total gross weekly income:	
Below £276 in England or £269 in Scotland	15 per cent
£276–£357.99 in England or £269–£364.99 in Scotland	7.5 per cent
£358 and over in England or £365 and over in Scotland	Nil
Student dwellings:	
All occupiers are either students excluded from entitlement to main CTR (see below) or on income-related ESA/PC. At least one must be a student and at least one on ESA/PC.	100 per cent

If you are jointly liable for the council tax with someone who is not your partner, the amount of second adult rebate is divided by the number of people liable, and you get your equal share of it.

Example

Oscar and Adam are joint tenants and are both liable for council tax. Oscar's mother (a second adult) gets PC and lives with them. The total second adult rebate is 25 per cent, but as there are two liable residents, Oscar gets 12.5 per cent.

Someone counts as a student excluded from entitlement to main CTR if they would be excluded if they were under pension age (see p155).

Unless you qualify for a 100 per cent second adult rebate, the maximum second adult rebate you can get is always 25 per cent of your council tax liability, even if you would have received a 50 per cent council tax discount, or would have been exempt from council tax altogether, were it not for the presence of two or more second adults in your home.

Certain income of a second adult can be ignored. This includes any personal independence payment, adult disability payment, disability living allowance, Scottish adult disability living allowance, child disability payment, attendance allowance or pension age disability payment they receive.[74]

Example

Ayla is the tenant of her flat. She is in a well-paid job, so lets her friend Josie stay with her without charging her rent. Josie earns £190 a week. Ayla's second adult rebate is 15 per cent of her council tax liability.

7. Band E–H council tax reduction: Scotland

If you live in a band E, F, G or H property in Scotland, you may qualify for a special type of council tax reduction (CTR), even if your income is higher than the usual CTR threshold. You qualify if:[75]

- you meet the general conditions for all CTR schemes on p152; *and*
- your property is in in council tax band E, F, G or H; *and*
- you and your partner do not have capital of more than £16,000, unless you or your partner get the guarantee credit of pension credit (PC); *and*
- the amount of band E–H CTR you would qualify for is more than the amount of main CTR or second adult rebate you would get (otherwise you get main CTR or second adult rebate instead).

Note: if you are a full-time student and the working-age rules apply, you cannot qualify for band E–H CTR unless you fall into an excepted group – eg, a lone parent or a student couple with dependent children.[76] If you are not entitled to CTR because of this rule but your partner is not a student, they may qualify for CTR instead.

Calculating band E–H council tax reduction

Entitlement to band E–H CTR depends on how your weekly income compares to a set threshold.[77]

Household type	***Income threshold***
Single person	£321 a week
Lone parent with dependent child(ren)	£479 a week
Couple (with or without dependent children)	£479 a week

If your weekly income is equal to or less than the relevant threshold, you qualify for maximum band E–H CTR (see below).

If your weekly income is more than either the relevant threshold, calculate the excess income (your income minus the threshold). Your band E–H CTR is calculated by deducting 20 per cent of the excess from your maximum CTR for a band E–H property (see below).

Your income and capital are assessed in the same way as for main CTR (see p166 and p172) and if you or your partner get the guarantee credit of PC, or if you get income-related employment and support allowance, you are treated as if you have no income, as all of your income is disregarded and you receive maximum band E–H CTR (but, in most cases, you woud qualify for a higher amount under main CTR, which will be awarded instead).

See p168 for how your income is calculated if you or your partner get universal credit.

Maximum council tax reduction for band E–H property

Follow these steps to calculate your weekly maximum CTR for band E–H CTR.

Step 1: calculate your council tax liability without CTR. This is the annual council tax due on your property after deducting any discount or disability reduction. If you are jointly liable for the council tax with someone who is not your partner, divide the result equally between you.

Step 2: divide the amount from Step 1 by:

- 1.075 if your property is in council tax band E;
- 1.125 if your property is in council tax band F;
- 1.175 if your property is in council tax band G;
- 1.225 if your property is in council tax band H.

This gives the band D equivalent charge.

Step 3: deduct the figure obtained in Step 2 from the figure obtained in Step 1, divide the answer by the number of days in the tax year and multiply by seven to get your weekly maximum CTR.

8. Extended and continuing reductions

In some cases, your main council tax reduction (CTR), second adult rebate or band E–H CTR can continue at the same rate for four weeks after you or your partner stop getting certain benefits, because you start work or your earnings or hours of work increase, or because you move onto pension credit (PC).

This applies to pension-age applicants in England, Wales and Scotland, and to working-age appliants in Wales and Scotland. Check your local scheme if you are a working-age applicant in England.

Extended reduction

If you are entitled to CTR, you may qualify for an extended reduction if you or your partner have been on employment and support allowance (ESA) for at least 26 weeks and this ends because you start work or increase your hours or pay (and the increase is expected to last at least five weeks).[78]

If you qualify, you receive the same amount of CTR as you did before the change, for up to four weeks (in England, the amount depends on your local scheme). This only applies if it exceeds the amount of CTR you or your partner would get based on your new income. After four weeks, your CTR is recalculated based on your updated financial circumstances.

Report the change in your circumstances to your local authority, and it will assess whether you are entitled.

Continuing reduction on claiming pension credit

To avoid delays in reassessing your CTR when you move from income-related ESA onto PC, provided you otherwise continue to qualify for CTR you continue to receive it, normally at the same rate as before this happened, for a period of four weeks.[79] You qualify for a continuing reduction if:

- your partner has claimed PC and the DWP has certified this; *or*
- your income-related ESA ceased because you reached pension age (see p155). The DWP must certify this and that you are required to claim or have claimed PC (or are treated as having done so).

9. Applications, decisions and awards

You should apply for council tax reduction (CTR) as soon as you think you might be entitled.

If you are not eligible, you may still apply for a discretionary reduction (see p135).

Do you get universal credit?

CTR is not included in your universal credit (UC) claim, even if you get the housing element of UC. You need to apply directly to your local council.

Making an application

You can make an application for CTR:[80]

- in writing on a properly completed application form (available from your local authority or its website); *or*
- online (Scottish councils do not need to make this option available); *or*
- by phone, if the local authority has published a number for this purpose.

If you are applying in writing, you must apply to your local authority's designated office. You must provide any information and evidence reasonably required. You can claim in some other written form (eg, by letter), as long as it contains all necessary information and evidence. An application made on a form provided by a local authority is properly completed if it is completed in accordance with the instructions on the form, including providing information and evidence.[81]

In England and Wales, in most cases, you must provide your (and you partner's) national insurance (NI) number, or provide information to allow the local authority to trace your NI number, or you must apply for an NI number and show that you have made the application and provide the evidence required to allow one to be allocated.[82]

In Scotland, a local authority can treat information in a UC application as an application for CTR, if you have a liability for council tax.[83]

Check with the local authority that your application has been received. If you apply in writing, keep a copy of your application and proof of posting or receipt.

Applying in advance

Unless you live abroad, you can apply in advance if you think you are going to become eligible for CTR in the future – eg, because you know that you are going to have a drop in income or will become liable for council tax.

If you are not yet liable for council tax but will become liable within eight weeks (in England or Scotland) or 13 weeks (in Wales), and you make an application for CTR at any time within that time, the local authority should treat your CTR application as made on the date your council tax liability starts.[84]

In England, if the pension-age rules apply to you, you can apply up to 17 weeks before you become eligible for CTR. In England or Scotland, you can also apply up to 17 weeks in advance if you or your partner will reach pension age (see p155) within 17 weeks. If you live in Wales, or if the working-age rules apply to you and you live in England or Scotland, you can make an application up to 13 weeks before you become eligible for CTR.[85]

Providing further information

Your claim start date is usually based on when your application is received, not when you provide all your evidence. You should submit your application as soon as possible, even if you do not yet have all the required evidence. If the local authority requests further information, you must supply it within one month of the request, or within a longer period if the council considers it reasonable.[86]

Applications by couples

If you are part of a couple (see p149), either of you can apply for CTR. Who applies should be agreed between you. If you cannot agree, the local authority may decide who is the applicant.[87] **Note:** in some cases, who makes the application can affect your entitlement – eg, if you have limited capability for work-related activity but your partner does not, an enhanced disability premium is only included in your applicable amount if you are the applicant.

Amending and withdrawing applications

You may amend your application at any time before a decision is made on it. This allows you to include new information or changes in circumstances or to correct any errors. Any amendments are treated as if they were included in your original application.

You may withdraw your application at any time before a decision is made. A notice of withdrawal has effect from when the local authority receives it.

Notification of decisions

In England and Wales, your local authority must make its decision within 14 days, or as soon as reasonably practicable after that. It must notify you and any other person affected of the decision in writing.[88]

Backdating

CTR can be backdated in some situations. If you are a **working-age** applicant:

- in England, check your local authority's CTR scheme for details;
- in Wales, as a minimum, your local authority must allow up to three months' backdating if you have continuous good cause for your late application. Local authorities are permitted to allow longer and may also set more generous criteria for backdating;[89]
- in Scotland, your application can be backdated for up to six months if you have continuous good cause for your late application.[90]

Examples of good cause include being too ill to claim or being wrongly advised.

If you are **pension age**, CTR can be backdated for up to three months from the date you applied, so long as you were entitled throughout. There is no need to show good cause.[91] This can be extended where you have made a claim for the guarantee credit of pension credit (PC) and apply for CTR within one month of this claim being awarded, but your award of CTR cannot begin more than three months before your claim for PC was made.[92]

Reporting changes in circumstances

You must report any change in your circumstances that you might reasonably be expected to know might affect your right to, or the amount of, CTR.[93] You, or someone acting on your behalf, must notify the authority of any changes between the making of an application and a decision being made on it. After the decision is made, you must report any changes while you are receiving CTR.

Examples of changes that you must inform the local authority about

You change your address.

Someone joins or leaves your household.

The income or capital of anyone in the property changes so as to affect your CTR.

There is a change in benefits you receive.

Someone in the property starts or stops employment.

The ownership of the property changes.

In England and Wales, you must report the change within 21 days of the change occurring or, if later, as soon as reasonably practicable after the change occurs.[94] In Scotland, there is no set time limit to report changes. Do this promptly to the office handling your application. It is always best to report a change in writing and keep a copy. You can also report a change by phone, online or by email, if permitted by your local authority.

You may be able to report a birth or death using the Tell Us Once service. Ask your local register office whether this is available in your area.

If you fail to report a change in circumstances, your CTR may be stopped and you become liable to pay the tax for the period concerned. If you are considered to have deliberately acted falsely or dishonestly, you may be prosecuted for an offence.

If you move to a new local authority area, report this change to your old authority and apply for CTR from your new local authority.

Note: whether a delay in reporting a change is reasonable depends on the circumstances. For example, if a mental health problem makes it hard for you to deal with your finances, it may be reasonable that it takes you longer to report changes. However, if support was available (eg, from a friend or adviser) and you did not use it, a delay is less likely to be considered reasonable.

If you have been awarded too much council tax reduction

CTR is not a payment to you – it is a reduction in your council tax liability. Therefore, if you are awarded too much CTR, there is no legal concept of 'overpayment', just an adjustment in liability. Your local authority will recalculate your CTR and increase your council tax liability to reflect the correct amount.

In England and Wales, this applies even if the council made the error, unless its local CTR scheme says otherwise. You could apply for a discretionary reduction (see p186) if you cannot afford to pay the increased council tax.

In Scotland, if you were awarded too much CTR for a past period (called an 'overentitlement'), any council tax arrears which resulted from the adjustment of your CTR cannot be recovered from you if:[95]

- the error was the local authority's fault (or someone acting on its behalf); *and*
- you did not cause or 'materially contribute to' the mistake; *and*
- you could not reasonably have known that you were getting too much CTR, either at the time or when later notified of your entitlement.

When your entitlement ends

Your CTR award continues indefinitely, and you do not need to reapply every year. However, if your circumstances change and you no longer qualify for CTR, it normally ends on the Sunday on or after the change occurs if you live in England and the pension-age rules apply to you or if you live in Scotland. In Wales, your CTR ends on the date the change occurs.[96]

---

10. If you disagree with a council tax reduction decision

Challenging a decision about your council tax reduction

England and Wales

You have a right to appeal decisions made by the local authority about:[97]

- whether you are entitled to council tax reduction (CTR);
- the amount of CTR you have been awarded;
- discretionary decisions under section 13A of the Local Government Finance Act 1992 (see p135).[98]

Your local authority scheme should include details of your appeal rights. This information should also be included in the written decision you receive about your CTR award.[99]

Before you can appeal a decision, you must first write to the local authority to explain what you disagree with and why – eg, you disagree with the amount of CTR awarded because the council has established the wrong facts or did not apply the regulations properly. This may be referred to as a 'notice of appeal'. The authority must respond in writing either rejecting your challenge, with reasons, or stating the steps it will take to resolve the issue – eg, looking at the matter again, or awarding the reduction to which you are entitled.[100]

There are time limits.

- In England, because CTR and housing benefit (HB) are administered together, if you are challenging a decision that affects both, it makes sense to write to the local authority within one month of the decision (the time limit to ask the authority to revise its HB decision). In other cases, it is advisable to do so within a month, or if a time limit is given in your local authority's CTR scheme, within that time limit. However, as there is no time limit given in the legislation, if

your local authority refuses to consider your notice of appeal on the grounds that it is late, seek advice.
- In Wales, the time limit for submitting your notice of appeal is one month from the date of the decision or of the written explanation of that decision.[101]

If you are not satisfied with the local authority's response, or if it fails to respond within two months, you can appeal to the Valuation Tribunal for England or the Valuation Tribunal for Wales. You should do this within a further two months (see Chapter 11).[102]

If you do not start your appeal within this time limit, the valuation tribunal may dismiss your appeal, unless you can show there were reasons beyond your control which prevented you from doing so.[103]

In exceptional cases, you may be able to apply to the High Court for judicial review if the local authority failed to properly consider your application and did not follow a lawful review process (see p318).[104]

Scotland

If you disagree with a decision your local authority has made about your CTR application, you can ask it to review its decision. You must request a review within two months of the decision date, stating what you disagree with and why.[105]

The local authority must respond in writing within two months of receiving your request, either by revising the decision or confirming it remains the same.[106]

If you are still dissatisfied after the review, or if the council fails to respond within two months,[107] you can apply for a further review by the Local Taxation Chamber (LTC) (part of the First-tier Tribunal for Scotland).

You appeal to the LTC in writing, preferably using Form D (available from localtaxationchamber.scot/apply). You must submit it within 42 days of the local authority's review decision notification. You appeal must include:[108]
- your name, address and email; *and*
- the name, address and email of your representative, if you have one; *and*
- where applicable, any other specified address (which can be an email address) for receipt of any documents from the LTC in connection with the appeal; *and*
- a clear statement that it is a 'notice of appeal'; *and*
- your reasons (grounds) for the appeal; *and*
- a statement saying if you want a hearing; *and*
- any supporting evidence; *and*
- your (or your representative's) signature; *and*
- a copy of your review request to the council and its review decision (if received).

If you miss the 42-day time limit, explain why your appeal is late. The LTC must treat any such statement as a request for extending that time limit.[109]

Challenging the local authority's scheme

If you want to challenge the local authority's CTR scheme (eg, because you think the scheme's content or the way it was adopted is unlawful), you can only do so by judicial review.[110] For information on judicial reviews, see p318.

11. Discretionary reductions

In England and Wales, local authorities have the additional discretionary power to reduce the amount of council tax owed in any individual case under section 13A of the Local Government Finance Act 1992. See p135 for the details.

Notes

1. **What is council tax reduction**
1 **E** s13A (2)(a) and (b) LGFA 1992
W s13A(i)(c) LGFA 1992
R (Winder & Ors) v Sandwell MBC [2014] EWHC 2617 (Admin)
2 **E** Sch 1A para 2 LGFA 1992
W Sch 1B para 3(7) LGFA 1992; reg 14 CTRSPR(W) Regs
3 **E** Reg 2 and 6 CTRS(PR)(E) Regs
W Reg 2 and 6 CTRSPR(W) Regs
S Reg 6 CTR(S) Regs; regs 2 and 4 CTR(SPC)(S) Regs
4 **E** Reg 4 CTRS(PR)(E) Regs
W Reg 4 CTRSPR(W) Regs
S Reg 5 CTR(S) Regs; reg 2 CTR(SPC)(S) Regs
5 **E** Reg 5 and Sch 1 paras 4, 8 and 11 CTRS(PR)(E) Regs
W Regs 5 and 9 and Schs 1 and 6 CTRSPR(W) Regs
S Reg 5 CTR(S) Regs; regs 8, 21 and 48 CTR(SPC)(S) Regs
6 **E** Reg 14 and Sch 1 paras 1-4 CTRS(PR)(E) Regs
W Regs 21-25 CTRSPR(W) Regs
S Reg 47 CTR(S) Regs
7 **E** CTRS(PR)(E) Regs
W CTRSPR(W) Regs
8 **E** Sch 1A para 5(1) LGFA 1992
W Reg 18 CTRSPR(W) Regs
9 s66(2)(ba) LGFA 1992

2. **Eligibility conditions**
10 **E** s13A(1) LGFA 1992; regs 11(2), 12, 13 and Sch 8 para 7 CTRS(PR)(E) Regs
W s13A(1) LGFA 1992; regs 28-30 CTRSPR(W) Regs
S s80 LGFA 1992; regs 16, 19 and 66 CTR(S) Regs; regs 16, 19 and 40 CTR(SPC)(S) Regs
11 *R (on the application of Williams) v Horsham DC* [2004] *The Times*, 29 January
12 R(H) 9/05
13 **E** Sch 1 para 5 CTRS(PR)(E) Regs
W Reg 26 CTRSPR(W) Regs
S Reg 15(3) CTR(S) Regs; reg 15(3) CTR(SPC)(S) Regs
14 **E** Sch 1 para 5(2) and (3)(i) CTRS(PR)(E) Regs
W Reg 26(2)(a) and (3)(i) CTRSPR(W) Regs
S Reg 15 CTR(S) Regs; reg 15 CTR(SPC)(S) Regs
15 **E** Reg 13 CTRS(PR)(E) Regs
W Reg 29 CTRSPR(W) Regs; Sch para 20 CTRS(DS)(W) Regs
S Reg 19 CTR(SPC)(S) Regs; reg 19 CTR(S) Regs
16 Reg 19(2) CTR(SPC)(S) Regs; reg 19(2) CTR(S) Regs

3. Pension-age rules

17 **E** Reg 14 and Sch 1 paras 1-4 CTRS(PR)(E) Regs
W Regs 21-25 CTRSPR(W) Regs

18 **E** Reg 3 CTRS(PR)(E) Regs
W Reg 3 CTRSPR(W) Regs
S Reg 3 CTR(S) Regs; reg 12 CTR(SPC)(S) Regs

4. Working-age rules

19 **E** Reg 3(b) CTRS(PR)(E) Regs
W Reg 3(b) CTRSPR(W) Regs
S Reg 3 CTR(S) Regs

20 s13A(2) and Sch 1A para 2 LGFA 1992

5. Main council tax reduction

21 **W** Regs 22-25 and 31 and Sch 11 CTRSPR(W) Regs
S Regs 14(3)(b) and 20 CTR(S) Regs

22 **E** Sch 1 para 7 CTRS(PR)(E) Regs
W Sch 1 para 2 and Sch 6 para 4 CTRSPR(W) Regs; reg 27(1) CTRS(DS)(W) Regs
S Reg 79(4) CTR(S) Regs; reg 47 CTR(SPC)(S) Regs

23 **E** Sch 1 para 7(3)-(5) CTRS(PR)(E) Regs
W Sch 1 para 2(3)-(5) and Sch 6 para 4(3)-(5) CTRSPR(W) Regs
S Reg 79(2), (4) and (5) CTR(S) Regs; reg 47(2) and (3) CTR(SPC)(S) Regs

24 **E** Reg 6 CTRS(PR)(E) Regs
W Reg 6 CTRSPR(W) Regs
S Reg 12 CTR(S) Regs; reg 2 CTR(SPC)(S) Regs

25 **E** Reg 7 CTRS(PR)(E) Regs
W Reg 7 CTRSPR(W) Regs
S Reg 7 CTR(S) Regs; reg 10 CTR(SPC)(S) Regs

26 **E** Reg 8 CTRS(PR)(E) Regs
W Reg 8 CTRSPR(W) Regs
S Reg 12 CTR(S) Regs; reg 11 CTR(SPC)(S) Regs

27 **E** Reg 9 CTRS(PR)(E) Regs
W Reg 9 CTRSPR(W) Regs
S Reg 90 CTR(S) Regs; reg 3 CTR(SPC)(S) Regs

28 **E** Sch 1 para 8(6) CTRS(PR)(E) Regs
W Sch 1 para 3(6) and Sch 6 para 5(6) CTRSPR(W) Regs
S Reg 90(6) CTR(S) Regs; reg 48(6) CTR(SPC)(S) Regs

29 **E** Sch 1 paras 7 and 8 CTRS(PR)(E) Regs
W Sch 1 para 3(7) and (8) and Sch 6 para 5(7) and (8) CTRSPR(W) Regs
S Reg 90(7) and (8) CTR(S) Regs; reg 48(7) and (8) CTR(SPC)(S) Regs

30 **E** Sch 1 para 8 CTRS(PR)(E) Regs
W Sch 1 para 3 and Sch 6 para 5 CTRSPR(W) Regs
S Reg 90(1) CTR(S) Regs; reg 48(1) CTRS(SPC)(S) Regs

31 **E** Sch 1 para 8 CTRS(PR)(E) Regs
W Sch 1 para 3(9) and Sch 6 para 5(9) CTRSPR(W) Regs; reg 28(9) CTRS(DS)(W) Regs
S Reg 67(9) CTR(S) Regs; reg 48(9) CTR(SPC)(S) Regs

32 **W** Sch 6 para 3 CTRSPR(W) Regs
S Reg 35 CTR(S) Regs

33 **E** Sch 1 para 6 CTRS(PR)(E) Regs
W Sch 1 para 1 and Sch 6 paras 1-3 CTRSPR(W) Regs; regs 23-25 CTRS(DS)(W) Regs
S Reg 20 CTR(SPC)(S) Regs

34 **E** Sch 2 CTRS(PR)(E) Regs
W Sch 2 CTRSPR(W) Regs; Sch 3 CTRS(DS)(W) Regs
S Sch 1 CTR(S) Regs; Sch 1 CTR(SPC)(S) Regs

35 Reg 5(2) Council Tax Reduction Schemes (Prescribed Requirements) (England) Regulations 2025 No.39

36 **W** Sch 8 para 14 and Sch 9 para 8 CTRSPR(W) Regs
S Sch 3 para 16 CTR(S) Regs

37 *Sakar v LB Hackney* [2024] EWHC 2081

38 **E** Sch 1 para 17 CTRS(PR)(E) Regs
W Sch 1 paras 11 and 18 and Sch 6 para 20 CTRSPR(W) Regs
S Regs 38 and 42 CTR(S) Regs; reg 28 CTR(SPC)(S) Regs

39 **E** Sch 1 para 16(3) CTRS(PR)(E) Regs
W Sch 1 CTRSPR(W) Regs
S Regs 27-33 CTR(SPC)(S) Regs

40 **E** Sch 1 para 13 CTRS(PR)(E) Regs
W Sch 1 para 7 CTRSPR(W) Regs
S Reg 24 CTR(SPC)(S) Regs

41 **E** Sch 5 CTRS(PR)(E) Regs
W Sch 4 CTRSPR(W) Regs
S Sch 3 CTR(SPC)(S) Regs

42 Reg 34 CTRSPR(W) Regs

43 **E** Sch 5 CTRS(PR)(E) Regs
W Sch 4 CTRSPR(W) Regs
S Sch 3 CTR(SPC)(S) Regs

44 **W** Sch 6 para 9 CTRSPR(W) Regs
S Reg 42 CTR(S) Regs

45 Regs 40 and 43 CTR(S) Regs

46 **W**Sch 6 para 17(2) and Sch 9 CTRSPR(W) Regs
S Reg 57 CTR(S) Regs

47 **W** Sch 9 CTRSPR(W) Regs
S Regs 57-63 CTR(S) Regs

48 Sch 9 para 49 CTRSPR(W) Regs

49 **W** Sch 6 para 27(5) CTRSPR(W) Regs
S Reg 67 CTR(S) Regs
50 **W** Sch 6 para 28 CTRSPR(W) Regs
S Reg 70 CTR(S) Regs
51 **E** Sch 1 paras 18 and 23 CTRS(PR)(E) Regs
W Sch 1 para 12 and Sch 6 para 14 CTRSPR(W) Regs
S Regs 49(4) and 50(2)(j) CTR(S) Regs; reg 32 CTR(SPC)(S) Regs
52 **E** Sch 1 para 20 CTRS(PR)(E) Regs
W Sch 1 para 14 and Sch 6 para 11 CTRSPR(W) Regs
S Reg 40 CTR(S) Regs; reg 34 CTR(SPC)(S) Regs
53 **E** Sch 1 para 18(1)(b) and (2) CTRS(PR)(E) Regs
W Sch 1 para 12(1)(b) and (2) and Sch 6 para 14(1)(b) and (2) CTRSPR(W) Regs
S Regs 49(3) and 50(3) CTR(S) Regs; reg 32(1)(b) and (2) CTR(SPC)(S) Regs
54 **E** Sch 4 CTRS(PR)(E) Regs
W Schs 3 and 8 CTRSPR(W) Regs
S Regs 49(6)(d) and 50(3)(i) and Sch 3 CTR(S) Regs; Sch 2 CTR(SPC)(S) Regs
55 **E** Sch 4 CTRS(PR)(E) Regs
W Schs 3 and 8 CTRSPR(W) Regs
S Reg 50(3)(ii) and Sch 3 para 15 CTR(S) Regs; Sch 2 CTR(SPC)(S) Regs
56 **E** Sch 1 para 24(3) CTRS(PR)(E) Regs
W Schs 1 para 18(3) and 6 para 20(3) CTRSPR(W) Regs
S Reg 38(2), (3) and (4) and 42(2), (3) and (4) CTR(S) Regs; reg 28(3) CTR(SPC)(S) Regs
57 **E** Sch 1 para 25 CTRS(PR)(E) Regs
W Sch 1 para 19 and Sch 6 para 21 CTRSPR(W) Regs
S Regs 77 and 78 CTR(S) Regs; reg 29 CTR(SPC)(S) Regs
58 **E** Reg 11(2) and Sch 1 paras 31-37 CTRS(PR)(E) Regs
W Reg 30 and Sch 1 paras 25-31 and Sch 6 paras 26-33 CTRSPR(W) Regs
S Regs 66-73 CTR(S) Regs; regs 40-46 CTR(SPC)(S) Regs
59 **E** Sch 1 para 13 CTRS(PR)(E) Regs
W Sch 1 para 7 and Sch 10 para 8 CTRSPR(W) Regs
S Reg 69 and Sch 4 CTR(S) Regs; reg 24 CTR(SPC)(S) Regs
60 **W** Sch 6 para 9(6) CTRSPR(W) Regs
S Regs 47(2) and 69 CTR(S) Regs
61 *JRL v SSWP (JSA)* [2011] UKUT 63 (AAC)
62 **E** Sch 1 para 36 CTRS(PR)(E) Regs
W Sch 1 para 30 and Sch 6 para 32 CTRSPR(W) Regs
S Reg 68 CTR(S) Regs; reg 46 CTR(SPC)(S) Regs
63 **E** Sch 6 Part 1 CTRS(PR)(E) Regs
W Schs 5 and 10 CTRSPR(W) Regs
S Sch 4 CTR(S) Regs; Sch 4 CTR(SPC)(S) Regs
64 **E** Sch 1 para 34 CTRS(PR)(E) Regs
W Sch 1 para 28 and Sch 6 para 30 CTRSPR(W) Regs
S Reg 71 CRT(S) Regs; reg 44 CTR(SPC)(S) Regs
65 **E** Sch 1 para 34(2) CTRS(PR)(E) Regs
W Sch 1 para 28(2) CTRSPR(W) Regs
S Reg 44(2) CTR(SPC)(S) Regs
66 **E** Sch 1 para 35 CTRS(PR)(E) Regs
W Sch 1 para 29 and Sch 6 para 31 CTRSPR(W) Regs
S Reg 72 CTR(S) Regs; reg 45 CTR(SPC)(S) Regs
67 **E** Sch 1 para 37 CTRS(PR)(E) Regs
W Sch 1 para 31 and Sch 6 para 33 CTRSPR(W) Regs
S Reg 63 CTR(S) Regs; reg 27(2) CTR(SPC)(S) Regs
68 **E** Sch 1 para 17(1) CTRS(PR)(E) Regs
W Sch 1 para 11(1) and Sch 6 para 13(1) CTRSPR(W) Regs
S Regs 39 and 43 CTR(S) Regs; reg 31(1) CTR(SPC)(S) Regs

6. **Alternative maximum council tax reduction (second adult rebate)**

69 **E** Sch 1 para 4 CTRS(PR)(E) Regs
S Reg 13(3) and (7) CTR(S) Regs; reg 14(6) and (7) CTR(SPC)(S) Regs
70 CH/48/2006
71 **E** Sch 1 para 4 and Sch 3 CTRS(PR)(E) Regs
S Regs 13 and 91 CTR(S) Regs; regs 14 and 56 CTR(SPC)(S) Regs
72 **E** s6(5) and Sch 1 LGFA 1992; Sch 1 para 4(3) CTRS(PR)(E) Regs
S s99 LGFA 1992; regs 13(7) and 92 CTR(S) Regs; regs 14(7) and 57 CTR(SPC)(S) Regs
73 **E** Sch 3 para 12 CTRS(PR)(E) Regs
S Sch 2 para 12 CTR(S) Regs; Sch 5 para 12 CTR(SPC)(S) Regs
74 **E** Sch 3 para 2 CTRS(PR)(E) Regs
S Sch 2 para 2 CTR(S) Regs; Sch 5 para 2 CTR(SPC)(S) Regs

7. **Band E-H council tax reduction: Scotland**
75 Regs 14 and 20 CTR(S) Regs; reg 14A CTR(SPC)(S) Regs
76 Regs 14(3)(b) and 20 CTR(S) Regs
77 Reg 14(5)(a)(ii) CTR(S) Regs; reg 14A(5)(a)(ii) CTR(SPC)(S) Regs

8. **Extended and continuing reductions**
78 **E** Sch 1 paras 87-105 CTRS(DS)(E) Regs
W Sch 1 para 32 and Sch 6 paras 34 and 39 CTRSPR(W) Regs
S Regs 80 and 85 CTR(S) Regs; reg 49 CTR(SPC)(S) Regs
79 **E** Sch 1 para 43 CTRS(PR)(E) Regs
W Sch 1 para 37 CTRSPR(W) Regs
S Reg 55 CTR(SPC)(S) Regs

9. **Applications, decisions and awards**
80 **E** Sch 7 paras 2-3 CTRS(PR)(E) Regs
W Sch 12 paras 2-3 CTRSPR(W) Regs; Sch 1 paras 2-3 CTRS(DS)(W) Regs
S Regs 23 and 25 CTR(S) Regs; regs 63 and 64 CTR(SPC)(S) Regs
81 **E** Sch 7 para 4 CTRS(PR)(E) Regs
W Sch 12 para 4 CTRSPR(W) Regs; Sch 1 para 4 CTRS(DS)(W) Regs
S Reg 23(6) CTR(S) Regs; reg 63(6) CTR(SPC)(S) Regs
82 **E** Sch 8 para 7 CTRS(PR)(E) Regs
W Sch 13 para 5 CTRSPR(W) Regs
83 Reg 24 CTR(S) Regs
84 **E** Sch 8 para 5(6) CTRS(PR)(E) Regs
W Sch 13 para 2(6) CTRSPR(W) Regs
S Reg 26(3) CTR(S) Regs; reg 65(2) CTR(SPC)(S) Regs
85 **E** Sch 8 para 5(6)-(7) CTRS(PR)(E) Regs
W Sch 13 para 2(6)-(7) CTRSPR(W) Regs; Sch para 108(6) and (7) CTRS(DS)(W) Regs
S Reg 26(6) CTR(S) Regs; reg 65(2) and (3) CTR(SPC)(S) Regs
86 **E** Sch 8 para 5(5)(c) CTRS(PR)(E) Regs
W Sch 13 paras 2(4) and (5)(c) and 5(4) CTRSPR(W) Regs; Sch para 111(4) CTRS(DS)(W) Regs
S Reg 27(1) CTR(S) Regs; reg 66(1) CTR(SPC)(S) Regs
87 **E** Sch 8 para 4(1) CTRS(PR)(E) Regs
W Sch 13 para 1 CTRSPR(W) Regs; Sch para 107(1) CTRS(DS)(W) Regs
S Reg 22 CTR(S) Regs; reg 61 CTR(SPC)(S) Regs
88 **E** Sch 8 paras 11 and 12 CTRS(PR)(E) Regs
W Sch 13 paras 8 and 9 CTRSPR(W) Regs; Sch para 114 CTRS(DS)(W) Regs
89 **W** Sch 13 para 4 CTRSPR(W) Regs
90 **S** Reg 26(7) and (8) CTR(S) Regs
91 **E** Sch 8 para 6(2) CTRS(PR)(E) Regs
W Sch 13 para 3(1) CTRSPR(W) Regs
S Reg 62(1) CTR(SPC)(S) Regs
92 **E** Sch 8 para 6(3) CTRS(PR)(E) Regs
W Sch 13 para 3(2) CTRSPR(W) Regs
S Reg 62(2) CTR(SPC)(S) Regs
93 **E** Sch 8 para 9 CTRS(PR)(E) Regs
W Sch 13 para 7 CTRSPR(W) Regs
S Reg 31 CTR(S) Regs; reg 69 CTR(SPC)(S) Regs
94 **E** Sch 8 para 9(2) CTRS(PR)(E) Regs
W Sch 13 para 7(2) CTRSPR(W) Regs
95 Reg 21 CTR(S) Regs; reg 19A CTR(SPC)(S) Regs
96 **E** Sch 1 para 46(1) CTRS(PR)(E) Regs
W Sch 1 para 37(1) and Sch 6 para 46(1) CTRSPR(W) Regs
S Reg 34(1) CTR(S) Regs; reg 59(1) CTR(SPC)(S) Regs

10. **If you disagree with a council tax reduction decision**
97 **EW** s16 LGFA 1992
E Sch 7 para 8(1) CTRS(PR)(E) Regs
W Sch 12 para 8 CTRSPR(W) Regs; Sch 1 para 8 CTRS(DS)(W) Regs
98 *SC and CW v East Riding of Yorkshire Council* [2014] VTE Appeal No.2001M113393 and 2001M117503
99 **E** Sch 1A para 2(6) LGFA 1992; Sch 8 para 12(4) CTRS(PR)(E) Regs
W Sch 1B para 5(1)(b) LGFA 1992; Sch 14 para 3 CTRSPR(W) Regs; Sch 10 para 3 CTRS(DS)(W) Regs
100 **E** Sch 7 para 8(2) CTRS(PR)(E) Regs
W Sch 12 para 9 CTRSPR(W) Regs
101 Sch 12 para 8(2) CTRSPR(W) Regs; Sch 1 para 8(2) CTRS(DS)(W) Regs
102 **E** Sch 7 para 8(3) CTRS(PR)(E) Regs; reg 21 VTE(CTRA)(P) Regs
W Sch 12 para 10 CTRSPR(W) Regs; reg 29 VTW Regs
103 **E** Reg 21 VTE(CTRA)(P) Regs
W Reg 29 VTW Regs
104 *Norman and another v East Dorset DC* [2012] EWHC 3696 (Admin)
105 Reg 93 CTR(S) Regs; reg 70A(2) CTR(SPC)(S) Regs
106 Reg 93(4) CTR(S) Regs; reg 70A(4) CTR(SPC)(S) Regs
107 Reg 94(1) CTR(S) Regs; reg 70B(1) CTR(SPC)(S) Regs; r41(4) FTTSLTC(RP) Regs
108 r41(3) FTTSLTC(RP) Regs
109 r41(5) FTTSLTC(Rp) Regs
110 s66(2)(ba) LGFA 1992

Chapter 9

Bills and payments

This chapter covers:

1. Who is liable to pay the bill

Chapter 5 identified who is liable for council tax. However, no one is required to pay council tax until a bill has been issued.[1] As council tax is a property-based tax, there is no legal duty on individuals to notify the local authority that they may be liable. Instead, the onus is on the local authority to issue bills to those it identifies as liable.

If the local authority cannot establish the name of a liable person after making reasonable enquiries, the bill may be addressed to 'the resident', 'the council taxpayer', 'the managing agent' or 'the owner'.[2] Bills can be issued to individual taxpayers or companies, including companies liable as owners of a dwelling.

The liable person's spouse or partner, and anyone who shares the same legal interest in the dwelling, is jointly liable for the bill (see p95). In Scotland, a person who is jointly liable need not be named on the bill to be held responsible for payment.[3] In England and Wales, however, local authorities must issue a 'joint taxpayers' bill' before requiring payment from someone who is jointly liable who has not previously been included on a bill.[4] It must serve this within six years of the first day of the financial year to which it relates. The liable people must decide between themselves how they divide the cost.

Joint liability means that both or all jointly liable taxpayers can be held individually or collectively liable to pay the whole amount. You can appeal a decision on 'joint and several liability' (see Chapter 11).

Proposals to change aspects of billing have been raised in a 2025 consultation paper.[5]

Payments after a death

Relatives are not personally liable for a deceased person's council tax debt unless they were jointly and severally liable with the deceased. Similarly, executors or administrators are not personally liable for the debt, and no payment is due until a demand notice is served.[6] See p215 for more about outstanding liabilities after a death.

2. When bills should be issued

Local authorities must serve a council tax bill on each chargeable dwelling every financial year. In England and Wales, this should be done 'as soon as practicable' after the local authority sets the council tax for the year.[7] In Scotland, the bill should be issued as soon as practicable after the local authority has set a council tax and knows the water charge for the year.[8] This demand for water charges must be included in any council tax notice issued by the local authority.[9]

Most local authorities aim to send out council tax bills by mid-March, with the payment falling due from 1 April.

If you pay by direct debit, you may be offered a choice of payment dates in April to make your first payment. If you change your direct debit date, the local authority should inform you of any changes to the amount due.

Authorities must send separate bills for different financial years and for different dwellings, even if the same person is liable for both.[10] **Note:** some outsourced billing services have issued multiple bills for the same period showing different amounts. This can cause confusion and problems during enforcement if it is unclear which bill is valid. Authorities should ensure they comply strictly with billing rules.

In England and Wales, however, a single bill may cover both the current and preceding financial years if it is for the same dwelling.[11]

In Scotland, where the local authority believes that a person is liable for water and/or sewerage charges that have not yet been billed, it must include those charges in the bill.[12] Before doing so, the local authority must take reasonable steps to ascertain liability.[13]

From 1 April 2023, local authorities in Scotland are responsible for the collection of charges in place of Scottish Water.[14]

Late bills

A local authority must issue a bill (also known as a 'demand notice') as soon as reasonably practicable.[15] If there is a significant delay, the authority may lose the right to recover the amount owed. In one case concerning non-domestic rates, the local authority delayed seven years before serving demand notices.[16] When the ratepayers failed to pay, the local authority obtained liability orders. However, the High Court quashed the liability orders, describing the delay as inexcusable.

The High Court has considered the effect that serving a bill late has on validity.[17] Ordinarily, mere delay is not sufficient to invalidate a notice, even if it is sent several years after the tax fell due. It ruled that the test was to look at the length of the delay and its impact on the taxpayer. The key test is whether 'prejudice' has been caused. Prejudice is different from inconvenience and must be substantial. It can be caused in a number of ways. The court said there was also a public interest in ensuring that local taxes are collected, which had to be considered.

Prejudice caused by late billing

Prejudice could arise for someone on a low income who receives council tax bills for previous financial years that do not consider any potential past entitlement to a council tax reduction (CTR) or council tax benefit (CTB). Indeed, any application for CTR or CTB for earlier financial years will be subject to the benefit backdating rules. Arguably, prejudice is caused to anyone who effectively loses a right to claim CTR or CTB which might have covered the total liability for the year concerned.

Similarly, if you have been unable to claim under a CTR scheme since 1 April 2013 because of failure to supply a demand notice in time, it would be possible to challenge the bill as invalid as it has caused prejudice – ie, the loss of the opportunity to apply for CTR.

Prejudice may also arise from the failure to be given, as soon as practicable, the information accompanying the demand notice (see p198). Prejudice may arise from being unable to make provision from a limited income for paying the bill or from the loss of the right to pay in instalments or loss of an appeal right. The longer the delay in serving a demand notice, the more likely it is that you will be able to show some procedural or substantive prejudice.[18]

Challenging late issue of a bill

If you want to challenge the late issue of a bill, do so before the magistrates' court issues a liability order.[19] In theory, this should also be the case before the sheriff court in Scotland, but the difficulty is that the Scottish summary procedure does not give advance notice to the council taxpayer.

Another possible remedy is to lodge an appeal with the valuation tribunal or Local Taxation Chamber. This can be done under section 16 (section 81 in Scotland) of the Local Government Finance Act 1992, which allows appeals relating to 'any calculation' of council tax (see p263). The right to appeal arises as soon as you become aware of the bill. If liability order proceedings have commenced, it is always best to attend the magistrates' court (or sheriff court) and raise the issue of late billing and any prejudice caused.

Reducing council tax if a bill is late

In England and Wales, a local authority has the power to reduce an individual council tax bill (see p135). If a bill is served late, perhaps years after the original liability arose, you can apply to the local authority for a discretionary reduction in the amount due. The authority may grant this for any council tax liability, no matter when it arose.[20]

Late service of a bill may amount to maladministration (see p301) and cause hardship. While a late bill is not automatically invalid, the local authority is expected to act sympathetically and reasonably, particularly where the delay results in hardship or prejudice, such as a shortened time to pay or missed entitlement to reductions. If a council has an anti-poverty strategy, it is expected to act in line with it.

Retrospective changes caused by late entry in the valuation list

In some cases, a late bill arises from a late entry or alteration in the valuation list. This may be be due to an error by the Valuation Office Agency (VOA) – eg, failing to record a newly built property promptly, or later concluding a dwelling existed at an earlier date than previously assessed.

Sometimes, a billing authority may attempt to recover a sum of council tax for previous years, based upon the backdated entry. In such cases, it can be argued that the effective date of the entry should be treated as the date the VOA altered the list, not the earlier date when the property was considered to have come into existence.[21]

Making a complaint

If you receive late billing for which you are not responsible, make a formal complaint to the local authority. In practice, many billing authorities will withdraw a late bill rather than face a formal complaint investigation. You should also be prepared to appeal either to the valuation tribunal (England or Wales) or the Local Taxation Chamber (Scotland) if there is a question of CTR entitlement (see Chapters 8 and 11). Note the time limits and do not delay in making your appeal.

The tribunal examines why the billing was delayed and who made the decision to retrospectively reopen your account for a financial year previously considered closed. A local authority should have valid reasons for revisiting an earlier year.

The Ombudsman investigates late billing cases as maladministration (see p300).[22]

Where a bill arises from changes caused by retrospective alteration in the valuation band, see above.

3. How the bill is calculated

Liability for council tax is calculated on a daily basis.[23] Despite this daily liability, your annual bill is issued at the start of the financial year and based on assumptions, which are corrected later if necessary (see p195).

If you need to correct a bill, keep in mind that there is a right of appeal if the local authority declines to make the correction.

The local authority must estimate the chargeable amount by taking the relevant amount of council tax for that dwelling (depending on its valuation band), and then make the following assumptions.

- The same person will be liable for every day.
- The dwelling's valuation band will not change and it will remain a chargeable dwelling throughout the year.
- Any reduction under the disability reduction scheme (see Chapter 6) has been properly calculated and applies throughout the year.
- The discount status remains unchanged throughout the year.
- Any council tax reduction (CTR) applies throughout the year.[24]
- In Scotland, liability for Scottish Water charges applies throughout the year.[25]

If more than one reduction applies, they should be applied in the following order:

- disability reduction;
- discount;
- any reduction under a CTR scheme and/or any discretionary reduction.

If you are awarded 100 per cent CTR, the local authority must ensure this is is equal to your liability.

The bill can also take into account any credits from past periods, penalties due and any alleged overpayment of council tax benefit (CTB) pre-2013 or tax which remains unpaid due to the removal of CTR after it is awarded. **Note:** it is not possible to be overpaid an amount of CTR (see p183).

It is questionable whether any claim of excess CTB overpayment from earlier financial years may be recovered through the liability order system in the magistrates' court, such claims being outside a literal interpretation of the enforcement regulations. The recoverability of such sums may be challenged by an appeal to the First-tier Tribunal (Social Security and Child Support). If recoverable, they may be enforced via the county court system.[26] When CTB existed, it operated in tandem with the housing benefit system, with excess payments recoverable as a civil debt through the county court.

Has your liability ended mid-year?

Special rules apply if a bill is for a period earlier in the financial year and, on the day it is issued, you are no longer liable for council tax at that address. The bill will either:

– require payment of the amount due up to the last day of liability (calculated as described above but based on the actual, not estimated, circumstances); *or*
– if you are due a credit, require the amount payable (if any) after the credit has been offset against the chargeable amount.[27] This could apply, for example, following a delay in recalculating a reduction or, in theory, where a referendum over the level of council tax is held.

The authority usually requests such payments as a lump sum.

In-year changes to assumptions

It may become clear during the year that an estimated amount has been based on an incorrect assumption – eg, your entitlement to a discount may change partway through the year. If so, the local authority should now calculate the appropriate amount that appears due for the year.[28] If:

- the new amount is **higher than** the estimated amount, the local authority should bill you and give you at least 14 days to make the interim payment;
- the new amount is **lower than** the estimated amount, the local authority should notify you accordingly and make an interim repayment (but see below).

In England and Wales, if you move home within the same local authority area and have overpaid for the first home, and you are now liable for council tax at the second home, the local authority may credit the overpayment against your new liability, rather than refund you. This is likely to be done unless you specify otherwise to the authority. If you overpaid a lump-sum payment, the local authority should make an interim repayment in the usual way.[29]

If you have made payments under the statutory instalment scheme, see p203.

In Scotland, if an overpayment of council tax has occurred because you are no longer liable to make payments, you can ask the local authority to refund you. The council may hold onto the overpayment until you request a refund, and may seek to credit the overpayment against any subsequent balance due.[30]

In England, further rules apply about changes in the tax payable due to any local referendum (see p199).[31]

Incorrect payments

The actual amount owed to the local authority will only be known for certain at the end of the financial year or when your liability ends. If a previous bill was issued containing payments that do not reflect the actual liability, the authority must issue a new bill with the correct amounts. The local authority should, as soon as practicable after the end of the year (or the part of a year), serve a new bill on you as the liable person. This should state the actual amount due and adjust the amount(s) required to be paid under the previous bill.[32]

If the amount stated in the new notice is greater than the amount previously required, you must pay the difference within a period specified by the local authority. The local authority must allow at least 14 days following the issue of the new bill.[33]

If you have overpaid council tax and require a refund, the authority must arrange this. In most cases, the local authority may either repay the amount in question to you or credit it against any future council tax liability.[34] However, if the overpayment has arisen because you are no longer liable to make payments on one dwelling, but are immediately liable to make payments to the same local authority on another dwelling and you have not made a lump-sum payment, the local authority may require the amount of any overpayment to be credited against the new liability.[35]

In England and Wales, if the local authority is required to repay a sum but does not do so, you can take recovery action using the money claims procedure in the county court.[36]

Where the local authority refuses to repay the overpayment, following the decision in *Lone v Hounslow London Borough Council*[37] you must obtain a ruling from the valuation tribunal before taking recovery action. Civil proceedings may then be brought, if necessary, to enforce any repayment following the tribunal's decision if an overpayment or repayment situation has arisen (see p317).[38]

You can use the small claims procedure of the county court for sums of up to £10,000. You can follow a similar procedure in Scotland for up to £5,000. You can also complain to the Ombudsman (see p300).

See also excessive amounts of council tax on p199.

4. How bills are served

Before you are required to pay council tax, the local authority must serve you a bill.[39] This means the council has done what is reasonably necessary for you to know about the bill – actual receipt is not required. A bill may be considered legally served if it is:[40]

- posted to your usual or last known address; *or*
- hand delivered to:
  - the liable person at their usual or last known address; *or*
  - another person at the chargeable dwelling; *or*
- fixed to a visible part of the dwelling; *or*
- emailed, but only if you have agreed to this.[41]

If posted or left at the address, the date of issue is the date the bill was posted or left at the address. If delivered by hand, the actual delivery date is the date of issue. The bill should include the date of issue, which determines such matters as when payments become due.[42]

Local authorities should ensure that when a bill is sent by post, the first instalment due is payable at least 14 days after the day on which it is delivered to the post office. Councils (or their outsourced billing agents) should keep records of when bills are posted or delivered so that they can prove the date of issue later.

If the bill has not been received at the correct address, the local authority must serve it again if it wishes to initiate enforcement proceedings (see Chapter 10). If the bill is undelivered (eg, marked 'gone away'), the local authority should investigate who should now be liable. Ignoring such returns may give rise to late bill appeals.

A document sent by first-class post is deemed served two days after posting.[43]

If enforcement is started without proper service of the bill, it may be legally challengeable. You must be made aware of the notice of proceedings if enforcement is commenced.[44]

Failure of service

Failure of service of demands (or summonses based upon non-payment of demands) will provide grounds to have any liability order set aside.[45] If a process server or agent deliberately fails to serve a notice, it is treated seriously by the courts. The affected taxpayer can apply to have enforcement proceedings cancelled. The individual process server and their supervising principal may face contempt of court charges.[46]

Service of notices by social media is not legally permitted.[47] Any attempt to serve documents this way is invalid and can be challenged.

5. Information the bill should contain

The bill must contain certain prescribed information. There are minor variations between England, Wales and Scotland. Local authorities can decide the exact wording and how the information appears on the bill.

Information provided on council tax bills[48]

- The name of the liable person – or the 'council taxpayer' if the liable person is not known.
- The date of issue.
- The period covered by the bill.
- The address of the chargeable dwelling.
- The dwelling's valuation band.
- The total amount payable (including Scottish Water charges in Scotland) per chargeable dwelling broken down per tier (eg, district, county, parish/community).
- How the bill should be paid.
- In England and Wales, a reference to the billing authority's discretionary power to reduce bills under section 13A(1) of the Local Government Finance Act.[49]

- The calculation breakdown showing any discounts, disability reduction, discount/premium and variation of discount/premium or council tax reduction (CTR), the reason for it and the period covered.
- In England, the percentage change in council tax from the previous year, expressed to one decimal place.
- The gross expenditure of each billing and precepting authority for the year and the previous year, and the reasons for any difference between the figures for the previous and current year.
- The opinions of the billing authority and precepting authority of the effect that its gross expenditure has on the level of council tax set for the relevant year.[50]
- A statement of your duty to inform the local authority of anything that affects entitlement to a discount and that if you do not comply with this duty, without a reasonable excuse, the local authority may impose a financial penalty.[51]
- The amount (if any) to be credited against the amount of council tax which would otherwise be payable for the relevant year.
- The amount of any penalty. (Scottish civil penalties are usually issued as a separate bill.)
- Council tax arrears from the preceding year(s), but only to the extent that they have not already been billed for. (In Scotland, arrears are usually issued as a separate bill.)
- The contact details (address, phone number and email) for enquiries.
- Any CTR applicable, explaining the amount of CTR and the reasons for it.[52]
- An explanation of the duty to report changes of circumstances[53] and the possible consequences of failing to notify relevant changes in circumstances.
- In Wales, references to certain provisions of the Local Government Finance Act 1992.[54]
- In Scotland, the average Scottish council tax charge (excluding water charges) for a Band D property for the current year and for a Band D property in the previous year.
- In Scotland, if the council tax bill also includes water or sewerage charges, it must contain: the gross amount payable as water charges and as sewerage charges; the amount of any reductions applied to the gross amounts in any statement issued under the Water Industry (Scotland) Act 2002;[55] the net amount payable as water charges and sewerage charges; and contact details of the local authority and opening times.[56]

Bills served after the end of the year in question, or with another bill for another period, are not required to contain all the above information.[57]

Explanatory notes and accompanying information

The bill should be accompanied by a set of explanatory notes providing key information on: valuation and banding, exempt dwellings, disability reductions, discounts, appeals and the local CTR scheme. The billing regulations distinguish between information a demand notice is required to contain and information it is required to supply with a demand notice.[58]

Additionally, in England and Wales, bills issued before the end of the financial year to which they relate must be accompanied by information explaining the local authority's income and expenditure. Bills served after the end of the financial year concerned or with another bill are not required to contain all the specified information.[59]

A local authority may publish the information on its website rather than include the information with a demand notice.[60] The website address must be provided in the demand notice's explanatory notes. It must also be stated that there is a right to request, in writing, a printed copy of that information free of charge and that the authority must supply it as soon as reasonably practicable.[61]

Local authorities must also include information about the annual percentage changes in council tax between the previous year and the relevant year. In England, if the valuation band of a dwelling has changed, the bill must show the percentage difference between the amounts calculated in the relevant year and the previous year.[62]

Invalid bills

A bill may be invalid if it does not contain all the required information. Nevertheless, if the failure to comply with these requirements arose because of a mistake and the amount to be paid is demanded correctly, the bill is treated as valid. Failure to include all the information is unlikely to prevent a bill from being payable.[63] The local authority must issue a correction and a statement of the matter omitted from the bill as soon as practicable after the mistake has been found and send it to you.[64] However, there may be situations where the details contained in the bill are confusing or contradicted by amounts stated in other demands. It may be that the bill should be treated as invalid. If the amount stated in the bill is incorrect, it should be challenged immediately with the local authority and an appeal commenced (see Chapter 11).[65] If the local authority or an outsourced company acting on its behalf does not respond, make a formal complaint and ensure that it is acknowledged. To render a bill invalid so as to provide a defence against non-payment, the bill must fail to include information and must cause significant prejudice affecting understanding of the rights of the individual or liability to pay.[66]

Excessive amounts of council tax and referendums

In England, if a local authority's relevant basic amount of council tax is excessive, it is required to include a footnote on the demand notice stating the increase is excessive and that a referendum will be held, with further details to follow.[67]

A local referendum must be held if a billing authority's relevant basic amount of council tax for the year qualifies as excessive based on principles set by the Secretary of State.[68] The thresholds are set annually via *The Referendums Relating to Council Tax Increases (Principles) (England) Report*.[69]

Even though the demand notice is valid, the local authority cannot take enforcement action for the excessive portion of the bill unless the increase is approved by a referendum.

The authority may not issue a liability order or take enforcement action (eg, an attachment of earnings order) for an additional amount unless it is approved by a referendum. The 'additional amount' is the difference between the amount on the bill and the capped amount and/or any substituted amount applicable following a referendum.[70]

If the excessive amount is not approved in a referendum, it is held to be void, or if no referendum is held, a substitute non-excessive amount takes effect, and a local authority may issue a further revised demand notice.[71] The local authority can take no recovery action for the amount that has been declared excessive following a referendum.[72]

If you request a fresh bill, the local authority must provide it. This also appears to have consequences for enforcement as, if the local authority does not issue a fresh bill, the sum cannot be enforced as the local authority will be unable to prove it has followed the rules on billing that are essential for applying for a liability order (see Chapter 10).[73]

Where the referendum result is to approve the level of council tax originally set by the local authority, the original demand notice is enforceable.[74]

6. Payment arrangements

The local authority may adopt a variety of different payment arrangements, including:

- payment in instalments (see below);
- special arrangements (see p204);
- discounted lump-sum payments (see p205);
- discounts for non-cash payments (see p205);
- in Scotland, the local authority may delegate collection to a housing body, which then sets its own payment arrangements.[75]

Instalments

Most taxpayers have the right to pay by instalments.

In England and Wales, if the bill is issued:[76]

- on or before 30 April in the relevant year, payments under the statutory scheme are made in 10 monthly instalments from April to January. **Note:** in June 2025, the government announced a consultation on changing the statutory number of instalments from 10 to 12 in England. If enacted, it is not expected to be implemented before 1 April 2027;[77]

- from 1 May onwards, the monthly instalments must equal one less than the number of whole months remaining in the financial year (see below);
- between 1 January and 31 March in the relevant year, the full amount is payable in a single instalment on the date specified on the bill.

The instalments must be paid in consecutive months, but the local authority may choose the month to start and state this on the bill.[78]

Number of instalments

Month in which demand notice is issued	*Number of instalments*
April (or before)	10
May	9
June	8
July	7
August	6
September	5
October	4
November	3
December	2
January	1
February	1
March	1

In England, where the total amount is calculated based on a discount which varies during the year (eg, where the local authority changes the classification of dwellings entitled to discounts), the monthly instalments do not need to be equal, but shall be as specified in the notice.[79]

In Scotland, a local authority cannot demand the first instalment in the same month the bill is issued. If the bill is issued:[80]

- before 1 April in the relevant year, the local authority determines when the first of the 10 instalments is due – this can be either in April or May;
- from 1 April onwards, the monthly instalments must equal one less than the number of whole months left in the financial year;
- between 1 December and 31 March in the relevant year, the full amount is due in a single instalment on the date specified on the bill.

Paying in 12 instalments

In England, you have a legal right to request to pay your council tax bill in 12 monthly payments, rather than a maximum of 10.[81] **Note:** you must make the request yourself – councils are not required to offer 12 months unless you ask.

Details on how to request 12 instalments should be included in the explanatory notes that come with your annual demand notice sent at the beginning of the financial year.[82] Where your request is made between 1 January and 15 April in the year the financial year begins, the number of instalments is 12. If your request is made on or after 16 April of the year in question, the number of monthly instalments is the number of whole months remaining in the relevant year after the issue of the notice.[83] Effectively, in any case arising after 16 April, you are able to spread the remaining year's liability over as many months as remain, which also means treating February and March as instalment months.

Example

Maria wants to pay in 12 monthly instalments for the new tax year. She must request this from the local authority between 1 January and 15 April. However, Maria does not make her request until 6 June. She has nine instalments to pay (July to March).

Some Scottish and Welsh councils allow 12 monthly instalments at their own discretion.

Amount of the instalments

The amount of the instalments is worked out by dividing the total amount of the bill by the number of instalments. If this gives an amount which is a multiple of a pound, the instalments will be of that amount.[84]

Example

Manish's council tax is £1,200, payable in 10 instalments. The amount of each instalment is £120. If he is able to pay in 12 instalments, the monthly amount is £100.

If the division does not result in an amount which is a multiple of a pound, the amount payable is divided by the number of instalments and rounded to the nearest pound. Amounts ending in 50p should be rounded up. This amount is the amount of the instalments other than the first. This first amount is multiplied by the number of instalments less one, and the resulting amount is subtracted from the total amount payable. The amount remaining is the amount of the first instalment.[85]

Example

Bethan's council tax liability is £500 and she will pay in nine instalments.
The amount of all but the first instalment is £56 (£500 ÷ 9 = £55.5555).
The first instalment is £52 (£500 – (£56 x 8 instalments)).

If you only have a small amount of council tax to pay, the instalment method is an expensive way for the local authority to collect it. Consequently, local authorities have the power not to accept any instalment for less than £5. If the calculation of instalments would produce an instalment of less than £5, the local authority may require that the second instalment be added to the first and that the number of instalments be reduced by one. If the total amount payable is less than £10, the local authority may request payment of that amount in a single instalment. If the total amount payable is £10 or more, the local authority may reduce the number of instalments to the greatest number that allows individual instalments of at least £5.[86]

If you make a request during the financial year, the local authority must issue an instalment notice as soon as reasonably practicable.[87]

Instalments when liability ends mid-year

Once you are no longer liable for council tax (and for Scottish Water charges in Scotland), no further instalments are due under the statutory schemes. If you were jointly liable, whether named on the original bill or not, this only applies when everyone who was liable is no longer liable. In England and Wales, if the only person(s) who is liable is someone not named on the original bill, the local authority must issue a joint taxpayers' notice on them.[88]

When someone stops being liable, the local authority must serve a notice stating the actual amount due up to the day liability ended. This should be sent to at least one of the people who were jointly liable as soon as practicable after liability ends.[89]

Settling the final account[90]

If you have paid more than you owed, you may request a refund of the overpayment from the local authority. If no refund is requested, the local authority may decide to repay it or to credit it against your subsequent liability on another dwelling. It cannot be used to meet any other debt recoverable by the local authority, such as an overpayment of housing benefit.

If there is an underpayment (ie, you paid less than you owed), the local authority will issue a bill requiring the liable person to pay the outstanding amount. The authority must allow at least 14 days from issuing the bill for this amount to be paid.

If the formerly liable person becomes, once again, liable for council tax to the local authority in the same financial year, the matter is dealt with afresh. Any previous overpayment of tax by the liable person may, however, be credited against the subsequent liability.

Instalments when liability changes mid-year

The instalment schemes are based on the assumption that your circumstances will remain the same throughout the year. Liability may change, however, because:[91]

- there is a change to a joint liability or from a joint liability to sole liability; *or*
- the dwelling's valuation band changes (see Chapter 3); *or*
- the dwelling becomes exempt (see Chapter 4); *or*
- entitlement to a disability reduction changes (see Chapter 6); *or*
- entitlement to a discount/variation changes (see Chapter 7); *or*
- entitlement to a council tax reduction (CTR) changes (see Chapter 8); *or*
- a premium is imposed (see p137); *or*
- the council tax changes due to budgets being capped by central government; *or*
- liability to pay Scottish Water charges in Scotland changes.

The local authority must adjust the remaining instalments (if any) as soon as practicable after the change of circumstances. As many adjustments may be made as the circumstances require. The local authority must also serve a revised bill (an adjustment notice) each time an adjustment is made. This should state the:

- revised estimated liability for the relevant year, assuming no further changes; *and*
- amount of any instalments that remain 14 or more days after the issue of the notice.

In England and Wales, if a change increases the amount due, the remaining instalments must follow the rules for the statutory scheme (see p200). In Scotland, the local authority has the discretion to set the amount of each remaining instalment. If no further instalments are due, the additional amount must be paid as a lump sum within a period set by the local authority. The local authority must give you at least 14 days from the date the bill was issued to pay the amount owing. In Scotland, at least two instalments must fall to be paid under the demand notice concerned, in accordance with the statutory instalment scheme or any agreement with the council.[92]

If the revised amount is less than what you have already paid, you should request that the overpayment be refunded. If you do not make such a request, the local authority may decide to repay it or credit it against your subsequent liability.[93]

If a local authority revises its estimate of your council tax liability, when adjusting the remaining instalments it must take into account any amounts paid before the day on which the adjustment takes effect that were due to be paid after that day.[94]

Special payment arrangements

A local authority may agree that you can pay your council tax in a particular way.[95] These are outside the standard statutory instalment schemes and are often used when someone is experiencing financial difficulty. They may allow payments to be ended or adjusted. They may also allow for a fresh estimate to be made if the original estimate turns out to be wrong.

You may enter into these special payment arrangements before or after a bill has been issued, although in England and Wales, if there is joint liability, the arrangement can only be entered into with someone named on the bill. If you start the special arrangement after the bill has been issued, the local authority may make provision for dealing with any sums paid by instalments.

A bill issued under a special arrangement requires payment:

- within a set period of not less than 14 days after the day the bill is issued; *or*
- by instalments at intervals specified on the bill.

Note: the usual enforcement procedures (see Chapter 10) do not apply to special agreements. The local authority should set out procedures to be followed in the event of non-payment.

If you are facing financial hardship, see p186.

Discounts for lump-sum payments

Local authorities may encourage payment by lump sums, as this improves cash flow and reduces collection costs. The local authority can offer a discount if you pay your entire annual bill up front.[96] Not all councils offer this. Contact your local authority to ask if it offers a discount and what its terms are.

Discounts for non-cash payments

Various methods are available to pay council tax, but some are more cost-effective for local authorities than others. From the local authority's point of view, direct debit has the most advantages, and direct debit mandate forms are often sent with demand notices to encourage the use of this payment method. In addition, the local authority can offer a discount to taxpayers if they use such non-cash methods of payment.[97]

The local authority should consider the costs and benefits of such arrangements. It must decide the size of the discount and when non-cash payments are to be accepted on or before the date it first sets the council tax for the year.

If an adjustment is needed to the amount paid and the amount has been paid by a discounted non-cash payment, the instalment or other payment on which the discounted amount was accepted must be treated as having been paid in full. Any sum to be repaid, or credited against any subsequent liability, however, is reduced by the same proportion as was allowed for the discount.

If you have debts from previous years

When you owe council tax from a previous year, any new payment you make may be automatically allocated to your current year's bill – unless you clearly specify otherwise. You must do this, even if the local authority has suddenly issued a bill for an earlier liability period.

To ensure your payment goes towards the correct year, if paying:

- online or by bank transfer, use the correct reference number for the year;
- by cheque, write the year the payment is for on the back and include a written note;
- by phone or in person, state clearly the year you are paying for and ask for written confirmation.

If you do not, you could face enforcement action, as most computer systems usually default the total payment to the current year while the older bill remains uncredited.

The local authority can allow you to repay council tax arrears from previous years by instalments.

In Scotland, if you pay between 1 April and 31 March, payments will default to the current financial year, unless you quote a reference number that includes the correct year reference. Some Scottish taxpayers have, upon receiving a new council tax bill in February, started to make payments in March, which causes the payment to be defaulted to the terminating financial year. The new tax year reference numbers are not 'live' until 1 April.

If the local authority has obtained liability orders in earlier years, it is likely to include sums in costs. You may be able to challenge these (see p220).

If the local authority repeatedly allocates payments to different years so as to create or allow indebtedness to continue, complain as this is likely to be maladministration (see p301).

7. Penalties

A local authority may impose a civil penalty if you:

- fail to respond to a request for information to identify the liable person (see Chapter 5); *or*
- fail to notify the local authority that a dwelling is no longer entitled to an exemption (see Chapter 4); *or*
- fail to notify the local authority that you are no longer entitled to the same level of discount or premium (see Chapter 7); *or*
- fail to advise the local authority in good time that an assumption used to apply a discount/variation is incorrect; *or*
- knowingly make a false declaration about the non-occupation of a dwelling to obtain a discount/variation or avoid increased council tax liability.

In deciding to impose a penalty, the local authority is expected to act reasonably and proportionally.[98]

The local authority may collect a penalty by including it on your council tax bill (see p197) or sending a separate bill.[99] The bill should outline the reason for the penalty, along with general information about penalties.[100]

If a separate bill is sent, the local authority must allow at least 14 days for payment.

If the imposition of a penalty is under appeal or, in England and Wales, subject to arbitration:[101]

- no bill can be issued to recover a penalty;
- no payment is required until the appeal/arbitration is resolved.

In Scotland, a civil penalty may be imposed for failure to comply with a Local Authority Information Notice or an Assessor Information Notice. As in England and Wales, penalties can be collected as part of the council tax and water charges bill or by sending a separate notice requiring payment after 14 days or another period set by the local authority.[102] No penalty is recoverable while the penalty is subject to an appeal.[103]

Grounds on which a penalty may be quashed

Local authorities have the discretion to quash a penalty, and there is also a right of appeal to an independent tribunal. You may not be liable to a penalty if you have a reasonable excuse for not notifying the local authority. The words 'reasonable excuse' should be given their plain and ordinary meaning and include whether there are circumstances beyond your control.[104]

The evidential burden is on both parties. You must show that you had a reasonable excuse for the failure to notify, however, the billing authority needs to evidence that it had a legal basis to impose a penalty in the first place.[105]

What is reasonable depends upon the facts and circumstances of each case. Tribunals are unlikely to uphold penalties where there is no criminal intent, wilfulness or recklessness. Tax avoidance aimed at reducing liability should not be confused with tax evasion. The fact that a billing authority does not believe you does not amount to proof of factual wrongdoing.[106]

The penalty proportions of the instalments on the bill are not payable until the appeal or arbitration is finally disposed of, abandoned or fails.[107]

If you pay a penalty and it is later quashed by the local authority or following an appeal, the local authority must repay it. It can do this by deducting an amount from any other penalty, council tax and, in Scotland, Scottish Water charges owed to the local authority and repaying any balance.[108]

Not all changes in circumstances affect your council tax reduction (CTR) award and therefore do not attract a financial penalty. For example, a £70 penalty under regulation 13 of the Council Tax Reduction Schemes (Detection of Fraud and Enforcement) (England) Regulations 2013 was quashed when the local authority failed to show that the taxpayer's failure to report a change had resulted in any increase in CTR entitlement.[109]

The billing authority must produce evidence that its local CTR scheme permits penalties. If it fails to produce a copy or extract of the scheme, a tribunal may find it had no authority to impose the penalty.[110]

A penalty may be quashed if it is disproportionate in the circumstances. However, that does not mean a tribunal may not make an adverse finding against a taxpayer on other issues under appeal.[111]

If the penalty is excessive compared with the matter complained of, or unreasonable in the circumstances (eg, if you are terminally ill or have mental health problems), you should appeal to the valuation tribunal or, in Scotland, to the Local Taxation Chamber.

You can also make a complaint to the Ombudsman (see p300).

8. Appeals against the amount of the bill

If you disagree with the calculation of the amount you are liable to pay, you should initially write to the local authority. You can dispute actual and estimated amounts as the right of appeal is against 'any calculation' in council tax shown on the bill.[112] Clearly explain what part of the bill you disagree with and why you think it is wrong – eg, 'I applied for a disability reduction but it has not been awarded.'

There are some exceptions to this, such as the setting of the level of tax for each band by the council or court costs. These must be challenged in the court that imposed them – eg, the magistrates' court. However, if such charges are wrongfully included in your council tax bill or not permitted by law, you may still have grounds to dispute them.[113]

The local authority must respond in writing within two months. If it does not, or if you are dissatisfied with the response, you can appeal to the valuation tribunal or, in Scotland, the Local Taxation Chamber. You should usually do this within four months of the date you first raised the grievance with the local authority.

You cannot appeal on the basis that any assumption the local authority is required to make about the future may prove to be inaccurate.[114]

You should usually still pay the council tax bill while the appeal is pending, subject to any agreement you make with the local authority. However, if the local authority has applied for a liability order in the magistrates' court, apply for an adjournment of the liability order hearing if a formal appeal is underway.[115]

Notes

1. Who is liable to pay the bill

1 **EW** Reg 22 CT(AE) Regs; *R (on the application of Waltham Forest LB) v Waltham Forest Magistrates' Court* [2008] EWHC 3579 (Admin); CO/2347/2007
S Reg 18 CT(AE)(S) Regs
2 **EW** Reg 2(2) and (3) CT(AE) Regs
S Reg 19(2) CT(AE)(S) Regs
3 Reg 18 CT(AE)(S) Regs
4 **EW** Reg 28 CT(AE) Regs
5 MHCLG, *Modernising and Improving the Administration of Council Tax,* 20 June 2025
6 Reg 58(3) CT(AE) Regs

2. When bills should be issued

7 **EW** Reg 19 CT(AE) Regs
8 Reg 17 CT(AE)(S) Regs
9 Reg 6(1) Water and Sewerage Services to Dwellings (Collection of Unmetered Charges by Local Authority) (Scotland) Order 2023 SSI No.52
10 **EW** Reg 18 CT(AE) Regs
S Reg 19 CT(AE)(S) Regs
11 **EW** Reg 18 CT(AE) Regs
12 Reg 6(1) WSSD(CUCLA)(S)O
13 Reg 6(3) WSSD(CUCLA)(S)O
14 Reg 3 WSSD(CUCLA)(S)O
15 **EW** Reg 19 CT(AE) Regs
16 *Encon Insulation Ltd v Nottingham City Council* [1999] RA 382
17 *North Somerset DC v Honda Motor Europe Ltd; North Somerset DC v Chevrolet United Kingdom Ltd; North Somerset DC v Martin Graham* [2010] EWHC 1505 (QB)
18 *R (on the application of Waltham Forest LB) v Waltham Forest Magistrates' Court* [2008] EWHC 3579 (Admin); CO/2347/2007
19 *Regentford Ltd v Thanet DC* [2004] EWHC 246 (Admin), [2004] RA 113 (QBD)
20 *Morgan v Warwick DC* [2015] RVR 224
21 Reg 11(6) CT(ALA)(E) Regs; *RG v Dawn Bunyan* [2022] VTE Appeal No.VT00007677; see *Valuation in Practice,* No.66, November 2022
22 Ombudsman Report 13019622, Derby City Council, 30 October 2014

3. How the bill is calculated

23 **EW** s2(2)(d) LGFA 1992
S s71(2)(d) LGFA 1992
24 **EW** Reg 20 CT(AE) Regs
S Reg 20 CT(AE)(S) Regs
25 Reg 20 CT(AE)(S) Regs
26 *CJ v Stratford-on-Avon* [2011] UKUT 357
27 **EW** Reg 20 CT(AE) Regs
S Reg 20 CT(AE)(S) Regs
28 **EW** Regs 24 and 25 CT(AE) Regs
S Regs 23 and 24 CT(AE)(S) Regs
29 **EW** Reg 24 CT(AE) Regs
30 Reg 27(4) CT(AE)(S) Regs
31 Regs 21A and 21b CT(AE) Regs
32 **EW** Regs 24, 25 and 31 CT(AE) Regs
S Regs 23, 24 and 27 CT(AE)(S) Regs
33 **EW** Regs 24, 25 and 31 CT(AE) Regs
S Regs 23, 24 and 27 CT(AE)(S) Regs
34 **EW** Regs 24, 25 and 31 CT(AE) Regs
S Regs 23, 24 and 27 CT(AE)(S) Regs
35 **EW** Reg 24 CT(AE) Regs
S Reg 23 CT(AE)(S) Regs
36 **EW** Reg 55 CT(AE) Regs; *Espressa Management Limited v LB Croydon* [2025] VTE VT00016268, judgment of President Gary Garland
37 *Lone v LB Hounslow* [2019] EWCA Civ 2206
38 See *Lone v LB Hounslow* [2020] 1 WLR 952, paras 25 and 43-45

4. How bills are served

39 *Regentford Ltd v Thanet DC* [2004] All ER (D) 285
40 **EW** Reg 2 CT(AE) Regs
S s192 Local Government (Scotland) Act 1973; regs 1(3) and 20 CT(AE)(S) Regs
41 **EW** Reg 2(4) CT(AE) Regs
42 **EW** Reg 17(4) CT(AE) Regs
43 s7 Interpretation Act 1978
44 *R (on the application of Clark-Darby) v Highbury Corner Magistrates' Court* [2001] All ER (D) 229
45 *Chowdhury v Westminster City Council* [2013] EWHC 1921

46 *Myers v Elman* [1940] AC 282; *Cranfield and another v Bridgegrove Ltd; Claussen v Yeates; McManus v Sharif; Murphy v Staples UK Ltd; Smith v Hughes and another* [2003] EWCA Civ 656 (CA); judgment of District Judge Madge, Peterborough Crown Court Case No.S20120266, 29 November 2012 – process server jailed for contempt
47 *Sharpe v Wakefield* [1888] 22 QBD at 239

5. **Information the bill should contain**
48 Schs 1 and 2 CT(DN)(E) Regs, as amended by The Council Tax and Non-Domestic Rating (Demand Notices) (England) (Amendment) Regulations 2023 No.13
49 Sch 1 para 18 CT(DN)(E) Regs 2011
50 Sch 2 paras 2-6 CT(DN)(E) Regs
51 **E** Sch 2 CT(DN)(E) Regs
W CT(DN)(W) Regs
52 **E** Reg 19(1)(a) CT(DN)(E) Regs 2011
W CT(DN)(W) Regs
53 **E** Reg 19A CT(DN)(E) Regs 2011
W Sch 1 para 8A CT(DN)(W) Regs
54 Reg 2(2)(b) CT(ND)(W) Regs amended by reg 9 of the Government Finance (Consequential and Miscellaneous Amendments and Revocations) (Secondary Legislation) (Wales) Regulations 2024 No.998
55 s29(D) Water Industry (Scotland) Act 2002
56 Water and Sewerage Services to Dwellings (Collection of Unmetered Charges by Local Authority) (Scotland) Order 2023 SSI No.52
57 Reg 5 and 6 CT(DN)(E) Regs 2011
58 Schs 1 and 2 CT(DN)(E) Regs 2011
59 Reg 5(2) CT(DN)(E) Regs 2011
60 Reg 2(4A) CT(AE) Regs, as amended by reg 3(b) CT(AE)(A)(No.2)(E) Regs
61 Reg 2(4C) CT(AE) Regs
62 Sch 1 paras 13 and 14 CT(DN)(E) Regs
63 *McGrath v Camden LBC* [2020] Business Law Reports 64
64 Reg 7 CT(DN)(E) Regs 2011
65 s16 LGFA 1992
E Reg 4C CTNDR(DN)(E) Regs
W Reg 5 CT(DN)(W) Regs
S Reg 29 CT(AE)(S) Regs
66 *McGrath v Camden LBC* [2020] EWHC 369 (Admin) QBD; *SSHD v SM (Rwanda)* [2018] EWCA Civ 2770
67 s52ZB LGFA 1992; Mark Sandford, *Council Tax: local referendums*, Research Briefing, House of Commons Library, 4 January 2023
68 s52ZC(2) and (3) LGFA 1992
69 *The Referendums Relating to Council Tax Increases (Principles) (England) Report 2025-26*, HC 624, 3 February 2025
70 Reg 21A(5) CT(AE) Regs
71 Reg 21A(3)(a) CT(AE) Regs
72 Reg 21A(2) CT(AE) Regs
73 Reg 21A(3)(b) CT(AE) Regs
74 s52ZH LGFA 1992

6. **Payment arrangements**
75 Sch 2 para 19 LGFA 1992
76 **EW** Sch 1 Part I CT(AE) Regs
77 **EW** Reg 21 and Sch 1 Part I CT(AE) Regs
S Reg 21 and Sch 1 CT(AE)(S) Regs
78 **EW** Sch 1 Part I CT(AE) Regs
S Sch 1 CT(AE)(S) Regs
79 Sch 1 para 2(3B) CT(AE) Regs, as inserted by reg 2(14) CT(AE)(A)(No.2)(E) Regs
80 Sch 1 Part I CT(AE)(S) Regs
81 Reg 21(1A) CT(AE) Regs
82 Sch 1 para 27 LGFA 1992
83 s11A LGFA 1992; para 2(3A) and Sch 1 CT(AE) Regs
84 **EW** Sch 1 Part I CT(AE) Regs
S Sch 1 Part I CT(AE)(S) Regs
85 **EW** Sch 1 Part I CT(AE) Regs
S Sch 1 Part 1 CT(AE)(S) Regs
86 **EW** Sch 1 CT(AE) Regs
87 Reg 21(1C) CT(AE) Regs
88 **EW** Reg 28 CT(AE) Regs
89 **EW** Sch 1 Part III CT(AE) Regs
S Sch 1 Part II CT(AE)(S) Regs
90 **EW** Sch 1 Part III CT(AE) Regs
S Sch 1 Part II CT(AE)(S) Regs
91 **EW** Sch 1 Part III CT(AE) Regs
S Sch 1 Part II CT(AE)(S) Regs
92 Reg 24 CT(AE)(S) Regs
93 **EW** Sch 1 Part III CT(AE) Regs
S Sch 1 Part II CT(AE)(S) Regs
94 **EW** Sch 1 Part III CT(AE) Regs
95 **EW** Reg 21 CT(AE) Regs
S Reg 21 CT(AE)(S) Regs
96 **EW** Reg 25 CT(AE) Regs
S Reg 24 CT(AE)(S) Regs
97 **EW** Reg 26 CT(AE) Regs
S Reg 25 CT(AE)(S) Regs

7. **Penalties**

98 *Associated Provincial Picture Houses v Wednesbury Corporation* [1948] 1 KB 223
99 **EW** Reg 29 CT(AE) Regs
S Reg 26 CT(AE)(S) Regs
100 Sch 1 CCTNDR(DN)(E) Regs
101 **EW** Reg 29 CT(AE) Regs
S Reg 26 CT(AE)(S) Regs
102 Reg 26(1) CT(AE)(S) Regs
103 Reg 26(2) CT(AE)(S) Regs
104 *World of Enterprise Ltd v Revenue and Customs* [2011] UKFTT 719 (TC)
105 *Kirsty Poole v Uttlesford DC* [2020] VTE Appeal No.00000680, paras 13-14
106 VTE Appeal Nos.0665M130018/254C and 0665M132093/254C [2014]
107 **EW** Reg 29 CT(AE) Regs
S Reg 26 CT(AE)(S) Regs
108 **EW** Reg 29 CT(AE) Regs
S Reg 26 CT(AE)(S) Regs
109 *Kirsty Poole v Uttlesford DC* [2020] VTE Appeal No.00000680
110 *Kirsty Poole v Uttlesford DC* [2020] VTE Appeal No.00000680
111 *Taxpayer v Warrington BC* [2015] VTE Appeal No.MO137634

8. **Appeals against the amount of the bill**

112 **EW** s16(2) LGFA 1992
S s81 LGFA 1992
113 *Attfield v Barnet LBC* [2013] EWHC 2089
114 **EW** Reg 30 CT(AE) Regs
115 *Wiltshire Council v Piggin* [2014] EWHC 4386 (Admin)

Chapter 10

Enforcement

This chapter covers:

1. Introduction

This chapter outlines the statutory enforcement process used by local authorities to recover unpaid council tax. The process differs between Scotland and England and Wales, although some aspects, such as benefit deductions, are common to all nations.

The local authority can agree a special payment arrangement with you (see p204). This is often the most suitable approach if you are in arrears. **Note:** if you do not keep to the agreement, the local authority can begin recovery action.

Some enforcement functions can be performed on behalf of the local authority by subcontractors. However, only the local authority itself can apply to have a debtor committed to prison.[1]

Note: at any stage of enforcement, recovery action must stop if the full outstanding amount (including costs) is paid.

For further information about enforcement actions, see CPAG's *Debt Advice Handbook* and *Debt Advice Handbook Scotland*. Both are available free at cpag.org.uk/handbooks.

2. Statutory enforcement in England and Wales

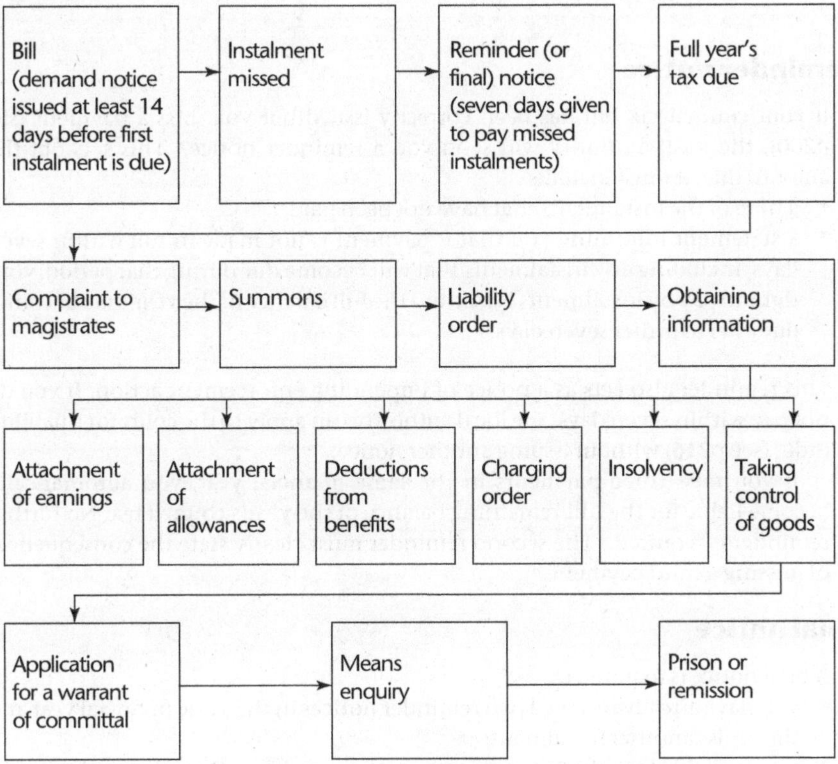

Council tax collection protocol and local authority enforcement policies

The *Council Tax Protocol: Revised collection of council tax arrears good practice protocol*, issued by the Local Government Association and Citizens Advice, promotes best practice in the recovery of council tax. It encourages co-operation between billing authorities and advice agencies, including the use of enforcement agents. However, it does not refer to other enforcement methods such as bankruptcy and charging orders.[2] The full protocol is at citizensadvice.org.uk.

Local authorities should also publish their own debt collection policies, which they are expected to follow.[3] Failure to have a written bankruptcy policy is likely to be maladministration.[4] Maladministration can also arise if the authority fails to consider other methods of enforcement as an alternative to bankruptcy, especially if it fails to assess vulnerability.[5] A local authority is at fault if it states it has suspended, or will suspend, enforcement action but continues it.[6] In some cases, such failures arise because enforcement functions are outsourced to subcontractors (for whom the council is responsible and is required to monitor).

The government has also issued good practice guidance for local authorities.[7]

The actual policy adopted by a billing authority is generally a matter for the authority itself.

Reminder notice

If your council tax bill has been correctly issued but you miss a payment (see p200), the local authority will send you a reminder notice.[8] This sets out the amount due. It must include:

- a note of the instalments that have not been paid;
- a statement informing you that if payment is not made in full within seven days, including any instalments that will become due during that period, your right to pay by instalments is lost and the full balance of the year's tax becomes due after a further seven days.

This reminder also acts as a notice of impending enforcement action. If you do not pay within seven days, the local authority can apply to the court for a liability order (see p216) without issuing another notice.

If you miss three payments in the same financial year, you automatically become liable for the full remaining balance of the year's council tax. No further reminder is required.[9] The second reminder must clearly state the consequences of missing a third payment.[10]

Final notice

A final notice is required if:

- you have already received two reminder notices in the same financial year and then miss another instalment; *or*
- you are liable to make only one payment under a council tax demand notice.

The final notice should state all amounts the local authority intends to recover on a liability order (see p216), unless this amount is identical to that on the second reminder.[11] In the case of joint taxpayers, the final notice may be addressed to all of them.[12]

Once the outstanding amount becomes due – either after a reminder or seven days after a final notice – the local authority can apply to the magistrates' court for a liability order (see p216).[13]

Joint liability

If a bill has been issued in joint names, the local authority may recover the full amount of unpaid tax from any one of the people who are jointly liable. If no joint bill has been issued, the authority must first send a notice to those who are jointly liable but have not previously received a bill. No recovery action can be taken against them until this notice has been sent.

The jointly liable person must be given at least 14 days to pay the bill. If no payment is made, a reminder must be served. If still no payment is made after seven days, the authority can then apply to a magistrates' court for a summons for a liability order. A further 14 days must be given between any summons and hearing where a liability order may be granted (see p216).

A liability order may be sought solely against the person to whom the bill was originally sent (even if no joint bill has been sent), or against both that person and a jointly and severally liable person. Otherwise, it is not possible for a summons to cover more than one person.

Write-offs and payments

A local authority may choose to write off a debt in certain situations – eg, when it is not cost-effective to pursue or if the taxpayer is experiencing financial hardship. It could, for instance, be appropriate to write off liability if a person dies shortly after the financial year begins, resulting in only a small amount being owed.

Even though some local authorities may claim they do not have this power, they do under section 13A(1)(c) of the Local Government Finance Act 1992, which allows an authority to reduce any sum that may be owed in council tax as it thinks fit. This power can be used whether or not a reduction has already been awarded under the local authority's council tax reduction scheme.[14] It can also apply regardless of when the liability arose.[15] A wider power also exists allowing the write-off of any sum under the general financial powers of a local authority.[16]

Outstanding liabilities on death

When a person dies, any outstanding council tax becomes a debt of their estate.[17] It can be recovered once the billing authority has served a payment notice. No liability order is required.

The executors or administrators have the right to take any legal steps which the deceased could have taken in relation to the debt, such as applying for a discount or exemption or starting an appeal.[18] The executor can recover overpayments of council tax.[19]

The executor or administrator cannot be personally liable for the debt, nor can any relatives or beneficiaries of the deceased be pursued for payment. No liability arises unless the executor or administrator is first served with a demand.

If enforcement action started before the billing authority became aware of the death, any court or other costs incurred after the death are not enforceable. You should challenge the imposition of any costs.[20]

Information and publicity about summonsed people

A council should not normally publish the names of individuals who are experiencing difficulty paying their council tax. This information is private and should not be released under Freedom of Information legislation or disclosed in any other way, unless it is in accordance with a permitted regulatory purpose. This does not prevent proceedings from being reported by the media if a non-payment case reaches court.[21]

Different rules apply to elected councillors. In general, councillors cannot rely on the data protection exemption under section 40(2) of the Freedom of Information Act 2000.[22]

If a council or an enforcement agent wrongly discloses protected information about a taxpayer (eg, by incorrectly naming them as a local tax defaulter[23]), this may give rise to a claim for damages.[24]

3. Liability orders (England and Wales)

A liability order issued by a magistrates' court gives a local authority options to recover the amount of council tax owed (see p227). It is not a judgment debt for the purposes of Part 70 of the Civil Procedure Rules or the Magistrates' Court Act 1980. This means it cannot be enforced as a judgment debt in the county court or High Court.[25]

A local authority must follow the rules on billing; it cannot obtain an order if it has not issued a reminder or final notice, as described on p214. Before applying for a liability order, the local authority should, as a matter of good practice, check whether you:

- are entitled to council tax reduction (CTR) (see Chapter 8);
- have made a claim for CTR that has not yet been processed (see p217);
- have appealed or are seeking a review (see Chapter 11);
- are owed a refund for a previous period;
- have made a claim for a discretionary reduction (see p186).

Some local authorities fail to carry out proper checks to communicate adequately between the council tax department and the section handling CTR. This is particularly problematic for people in low-paid or unstable employment who move in and out of benefit entitlement. Delays in awarding discounts or CTR and delays by the DWP in processing benefit awards can lead to people being wrongly recorded as council tax debtors and enforcement proceedings starting. In such cases, the local authority should suspend recovery action. It should also consider refunding any costs added due to its own delay or error. However, in practice, it can be difficult to persuade council officers (or staff from outsourced enforcement companies) to pause recovery. If you are in this position:

- consider appealing, although it can take time to obtain a hearing;
- ask for an alternative payment arrangement in exchange for withdrawing proceedings. Many local authorities will still seek to obtain a full liability order, as this allows them to enforce payment if the arrangement is broken.

If the local authority does not act reasonably and a summons is issued, go to the court, explain the situation to the magistrates and ask for an adjournment.

If your council tax reduction has yet to be determined

If you receive a summons before your application for CTR has been determined, apply to the magistrates' court for an adjournment of the hearing (see p222).

The decision to seek a liability order is discretionary.[26] The local authority must consider the relevant facts of the individual case and not act unreasonably.[27] If a local authority proceeds to seek a liability order while knowing that a CTR claim is pending, this may represent an unreasonable exercise of discretion. Even if the process is automated, it remains a legal decision. It is arguable that Parliament did not intend for support systems to be undermined by the imposition of liability orders and court costs while CTR claims are outstanding. Such a case can clearly be made in the case of pensioners, such as those entitled to the guarantee credit of pension credit. Arguably, the function of the local support system is to provide support for local taxpayers, not to create debt.

A magistrates' court could decline to issue the order if the local authority has not determined CTR or an application for a discretionary reduction (see p186).

The courts have applied a test of 'substantial prejudice' to taxpayers in cases where bills and summonses are issued late.[28] Where substantial prejudice is found, the authority may be prevented from recovering the debt. Examples of substantial prejudice include:

- when a bill or summons is sent early, before CTR has been assessed;
- when a bill or summons has been issued late and it is now too late to apply for CTR;
- loss of CTR due to the rules preventing backdating, where entitlement would otherwise have existed;
- loss of a right of appeal due to delay;
- having to move home or being unable to meet other payment demands.

It may also be possible to object to a liability order on human rights grounds. The European Court of Human Rights considers that there must be clarity in court orders and judgments.[29] If a liability order is granted while CTR entitlement remains undetermined, the amount of liability is not fixed and may later be revised. This lack of clarity could potentially form the basis of a human rights argument. However, the matter has yet to be tested.

Readjusted bills

It is often unclear why a readjusted bill has been issued, particularly if it relates to liability from several years ago. This may cause particular problems for people who are entitled to CTR but whose circumstances change over time.

If you receive a readjusted bill, request an explanation for the readjustment. Experience suggests this may prompt the local authority to re-examine the amount being claimed. Be prepared to take an appeal to a valuation tribunal to challenge any readjustment, particularly if CTR has already been awarded.

If a discretionary reduction is refused, or if the local authority is trying to enforce a bill with no lawful basis, you should attend the magistrates' court and challenge the bill, arguing that either you have paid your liability for the year in question or you have been caused prejudice.

Have you been caused prejudice?

The issue of a late bill, which has caused prejudice, is a defence to an application to make a liability order. In *North Somerset District Council v (1) Honda Motor Europe Ltd and (2) Chevrolet United Kingdom Ltd and (3) Martin Graham,*[30] the local authority delayed sending out bills for local taxes payable between 2002 and 2007. The High Court accepted the argument that the failure to serve the business rates as soon as practicable after 1 April in the relevant financial year rendered the notices invalid.

The court held that no duty existed on the taxpayer to pay the rates until a correct demand notice was served. Relevant factors to be considered are the length of the delay and the prejudice to the taxpayer which could arise in any number of ways.

Prejudice is considered different from inconvenience and must be 'substantial' and certainly not technical or contrived.

The judgment shows that the courts will look beyond the simple failures to serve notices and consider both the overall conduct of the local authority and the impact that procedural defects may have on taxpayers.

Significantly, the court recognises (paragraph 34) that the defendants are entitled to raise an issue of invalidity by way of defence at both the magistrates' court and as an administrative decision: 'Had the Council sought to enforce the notices by way of complaint in the Magistrates' Court the same defence could have been raised.'[31] This means that an objection should be made before the magistrates' court.

Time limits

A local authority must apply to the magistrates' court for a liability order within six years of the council tax bill being issued. However, once a liability order is granted, there is no statutory time limit for the local authority to enforce it.

In *Bolsover District Council and Another v Ashfield Nominees Ltd and Another*, the court allowed a local authority to use insolvency proceedings against a company based on a liability order over six years old. However, enforcement of an older liability order against an individual could be seen as an abuse of process and maladministration, particularly where there has been a significant delay.

If a council seeks to enforce liability from a previous year, the Valuation Tribunal for England (VTE) or the Valuation Tribunal for Wales (VTW) can still determine the matter.

The Ombudsman has ruled it unacceptable for a local authority to attempt to enforce a liability order without retaining the relevant paperwork.[32] Even where a debt is lawfully owed, recovery may be unjust if the authority cannot produce evidence due to excessive delay or loss of records.

Where bills or reminders are served late, any resulting liability order may be dismissed by the magistrates' court if the delay has caused prejudice (see p191). A discretionary reduction under section 13A of the Local Government Finance Act 1992 may be used to reduce or remove liability where other benefits or reductions are not available (see p186).

Extensive delays could be considered maladministration and you can complain to the Ombudsman (see p300).

The principle that delay can render enforcement unjust was supported by a Court of Appeal ruling under the former rating system, where a 12-year delay by a local authority in pursuing liability was held to be unreasonable, giving rise to a judicial review claim.[33]

Obtaining a liability order

Until 2020, local authorities were required to apply to the magistrates' court for a summons, which had to be signed by a magistrate or justices' clerk. Since 1 January 2020, this is no longer necessary – the summons can now be issued without a signature, provided it is done by a delegated officer. This has been approved by the High Court.[34] However, the court cannot delegate the issue of the summons to the local authority so that the court process is bypassed entirely by the council issuing its own summonses.[35]

Regulations allow a summons to be addressed jointly to two or more taxpayers. However, principles of natural justice require that each individual receives their own summons to ensure proper notice of the hearing. If a single reminder is issued to jointly liable individuals, the local authority must still produce separate summonses for each person it intends to pursue with a liability order.

The summons instructs you to attend the court to explain why you have not paid.[36] There must be a minimum of 14 days between service of the summons and the hearing.[37] If you do not attend, a warrant for your arrest cannot be issued, but the hearing will still proceed in your absence.

While there is no prescribed format for a summons, it must state the outstanding amount and may also include any reasonable costs incurred.

The costs for issuing a liability order

Since 2018, the cost of issuing a summons in England and Wales is set at 50p per defendant.[38] However, many local authorities charge higher amounts – often £70 to £125 or more – for what is essentially a standardised, fully automated process.

This is likely to breach the intent of the regulations, which allow only reasonable permitted costs. For costs to be reasonable, local authorities must be able to justify how they are calculated. It has been held that a local authority cannot raise revenue without clear statutory authority.[39]

Have you been charged more than 50p for costs?

If your summons includes charges above 50p for issuing the notice, you are entitled to question the legality of those charges. It may be arguable that they are unlawful, breaching statutory provisions and wider constitutional principles. You should also query other amounts included in the summons to establish why they were incurred.

You can do this before the hearing, and if the local authority does not agree to reduce or drop the costs, the matter may be raised in court. The authority must provide a breakdown of the costs claimed in seeking the liability order, if requested by the court.[40]

The costs of the application are divided into two stages: those reasonably incurred before and after a hearing. If you pay the balance before the hearing, only pre-hearing costs should apply, and these should be lower.[41]

The magistrates have a discretion to reduce or refuse costs if they believe the amounts are unreasonable. However, even if you succeed in challenging the charges, you may not be awarded your own costs for defending the claim, due to limitations on cost recovery in these proceedings.

In Wales, the maximum that may be charged in costs when seeking a liability order is £70.[42]

Challenging the costs of a liability order

You can challenge the costs of applying for a liability order if they are unreasonable. Magistrates must be satisfied that:[43]

- the costs were actually incurred by the council; *and*
- the costs were directly related to obtaining your liability order; *and*
- it was reasonable to incur them.

In *Nicolson v Tottenham Magistrates' Court,* it was held that debtors are entitled to an explanation of the costs awarded.[44] The court ruled that costs must be clearly linked to the court process for obtaining the order and not to enforcement, administration or general council tax operations.

This means that only the essential costs of obtaining the liability order are recoverable. Simply because a local authority claims an item on a document described as a 'bill of costs', it does not mean it can be included as costs incurred in obtaining a liability order. You should carefully check any bill of costs and question items not clearly related to the court application itself (eg, IT, staffing or sending reminder letters). Legal costs must relate only to the steps involved in obtaining the liability order and not to any other legal proceedings – eg, the cost of obtaining warrants of committal.

A local authority must not require you to pay a sum for the costs of applying for a liability order if it has not yet obtained the order. It is unlawful for a council to issue a summons demanding payment of a sum that includes prospective liability order costs as a precondition for avoiding the hearing or further enforcement action.[45]

The council cannot collect the additional costs once you have paid the tax amount and the initial portion of the costs. Any attempt to do so may constitute an abuse of process, and the magistrates' court may dismiss any summons aimed at recovering those extra costs.[46]

Where a council claims costs, the sum awarded in costs is the net amount and should not include VAT.[47]

If the council uses an estimated cost model, it must disclose how costs were calculated and show that they were reasonably and properly incurred.

Serving the summons

A summons may be served, giving at least 14 days' notice, by:[48]

- posting it to your usual or last-known place of abode; *or*
- delivering it to you; *or*
- leaving it at your usual or last-known address; *or*
- in the case of a company, leaving it at, or posting it to, its registered office; *or*
- leaving it at, or posting it to, an address you have provided as somewhere service will be accepted; *or*
- electronic service (if this method has been agreed), including by sending to a legal representative.

The summons will be deemed served providing one of these methods is used and can be proven to have been used.

If you do not receive a summons for a liability order hearing and the magistrates' court makes the order in your absence, the High Court may quash the order on judicial review.[49] If a summons is not served, any liability order purportedly based upon it is invalid.[50]

Withdrawing the summons

Once issued, a summons can only be withdrawn by the court. The power is considered inherent to the court's jurisdiction. A summons cannot be withdrawn by the local authority that is a party to the case.[51] A summons may be withdrawn by the justices' clerk if both you and the council agree. If either party objects, it can only be withdrawn by a magistrate after both sides are heard in court.

Payment of the outstanding amount

If the outstanding amount, plus costs, is paid before the hearing, the local authority cannot continue with the application for a liability order.[52] However, if the amount outstanding has been paid or CTR awarded, but the costs remain unpaid, a liability order can still be made for the costs alone.[53] The local authority may be prepared to waive the costs, especially if the delay was caused by its own action or inaction.

Adjournments

You can apply to the magistrates' court for an adjournment of a council tax liability order hearing if there is an unresolved issue that could affect your liability. This could include situations like claiming an exemption, a pending or incorrect CTR application, or a matter that should be appealed to the valuation tribunal (see p262). Apply by writing to the justices' clerk.

In some cases, local authorities may request an adjournment for administrative reasons, but this raises concerns about natural justice, as the court cannot delegate its duties to a party involved in the case.

The granting or refusal of an adjournment is a judicial act and should be exercised fairly.[54] If a court fails to consider an application for an adjournment, any decision may be quashed by judicial review.[55] You should also lodge a complaint with the court concerned, and it is advisable to contact your MP.

If you do not get a response from the magistrates' court, call the listing department to check on the status, or go to the court in person to make your application.

Attending court

It is best to respond to any court summons and be prepared to attend the court hearing. Doing so ensures you have an opportunity to:

- challenge the application for a liability order;
- negotiate a payment arrangement or settlement directly with the local authority;
- prevent enforcement action from proceeding unchallenged.

Even if the billing authority says there is no need to attend court, it is in your interest to do so. If you do not attend, your case will likely be processed as part of a bulk administrative process, where liability orders are granted automatically for all non-appearances, without considering your individual circumstances. Often, simply attending (or being willing to attend) may result in an adjournment, giving you more time to settle the matter. If it cannot be adjourned, you must attend court if you wish to make representations. This is important if your debt is over £5,000, as a liability order could lead to bankruptcy proceedings, forming the legal basis for further enforcement.

The duty solicitors scheme at magistrates' courts is not available for liability order hearings.

The hearing

If no settlement is reached with the local authority, or if you want to challenge the basis of its claim, a court hearing must take place.

You have a legal right to attend the hearing, listen to the case against you and speak in your defence. The burden of proof is on the local authority to demonstrate that it has complied with the rules of billing, not upon you to show why you have not paid. If you are prevented from addressing the court or seeing the evidence, the hearing breaches natural justice, and you are entitled to appeal as the hearing was not fair.

The procedure for the hearing follows rule 14 of the Magistrates' Courts Rules 1981. You should be allowed to examine all the evidence produced by the local authority and ask questions in cross-examination. The court normally must comprise two justices of the peace or a single district judge.[56]

You may submit that there is 'no case to answer' if the local authority has failed to prove a required part of its case. If your submission succeeds, the court must refuse the liability order.

Hearings are generally open to the public. Online and telephone hearings are permitted under court rules, as long as access to justice is not affected.[57] This mirrors the approach allowed in the civil courts by the Civil Procedure Rules.[58]

Remote hearings should not proceed if technology issues affect your ability to participate fairly.[59]

Recording or filming court proceedings is prohibited. Only the presiding judge or magistrate can authorise any recording, and this is rare. Attempting to record without permission could lead to contempt of court proceedings.

Representatives

You can represent yourself without a legal representative. In addition, you have the right to bring someone with you to support you during the hearing – eg, an adviser who is not a lawyer.[60] They can sit with you in court and help by taking notes, prompting and giving you advice on the conduct of the case. They are known as a 'McKenzie friend'. Tell the court in advance about the adviser. Anyone considering attending court as a McKenzie friend should read the practice guidelines available at judiciary.uk. The court may also exercise a discretion to allow a non-lawyer to represent an otherwise unrepresented person, but only if it is in the interests of justice.[61]

Grounds for granting a liability order

An order must be made if the magistrates are satisfied that:[62]

- the sum is lawfully payable by the person concerned; *and*
- it has not been paid.

The local authority must satisfy the court that:

- the council tax has been properly fixed by the local authority; *and*
- the bill was issued in accordance with the regulations; *and*
- full payment has not been made by the required date; *and*
- a reminder, second reminder or a final notice has been issued; *and*
- the sum remained unpaid seven days after the notice was issued and the full amount then became due; *and*
- the summons has been served at least seven days after the reminder or final notice; *and*
- the full sum claimed (including any costs) has not been paid at the time of the hearing.

You may be able to challenge the liability order if:

- the amount has not been demanded in accordance with the regulations – eg, the local authority failed to follow the correct time periods in serving bills and reminders;
- two bills have been issued for the same liability;
- the bill or notices were issued late (see p218 and Chapter 9);
- instalments were not correctly calculated in accordance with the regulations (see Chapter 9);
- the amount has already been paid;
- you are not the person named on the summons;
- the council tax charge is not in accordance with the rate set by the local authority;
- the hearing is scheduled less than 14 days following the issue of the summons;
- you have properly requested to pay by instalments, but the local authority has failed to comply with the statutory scheme;[63]
- you are owed a refund of overpaid council tax;[64]
- you are an undischarged bankrupt;[65]
- you are subject to an individual voluntary arrangement (IVA).[66]

Some matters must be resolved through an appeal to the VTE/VTW (see p263) – eg, liability disputes, whether the dwelling is chargeable or entitlement to a discount, exemption or discretionary reduction.[67]

However, magistrates do have a role in considering lawful objections based on set-off or legal preclusion.[68]

Practices can vary greatly between courts. However, if you can provide credible evidence of a serious objection to the alleged liability, many courts will grant an adjournment to allow further consideration. This is especially likely if you have lodged an appeal with the VTE/VTW.[69] Unless agreed in advance, an application for an adjournment must be made in the courtroom on the 'return day' of the summons. Wherever possible, contact the court in writing to request an adjournment, and also inform the local authority.

Evidence

The local authority can use any statement contained in a document, including a computer-generated statement, provided:[70]

- the document forms part of a record compiled by the authority;
- direct oral evidence of any fact stated in it would be admissible;
- if the document was generated using automated software, it is accompanied by a certificate validating that the system was working correctly.

If the document is produced in court, you can ask the officer to present the certificate for inspection. If it is not provided, the automated evidence will be inadmissible, and the local authority cannot prove its case.[71]

Any direct evidence you provide, including documents or statements, is also admissible.[72]

It is important not to rely on legal arguments, caselaw or statutory references generated by AI tools (eg, ChatGPT) unless you have verified them yourself.[73]

If your documents include hearsay (statements made by someone not present in court), you must give 21 days' notice to the clerk and to the local authority.[74] This is a potential problem, as you may only receive 14 days' notice of a summons. However, one solution is to send copies of the documents to the local authority well in advance, so they become part of the authority's records.

If there is a history of maladministration of billing and reminder notices by the local authority, the magistrates may order the billing authority staff to explain what has happened. In exceptional circumstances, the High Court may also intervene.[75]

The liability order

The court may issue a liability order:[76]

- for one person for one amount; *or*
- for multiple people and multiple amounts, grouped together in what is known as a schedule.[77]

In *Kofa v Oldham*, Mr Justice Fordham expressed the opinion that there was no need for a court-issued order. However, a court granting enforcement must be satisfied that a liability order has been made.[78]

A liability order is indended to identify the aggregate amount recoverable, including costs. However, issues can arise if a magistrates' court issues the liability order orally, without providing a written order. This makes it unclear how the full amount can be enforced. If the full sum claimed has been reduced (eg, because CTR has been awarded), the liability order will be for a greater sum than the amount payable. In such cases, the excess amount should be treated as paid. However, if you owe more than the amount specified on the order, the local authority can only enforce up to the sum stated in the liability order. To enforce any outstanding balance, it would need to seek a new order.

If the court fails to provide a stamped and sealed order, the local authority may struggle to prove that a valid order exists or existed. Without a proper order, it would be difficult to demonstrate that the magistrates were satisfied the local authority had met all necessary legal requirements for issuing the order.

In practice, the courts seldom issue individual liability orders. The judge or chair of the magistrates normally just signs a certificate attached to the list of non-payers, but in a form that does not comply with the regulations – without the stamp or seal of the court or any form laid down in regulations since 2003.

This is a serious flaw in the proceedings identified by the Court of Appeal.[79] Until 2012, many courts did not keep proper records of liability order hearings or the orders issued, leaving local authorities to maintain records which could be wrong and incapable of independent verification. This has also been identified as a serious omission in enforcement by the High Court.[80]

A distinction may be drawn between making the liability order and issuing it. The lack of an adequate and independent record may be a breach of human rights under Article 6 of the European Convention on Human Rights, regarding the determination of a citizen's civil rights and obligations.[81]

If a liability order has been issued but the billing authority later sends a notification with an adjustment to payments (such as for a lump sum payment or a joint taxpayers notice), the amount that can be recovered may be updated based on this new information. This adjustment can be made without the need to return to court for a new order.[82]

Setting aside a liability order

A magistrates' court has the power to set aside (quash) a liability order if:[83]

- the local authority applies and accepts that the order should not have been made; *or*
- you show that the court acted in excess of jurisdiction[84] – ie, it made an order when it had no legal power to do so.

A potential drawback for the council taxpayer is that the right to quash the order given to the council is wholly reliant on the local authority's willingness to make the application. You could challenge unreasonable refusals to quash liability orders, by judicial review. You could also make a complaint of maladministration (see p300). In the meantime, you remain subject to the order.

The High Court ruled that the following apply when deciding to set aside a liability order.[85]

- There must be a genuine and arguable dispute about the liability to pay.
- There must have been a substantial procedural error, defect or mishap for the liability order to have been made.
- The application to set aside was made promptly after the defendant had notice of its existence.

In *Mustafa v London Borough of Bromley*, it was held that the essence of such situations 'is that there has been some unusual and unexpected combination of circumstances such that justice requires that the order be set aside'.[86]

'Promptly' is usually interpreted as within three weeks of your learning about the liability order (some leeway exists if you have a disability). Cases in which liability orders have been made years earlier and in which the debtor, after learning of them, fails to apply for months or years to set aside will be unsuccessful because of lack of promptness.[87]

How to apply to set aside

There is no prescribed form for making an application to set aside a liability order, but a letter can be sent to the court's clerk.[88] Include:

- the date and reference of the liability order;
- the reasons you are applying to have it set aside;
- any supporting evidence such as CTR applications, notices not received, correspondence or payments made.

Ask for a hearing to consider the application.

This is crucial if a local authority is seeking to enforce a liability order through bankruptcy proceedings, unless the matter is also being challenged through the valuation tribunal (see p241). Therefore, it may also be necessary to lodge an appeal with the VTE/VTW. See Chapter 11 for more information on appeals. Costs may be awarded to the successful party if a set-aside application is contested.[89]

4. Recovery methods (England and Wales)

The liability order gives the local authority the power to:

- obtain information about your financial circumstances (see p228);
- make an attachment of earnings order (see p229);
- make an attachment order on an elected member's allowances (see p231);
- apply to the DWP for third-party deductions to be made from your universal credit (UC), income-related employment and support allowance (ESA) or pension credit (PC) (see p231);[90]
- use enforcement agents (previously known as bailiffs) to take control of your goods (see p232);

- apply for a charging order (see p240);
- apply to bankrupt you (see p241).

Only one recovery method at a time may be pursued.[91] In joint liability cases, the local authority may pursue only one person at a time.[92] So if, for example, one of the joint taxpayers is the subject of an attachment of earnings order (see p229), the local authority cannot take control of the goods of the other.

Providing information

Once the liability order has been made and for as long as the amount in question remains unpaid, the local authority may request you to provide the following information:[93]

- the name and address of your employer;
- your earnings or expected earnings;
- statutory deductions from pay (these must be disregarded when calculating the amount to be deducted under an attachment of earnings order);
- your payroll number;
- details of existing attachment of earnings orders;
- details of other sources of income – eg, occupational pension, benefits;
- whether someone else is jointly liable for the debt.

You do not have to supply the information if the request is not made in writing, or if the information is not in your possession or control. Similarly, you are not required to provide any information which is not prescribed by the regulations – eg, your vehicle number plate. Otherwise, you must provide the information within 14 days of the request being made.[94]

You have no duty to update the local authority of a change of circumstances unless it makes a fresh request for the relevant information, but you do have to inform it about any change in your circumstances as regards your ongoing liability (see Chapter 5) and entitlement to council tax reduction (CTR – see Chapter 8).

If more than one person is named on the council tax account, the local authority can:

- request the same information from each person;
- enforce the order against either or both individuals, though only one enforcement method can be used at a time.

If you fail, without a reasonable excuse, to supply the requested information, you are guilty of a criminal offence and may be fined by the magistrates' court up to a maximum of level 2 (£500).[95] If you 'knowingly or recklessly' supply false information, you could be found guilty of a criminal offence and fined up to a maximum of level 3 (£1,000).[96]

Attachment of earnings order

An attachment of earnings order allows the local authority (that holds a liability order) to instruct your employer or pension provider to make regular deductions from your wages, statutory sick pay (SSP) or occupational pension.[97] The employer then sends the deducted amount to the council to repay the council tax debt. Certain costs arising from unsuccessful enforcement activity may also be recovered by an attachment of earnings order.

Attachment of earnings orders are a practical and, in many cases, preferable alternative to taking control of goods (see p232). However, the decision to use this method of recovery is discretionary and the local authority must consider all the relevant factors before deciding to adopt this method. Normally the local authority offers you the opportunity to pay by instalments before using an attachment of earnings order.

A local authority cannot have more than two council tax attachment of earnings orders against a person at one time.[98]

In addition to each amount deducted, the employer can deduct a further £1 towards administration costs each time a deduction is made.

Local authorities are encouraged to assess the individual's means. Government guidance states: 'Wherever possible, attachments should only be made after reviewing an individual's total debts and other ongoing commitments such as utility bills, mortgages or rent and support of dependents.'[99]

The order

The attachment of earnings order must specify:

- confirmation of the liability order and the outstanding amount;
- the rate at which deductions are to be made from net earnings (see p230);
- the period within which each deduction made is to be paid to the local authority – ie, within 19 days of the end of the month in which the deduction is made.

The order must be signed by the proper officer at the local authority. A facsimile signature is acceptable.

The attachment of earnings order remains in force until:

- the debt (including any costs) is fully paid; *or*
- it is cancelled by the issuing authority.[100]

The local authority may cancel the order on its own initiative or following an application by you or your employer.[101]

Notifying employment changes

While an attachment of earnings order is in force, you must notify the local authority in writing if you leave a job or become employed or re-employed. You must do this within 14 days of the day on which you leave, start or recommence the employment, or (if later) the day on which the local authority informs you that the order has been made.[102] If you do not comply, without a reasonable excuse, you commit an offence and may be fined.[103] If you make a statement that you know to be false, you may also be found guilty of an offence.[104]

The deductions to be made

The deductions are made from your net earnings[105] – ie, after income tax, class 1 national insurance and pension contributions have been deducted.[106] Earnings include your wages/salary, overtime, bonuses, commission, SSP and any other payment under your contract of service.[107]

The amount deducted depends on how often you are paid. If you are not paid weekly or monthly, or are paid on an irregular basis, a daily rate is used. If you are paid monthly, you may be worse off than in the other two situations, as the deduction amount is set by multiplying the weekly amount by four. Special rules cover more unusual payment arrangements.

Deductions from weekly net earnings[108]

Monthly	*Weekly*	*Daily*	*Deduction rate*
Up to £300	Up to £75	Up to £11	0%
£300.01 to £550	£75.01 to £135	£11.01 to £20	3%
£550.01 to £740	£135.01 to £185	£20.01 to £27	5%
£740.01 to £900	£185.01 to £225	£27.01 to £33	7%
£900.01 to £1,420	£225.01 to £355	£33.01 to £52	12%
£1,420.01 to £2,020	£355.01 to £505	£52.01 to £72	17%
£2,020.01 and over	£505.01 and over	£72.01 and over	17% of this threshold and 50% of the remainder

You can negotiate with the local authority and your employer for a lower deduction than the statutory amount.

If your earnings fluctuate, your employer must adjust the deduction accordingly.

Priority of attachment of earnings orders

There is a priority for attachment of earnings orders if more than one has been made against you.[109] Council tax attachment of earnings orders should be dealt with one at a time and in the order in which they are made. If an order is already in force (eg, for child support arrears), a council tax order is applied to the balance of pay remaining after the other deductions have been made. If an order for council tax is in effect when another order is made, the council tax order should continue to be met and the balance considered attachable for the other order.

Complaints about attachment of earnings orders

The Ombudsman will not investigate the decision to apply for an attachment of earnings order but may look into errors in how it is carried out, especially if it is deemed 'disproportionate and heavy-handed'.[110] A council is not at fault for seeking an order if you were allowed to make a settlement but failed to do so.[111] However, it is at fault if it gives you incorrect advice that prevents you from making a reasonable payment offer.[112]

Councillors' allowances

If you are a local authority councillor (but not a member of the Court of Common Council of the City of London), the local authority can deduct 40 per cent from your allowances – eg, for attending meetings and for special responsibilities. This is discretionary, and the authority must consider all the relevant factors.

Note: if an elected member fails to pay council tax within two months of the due date, they cannot vote on matters influencing the setting of the local authority's council tax.[113]

The Information Commissioner has ruled that Freedom of Information Act requests regarding councillors summoned for unpaid council tax should be disclosed due to public scrutiny expectations.[114]

Deductions from benefits

In England, Wales and Scotland, if a liability order (in Scotland, a summary warrant or decree from the sheriff court) has been obtained, the local authority may apply for third-party deductions to be made from your UC, PC or income-related ESA.[115] This is a discretionary decision and the local authority must take all the circumstances of the case into account before deciding to pursue it.[116]

The maximum amount that can be deducted for council tax arrears from:

- UC is 5 per cent of your monthly standard allowance – ie, in 2025/26:

Single claimant	
Under 25	£15.85
Over 25	£20.01
Joint claimants	
Both under 25	£24.88
One or both 25 or over	£31.45

- PC or income-related ESA is £4.55 a week.

If you disagree with a decision about deductions, you can challenge it by asking for a mandatory reconsideration and then appeal.

There are also restrictions if deductions are being made for other debts. See CPAG's *Welfare Benefits Handbook* for details about the rules.

Deductions from benefit can only be made in respect of one application from the local authority at any given time. If the local authority makes a second application before the sum specified in the first application has been fully recovered, the second has to wait until the first has been cleared.[117]

As far as is practicable, you and the local authority should be notified of the decision in writing within 14 days. You should also be notified of your right to appeal against the decision.

When you have paid the debt, the local authority must notify the DWP within 21 days, or as soon as practicable after that.[118]

The DWP must notify you in writing of the total amount deducted under any application if you request this information in writing or the deduction ends.[119]

Taking control of goods

The seizure of goods and their sale at auction to pay off debt is a remedy that local authorities have long used in local taxation.

Schedule 12 to the Tribunals, Courts and Enforcement Act 2007 and the Taking of Control of Goods Regulations 2013 set the rules about taking control of goods and what enforcement agents can and cannot do. These rules govern council tax enforcement against goods.[120] The government prefers to refer to bailiffs as 'enforcement agents' but the term 'bailiff' remains in common use, including by bailiffs themselves.

There are several different types of enforcement agent:

- county court bailiffs are civil servants enforcing judgments (usually not council tax);
- High Court enforcement officers are privately authorised officers who enforce High Court judgments;
- local authority enforcement agents are employed directly by councils or contracted private firms to collect council tax debts.

They all enforce liabilities by taking control of goods.

It is good practice for local authorities to consider other methods (such as attachment of earnings orders or deductions from benefits) in preference to taking control of goods as an initial enforcement option. If some other method of recovery is in force, the local authority has no power to take control of goods.[121]

Local authorities must issue a written notice at least seven days before visiting to take control of goods.[122] Sundays, bank holidays, Good Friday and Christmas Day do not count in calculating the seven-day period.[123]

Some councils require enforcement firms to operate a longer notice period. The government has proposed reforms that would extend the minimum notice period from seven days to 28 days. It claims this should give people in debt sufficient time to get debt advice, to assess their ability to pay and to agree a repayment plan.

The written notice must mention *all* of the following:[124]

- your name and address; *and*
- the reference number(s); *and*
- the date of notice; *and*
- details of the liability order; *and*
- the amount of any enforcement costs incurred up to the date of notice; *and*
- the possible additional costs of enforcement if the sum outstanding should remain unpaid as at the date mentioned; *and*
- how, and between which hours and on which days, payment of the sum outstanding may be made; *and*
- a contact phone number, address and the hours available for the enforcement agent or their office; *and*
- details of the debt to enable the debtor to identify the debt correctly; *and*
- the amount of the debt, including any interest due; *and*
- the date and time to pay by to avoid enforcement.

The seven-day notice may be served by post, email or fax or be hand delivered or affixed to the property (if no letterbox).[125]

Codes of practice

Local authorities must ensure their enforcement agents are properly authorised and follow the law.[126] In addition to national standards, councils may have their own codes of practice. Failure to follow these may be maladministration and grounds for a complaint to the Ombudsman (see p300).[127]

Vulnerable households

Enforcement agents must take extra care when dealing with vulnerable people. The regulations restrict the steps that enforcement agents may take when encountering individuals who may be classed as vulnerable. While not defined in the regulations, vulnerability is explained in the *Taking Control of Goods: national standards*, which says you are vulnerable if, because of your age, health or disability, you cannot safeguard your personal welfare or that of other members of your household.[128] See p326 for examples of groups who could be considered vulnerable. Vulnerability can be temporary – eg, during illness or injury. The enforcement officer must assess the situation they find at the property and decide whether to proceed.

Note: agents are not permitted to carry out the taking control of goods procedure if a child or vulnerable person is the only person present in the dwelling.

Is someone in the household vulnerable?

Inform the local authority and enforcement agent in writing as soon as possible and:

– include medical evidence, support letters, or any relevant documentation;

– request that enforcement action be suspended or stopped;
– insist they follow vulnerability protocols under the national standards.

Goods

Goods are property of any description other than land.[129] An enforcement agent can only take control of goods which belong to you[130] on premises that they have power to enter or that are on the highway.[131] If goods are jointly owned, the enforcement agent must obtain full details of the co-owner and they must be included in subsequent proceedings and be paid their share of the proceeds of any sale.

Exempt goods

The following are exempt and cannot be taken into control:[132]

- your only or principal home. This can include a houseboat, tent, caravan, mobile home or vehicle if it is your home;[133]
- items or equipment (eg, tools, books, phones, computers and vehicles) that you need for your employment, business, trade, profession, study or education. The total value of these items must not exceed £1,350;
- clothing, bedding, furniture, household equipment, items and provisions reasonably required to satisfy your basic domestic needs and those of every member of your household. These include:
  - a cooker or microwave, but not both;
  - a refrigerator;
  - a washing machine;
  - a dining table and enough dining chairs for all household members;
  - beds and bedding sufficient for every member of the household;
  - a landline phone or a mobile phone (if no landline);
  - medical and care equipment reasonably required for the care of any member of the household, or for safety or security – eg, an alarm system;
  - sufficient lamps or heaters to meet basic lighting/heating needs;
- any item or equipment reasonably required for the care of a person under the age of 18, a disabled person or an older person;
- assistance dogs (including guide dogs, hearing dogs and disabled aid dogs), sheep dogs, guard dogs and domestic pets;
- a vehicle displaying a valid Blue Badge or clearly used by a disabled person;
- fixtures – ie, things attached to the property, including anything plumbed in or that forms part of the property. This includes light and electrical fittings, baths, hobs, stoves, shelves and built-in wardrobes;
- goods that are in use whose seizure would likely result in a breach of the peace.[134]

Items belonging to children or used exclusively by them cannot be taken.[135]

Goods that are unlawful to use (such as unlicensed motor vehicles) are exempt from seizure.[136]

Lawful entry to premises

Time

In general, entry should only take place between 6am and 9pm on any day of the week.[137]

Place

An enforcement agent can only enter a property where they reasonably believe you live or run a business. This typically means your primary home or the place where council tax is paid. Enforcement agents cannot enter properties owned by relatives or neighbours unless you live or work there.[138] **Note**: 'premises' can include vehicles, vessels, tents and other movable structures. However, agents cannot seize goods on private land like car parks without a court order. Clamping cars other than on your property or on the highway is not lawful.

If an enforcement agent cannot prove a valid liability order, their authority to enforce is questionable.[139]

Virtual seizure and controlled goods agreements

In some cases, enforcement agents may offer to arrange a controlled goods agreement remotely – eg, by email or phone. This is sometimes called a 'virtual seizure'. Consequently, an enforcement agent may enter into a controlled goods agreement within the meaning of Schedule 12 to the Tribunals, Courts and Enforcement Act 2007 with a debtor, whether or not the agent enters.[140] However, this is only a decision of a Master in the High Court and if no consent is given and no agreement is signed and the enforcement agent has not entered the premises, then no seizure has taken place.[141]

Method of entry

The enforcement agent must enter a property peacefully through an unlocked door or other usual entrance.[142] They should be clear as to why they are seeking entry to the premises. Enforcement agents cannot obtain a court order to gain entry to any property for council tax debts, nor can an occupier be sent to prison merely for refusing entry. You are entitled to use reasonable force in resisting agents who try unlawfully to push their way in.[143]

Identification

The enforcement agent must show evidence of their identity and authority to enter, which you can request before or during the visit.[144]

Ways of taking control

To take control of goods, an enforcement officer must do *one* of the following:[145]

- enter into a 'controlled goods agreement'; *or*
- secure the goods on the premises; *or*
- secure the goods on the highway; *or*
- remove the goods and secure them elsewhere.

Controlled goods agreements

A 'controlled goods agreement' lets an enforcement agent list your possessions without removing them from your home. You must not remove or dispose of the goods, nor permit anyone else to do so, until the debt is paid.

The agent must not enter into a controlled goods agreement if you do not understand it due to language, learning or mental health problems.[146]

To be enforceable, a controlled goods agreement must be signed. If the document has been misrepresented, the signature is not effective.[147]

It must be signed by both you (or someone acting for you) and the agent, and include:[148]

- your name and address;
- the agreement date and reference;
- the names of all persons entering into the agreement;
- the enforcement agent contact details and office hours;
- a list of the goods and their description, including;
  - the manufacturer, model and serial number of the goods;
  - for vehicles, the manufacturer, model, colour and registration;
  - the material, colour and usage, and (where appropriate) any other identifying characteristic, of the goods;
- the repayment terms.

You must be given a copy of the signed agreement.

Securing the goods

The enforcement agent may secure goods on premises – eg, in a cupboard, room, garage or outbuilding.[149] They may immobilise vehicles. Separate rules and notice provisions apply to taking goods from the highway.[150] The enforcement agent must keep the goods in the same condition they found them. This means that secure storage should prevent damage or deterioration of the goods for so long as they remain in the agent's control.[151]

If the agent has already taken control of goods but has not yet removed them, they have the legal right to re-enter your premises. They can use forced entry under these circumstances, but you must be notified before any forcible entry.[152] The notice must be given by the enforcement agent personally (not by post) or left in a prominent place.[153]

Removing the goods

Additional information and notice and an inventory are issued if goods are removed,[154] including a notice giving the date of removal of the goods to storage or for sale, the daily and weekly charges and the procedure for collection by, or on behalf of, the debtor.[155] Removal is rare, as auction prices seldom cover enforcement or auction fees and subsequently leave the debt outstanding. Household items also require safety certificates to sell. Enforcement agents typically prefer to arrange payment or a controlled goods agreement instead.

Selling goods

Taking control of goods provides security in case you fail to pay. Enforcement officers have a general duty to sell the goods for the best price. They must obtain a valuation and allow you (or a co-owner) to get an independent valuation if desired. They must give at least seven days' notice of the sale, within 12 months. This period can be extended (repeatedly, if necessary). This allows you to make instalment payments to discharge the debt.

Note: a sale cannot be completed if a third-party claim to ownership is outstanding.[156]

After the sale

Immediately after the sale, the enforcement officer must provide you and any co-owner with a statement detailing the items sold and the sum received for each. It must also state how the sale proceeds are applied to the costs and to your debt. Any recoverable expenses incurred by the enforcement officer should be listed.

Fees

Fees

Compliance stage fee: £75

Upon receipt of an instruction from the authority, the enforcement agent must send a notice of enforcement giving you a minimum of seven clear days' notice that a visit will take place to take control of goods.

This fee is payable for each liability order/warrant of control.

Enforcement stage fee: £235 (plus 7.5 per cent of the value of any council tax debt that exceeds £1,500)

This fee becomes chargeable when the debt is not paid during the compliance stage or when a payment arrangement is broken and an enforcement agent visits the property to remove goods.

Sale stage fee: £110 (plus 7.5 per cent of the value of the debt that exceeds £1,500)[157]

This fee is charged when an enforcement agent attends the premises to remove goods and arrange for their sale. Additional charges may be applied relating to the removal. These include storage and locksmith's fees.

As soon as one of these stages begins, the enforcement agent is likely to demand the fee, even though they may not have completed all the activities covered by the stage. Fees should only be charged for steps actually taken.

Where a liability order has been made against more than one person in respect of an amount, only one compliance fee is payable and no additional charge may be imposed against the other persons. A single charge for the compliance stage is treated as the charge covering the others, as well as the first named person.[158]

Where you fall into a vulnerable category (see p233), the enforcement agent is required to give you 'an adequate opportunity to obtain assistance and advice prior to removal of the goods'. The enforcement stage fee is not recoverable if the enforcement agent does not do this.[159]

Enforcement agents can only impose the above charges, plus the outstanding amount due under the liability order. The enforcement agent and the local authority cannot charge for other matters, such as writing letters or making arrangements to pay.

Challenge any questionable charges first with the enforcement agents, then with the local authority using its formal complaints procedure. If neither resolves the matter, you can make a complaint to the Ombudsman (see p300).[160] For example, if you make an arrangement with the enforcement agent and no goods are taken, there should be no charge for their removal.[161]

Fees are recoverable from the proceeds of sale of the seized goods or may be paid by the local authority.[162] Legislation states that fees may be recovered from you, but no mechanism is clearly set out to enforce payment; the legislation envisages that the sums claimed are only payable where the steps for which they are levied are actually taken, meaning that goods have to be taken away and sold at auction. In such cases, the sums are then deducted from the proceeds of sale.[163]

You can take any dispute over the fees to the civil courts.[164] If you think you have been overcharged by enforcement agents, you can also make an application in the county court, but you will be expected to first obtain a ruling from a valuation tribunal if the local authority disputes the amount.[165] For more information, see Chapter 12.

Return of the council tax debt to the local authority

Some local authorities wrongly claim that once a debt is with an enforcement agent, it cannot be returned to them. This is incorrect, as enforcement agents work for the local authority and follow its instructions. The only powers they have are to take control of goods, not to make financial decisions. Regulations allow payments to be made directly to the local authority at any time.[166]

If a local authority refuses to reconsider a debt returned from enforcement agents, you can challenge this by complaining to the district auditor. Mentioning the possibility of involving the auditor often prompts the authority to reconsider its actions.

Remedies against wrongful enforcement

If you are unhappy with an enforcement officer's conduct, you can threaten or take court action, or make a complaint.

Many enforcement officers now wear body-worn video cameras that record all visits to premises. You can ask for the footage to help resolve a dispute.

If enforcement agents wrongly seize goods, you, and any third party (eg, your landlord or a relative) may take legal action. The most common ground for action is when enforcement agents have taken control of the wrong person's goods, such as those belonging to a non-liable person.[167]

You, a creditor or co-owner of any goods are entitled to make an application to the court. In a dispute about the amount of proceeds payable to the co-owner of the goods, the court determines the matter.[168]

You may take proceedings in the county court or High Court, where you can seek remedies like the return of goods, payment of damages, or an injunction.[169] Claims under £10,000 can be made via the small claims track, where legal costs are not awarded.

Regulations provide that only 'fit and proper' persons are authorised to act as enforcement agents.[170] To challenge an enforcement agent's conduct, you can file a complaint about their fitness to practice with the county court using the EAC2 form.[171] If the agent is found unfit, their certificate may be suspended or cancelled, and goods may be returned. The enforcement agent, or the company they work for, could be liable for damages for wrongful acts. Individual enforcement agents may have a defence to a claim if they have a reasonable belief that what was done was not in breach of Schedule 12 or the liability order was not defective,[172] but the council as creditor may be held liable for damages for breaches of the Tribunals Courts and Enforcement Act 2007.[173]

If harm or damage caused by an enforcement agent is valued below £10,000, you may pursue a claim through the county court, to be allocated to the small claims track. For example, if you are owed money or should be paid compensation, you can start a claim through the county court using Form N1, with the amount limited to a maximum of £10,000 for the small claims track. You can take the action against the enforcement agent individually, the company employing the enforcement agent or the local authority.[174] The small claims track is a more attractive option, as neither side can claim legal costs.

The complaint must provide details and can include documentary evidence in support (which may include digital images) which explain the reason or reasons why the certificated person is not a fit person to hold a certificate to be an enforcement agent.[175]

You can find leaflets explaining how to bring a claim in the county court at your local county court or at hmctsformfinder.justice.gov.uk.

The Enforcement Conduct Board

The Enforcement Conduct Board (ECB) is a regulator formed in 2022. It is currently a non-statutory regulatory body aiming to oversee the enforcement and debt collection industry and hold it to greater account. The ECB is independent of government and the industry, and is funded by a voluntary levy.[176]

The ECB can conduct audits and reviews of firms' policies, procedures and compliance. It applies to all enforcement activities, not just council tax.

To be ECB-accredited, firms must:

- follow professional standards and comply with the law and the ECB's professional values;
- pay the annual levy and submit regular data returns to the ECB;
- co-operate with the ECB monitoring and information requests;
- handle complaints properly, including complying with remedies the ECB recommends.

The ECB accreditation scheme is voluntary but most of the larger firms have signed up to it. At the time of writing, 96 per cent of the market share of enforcement activity has signed up.

From 1 January 2025, if you are unhappy with the conduct of an ECB-accredited firm, and their internal complaints process has not resolved the issue, you can escalate your complaint directly to the ECB.

The ECB has signed a Memorandum of Understanding with the Local Government and Social Care Ombudsman to improve the handling of complaints about enforcement agents acting on behalf of local authorities. The agreement sets out how the two organisations work together to ensure complaints are properly handled and enable data to be shared.

Charging orders

A charging order effectively secures a debt against property you own (fully or partly) in a similar way to a mortgage. It cannot be used if you are a tenant or licensee.

The local authority can apply for a charging order if:[177]

- it obtained one or more liability orders for the debt; *and*
- the total council tax arrears are at least £1,000 (usually used for debts of over £5,000).

A charging order cannot be used against any other property owned or occupied by you. A charging order can only be placed on the home you owe tax on (not other properties), and once in place, other enforcement methods (like enforcement agents) should not be used.[178]

Charging orders in the county court proceed through the Civil National Business Centre (CNBC). You should take part in proceedings and can apply to the valuation tribunal to challenge liability or calculation of the tax.

If the dwelling is used as a family home, the court has an overarching duty to consider Article 8 of the European Convention on Human Rights (ECHR) (right to respect for private/family life) and balance this against the council's right to recover the debt.[179] The court must also consider:[180]

- your personal circumstances; *and*
- the interests of any other creditor; *and*
- whether anyone would be 'unduly prejudiced' by the order.

You or any party with an interest in the property can apply to the court to discharge or vary the order[181] – eg, if the debt or your circumstances have changed. Applications are transferred from the CNBC to your local county court.[182]

If the debt remains unpaid, the council can ask the court for an order for sale. These are rarely granted if the home is occupied or jointly owned. Courts weigh the family's rights under the ECHR against the council's right to recover the debt. Even when granted, a sale can be postponed.

See CPAG's *Debt Advice Handbook* for more information.

Bankruptcy proceedings

If the local authority has obtained a liability order, it can apply for bankruptcy if you owe at least £5,000. It may combine multiple debts into one application.

People with unmanageable debts sometimes apply for their own bankruptcy, especially if they do not have assets. Always discuss your circumstances with a debt adviser before applying for bankruptcy.

The trustee in bankruptcy (appointed by the Official Receiver or insolvency practitioner) will handle your financial affairs, and bankruptcy lasts 12 months. After that, you are discharged from debt. Bankruptcy also stops other enforcement actions, including imprisonment.[183]

If you are facing bankruptcy proceedings, you should obtain professional advice as quickly as possible. A local authority will only apply to make you bankrupt if you have assets that can be sold to pay the debt. For homeowners, bankruptcy could lead to the loss of your home, and the legal costs will be added to your debt. However, bankruptcy proceedings may give you a chance to dispute council tax liability or correct miscalculations (eg, exemptions, CTR eligibility). While a formal appeal is ongoing, the council should halt recovery actions.

Useful guides

The Insolvency Service's guide to bankruptcy is at gov.uk/government/organisations/insolvency-service.

CPAG's *Debt Advice Handbook* is free to access at cpag.org.uk/handbooks.

Support Through Court provides advice if the local authority is proceeding through the High Court (helpline: 0300 081 0006; supportthroughcourt.org).

The Local Government and Social Care Ombudsman has a factsheet at lgo.org.uk/make-a-complaint/fact-sheets/benefits-and-tax/bankruptcy.

Evidence of the bankruptcy debt

The local authority must prove the existence of a valid liability order.[184] The High Court has indicated that it will consider whether the debt can be substantiated, which may be a debtor's only route to challenge the claim.

Often, magistrates' courts do not produce properly signed or sealed liability orders, especially when local authorities use automated bulk summons systems (see p226). These may not generate an individual, signed copy of the order.

If you were not notified of the liability order hearing, ask the local authority to produce the order.[185] If it cannot provide a properly signed or stamped document, the court may reject the application as the order was not lawfully obtained.

Paying the debt

You can avoid bankruptcy by paying the debt before the bankruptcy order is made. The court may grant an adjournment if you show a realistic plan to pay – eg, by borrowing the funds.[186] However, repeated adjournments are unlikely. Even if you clear the council tax, you may still be liable for bankruptcy costs.

The bankruptcy hearing

It is essential to attend any hearing, otherwise you risk being made bankrupt in your absence. You can bring a representive (if you have one). Legal aid may be available if your home is at risk, but it can be hard to access.

The court must ensure that exercising its discretion to make a bankruptcy order does not cause injustice.[187] You can argue that:

- you are able to pay the debt;
- you made a reasonable offer that the council unreasonably refused;[188]
- there is a set-off, counterclaim or payment made already;
- a genuine appeal is lodged with the valuation tribunal.[189]

Use a witness statement to set out your financial position, explain your reasons and include any supporting evidence. You can cross-examine the local authority's case.

By the time the bankruptcy petition reaches court, it is often too late to challenge the liability order by applying to the magistrates' court or the High Court. Most challenges should be made via the valuation tribunal,[190] though in rare cases the court may examine liability issues.[191]

Make sure the amounts and dates in the petition match the liability order. Courts often wrongly assume liability could be disputed at the liability order hearing.[192]

If a statutory demand failed to refer to your right to apply to set it aside, or if your earlier arguments were rejected, you can still raise them at the petition stage.[193]

The court might adjourn proceedings if you have appealed to the valuation tribunal. The appeal should be brought promptly. An adjournment is much more likely where you have appealed in time and a decision of the tribunal can be expected reasonably soon than if you made an out-of-time appeal.[194]

An adjournment may also be granted if you show a realistic prospect of settling the debt, and should not be unreasonably refused if you have evidence of making payments or attempts at making payment. Factors that may be taken into account include a lack of legal advice and confusion on what may be required.[195]

If your appeal has no real prospect of success, the court is likely to proceed with the bankruptcy. Otherwise, it may adjourn or dismiss the petition depending on the circumstances.[196]

Appeals on a point of law against a bankruptcy order

Where the county court makes a bankruptcy order which involves an error of law, you must apply to the High Court.[197] File a notice of appeal at the Royal Courts of Justice in London within 14 days of the bankruptcy judgment. You can read a practice direction about proceedings at www.justice.gov.uk/courts/procedure-rules/civil/rules/insolvency_pd.

You must provide details of the county court that made the order and a copy of any judgment. You must obtain a transcript of the hearing and prepare a skeleton argument and chronology (the requirement to serve these with the notice of appeal may be waived if you are unrepresented, although you will be required to do this later).[198]

You can ask the High Court to stay (pause) the bankruptcy proceedings until your appeal is heard. Legal aid may be available if your home is at risk.

Your appeal should explain where the county court judge erred in law. Grounds may include that the local authority could not produce a valid liability order, the evidence does not prove the case, or there has been a material irregularity during the proceedings.[199] A petition can also be dismissed if it is an abuse of process in being created for an extraneous purpose.[200]

Where a bankruptcy order is made, the trustee in bankruptcy has three years to take action to sell or secure your interest in the property. If this is not done, your interest in the property returns to you automatically.[201] The three years start from the date that the bankruptcy application was lodged, not the date of the hearing.[202]

After one year, courts are more likely to favour creditors' interests unless there are exceptional circumstances (eg, serious illness).[203]

Annulment and rescission of bankruptcy orders

After the bankruptcy order has been made, you can apply to have it annulled (cancelled) under the Insolvency Act 1986, if certain conditions apply.

Annulment may be justified where:[204]

- the local authority cannot provide a proper account;
- the local authority has failed to follow its own criteria;
- the local authority could have pursued other recovery methods;

- there is a failure to serve documents;
- it is disproportionate in the circumstances;
- the amount of the debt has been paid.[205]

Apply to the court that made the order and send a copy to the Official Receiver. Alternatively, you can seek rescission of the order.[206]

Annulment or rescission is a discretionary decision for the court, even if the liability has been quashed or the property removed from the valuation list. Appeals are rare unless the decision is clearly unreasonable.[207]

Get specialist advice on these issues.

Adjournment of the bankruptcy petition

In *Okon v London Borough of Lewisham*, the court held that a judge should adjourn a bankruptcy hearing if a valuation tribunal appeal is pending.[208]

Many debtors only realise there was improper service of documents after a bankruptcy order is made, often after receiving legal advice. Councils often use outside agents, and complaints about poor or failed service in council tax cases (including bankruptcy or charging orders) are increasing.[209] Improper service can be the basis of an appeal or a complaint to the court.

Failure of service of documents where a debtor has moved away or even never occupied a property may be an issue. If you do not get served with key legal documents in council tax cases, it is very serious and needs a legal response. Knowing about the case against you is crucial to getting justice. You must know about a case against you and at least have an opportunity to attend. Instead of using the post, these documents get served personally by a process server.

Any deliberate failure to serve documents is a contempt of court or perjury because the process server or solicitor has misled the court.

Imprisonment

England is the only country in Europe where a person can be imprisoned for unpaid local tax. Wales and Scotland do not allow imprisonment for council tax arrears. Wales abolished it in April 2019 with no rise in default rates.[210]

While the power to imprison remains in England, its use is rare – around 100 people a year were imprisoned as of 2016.[211] It is not a punishment, but a last resort to force payment from someone who can pay but refuses.[212]

English local authorities can apply to the magistrates' court for a warrant committing a debtor to prison.[213] A local authority can only seek a warrant of commitment if it has been informed that an attempt to recover the debt by enforcement agents has been unsuccessful. If it appears to the local authority that (for whatever reason) no or insufficient sums can be recovered, it can proceed to seek committal. If there has been no attempt to seize goods, imprisonment is not available.

If a subcontractor is collecting the debt, the council must terminate enforcement before seeking imprisonment.[214]

The cost of applying for a warrant is £212 from 8 April 2025.[215]

The maximum sentence is three months,[216] used only in extreme, deliberate non-payment cases.[217]

If you are threatened with imprisonment

Contact the local authority immediately in writing. Set out your financial circumstances and ask the local authority to use its power under section 13A(1)(c) of the Local Government Finance Act 1992 to reduce or remit the debt where there is financial hardship (see p135).

Imprisonment is intended as a last resort where no other method of enforcement and recovery of the debt is available. Alternatives should be properly considered (eg, deductions from benefits) by the magistrates' court.

Means inquiry

Before issuing a warrant of commitment to prison, the magistrates' court must conduct a formal means inquiry to assess your financial situation. This includes questioning your income, outgoings, debts and savings to understand why you have not paid. To enable such an inquiry, you may be summoned to appear before a magistrates' court.[218]

The magistrates' court must properly assess your means. If it fails to do so, the committal order can be quashed on appeal to the High Court. If you get means-tested benefits, point out that your financial circumstances have already been assessed and found to be limited. The High Court has held that a committal order is wrong where benefit deductions are available.[219] The same also applies where an attachment of earnings would be available.[220]

A typical error in many means inquiries is failing to ask the debtor if they have any savings or capital. A lack of accessible savings or capital is likely to mean that you cannot pay the sum immediately. If you simply do not have enough money to pay on the day, the warrant should not be issued[221] as the purpose of committal is coercive and not intended as a punishment or as a deterrent to other non-payers.[222] This principle also applies to any decision to issue a warrant that has previously been suspended on terms. Magistrates should not simply assume that a failure to keep to an order results from wilful refusal.[223]

A warrant to commit you to prison is only issued if the court is satisfied that failure to pay is due to:

- your wilful refusal – eg, you deliberately decide not to pay even though you can; *or*
- your culpable neglect – eg, you have spent available income on non-essential items rather than paying your debt;[224] *and*

- you have the means on the day of the hearing to pay the debt.[225]

Only a failure by you to pay council tax that is 'blameworthy' is considered to be wilful refusal or culpable neglect. You should not be at risk of imprisonment if you cannot pay because you do not have enough income, or the failure arose through illness, job loss, a domestic disaster such as a fire or flood, unexpected pregnancy, being forced from a property as a result of domestic abuse, or a failure to pay benefit. In such cases, the court should make an application to remit the debt (see below).

Even if wilful refusal or culpable neglect is found, the court must still assess whether issuing the warrant is reasonable. If you make a realistic offer of payment, the court should accept it.[226] If you are seriously ill and cannot attend the hearing, the court should avoid imprisonment without further investigation.[227]

Mothers with young children

Under Article 8 of the European Convention on Human Rights, the court must:
- consider the impact of imprisonment on children;
- ensure the committal is proportionate to the amount owed;
- avoid imprisonment where alternatives exist or where the debt is small.

In *R (Stokes) v Gwent Magistrates' Court*, the High Court held that jailing a young mother for 12 days for a debt of £455 violated Article 8, highlighting the disproportionate nature of imprisonment for small amounts.[228]

Courts must carefully weigh the effect on family life, especially in cases involving mothers with young children.[229]

Remission of the debt

If you are unable to pay or have very old debts, the magistrates' court can remit (cancel) the debt, in part or in full.[230] The council tax debt is extinguished for the financial year in question, but not for subsequent years.

Partial remission can occur if a payment plan would result in an unreasonably long repayment period (more than three years).[231] However, the court may choose to postpone the warrant to a specific date and review payment terms if it seems the debt will not be cleared in three years.

Once imprisonment terms are set, no remission is possible. If you cannot meet the payment terms, inform the court, which may postpone the warrant indefinitely. Alternatively, you can request that the High Court quashes the warrant if there was a defect in the means inquiry.[232]

Challenging a decision to imprison

You can challenge a decision to imprison by way of a case stated appeal (within 21 days) or by judicial review (within three months).[233] In practice, if the warrant of commitment has been issued and you are already in prison, judicial review is the preferred route of appeal, as the High Court can grant immediate bail to an imprisoned debtor, pending the full appeal hearing. Local authorities are expected to file witness statements or at least supply details of what led to the committal application. The High Court expects that the authority, when challenged, should set out what they did and why, so far as is necessary, fully and fairly to meet the challenge.[234]

5. Statutory enforcement in Scotland

Council tax enforcement in Scotland differs greatly from in England and Wales.

A key difference is the 20-year limitation in Scotland, compared with six years in England and Wales.[235] Although Scottish authorities can pursue council tax debts for up to 20 years, many councils choose not to. Also, Scottish authorities can only start enforcement once a bill has been issued or acknowledged, and a bill can only be issued retrospectively if you gave false information or deliberately avoided payment.[236]

Reminders and losing the right to pay by instalments

If an instalment under the statutory instalment scheme or any special agreement has not been paid by the due date, the local authority must serve a reminder notice on the liable person. It requires payment within seven days.[237] The notice must include:

- the instalment(s) due and the remainder balance for the year;
- a statement that failure to pay within seven days will result in losing the right to pay by instalments, making the full annual balance due.

Note: from 1 April 2025, only one reminder notice will be issued, requiring action within 21 days. No final notice will be sent.

If you receive two reminders during the financial year, a third missed payment makes the full balance due immediately, without another reminder.[238] The second notice must warn of this.

The local authority can only take recovery action for unpaid amounts, including the 10 per cent statutory surcharge and civil penalties.[239]

Local councillors with over two months' arrears may face voting restrictions. (see p231).[240]

Appeal to the Local Taxation Chamber

If you dispute liability to pay, the local authority must start the first stage of an appeal to the Local Taxation Chamber of the First-tier Tribunal for Scotland (LTC).[241] This enables the sheriff to refuse to grant a summary warrant or decree while the matter is being considered. You must serve a letter or notice on the local authority within 14 days of the reminder or final notice.

Summary warrant or decree

A summary warrant is a fast-track process used by local authorities to recover unpaid debts such as council tax, water charges or civil penalties. It allows enforcement without a court hearing, based solely on a certificate submitted by the local authority.[242] It results in rapid enforcement.

The sheriff must grant the warrant if the local authority certifies that:[243]

- a reminder notice was served and payment was not made within 14 days; *and*
- no appeal was lodged within 14 days, or any grievance has been addressed or time-barred; *and*
- the amount remains unpaid.

If multiple people are jointly liable, the warrant can show joint or individual liability.[244]

There is no requirement for the council or the sheriff court to give notice to you or allow the chance to challenge the debt before the warrant is granted.

A number of legal opinions consider that the summary warrant process may breach Article 6 of the European Convention on Human Rights (right to a fair hearing), since the debtor is not given a chance to present evidence or contest the debt.

Providing information

Once a summary warrant or decree for payment is issued, you must provide specified information the local authority requires.[245] The obligation lasts for as long as any part of the relevant amount remains unpaid. You must provide:

- your employer's name; *and*
- your employer's address – if the employer has no premises in Scotland, provide any Scottish business address of the employer; *and*
- your national insurance number; *and*
- your bank account details; *and*
- details of anyone else jointly liable, including full name and address of each other person jointly liable for the debt.

You must provide the information in writing within 14 days of the local authority's request.[246] Failure to comply could result in a civil penalty.

If a penalty has been issued due to non-compliance with a council tax-related request, recovery action must pause as soon as you lodge an appeal to the LTC. Enforcement cannot proceed until the appeal is decided or withdrawn.

Recovery methods

Once a summary warrant or decree of payment is issued, the local authority can recover unpaid council tax, Scottish Water charges and civil penalties, plus a 10 per cent surcharge (see p252), by either:

- an earnings arrestment (see p250); *or*
- deductions from benefits (see p231); *or*
- an arrestment and action of furthcoming and sale (see p251);[247] *or*
- sequestration (taking temporary possession) if the debt exceeds £3,000. For more information, see aib.gov.uk; *or*
- attachment and exceptional attachment orders. **Note:** special permission is needed from the sheriff for a special attachment to seize goods.

The summary warrant is enforced by sheriff officers or messengers-at-arms. Their fees and expenses are charged to you.[248] Before action, they must provide a Debt Advice and Information Package (DAIP), which explains your rights and where to get help.[249] It is available from aib.gov.uk.

A DAIP is a legal requirement before an attachment can occur.

When sheriff officers serve a document by leaving it at a household or place of business, they must ensure that is likely to catch your attention. It must be in a sealed, clearly marked envelope and bear the notice: 'This envelope contains a citation or intimation from [the specific sheriff court] and sealed by the sheriff officer.'[250]

It is important to inform sheriff officers in writing if you have appealed or dispute liability. **Note:** sheriff officers cannot demand entry to your home without a court order, known as an 'exceptional attachment order'. Entry must not be forced unless someone over 16 who understands what is happening is present.

Misconduct by messengers-at-arms is dealt with by the Court of Session. Misconduct by sheriff officers is dealt with by a sheriff. Penalties may include suspension, removal from office or a fine.[251]

Have you been contacted by a sheriff officer?

Act quickly, especially if you are in dispute or have lodged an appeal.

Inform them in writing of any pending appeals or liability disputes.

Get debt advice immediately – enforcement may be paused depending on your circumstances.

Challenging liability

If you dispute your liability or the amount the authority asks for, you should appeal promptly under section 81 of the Local Government Finance Act 1992 (see Chapter 11). This is particularly important if enforcement action is ongoing or likely. Simply writing or communicating with sheriff officers about a dispute has been ruled insufficient to be a valid notice of appeal.[252]

If a sheriff has already made a decision, you can appeal under section 110 of the Courts Reform (Scotland) Act 2014.

Representation at hearings

If you cannot afford a lawyer, you can be represented by a lay person (someone who is not legally qualified).[253] However, there are important restrictions and procedures. A lay representative can speak on your behalf, even in the Court of Session, but in summary warrant proceedings (which are closed and automatic), you cannot argue your case in the sheriff court. However, if the local authority applies for a normal decree, you can argue your case in court.

The lay person must formally apply to the court to obtain the appropriate approval to be heard.[254] You apply by submitting a motion to the court, attaching Form 4.3, signed by the lay person. The appointment is at the court's discretion, based on the interest of justice. Permission may be for a single or multiple specified hearings.[255]

The right to a McKenzie friend does not exist in Scotland.

Earnings arrestment

A sheriff officer can serve an earnings arrestment schedule on your employer, requiring them to deduct a prescribed amount from your net earnings every payday. The arrestment continues until the debt is paid off or you leave your job. It functions similarly to an attachment of earnings in England and Wales.

The amounts that can be seized by way of a diligence (court order) against earnings are known as an arrestment of earnings.

In 2022/23, over 454,000 earnings arrestments were executed in Scotland. Around 91 per cent were for unpaid council tax.[256]

Deductions are made based on your net income and follow set bands. These are updated annually and apply to arrestments from 6 April 2025 onward.[257] Older arrestments (pre-April 2018) may still follow previous rules unless your employer chooses to apply the new rates after being informed.[258]

Net monthly earnings	*Deduction*
£750.00 or less	Nil
£750.00 to £1,500.00	£10.00 or 15% of earnings over £750.00, whichever is greater
£1,500.00 to £2,500.00	£112.50 plus 20% of earnings over £1,500.00
Over £2,500.00	£312.50 plus 25% of earnings over £2,500.00
Over £3,750.00	£625.00 plus 50% of earnings over £3,750.00
Net weekly earnings	*Deduction*
£172.60 or less	Nil
£172.61 to £345.22	£2.30 or 15% of earnings over £172.61, whichever is greater
£345.22 to £575.37	£25.89 plus 20% of earnings over £345.22

£575.37 to £863.06	£71.92 plus 25% of earnings over £863.06
Over £863.06	£143.84 plus 50% of earnings over £863.06
Net daily earnings	***Deduction***
£24.65 or less	Nil
£24.66 to £82.19	£0.33 or 15% of earnings over £24.66, whichever is greater
£82.19 to £123.29	£3.70 plus 20% of earnings over £82.19
Over £123.29	£20.55 plus 50% of earnings over £123.29

When applying a percentage, the calculation should be to two decimal places and the result rounded to the nearest whole penny, with exact half pennies rounded down.[259]

The regulations make very specific provision for calculating percentages of both monthly and weekly earnings that should be followed to the letter.[260]

An arrestment and action of furthcoming or sale

'Arrestment' is the process by which money or goods held by a third party for a debtor may be frozen. It is usually used for bank accounts. If your bank account details are unknown, usually bank arrestments are initiated by serving letters on the main banks. If money is identified as held by a third party, an arrestment is served by an officer of the court, with a witness present, which freezes the funds. They cannot be withdrawn until the debt has been settled. You are typically asked to sign a mandate to release the money to the council. If you refuse to sign, the council must go to court to raise an action of furthcoming to access the funds.

Any money that remains in the account is released.

You cannot defend the action by disputing the debt, but you can defend it by showing that the arrestment was invalid, procedurally irregular or gained nothing.

Suspension of the summary warrant

This process allows you to apply to temporarily halt enforcement actions (such as arrestments or earnings arrestments) that arise from a summary warrant, but it is subject to strict conditions.

Before the sheriff makes any order for summary suspension, you must provide a caution (a financial bond) or other sufficient security to cover the council tax owed, any interest and any expenses the sheriff believes should be added.[261]

Time to pay orders

You can apply to a sheriff court for a time to pay order.[262] This allows you to pay council tax arrears in affordable instalments. While the order is in force, the local authority cannot enforce the debt.

The court must grant the order if it considers it is reasonable. It must take into account:

- the nature and reasons for the debt;
- whether the council offered help – eg, a payment plan;
- your financial circumstances;
- how reasonable your offer is;
- whether any refusal or any objection from the local authority is reasonable.

Sequestration and bankruptcy

A local authority may initiate bankruptcy proceedings (known as sequestration) to recover unpaid council tax under the Bankruptcy (Scotland) Act 2016.

To obtain a sequestration warrant, the local authority must provide evidence of the debt, usually via a certified extract from the summary warrant process.

A warrant of sequestration may be refused if the local authority fails to show clear evidence connecting the person to the debt or if the statutory process (eg, service of notices) was not properly followed.[263]

Enforcement costs

When a summary warrant is issued for unpaid council tax, a 10 per cent surcharge of the outstanding balance is automatically added to the debt.

If enforcement begins, sheriff officers or messengers-at-arms may charge fees set by the court, together with costs incurred in executing a summary warrant.

Fees for messengers-at-arms and sheriff officers[264]

Debt	Fee
£708 or under	£100.60
over £708 and under £2,845	£155.95
over £2,845 and under £28,648	10 per cent of the appraised value

Notes

1. Introduction

1 The Local Authorities (Contracting Out of Tax Billing, Collection and Enforcement Functions) Order 1996 No.1880

2. Statutory enforcement in England and Wales

2 Citizens Advice and the Local Government Association, *Council Tax Protocol:Revised Collection of Council Tax Arrears Good Practice Protocol*, 2017

3 Ombudsman Report 13004696, Plymouth City Council, 13 January 2014

4 Ombudsman Report 07B10432, Manchester City Council, 22 September 2009
5 Report on an investigation into complaint No.07N10432 [2010] BIPR 476 report by Jerry White 22 Sept 2010
6 Ombudsman Report 14000871, Sandwell MBC, 18 December 2014
7 MHCLG, *Council Tax Collection: best practice guidance for local authorities*, 2021
8 Reg 23 CT(AE) Regs
9 Reg 23(2) CT(AE) Regs
10 Reg 23 CT(AE) Regs
11 Reg 33 CT(AE) Regs
12 Reg 54 CT(AE) Regs
13 Reg 34 CT(AE) Regs
14 s13A(1)(c) LGFA 1992
15 *Morgan v Warwick DC* [2015] RVR 224
16 s151 Local Government Act 1972
17 Reg 58 CT(AE) Regs
18 Reg 58(8) CT(AE) Regs; see also *Evans v LB Havering* [2021] VTE VT00003285
19 Reg 58(4) CT(AE) Regs
20 See reg 58(2)(b) CT(AE) Regs
21 *DH v Information Commissioner and Another* [2016] UKUT 139 (AAC)
22 *DH v Information Commissioner and Another* [2016] UKUT 139 (AAC), paras 51-56 and 70
23 *Camden LBC v Toufexi* [1992] 14 January 1992
24 *Ali & Another v Channel 5 Broadcasting Ltd* [2019] EWCA Civ 677

3. **Liability orders (England and Wales)**

25 *Powys County Council v Hurst* [2018] EWHC 1684 (Admin), 4 July 2018, per Hickinbottom J
26 Reg 34 CT(AE) Regs
27 *Associated Provincial Picture Houses Ltd v Wednesbury Corporation* [1948] 1 KB 223
28 *North Somerset District Council v (1) Honda Motor Europe Ltd and (2) Chevrolet United Kingdom Ltd and (3) Martin Graham* [2010] EWHC 1505 (QB); *McGrath v Camden LBC* [2020] EWHC 369
29 *Hadjianastassiou v Greece* [1992] European Court Application No.12945/87
30 *North Somerset DC v (1) Honda Motor Europe Ltd and (2) Chevrolet United Kingdom Ltd and (3) Martin Graham* [2010] EWHC 1505 (QB)
31 *North Somerset DC v (1) Honda Motor Europe Ltd and (2) Chevrolet United Kingdom Ltd and (3) Martin Graham* [2010] EWHC 1505 (QB)
32 Ombudsman Report 13019622, Derby City Council, 30 October 2014
33 *R v Lambeth LBC ex parte Ahijah Sterling* [1986] RVR 27
34 r5 Magistrates' Courts (Amendment) Rules 2019 No.1367, amending Magistrates Court Rules 1981; see *R (on the application of Peacekeepers Foundation) v Liverpool and Knowsley Magistrates Court* [2025] EWHC 1493 (Admin)
35 Statement from Minister Bridget Prentice 22 *Hansard* Column 72WS, 22 October 2009
36 *Ratford and Haywards (Receivers and Managers) v Northavon DC* [1986] RA 137
37 Reg 35(2A) CT(AE) Regs
38 Sch 1 The Magistrates' Courts Fees Order 2008 No.1052; The Justices of the Peace and Authorised Court and Tribunal Staff (Costs) Regulations 2020 No.398
39 *Attfield v LB Barnet* [2013] EWHC 2089 (Admin)
40 *R (on the Application of Reverend Nicolson) v Tottenham Magistrates* [2015] EWHC 1252 (Admin)
41 Reg 34(5) and (7) CT(AE) Regs; *R (on the application of Reverend Nicolson) v Tottenham Magistrates* [2015] EWHC 1252 (Admin)
42 Reg 3 The Council Tax and Non-Domestic Rating (Amendment) (Wales) Regulations 2011 No.528
43 The Magistrates' Courts Fees (Amendment) Order 2013 No.1409; reg 34(7) CT(AE) Regs; *R (on the application of Reverend Nicolson) v Tottenham Magistrates* [2015] EWHC 1252 (Admin)
44 *R (on the application of Reverend Nicolson) v Tottenham Magistrates* [2015] EWHC 1252 (Admin), Mrs Justice Andrews
45 *R (on the application of Morley) v Surrey Heath BC and Guildford Magistrates' Court* [2025] EWHC 1678 (Admin). para 69 per Timothy Corner KC, sitting as a High Court judge

46 *R (Mathialagan) v Camberwell Green Magistrates' Court* [2005] EWHC Admin 929, [2004] RVR 212]; *R (Mathialagan) v Southwark LBC* [2005] RA 43; *R v Commissioner of Police Metropolis and Hooper* [2005] 1 WLR 1995
47 *R (on the application of Morley) v Surrey Heath BC and Guildford Magistrates' Court* [2025] EWHC 1678 (Admin), para 69
48 Reg 35 CT(AE) Regs; r99 Magistrates' Courts Rules 1981 552 as amended SI 2019 No.1367
49 In *R (on the application of Clark-Darby) v Highbury Corner Magistrates' Court* [2001] All ER (D) 229, the High Court quashed a liability order where the person had not received the notice of the hearing, as it was unjust to allow the order to stand
50 *Chowdhury v Westminster City Council* [2013] EWHC 1921
51 *DPP v Porthouse* [1988] 153 JP 57
52 Reg 34 CT(AE) Regs
53 Reg 34 CT(AE) Regs
54 *R v Kingston upon Thames Court ex parte Peter Martin* [1994] Imm AR 172
55 *Liverpool City Council v Pleroma Distribution Ltd* [2002] All ER (D) 302
56 Reg 2 CCCTNR(E)(MC) Regs
57 *R (on the application of Peacekeepers Foundation) v Liverpool and Knowsley Magistrates Court* [2025] EWHC 1493 (Admin)
58 *Hripsime Lake v Lancaster City Magistrates' Court and Lancaster City Council* [2023] EWHC 2727 (Admin)
59 See *Paling v Ipswich Magistrates' Court* [2018] EWHC 2739 (Admin)
60 *R v Leicester City Justices ex parte Barrow and another* [1991] 3 All ER 935; *Practice Guidance: McKenzie friends*, issued by Lord Neuberger, Master of the Rolls, 12 July 2010
61 *O'Toole v Scott* [1965] UKPC, reported as 14 [1965] AC 939; *Sims v Moore* [1970] 2 QB 327
62 Reg 34 CT(AE) Regs
63 *Evans v Caterham and Warlingham UDC* [1974] *The Times*, 29 January
64 *Hardy v Sefton* [2006] EHWC 1928; *R (on the application of Mohamed) v Southwark LBC* [2009] All ER (D) 233
65 *R (on the application of Mohamed) v Southwark LBC* [2009] All ER (D) 233 (Feb)
66 *Kaye v South Oxfordshire DC* [2013] EWHC 4165 (Admin)
67 Reg 57 CT(AE) Regs
68 *Espressa Management Limited v LB Croydon* [2025] VTE VT0001626825 March, decision of the Valuation Tribunal President Gary Garland
69 See *Wiltshire Council v Piggin* [2014] EWHC 4386 (Admin)
70 Reg 53(4) CT(AE) Regs
71 *Sutton v Islington LBC* [1997] CO/1784/94, 17 October 1997, unreported
72 The Magistrates' Courts (Hearsay Evidence in Civil Proceedings) Rules 1999 No.681
73 *Ayinde v LB Haringey* [2025] EWHC 1383 (Admin); *Hamad Al-Haroun v Qatar National Bank QPSC and QNB Capital LLC* [2025] EWHC 1588 (Comm)
74 rr3-6 The Magistrates' Courts (Hearsay Evidence in Civil Proceedings) Rules 1999 No.681
75 *Norman and another v East Dorset DC* [2013] All ER (D) 153
76 Regs 35 and 48 and Sch 2 Forms A and B CT(AE) Regs
77 Regs 35 and 48 and Sch 2 Forms A and B CT(AE) Regs
78 *R (on the Application of Sharon Kofa) v Oldham MBC* [2024] EWHC 685 (Admin); *LB Lambeth v Simon* [2007] BPIR 1629, Registrar Simmonds
79 *R (on the application of Mathialagan) v Southwark LBC and another* [2005] RA 43
80 See *LB Lambeth v Simon* [2007] BPIR 1629, 6 June 2007
81 Art 6 European Court of Human Rights; see also *Rommelfanger v Germany* (1989) 62 DR 151 and *Diennert v France* (1996) 21 EHRR 554
82 Reg 57(1) CTAE Regs
83 s82 LGA 2003
84 *Liverpool City Council v Pleroma Distribution Ltd* [2002] All ER (D) 302
85 *R (on the application of Newham LBC) v Stratford Magistrates' Court* [2008] All ER (D) 17
86 [2021] EWHC 404 (Admin)
87 *Gregory v Thames Magistrates' Court* [2019] EWHC 2125 (Admin)
88 *R (on the Application of Khan) v Feltham Magistrates' Court* [2017] EWHC 3042 (Admin), per Cockerhill, J
89 s64 of the Magistrates' Courts Act 1980; *R (on the Application of Khan v Feltham Magistrates' Court* [2017] EWHC 3042 (Admin) para 68

4. **Recovery methods (England and Wales)**

90 Reg 56 The Universal Credit (Consequential, Supplementary, Incidental and Miscellaneous Provisions) Regulations 2013 No.630
91 Reg 52 CT(AE) Regs
92 Reg 54 CT(AE) Regs
93 Reg 36 CT(AE) Regs
94 Reg 36 CT(AE) Regs
95 Reg 56 CT(AE) Regs
96 Reg 56 CT(AE) Regs
97 Reg 37 CT(AE) Regs
98 Reg 37(4) CT(AE) Regs
99 MHCLG, *Council Tax Collection: best practice guidance for local authorities*, 2021, s7
100 Reg 37a(2) CT(AE) Regs
101 Reg 41 CT(AE) Regs
102 Reg 40 CT(AE) Regs
103 Reg 56 CT(AE) Regs
104 Reg 56 CT(AE) Regs
105 Reg 38 and Sch 4 CT(AE) Regs
106 Reg 32(1) CT(AE) Regs; CT(AE)(A)(E) Regs
107 Reg 32 CT(AE) Regs
108 Sch 4 CT(AE) Regs; CT(AE)(A)(W) Regs
109 Reg 42 CT(AE) Regs
110 Complaint against Birmingham City Council, Ombudsman Report 13016986, 3 June 2014
111 Ombudsman Report 14006007, Ashford BC, 7 November 2014; Ombudsman Report 008317, Manchester City Council, November 2013
112 Ombudsman Report 14006452, Sandwell MBC, 19 November 2014
113 s106 LGFA 1992
114 IC-289435-S3R2 FOI Commissioner Decision on Liverpool City Council, 8 April 2024
115 CT(DIS) Regs, as amended by The Fines, Council Tax and Community Charges (Deductions from Universal Credit and Other Benefits) Regulations 2013 No.612
116 *SSWP v Timson* [2023] EWCA Civ 656 puts an additional duty on the DWP to consider the claimant's interests in the case of legacy benefits, and possibly also applies to UC
117 Reg 8(4) CT(DIS) Regs
118 Reg 8(6) CT(DIS) Regs
119 Reg 8(7) CT(DIS) Regs
120 The Tribunals, Courts and Enforcement Act 2007 (Commencement No.11) Order 2014 No.768
121 Reg 52 CT(AE) Regs
122 Reg 6 TCG Regs
123 Reg 6(2) TCG Regs
124 Reg 7 TCG Regs
125 Reg 8 TCG Regs
126 Part 3 TCEA 2007
127 Local Government Ombudsman Report, 96/A/3626
128 Ministry of Justice, *Taking Control of Goods: national standards*, 6 April 2014, para 74
129 Sch 12 para 3(1) TCEA 2007
130 Reg 45 CT(AE) Regs, as amended by art 7 The Tribunals, Courts and Enforcement Act 2007 (Consequential, Transitional and Saving Provision) Order 2014 No.600
131 Sch 12 para 9(a)-(b) TCEA 2007
132 Reg 4 TCG Regs
133 Reg 5(1) TCG Regs
134 Reg 10 TCG Regs
135 Ministry of Justice, *Taking Control of Goods: national standards*, 6 April 2014, para 64
136 *Uttlesford DC v Barnes* [1997] Lexis citation 3623 4 July 1997 Laws J
137 Reg 22 TCG Regs
138 Sch 12 para 14(6) TCEA 2007
139 *Leighton v Bristow & Sutor* [2024] RA 65 (HHJ Harrison, sitting as a Judge of the High Court, 20 September 2023
140 *Just Digital Marketplace Ltd v High Court Enforcement Officers Association* [2021] EWHC 15 (QB), per Master McCloud
141 *Just Digital Marketplace Ltd v High Court Enforcement Officers Association* [2021] EWHC 15 (QB); *Evans v South Ribble BC* [1992] QB 75
142 Ministry of Justice, *Taking Control of Goods: national standards*, 6 April 2014, paras 57-61
143 *Vaughan v McKenzie* [1969] 1 QB 557
144 Sch 12 para 26 TCEA 2007
145 Sch 12 para 13 TCEA 2007
146 Reg 14(2) TCG Regs
147 *Curtis v Chemical Cleaning and Dyeing Company* [1951] 1 KB 805
148 Reg 15 TCG Regs
149 Reg 16 TCG Regs
150 Reg 30 TCG Regs
151 Reg 34(1)(a) and (c) TCG Regs
152 Reg 26 TCG Regs; *Khazanachi v Faircharm Investments Ltd and others and McLeod v Butterwick* [1998] EWCA Civ 471
153 Reg 27 TCG Regs
154 Regs 32 and 38 TCG Regs
155 Reg 32(1)(c)-(e) TCG Regs

156 *Celador Radio Ltd v Rancho Steak House Ltd* [2018] EWHC 219 (QB); *Riaz v Designer Collection Europ Ltd* [2017] Employment Tribunal Case No.1800031/2017
157 Regs 4 and 5 and Table 1 TCG(F) Regs
158 Reg 54(11)(B) CT(AE), as substituted by reg 5 TCG Regs; see also para 11 art 7 The Tribunals, Courts and Enforcement Act 2007 (Consequential, Transitional and Saving Provision) Order 2014 No.600
159 Reg 12 TCG(F) Regs
160 Ombudsman Report 13012969, LB Haringey, 14 January 2014
161 Ombudsman Report 13011264, Hyndburn BC, 24 September 2014
162 Reg 4(2) TCG(F) Regs
163 ss50 and 62(1) TCEA 2007
164 Reg 16 TCG(F) Regs
165 *Lone v Hounslow* [2019] EWCA 2206
166 Reg 45 CT(AE) Regs
167 Reg 45(1) CT(AE) Regs
168 Sch 12 para 50(6)(a) TCEA 2007
169 Sch 12 para 66(5) TCEA 2007
170 Regs 3 and 4 Certification of Enforcement Agents Regulations 2014 No.421
171 gov.uk/government/publications/form-eac2-complaint-against-a-certificated-person
172 Sch 12 para 66(8)(a) and (b) TCEA 2007
173 *Burton v Ministry of Justice* [2024] EWCA Civ 681
174 Sch 12 para 66(6) TCEA 2007
175 Regs 9(3) Certification of Enforcement Agents Regulations 2014 No.421
176 enforcementconductboard.org
177 Reg 50(1)-(3) CT(AE) Regs
178 See Ombudsman Decision LB Bexley (19 010 618), 11 March 2020
179 That is, rights under Art 8(1) Convention for the Protection of Human Rights and Fundamental Freedoms 1950, TS 71 (1953), Cmd 8969, incorporated in s1(3) Sch 1 Pt I Art 8 Human Rights Act 1998
180 Reg 51(1) CT(AE) Regs
181 Reg 51(4) CTAE regulations; *R (on the application of Kofa) v Oldham Metropolitan Council* [2024] EWHC 685 (Admin)
182 CPR 73.10B(2)
183 *Re: Smith (a bankrupt) ex parte Braintree DC* [1990] 2 AC 215
184 *LB Lambeth v Simon* [2007] BPIR 1629
185 *Smolen v Tower Hamlets LBC* [2006] RVR 296
186 *State Bank of India v Dr Vijay Mallya* [2020] EWHC 96 (Ch)
187 *Eberhardt & Co Ltd v Mair* [1995] 1 WLR 1180
188 s271 IA 1986
189 *LB Waltham Forest v Zafar* [2014] EWHC 791 (Ch)
190 *Okon v LB Lewisham* [2016] EWHC 864
191 *Mohammed v Southwark LBC* [2006] RVR 124; see also *HMRC v Chamberlain* [2011] EWCA Civ 271, para 20, per Sir Andrew Morritt
192 s82 LGA 2003
193 *Clarke and another v Cognita Schools Ltd (trading as Hydesville Tower School)* [2015] EWHC 932 (Ch)
194 *Vieira v Revenue and Customs Commissioners* [2017] EWHC 936 (Ch)
195 *Patterson v Lewisham Bankruptcy* [2017] EWHC 632 (Ch)
196 *Vieira v Revenue and Customs Commissioners* [2017] EWHC 936 (Ch), para 84
197 r52.4 The Civil Procedure Rules 1998 No.3132
198 The Civil Procedure Rules 1998 No.3132; Practice Direction – Insolvency Proceedings, para 17.22(7B)
199 See *LB Lambeth v Simon* [2007] BIPR 1629, para 45
200 *Finnan v Finnan* [2020] BPIR 731; *Aabar Block Sarl and another v Maud* [2018] EWHC 1414 (Ch)
201 s283A IA 1986
202 *Sands & Anr v Sngh & Ors* [2015] EWHC 2219 (Ch)
203 s335 IA 1986; *Armstrong v Temblett & Anor* [2025] EWHC 1649 (Ch)
204 *Parveen v Manchester City Council and Helland*, 24 September 2007, Manchester County Court, District Judge Khan, unreported
205 *Adetula (Claimant) v Barking and Dagenham LBC* [2016] HC/2015/004349; [2017] EWHC 2279 (Ch)
206 s375 IA 1986
207 *Amin v (1) LB Redbridge (2) Atkinson (as a Trustee in bankruptcy of Anjam Amin)* [2018] EWHC 3100]
208 *Okon v LB* [2016] EWHC 864 (Ch)

209 *Broderick v Coventry City Council* [2020] EWHC 2083 (Admin); *UKI (Kingsway) Ltd v Westminster City Council* [2019] PTSR 128 (SC); *Lambert v (1) Forest of Dean DC (2) Nichols (3) Butler* [2019] BPIR 1220; *Yang v (1) The Official Receiver (2) Manchester City Council (3) Wright* [2018] BPIR 255; Report on an Investigation into Complaint (No.10 002 564) Against Torbay Council [2011] BPIR 1098; *Johnson v Tandrige DC* [2008] BPIR 405
210 The Council Tax (Administration and Enforcement) (Amendment) (Wales) Regulations 2019 No.220; Christians Against Poverty, *Taking On Client Poverty*, 23 May 2023
211 Written question 44494 2 September 2016 parliament.uk/business/publications/written-questions answers-statements/written-question/Commons/2016-09 02/44494
212 *Stevenson v Southwark LBC* [1993] RA 113; *R v Wellingborough Magistrates Court ex parte Gaunt* [1996] Lexis citation 3147, 31 January 1996, McCullough, J
213 Reg 47(1) CT(AE) Regs
214 Reg 73 The Local Authorities (Contracting Out of Tax Billing, Collection and Enforcement Functions) Order 1996 No.1880
215 Sch 3 The Court and Tribunal Fees (Miscellaneous Amendments) Order 2025 No.351
216 Reg 47(7) CT(AE) Regs
217 *R v Highbury Corner Magistrates' Court ex parte Uchendu* [1994] 158 JP 409
218 Reg 48(5) CT(AE) Regs
219 *R v Newcastle Justices Under Lyme Justices ex parte Massey* (1992) July 12, QBD) Dyson J
220 *R v Highbury Corner Magistrates' Court ex parte Edis* [1994] Lexis citation 2788 31 Jan 1994
221 *R v Poole Justices ex parte Benham* [1992] 156 JP 157
222 *Re: Smith (a bankrupt) ex parte Braintree DC* [1990] 2 AC 215
223 *R v Poole Justices ex parte Fleet* [1983] 1 WLR 973; *R v Horseferry Road Magistrates' Court ex parte Collins* [1986] CO/324/86; *R v Lewes and Crowborough Magistrates' Court ex parte Mackleden* [2002] RVR 363, para 15
224 Reg 47(2) CT(AE) Regs
225 *R v Poole Justices ex parte Benham* [1992] 156 JP 157
226 *R v Alfreton Justices ex parte Gratton, The Times*, 8 December 1993
227 *R v Gloucestershire Justices ex parte Daldry* [2000] RVR 242, per Keene, J, para 24
228 *R (on the application of Stokes) v Gwent Magistrates' Court* [2001] All ER (D) 125
229 *R v Petherick* (2012) 177 JPN 94, [2012] EWCA Crim 2214
230 Reg 48(2) CT(AE) Regs
231 *R v Newcastle-Upon-Tyne Justices ex parte Devine* [1998] RA 97
232 See *R (on the application of Wandless) v Halifax Magistrates' Court and Calderdale MBC* [2009] EWHC 1857 (Admin) QBD, reported as [2010] RVR 6
233 See *R v Poole Justices ex parte Benham* [1992] 156 JP 157
234 *R v Lancashire CC ex parte Huddleston* [1986] 2 All ER 941; *R v Gloucestershire Justices ex parte Daldry* [2000] RVR 242

5. Statutory enforcement in Scotland

235 Reg CT(AE) Regs; *China v Harrow UDC* [1954] 1 QB 178
236 s8 Prescription and Limitation (Scotland) Act 1973
237 Reg 22 CT(AE)(S) Regs
238 Reg 22 CT(AE)(S) Regs
239 s97 and Sch 8 para 1 LGFA 1992
240 s112 LGFA 1992
241 s81 LGFA 1992
242 Sch 8 para 2 LGFA 1992
243 Reg 30 CT(AE)(S) Regs
244 Reg 30 CT(AE)(S) Regs
245 Reg 31 CT(AE)(S) Regs
246 Reg 31 CT(AE)(S) Regs
247 Sch 8 para 2 LGFA 1992
248 Sch 8 para 4 LGFA 1992
249 s10 Debt Arrangement and Attachment (Scotland) Act 2002
250 Act of Sederunt (Sheriff Court Rules) (Miscellaneous Amendments) (No.2) 2011 No.289
251 s80 Debtors (Scotland) Act 1987
252 See *Polley v (1) West Lothian Council and (2) the Accountant in Bankruptcy* [2015] CSIH 19
253 s5A Court of Session Act 1988; s32A Sheriff Courts (Scotland) Act 1971
254 Act of Sederunt (Sheriff Court Rules) (Lay Representation) 2013 No.91
255 Reg 4.3 Act of Sederunt (Sheriff Appeal Court Rules) 2021 No.468
256 Alan McIntosh, 'Time for due diligence on debt recovery', *Journal of the Law Society of Scotland*, November 2024

257 Reg 1 and Sch The Diligence against Earnings (Variation) (Scotland) Regulations 2024 No.293
258 Explanatory Note, The Diligence against Earnings (Variation) (Scotland) Regulations 2024 No.293
259 Reg 2(b) and Sch The Diligence against Earnings (Variation) (Scotland) Regulations 2024 No.293
260 Reg 2(b) and Sch The Diligence against Earnings (Variation) (Scotland) Regulations 2024 No.293
261 s3(1)(a) and (b) Act of Sederunt (Summary Suspension) 1993; *Cowie v Martalo* [2011] GWD 32-676; *Derek Cooney v The Sheriff Clerk Glasgow and Glasgow City Council Respondent* [2018] CSIH 11
262 Part 1 Debtors (Scotland) Act 1987
263 Sch 8 LGFA 1992; ss2 and 7 Bankruptcy (Scotland) Act 2016
264 Sch 1 Act of Sederunt (Fees of Messengers-at-Arms) (No.2) 2002 No.566, as amended by Act of Sederunt (Fees of Messengers-at-Arms, Sheriff Officers and Shorthand Writers) (Amendment) 2018 No.126 and Act of Sederunt (Fees of Messengers-at-Arms and Sheriff Officers) (Amendment) 2021 No.225

Chapter 11

Appeals

This chapter covers:

1. Valuation tribunals

Appeals about council tax and related matters are handled by independent tribunals.

- In England, appeals are heard by the Valuation Tribunal for England (VTE).
- In Wales, appeals are heard by the Valuation Tribunal for Wales (VTW).
- In Scotland, appeals are heard by the Local Taxation Chamber (LTC) of the First-tier Tribunal for Scotland. This replaced the former Council Tax Reduction Review Panel and the Valuation Appeal Committees from 1 April 2023. The LTC also hears appeals about water charges.

These tribunals are free to use and cannot award costs against you. However, you must cover your own expenses. Tribunals are independent of local authorities and the Valuation Office Agency (VOA) or assessor.

Tribunals are less formal than courts, but parties must still follow procedural rules and deadlines. They provide a mechanism to review and correct any erroneous decisions affecting taxpayers.

In **England and Wales**, tribunal members serve in a voluntary capacity.[1] Members do not necessarily have any professional qualifications, but judges from the First-tier Tribunal (Social Security and Child Support) sometimes sit with the chairs of tribunals to hear council tax reduction appeals.[2] Tribunal administration is done by Valuation Tribunal Service staff from a centralised office. Tribunals in England and Wales sometimes sit at an administrative centre, but most hearings are now held online (see p282).

The Welsh government plans to reform the council tax appeals system, with regulations expected to come into force in early 2026.

In **Scotland**, the LTC chamber president is responsible for arranging business within the chamber. A list of members and their experience is at localtaxationchamber.scot/about. Members are unpaid. The LTC is assisted by a paid secretary who is usually a lawyer. LTC members cannot provide legal advice, but may signpost to advice services such as Citizens Advice or law centres.[3]

Clerks support tribunals with procedural advice but cannot advise on the merits of your case. The clerk is your point of contact and should be able to respond to requests for advice on procedures in advance of the hearing.

Useful information and guidance

You can find information on valuation matters and appeals at the VOA website (gov.uk/government/organisations/valuation-office-agency).

More information about appeals in England is at valuationtribunal.gov.uk. This includes summaries of recent valuation tribunal decisions and the *Consolidated Practice Statement* for the VTE.

The VTW's appeal guidance and best practice protocols are at valuationtribunal.wales.

In Scotland appeal procedures are outlined at localtaxationchamber.scot. If you lodged an appeal before 1 April 2023, see localtaxationchamber.scot/existing-appeals.

The overriding objective

Tribunals are part of the civil justice system and have an overriding objective to deal with cases fairly and justly.[4] This means the tribunal must:[5]

- use their legal powers appropriately;
- apply any practice statements or directions;
- interpret rules or practice directions to ensure appeals progress without unnecessary delay.

The fact that a liability order has been made in the magistrates' court for non-payment of council tax does not prevent the tribunal from reviewing liability.[6]

2. **Matters that can be appealed**

Appeals can be on:

- valuations (see p261);
- liability (see p263);
- discounts (see p263);
- disability reductions (see p263);

- exemptions (see p263);
- calculations on the amount of council tax (see p263);
- council tax reduction (CTR) decisions in Scotland (see p265);
- completion notices (see p266);
- penalties (see p266);
- discretionary reductions (see p267);
- incorrect amounts payable, including attempts to impose liability for past periods.

Valuation tribunals cannot hear appeals where another appeal route exists – eg, to the magistrates' court, county court or the High Court. If an appeal raises a matter that the tribunal has no power to consider, it will be struck out.[7]

It is vital to use the correct appeal route, as filing in the wrong tribunal can have serious consequences and may require the High Court to correct errors made by lower courts and tribunals.[8]

In England and Wales, some matters can only be dealt with by the High Court – eg, which classes of dwellings qualify for an exemption and the setting of council tax.

Valuations

Chapter 3 describes how you can make a proposal to the listing officer/assessor to alter the valuation list – eg, to put your home in a lower band.

England and Wales

When you make a valid proposal to the Valuation Office Agency, the listing officer has four months to decide whether to alter the list. During this time, you can negotiate about the banding. Before issuing a decision notice, the listing officer should discuss the proposal with you and any interested parties. The notice confirms either that the list will be altered or that the proposal is rejected.

A letter is sent with the notice explaining your right (and that of any interested party) to appeal. This is known as a decision letter or decision notice and should not be confused with informal correspondence, such as a general statement of opinion.

You and any interested party have three months from the date of the decision letter to appeal to the Valuation Tribunal for England (VTE)/Valuation Tribunal for Wales (VTW).[9] Late appeals may be accepted if the delay was beyond your control.[10]

Where this is not possible, it may be best to make a fresh proposal, particularly where there has been a change of facts.

The tribunal should list the appeal within six months of receiving the appeal notice and give you at least four weeks' notice of the hearing. The listing officer will prepare a presentation pack, typically including background information relating to the case and evidence of comparable property values. You may submit your own valuation evidence.

If a listing officer considers your proposal invalid, they can serve you with an invalidity notice (see p42). You can appeal against the invalidity notice (within four weeks) directly to the VTE/VTW. Your notice of appeal must be sent to the tribunal clerk and include a copy of the notice. If the invalidity notice does not already contain the following information, you must also include:[11]

- the address of the dwelling; *and*
- the reasons for the appeal against the invalidity notice; *and*
- the names and addresses of both the proposer (you) and the listing officer.

If the listing officer later withdraws the invalidity notice after an appeal has been started, they must inform the tribunal.[12]

If the listing officer agrees to the proposal or decides to alter the list, whether or not an agreement has been reached, the list must be altered within six weeks of the decision notice.[13]

Scotland

You can appeal to the Local Taxation Chamber (LTC) if you disagree with:[14]

- a decision that a dwelling is chargeable or that you are liable to pay council tax for it; *or*
- the calculation of how much council tax you are liable to pay.

You must submit your appeal directly to the LTC online portal within six months of your appeal notice (or two months for a penalty).[15]

The LTC acknowledges receipt of your appeal and may request further information from you or the assessor. If there is to be a hearing, you will receive at least 31 days' notice, unless both parties agree to a shorter period or there are urgent circumstances.[16] There is no strict deadline for the LTC to hear your appeal.

At least 14 days before the hearing date, you must send:[17]

- a list and copies of all documents you will rely on; *and*
- a list of any witnesses.

You can have a representative. They do not have to be legally qualified.[18]

Deciding which valuation applies

When determining a council tax banding, the tribunal must apply the same statutory valuation assumptions that were used in the original valuation (see p30). These assumptions apply regardless of whether a dwelling is in single or shared ownership.[19] The tribunal cannot question the legality or validity of the regulations themselves.

Example

Toby and Amara live in a shared-ownership flat with 25 years left on the lease. The tribunal must ignore any first value of shared-ownership properties and presume a 99-year lease.

Once the correct valuation assumptions are applied, the tribunal will consider whether the original valuation figure was wrong. An appeal is likely to succeed if you can show that:

- the assumptions were wrongly applied; *and*
- the correct value would place your home in a different valuation band.

Errors that may justify a change include mistakes about property size, number of rooms or nearby factors (eg, proximity to an industrial site).

If your appeal raises a complex, novel or contentious point of law (including principles of valuation), it may be heard by the president or a vice-president of the tribunal.

Liability, exemptions, reductions, discounts and amounts

You can appeal if you disagree with the local authority's decision about:

- who is a liable person, including whether it should be the owner (see Chapter 5);
- whether a dwelling is exempt (see Chapter 4);
- refusal of a disability reduction (see Chapter 6);
- refusal of a discount (see Chapter 7);
- your entitlement to CTR, or about the amount or the duration of an award (see Chapter 8);
- the amount you are required to pay;
- the removal of an existing exemption;
- the refusal of a discretionary reduction.

A person aggrieved by a decision has a right of appeal.[20] 'Aggrieved' means that there must be a legitimate reason for objecting to the decision. 'Person' means that the right of appeal is not necessarily limited to the taxpayer. The people who may appeal can include:

- someone who does not own or occupy the dwelling and is paying directly or indirectly – eg, a lodger or tenant or an ex-tenant;
- any taxpayer in the same area;
- anyone personally or financially affected;
- any person with property interests in the same billing authority area, even though they are not a taxpayer or owner;

- anyone who pays council tax indirectly through another charge to a council;
- anyone whose property or commercial interests are materially affected.

For example, it may be the owner or landlord of a building on which the council tax is levied and in which the actual taxpayer is resident, or the parent or guardian of a severely mentally impaired person who has been wrongly deemed liable by the local authority and is unable to appeal for themselves. It is not necessary for the person aggrieved to live in the borough.[21]

There are two stages to appeals on liability and calculation issues. The first stage involves writing to the local authority, stating which decision you dispute and why.[22] For example, it may be that you have been deemed a liable person for council tax when the property in which you live is actually a house of multiple occupation where the owner should be paying the council tax. The local authority has two months to respond, during which you can exchange further information.

A further appeal may be made to the VTE/VTW/LTC if the local authority:[23]
- rejects the appeal; *or*
- makes only partial changes; *or*
- fails to make a decision within the two-month period.

The local authority should normally inform you directly or publish information on its website of the right to appeal to the tribunal, but local authorities do not always do this.

You should mention your right of appeal in your initial letter. In the case of a dispute over liability, a calculation or an exemption, a letter could state: 'If you have not resolved this matter to my satisfaction by (two months), I intend to appeal to the valuation tribunal under section 16 of the Local Government Finance Act 1992.'

If you mention the right of appeal, it is important that you comply with the time limits laid down in section 16. For example, if the local authority issues a decision letter refusing your appeal you have eight weeks to lodge and appeal with the valuation tribunal from the date of the local authority's reply.

You can send copies of correspondence with the local authority in advance of your appeal. Mark them 'For information', date them clearly and state that you want an appeal to be listed if the issue is not resolved. This helps prove you appealed within the time limits if the authority misplaces your letter. Sending correspondence by email is recommended, as it provides an automatic receipt.

If you do not get a reply or acknowledgement, proceed with your appeal by contacting the tribunal directly. You can do this after eight weeks if there has been no reply. Send copies of all documents you intend to use to the local authority, even if it does not reply. You can also make a formal complaint about the failure of the authority to respond (see p299).

Example

Maddy, a student, loses her council tax exemption in year three of her degree. She writes to the local authority with proof of student status but gets no response. After two months, she appeals directly to the valuation tribunal.

England and Wales

You must normally appeal to the VTE/VTW within:[24]

- two months of the local authority's decision notice; *or*
- four months from your initial representation if the local authority has not responded.

The billing authority must issue a clear decision for the two-month limit to apply; vague or open-ended replies do not count.[25] To be safe, submit your appeal within eight weeks.

The tribunal president may accept a late appeal if the delay was due to circumstances beyond your control.[26]

It is important to distinguish between appeals to the VTE/VTW and appeals that go to the First-tier Tribunal for other social security benefits, such as DWP benefits, and for decisions about entitlement and calculations which were made for the council tax benefit system before 1 April 2013.

Scotland

Liability and exemption appeals

You must normally make an appeal within:[27]

- two months of the date the local authority notified you of its decision; *or*
- four months of the date you made the initial representation if the local authority has not responded.

You must apply direct to the tribunal.[28]

Council tax reduction appeals in Scotland

To appeal a determination by a local authority about an amount of CTR, you must first ask the local authority for an internal review within two months of the original determination.[29] This means writing to the local authority to request that it reconsiders its decision.

If you are still dissatisfied following a review, you have a further right of appeal to the LTC within 42 days of the date of the local authority notification.[30]

If the local authority does not respond within two months, you may also request a further review of a determination on an application.[31] See p185 for more details about LTC reviews.

Completion notices

When a new property is built or an existing one structurally altered, the local authority (or the assessor in Scotland) can issue a completion notice. This notice specifies the date from which the property is officially considered a dwelling for council tax purposes. The local authority can issue a completion notice if the work can reasonably be expected to be completed within three months.[32] The local authority can provide information about a completion notice, but only the tribunal can deal with the appeal.

England and Wales

You must usually make an appeal within 28 days of the competition notice being sent.[33] An out-of-time appeal may be allowed if you have failed to meet this time limit for reasons beyond your control.[34]

You, or someone on your behalf, should write to the clerk of the relevant tribunal,[35] explaining the reasons for your appeal. Include a copy of the completion notice.

Appeal forms are available from the relevant tribunal office. In England, you can register an appeal online at the Valuation Tribunal Service website. The clerk should notify you within two weeks that the appeal request has been received and send a copy to the local authority.[36]

The tribunal has the power to dismiss the appeal, confirm the completion date or set a different completion date. A tribunal may set a date which is longer than three months for the completion of the building work.[37]

Note that the criteria for council tax completion dates differ from those used for building control regulations.[38]

Scotland

You can make an appeal about a completion notice in writing to the LTC within 21 days of receiving the notice.[39] There is no power to consider out-of-time appeals. You must include:[40]

- a copy of the completion notice;
- a statement giving your reason(s) for appealing;
- any additional grounds you want to raise;
- any relevant supporting material;
- your, or your representative's signature.

Penalties

The local authority has the power to impose a penalty in certain instances if you fail to provide required information, or if you knowingly provide false information. While you can discuss the matter with the local authority, and it has the power to withdraw the penalty, you can also appeal to the tribunal. For more on penalties, see p206. Grounds for quashing a penalty include where:

- the local authority already has the information;
- you have valid reasons for withholding the information – eg, confidentiality;
- the information being demanded is excessive or impossible to comply with;
- the information is irrelevant or it is not within the remit of the local authority to seek.

England and Wales

You must normally appeal within two months of the penalty being imposed.[41] The tribunal president can allow an out-of-time appeal if you missed the time limit for reasons beyond your control.[42] The appeal is made by you, or someone acting on your behalf, writing directly to the clerk of the relevant tribunal. The letter should state the reasons for the appeal and the date you were notified of the penalty (if known).[43]

Appeal forms are available on the VTE/VTW websites. In England, you can register an appeal online at the Valuation Tribunal Service website.

The clerk should notify you within two weeks that the appeal request has been received and send a copy to the local authority.[44]

Scotland

To appeal to the LTC, you must write to the local authority within 28 days of the penalty being imposed.[45] If sent after 28 days, you must include a statement of reasons explaining the delay – this will be treated as an application to extend a time limit.[46] The appeal letter should contain:

- your full name and address;
- where applicable, the full name and address of your representative and an address for the receipt of documents;
- a clear statement that the notice is a 'notice of appeal';
- the ground(s) on which you are appealing;
- a copy of the written notice requesting a review that you sent to the authority;
- the local authority's decision about your review, if you have received it;
- a statement indicating whether you require a hearing;
- evidence you want the tribunal to consider;
- your signature (or your representative's);
- the date you were notified by the local authority of the penalty (if known).[47]

Discretionary reductions

In England and Wales, you can appeal against a local authority's refusal or decision about a discretionary reduction.[48] You have this right of appeal regardless of when you became liable for the amount.[49]

The tribunal will not consider whether the local authority has used its powers correctly and lawfully when deciding whether to grant a discretionary reduction. Following the decision in *SC and CW v East Riding of Yorkshire Council*,[50] the tribunal may look at the facts of your appeal (eg, your financial circumstances) and substitute its own decision if it is satisfied the authority made the wrong decision. At a hearing, you may be questioned about your financial position and the circumstances at the time of making the application for discretionary relief, including whether you applied under the local authority's CTR scheme. You may be asked whether you provided the billing authority with evidence at the right time for any CTR application. However, an award of a discretionary reduction is not dependent upon eligibility or entitlement to a CTR claim.

The tribunal applies principles which are similar, but wider, to judicial review, and considers whether the local authority has made an error of law, which means its decision should be quashed.

SC and CW v East Riding of Yorkshire Council

Mr and Mrs W

Mr and Mrs W, an unemployed couple with no savings, applied for a discretionary reduction. The council refused it. The couple had no surplus income and, by the local authority's own calculations, there was a shortfall of £72.34 in their income to meet existing liabilities and outgoings.

In the view of tribunal, the simple fact was that there was no surplus income to meet a council tax bill and that: 'It is difficult to imagine a clearer case for discretionary assistance'. It found that Mr and Mrs W were entitled to discretionary relief and there was no plausible or rational basis for limiting that relief to 12 weeks or any other period and 'that only full remission of the residual council tax for the year makes any sense in view of the absence of any funds to meet their liability'.

Mr and Mrs C

Mr and Mrs C were also a couple in a difficult financial position who applied for a discretionary reduction. The council refused it. Mrs C was disabled and her husband was her carer. They had one dependent child, but although they were 'a household existing at the very margins of viability' and 'in extremely hard-pressed financial circumstances', there was nonetheless a very small surplus of income over expenditure, which allowed very little latitude for contingencies or emergencies. However, because there was such a surplus, there was no basis in law for interfering with the council's decision to reject the application for discretionary relief, and their appeal was dismissed.

Principles of law by which the tribunal may quash a decision to refuse a discretionary reduction include the following.

- The authority got the facts wrong in a way that affects the decision.
- The authority failed to follow proper processes or procedures.
- The authority failed to properly apply the hardship test. The discretionary reduction is meant to include tackling hardship, and a local authority errs when it fails to give sufficient weight to this purpose.

- The authority failed to make an individual decision on your case. The local authority should look at your circumstances and not simply apply a general policy.
- The authority failed to follow its own guidance, which will usually mean a different decision will be substituted by the tribunal.[51]
- The authority has acted unreasonably[52] – eg, by:
  - failing to consider relevant facts;
  - considering irrelevant facts;
  - acting perversely or irrationally.

Failing to consider relevant facts occurs when the authority overlooks important information it should have considered when looking at your application. For example, it might not properly assess your income, neglect to apply a means test or ignore the impact of disability.

Considering irrelevant facts occurs when an authority bases its refusal on issues that should not affect the decision, such as your having just moved into a property, that you are unemployed or bankrupt, or have rent arrears.[53]

The authority has acted irrationally and perversely if it has refused a discretionary reduction in a way that no reasonable authority, following the correct process, would do. An example where an authority might act unreasonably in refusing a discretionary reduction is where the authority has created a liability by its own failure to award you a reduction at the correct stage, due to its own errors. Not having a clear policy on discretionary reductions also increases the likelihood that an appeal will succeed.

The tribunal may remit the matter to the billing authority for reconsideration.

The tribunal cannot hear challenges to the legality of the discretionary reduction scheme itself. This can only be done by judicial review. Tribunals cannot hear appeals about funding or financial support unrelated to the discretionary reduction scheme.[54]

3. How to appeal

You must appeal in writing, which is called a 'notice of appeal'. There are time limits for submitting your appeal. If you miss the time limit, you may be able to make a late appeal if you have a good reason (see p275).

If you want the tribunal to deal with your appeal quickly (known as expediting your appeal), make this clear and explain why your case is urgent.

England and Wales

You must appeal online with the valuation tribunal. The online form asks for details of you ('the appellant') and the council and/or Valuation Office Agency ('the respondent') and a summary of the grounds of appeal (limited to 1,200 characters). You or your representative must provide a contact address and an email address. Your appeal should state:[55]

- the reasons for the appeal; *and*
- the date you sent the first letter about the matter to the local authority; *and*
- the date (if any) you were notified of the local authority's decision.

Note: in some cases, the valuation tribunal administration may reject an appeal if it does not include a reply from the billing authority. However, if you have received no reply, the appeal can still proceed, provided that eight weeks have passed since your initial appeal letter.[56] If the administration staff do not accept this, ask for the matter to be referred to a tribunal clerk.

A summary should be sufficient. If your appeal arises under section 16 of the Local Government Finance Act 1992 regarding liability, exemption or discount or from a decision about your entitlement to council tax reduction (CTR), it must include the following:

- your full name and address; *and*
- the address of the property (if different to your home address); *and*
- the name of your local authority and the date you first wrote to it; *and*
- the date the authority refused your appeal (if it replied); *and*
- brief reasons why you consider the decision or calculation is wrong; *and*
- details of any related appeal regarding council tax benefit (pre-1 April 2013) or housing benefit, which arises from the same facts and which you made to the First-tier Tribunal for social security matters.[57]

If you fail to supply the information, you will be asked to provide it. If you do not supply the information within the time specified, your appeal will not be admitted.

If it is discovered at the hearing that you have omitted information which should have been supplied, the appeal could be struck out, but the tribunal can apply a 'common sense test'. The appeal should not be struck out if the error or omission is merely technical or due to a clerical error and no difficulty or prejudice has been caused to the billing authority. If the appeal is struck out, you may start a new appeal.

Directions to parties

When your appeal is accepted, both you and the other party will receive 'standard directions'. These are detailed instructions on how to proceed with your case. They explain what you must do and by when. If you fail to follow these steps, your evidence or submissions may be excluded.[58] The valuation officer and the local authority are also required to follow directions. The aim is to ensure that all parties and the tribunal have all the necessary information before a hearing is arranged. It is important to read the directions and comply with them as fully as possible, including any time limits. Contact the VTE/VTW if you are unsure about anything that is included within the instructions and directions.

Notice of receipt and directions (England)

When you begin your appeal online, you (or your representative) must supply an email address for correspondence. Once you have submitted your appeal, the Valuation Tribunal Service will send you an acknowledgement email confirming when it registered your appeal. It will also include a 'notice of receipt', which sets out what you (the appellant) and the respondent (the local authority or billing authority) must do to provide evidence. These instructions form part of the standard directions that both parties must follow.

The directions require you and the council to disclose your full case to the other party within four weeks of being sent the notice of receipt.

Any evidence submitted after the four-week deadline will only be considered if you can show a good reason why it was not available earlier.[59] This includes sending details of any documents, legal arguments and caselaw additional to those which you have already sent and which you may have put in with the four documents you can submit to the valuation tribunal using its online portal to begin the appeal.[60]

If the billing authority fails to comply with the standard directions within the specified time, its evidence will be excluded and it will be barred from taking any further part in the proceedings. The tribunal will issue a notice confirming this.[61]

Where the billing authority has been barred for failing to provide the information specified in the standard directions, the appeal is automatically allowed by default, without any consideration of the merits of the case. However, the tribunal's order will be delayed for 28 days in such a case. This is to allow the billing authority an opportunity to apply to the tribunal (which it must do within 14 days) for the appeal to be relisted for hearing on the grounds that it did not receive the notice of hearing, or that it did comply with the standard directions or for some other exceptional and compelling reason.

Following the steps set out in the practice statement could be difficult for vulnerable appellants. If this applies to you, apply to the tribunal for extra time to complete the steps required by the directions.

A failure to comply with any direction by a party may lead to:

- the appeal being struck out or dismissed; *or*
- the party being barred from participating further in the appeal; *or*
- a default judgment in the case of a CTR appeal.

Scotland

You must make an appeal to the Local Taxation Chamber (LTC) in writing,[62] usually using the approved form (available from localtaxationchamber.scot/apply). Read the accompanying guidance notes before completing the form. You can email your completed form and supporting documents to the LTC or send it to the address on the form.

LCT appeal forms and time limits

Form	Appeal	Time limit [63]
C1	Liability (calculation of liability, expemptions and discounts)	Four months from the date you notified the local authority
C2	Penalty notice	Two months from the date the penalty was imposed
C3	Completion notice	21 days from the date you received the completion notice
C-4a	Banding proposal deemed invalid	28 days from the date you received the notice that the appeal was invalid
C-4b	Banding proposal	12 weeks from the date you served the proposal to alter on the assessor
D	Council tax reduction	42 days from the date you received the decision from the local authority

The notice must include:[64]

- your full name, address and email address;
- where applicable, your representative's full name, address and email address;
- where applicable, any other specified address (including an email address) for receiving LTC documents related to the appeal;
- a clear statement that the notice is a 'notice of appeal';
- the ground(s) of appeal;[65]
- a statement indicating whether you require a hearing to be arranged;
- any evidence to support the appeal;
- your signature or thatof your representative.

If you have it, you should also include the written notification of the decision you want to be reviewed.

Within 14 days, the LTC must acknowledge receipt of your notice and send notice of the appeal to the respondent.[66]

The review can be dealt with based on written representations (ie, without a hearing) only if all the parties agree and the LTC considers it can decide the matter without a hearing.[67]

Where a hearing is to take place, each party must be given reasonable notice of the date, time and place (and any changes to that date, time and place).[68] The notice period for a hearing must be no less than 31 days, beginning with the date of issue of the notice, unless the parties consent to a shorter period or there are urgent or exceptional circumstances.

4. How appeals are dealt with

An appeal is normally dealt with by an oral hearing conducted by video link but, if all the parties agree, it can be dealt with by written representation (see p274).[69] In most cases, it is advisable to request an oral hearing so that you have the opportunity to present your case directly to the tribunal.

There is likely to be a wait of several months between the acknowledgement of your appeal, the submission of your documents and evidence and the hearing. Use this time to prepare for the hearing. The Valuation Tribunal Service's customer charter aims to list council tax liability and banding appeals within four months of registration.

In an appeal under section 16 of the Local Government Finance Act 1992 on liability, exemptions, discount or any calculation, the tribunal normally contacts you about two weeks before the hearing, and you must send copies of any documents you intend to use at the hearing well in advance to the tribunal and other parties to the appeal.

In **England**, the Valuation Tribunal for England (VTE) has the power to regulate its own procedures.[70] This includes the ability to:

- extend or shorten the time for complying with any regulation or directions;
- consolidate or hear together two or more sets of proceedings or parts of proceedings raising common issues, or treat an appeal as a lead appeal;
- permit or require a party to amend a document;
- require or allow a party or another person to provide documents, evidence, information or submissions to the VTE or another party;
- deal with an issue ias a preliminary issue;
- hold a hearing to consider any matter, including a case management;
- decide the form of any hearing;
- adjourn or postpone a hearing;
- require a party to produce a bundle of documents for a hearing;
- stay proceedings;
- suspend the effect of its own decision pending the determination by the Upper Tribunal or a court on an appeal or review.

In **Wales**, the Valuation Tribunal for Wales (VTW) has general powers to regulate its own procedures.[71]

In **Scotland**, the Local Taxation Chamber (LTC) can also regulate its own procedure. It may issue an order at any time in relation to the conduct or disposal of proceedings, including amending, suspending or setting aside an earlier order.[72] The LTC can:[73]

- extend or shorten the time for complying with any rule, practice direction or order;
- permit or require amendments to documents;

- order or permit a party to supply documents, information, evidence or submissions to the tribunal or to another party;
- deal with any proceedings as a preliminary issue;
- hold a hearing on any matter including case management;
- decide the form that proceedings may take;
- adjourn or postpone hearings either on request or on its own initiative;
- with the agreement of the parties, bring forward a hearing;
- require a party to produce a file of documents for a hearing;
- sist (suspend or stay) proceedings;
- suspend the effect of its own decision pending determination by the First-tier Tribunal, Upper Tribunal or other tribunal or order a rehearing.

Where appeals raise the same point of law or similar issues, the LTC can order the appeals to be conjoined.

Pre-appeal agreement

In **England**, the parties may reach an agreement before the appeal hearing (see p278) or before written representations are considered (see below). The agreement includes how the valuation list is to be altered and the listing officer must serve a copy of this on the VTE and on all the parties involved. The appeal is treated as withdrawn, and you do not need to take any further action. The alteration to the list must be made within six weeks.

In **Wales**, an appeal can be settled based on written representations if all the parties have given their consent in writing.[74]

In **Scotland**, the parties can agree to dispose of the appeal except for an appeal of a CTR decision.[75]

Consent orders

In England, parties may jointly apply for proceedings to be ended by a consent order. The application must be in writing and must include:

- the appeal number; *and*
- the existing entry in the list (rateable value, description and address); *and*
- full names of the parties; *and*
- the date(s) and amount(s) of any reduction, together with the entry (if different) that the list is to revert to if a temporary reduction is sought.

Applications for consent orders are considered by a senior member of the tribunal, who does not have to give reasons for their decision.[76]

Written representations

Written representations provide a relatively quick and effective way to resolve straightforward appeals. This means there is no hearing. The tribunal considers the case based on the written evidence and submissions provided by the parties and then issues its decision in writing. All parties (normally you, the listing officer/assessor and the local authority) must give their written agreement.[77]

There is no maximum time limit within which the tribunal must make its decision. Once it is agreed that the appeal will proceed in this way, the clerk serves notice on the parties, giving them at least 14 days (or less, if agreed) to send their written representations.[78] Any material submitted after the 14 days may be considered or rejected at the tribunal's discretion.[79] The tribunal may request more information or additional documentation from any party before reaching a decision, or it may decide an oral hearing is necessary.[80] Copies of all written material are sent to the other parties. There is then a further 14-day period for comments. The tribunal can:

- require any party to provide additional material; *or*
- order that the appeal be dealt with at a hearing; *or*
- proceed to reach a decision.

If additional information is required, copies must be provided to all parties. Each party may, within a tribunal-set period, supply a further statement in response.[81]

In Scotland, any party can withdraw their consent to deal with the appeal by written representation at any time before a decision is reached. This might happen, for example, if the other party's arguments are not as expected. If permission has been withdrawn, the appeal must be dealt with by an oral hearing.[82]

Pre-hearing review

In England and Wales, a tribunal chair may order a pre-hearing review to clarify the issues to be dealt with at the hearing, such as the procedure to be followed, evidence and time limits.[83] This may be done either at any party's request, or on the chair's own initiative. At least four weeks' notice must be given.

Extension of time limits

If you cannot meet a time limit at any stage of an appeal, apply to have it extended. Time limits can be extended in appeals about liability, completion notices, penalties and valuation bands.[84]

A request for an extension must be made to the tribunal president using the prescribed form.

An appeal can be pursued out of time if the president is satisfied there were circumstances beyond your control. You must therefore give a clear explanation for the delay. The tribunal might ask for more information from you or other parties before making a decision. In some cases, it may hold a hearing.

The president considers the following when deciding whether an extension should be granted:[85]

- when the notice was actually received;
- whether you were informed of the right of appeal and the 28-day limit;
- whether you have acted with all reasonable speed in the circumstances;
- your reasons (and any proof) for the delay, such as illness, absence from home or bereavement; *and*
- whether it would be contrary to the interests of justice or prevent a fair hearing not to permit the appeal to be heard.

When considering non-compliance, the tribunal must decide whether the breach was serious, if there was good reason and if it caused any disadvantage and also consider the interest of justice. The tribunal may apply tests used in the Upper Tribunal and the higher courts.[86]

A decision is sent to you and copied to all other parties (or potential parties). You normally have no further right of appeal against the decision to reject an application to extend the time limit. A further application can only be made if new information becomes available at the time of the original application. Where there has been a significant change in fact or law, it may be more appropriate to submit a new appeal.[87]

Expecting that an appeal could be settled by agreement with the valuation officer or the council is not likely to be a good reason for a delay in complying with the tribunal's directions.[88]

If you experience difficulty registering a liability appeal because the billing authority has not replied, refer to section 16 of the Local Government Finance Act 1992. The tribunal must register your appeal even if no reply has been received, provided that more than eight weeks have passed since you first wrote to the authority.

Lead cases

If appeals are made to the tribunal by more than one person about the same issues of fact or law (eg, a number of appeals about valuations in the same block of new flats), the tribunal can specify one or more of the appeals as a 'lead case'. It can then postpone making a decision on all other related appeals. The outcome of the lead case will normally apply to (and be binding on) the postponed appeals.[89] A copy of the decision must be sent to all affected parties.

If your appeal is not the lead case, you can apply in writing to the tribunal within one month to request a direction that the decision does not apply to, and is not binding on, your appeal.[90]

In Scotland, complex cases can be referred to the Upper Tribunal.[91] There is no provision for lead or complex appeals in Wales.

It is important that, in a lead case or group of appeals relating to the same building, a tribunal gives proper consideration to any distinguishing features of individual properties. The circumstances of each property must be considered.[92]

Withdrawing an appeal

In **England and Wales**, you may withdraw an appeal on a valuation matter by sending or delivering a notice to the VTE/VTW.[93] The tribunal must notify each party in writing that an appeal has been withdrawn.

In **England**, you can withdraw the appeal orally at the hearing. The tribunal must give its formal consent. In **Wales**, the appeal panel can withdraw your appeal at the hearing after considering representations.[94]

In **Scotland**, an appeal may be withdrawn by writing to the LTC, or at the hearing by asking the permission of the tribunal members.[95] If, after the appeal has started, the assessor agrees to the original proposal or the local authority decides not to contest the appeal, this is treated as a withdrawal of the appeal.

Reinstatement of an appeal

In **England**, it is possible to apply to reinstate an appeal after you have given notice to withdraw it. This might be appropriate, for instance, if an appeal has been withdrawn by mistake, if new advice or evidence has been obtained or if a ruling of another tribunal or the High Court might affect your case.

You must apply in writing to the VTE and within one month of either the date:[96]

- on which the VTE received the withdrawal notice; *or*
- of the hearing at which the appeal was withdrawn.

You should provide any supporting documentation and give your reasons.

In **Wales**, where an appeal has not been commenced in time, the tribunal president may authorise an appeal if satisfied the failure to begin the appeal in time has arisen due to circumstances beyond your control.[97]

In **Scotland**, where an appeal is withdrawn, you can make no further appeal relating to the same dwelling and based on the same matter and facts.[98]

Paying council tax while an appeal is pending

If you have been served a bill, you must make the payments required by the bill or by any subsequent agreement with the local authority. Making an appeal does not suspend your obligation to pay, although some local authorities may choose to pause recovery action while your appeal is being considered.

If an appeal is upheld, any overpayment of tax should be refunded or credited against future liability. If the billing authority refuses to repay the amount, you can ask the tribunal to issue an order for repayment.

In England and Wales, if the local authority applies for a liability order, the magistrates' court may agree to an adjournment if an appeal about liability has started. An adjournment should always be granted if there is a realistic prospect of success, especially if the authority seeks a committal order against you (see p244). This approach has been approved by the High Court.[99]

If the authority has obtained a liability order (a summary warrant or decree in Scotland), it is good practice to suspend recovery action until the appeal is decided. A failure to do so could be escalated to the Ombudsman (see p300).

If you appeal against a penalty imposed by the local authority (see p266), you do not have to pay the penalty until the appeal is resolved. If a sum in council tax relates to a previous year, it could also be argued that the matter should wait for a determination by the VTE/VTW/LTC.

If the local authority decides to cancel the penalty after your appeal has started, it will notify the tribunal, and your appeal will be considered withdrawn on the date the notice is served.[100]

Appealing as an interested person

An 'interested party' is anyone who is affected by the appeal. It includes:[101]

- the property's owner;
- a person who may be jointly or severally liable to pay council tax;
- a person other than an owner who would be liable to pay council tax if the dwelling were not an exempt dwelling or where the amount set were other than nil;
- any other person who pays council tax for the dwelling.

5. Appeal hearings

The president of the Valuation Tribunal for England (VTE) has issued a *Consolidated Practice Statement* (valuationtribunal.gov.uk/vte-guidance) for the conduct of proceedings. The Valuation Tribunal for Wales (VTW) has best practice protocols (valuationtribunal.wales/rules-and-protocols covering similar areas. These help interpret the procedural regulations and the steps to be taken when appealing, and give an idea of the tribunal's approach in specific situations. The Local Taxation Chamber (LTC) outlines its procedures on its website (localtaxationchamber.scot).

You should read the information that provides key details of how appeals should be prepared, particularly if you are a professional representative or acting in an official capacity. Taxpayers representing themselves are not expected to follow every step but must provide enough information for a fair process. Higher standards of preparation are expected from professional representatives and local authorities.

Most valuation tribunal hearings are open to the public, and it is a good idea to watch the tribunal in action to learn how proceedings operate. You can request a link to watch a hearing live, but recordings are not allowed.

Postponements

A hearing may need to be postponed where there is a good reason. Postponements can also occur if the tribunal has too many cases listed or if earlier hearings overrun.

Before a hearing begins, postponement requests are dealt with by tribunal staff, who must act in line with judicial and procedural principles.[102]

Either party may apply for a postponement in advance of the hearing date. The request must be made in writing as soon as possible, giving full reasons. The other parties must be notified. Your application should list your reasons and whether the other parties agree. In urgent cases, you can apply by phone.

The VTE states that postponements will not be granted automatically. They are only granted if there are exceptional and sufficient reasons, and if doing so is in the interests of justice. In Wales and Scotland, there are general powers to postpone.[103]

Examples of good reasons include:[104]

- illness of a party or representative (medical evidence should be provided where possible). If a representative has a long-term illness, it is expected that alternative arrangements for representation will be made;[105]
- unexpected or unforeseen events which prevent attendance – eg, major IT problems;
- new evidence or caselaw that requires consideration;
- documents or notices sent to an incorrect email address, causing delay.

The following are not accepted as good reasons:

- holiday commitments;
- ogoing or incomplete negotiations between the parties.

If good reasons are shown, postponement should normally be granted unless either the other party presents a stronger argument to the contrary or the interests of justice require it to be rejected.[106] Similar principles to those applied with granting adjournments may be expected to apply in law (see p222).

All parties are notified in writing (normally within three working days) of the decision, together with the reasons, provided there is sufficient time before the hearing.[107]

Notice of the hearing

In **England**, the VTE must give all parties reasonable notice of the hearing date and time.[108] This is normally 14 days, unless parties consent to a shorter period or there are urgent or exceptional circumstances.

In **Wales**, the tribunal clerk must give at least four weeks' written notice of the hearing's date, time and place. The clerk must publically display this information:[109]

- at the tribunal's office; *and*
- outside an office designated by the local authority for this purpose; *or*
- in another suitable place within the local authority's area.

In **Scotland**, the LTC must give at least 31 days' written notice, unless parties agree to alter this.[110]

There is no maximum time limit in which the tribunal must hear an appeal.

Representatives

On the day of the hearing, any party may:[111]

- represent itself; *or*
- be represented by a lawyer; *or*
- be represented by another person of their choice.

If you are representing yourself, you may have someone assist you – eg, a friend, a relative or an adviser.[112] In Scotland, if there are good and sufficient reasons, the LTC may refuse to permit a particular person to represent a party at a hearing.[113]

Remote hearings are to be treated in the same way as in-person hearings.

How the hearing is conducted

In **England and Wales**, the appeal is heard by two members, one of whom must be the chair and who must preside. The president, vice presidents and nominated senior members may sit alone as the tribunal. If all parties who attend the hearing agree, the appeal may be decided by two members in the absence of a chair.[114]

A council tax reduction (CTR) appeal must have a First-tier Tribunal judge as one of the panel if it involves a complex issue like right to reside or assessments of income or capital.[115]

In **Scotland**, the appeal is heard by:[116]

- the chamber president, a legal member or a judicial member; *and*
- one or two ordinary members – eg, a surveyor.

The chamber president, a legal member or a judicial member can sit alone to decide any matter in a non-list appeal case or a CTR case, or when the appeal is on the basis of written representations.[117]

Putting documentary evidence to the tribunal against listing officer decisions

The *Consolidated Practice Statement* provides for different rules and directions when you are appealing over a council tax banding and challenging a decision of the Listing Officer. The Valuation Tribunal Service states in the booklet *Council Tax Valuation: your appeal and preparing for your valuation tribunal hearing*: 'You should make sure that your case explains the issues that you and the Valuation

Office Agency (VOA) disagree about and the decision you want from the tribunal. Set out your arguments that support your case (including any legislation or case law) and enclose any evidence that you have to support this.' This is good advice because, although the tribunal allows you to give oral evidence to establish the facts, it often wants whatever you say to be confirmed by documentary evidence.

Serving documents on the listing officer

At least six weeks before the hearing,[118] you should receive the VOA's full case in response to the appeal, including arguments, evidence, legislation, caselaw and documents. Documents should be submitted by 5pm on the day they are due.[119] If the time specified by the regulations or a direction to do something ends on a day other than a working day, it is in time if it is done on the next working day.[120] 'Working day' means any day except a Saturday or Sunday, Christmas Day, Good Friday or a bank holiday.[121]

In **England**, if you wish to provide evidence, submit it to the other party at least four weeks before the hearing.[122] This may include caselaw or references to legislation. Anything sent after this deadline may not be considered by the tribunal unless you provide valid reasons for the delay.

At least two weeks before the hearing, the VOA must submit a bundle of documents, including any documents you have provided, to the tribunal and send you copies by email or post. If the VOA fails to comply, only documents provided by you and those in the decision notice will be considered.[123]

In **Wales**, there is no statutory requirement for advance evidence exchange beyond the Valuation Tribunal for Wales Regulations 2010.[124] However, the VTW expects parties to have discussed and exchanged evidence at least two weeks before the hearing .[125] Evidence must be shared with all parties in advance. If any party has not been given the opportunity to inspect, copy or extract information with at least 24 hours' notice, that evidence cannot be used.[126]

In **Scotland**, the LTC may issue directions regarding evidence.[127]

Submission of evidence

If you have already submitted evidence earlier in the appeal, simply refer to it and clarify which documents or arguments you rely on.[128]

It is important to send copies of any evidence in advance to the local authority or listing officer. For CTR appeals, send documents at least 14 days before the hearing. For liability appeals, discounts, exemptions or calculations, submit documents ideally one month before the hearing, unless otherwise directed by the tribunal.

Where documents may become available at a late stage, the tribunal has the discretion to admit or exclude such evidence.[129]

At least two weeks before the hearing, a billing authority may be required to electronically submit to the tribunal, and by either email or post to the appellant, a bundle of documents including any documents provided under any directions. A failure to do so may lead to evidence being excluded or a party being barred from taking further part in proceedings.

If you fail to follow a VTE rule or miss a deadline, the appeal can continue if the tribunal considers it just to do so.[130]

The tribunal may give directions to produce a bundle. This a collection of all documents, organised and numbered by page. Its purpose is to help the tribunal easily navigate and reference key evidence. It speeds up the tribunal process when all parties have copies of the documents in the same order. This is often the best way to present your evidence, whether or not the tribunal gives a direction.

Preparing a bundle

The simplest way to produce a bundle is to put the documents together in date order, although there is no specific rule that documents have to be in this order.

Include a front page with the following details:

- 'In the [Valuation Tribunal for England/Wales/Local Taxation Chamber]';
- appeal number;
- address of the property;
- your name as the appellant and the local authority/listing officer's name as the respondent.

You can also add your own statement or witness statement to the documents, which you can place at the beginning of the bundle.

For a remote hearing, you should send your bundle electronically. Only include essential documents to keep the file size manageable. Ensure it is paginated and indexed. In Wales, you should send it to the clerk and all other parties at least five working days before the hearing.[131]

Evidence that may be difficult to copy, such as photographs and large plans, can be shared on the day, but you should let the other parties know in advance about these.

Remote hearings

Remote hearings are now the default format for appeals in England, Wales and Scotland. In-person hearings are exceptional and granted only where justice cannot be achieved remotely.

In **England**, if the tribunal cannot decide an appeal on the papers (without a hearing), it will hold a remote hearing via video conference (Microsoft Teams), telephone or a hybrid (combination of both). You do not need to have the Teams app, the tribunal provides a secure joining link via email. A flexible approach must be followed at all times. Guidance is provided at valuationtribunal.gov.uk/how-remote-hearings-work.

An in-person hearing is only considered if the VTE president is satisfied that it is the most appropriate and fair way to resolve the case. The application form for an in-person hearing is at valuationtribunal.gov.uk/remote-hearing-faqs. Your application must include compelling reasons explaining why a remote hearing is not suitable.

In **Wales**, remote hearings are referred to as 'video hearings'. Unless a party requests in-person attendance, all parties attend by video link. There is a protocol for video hearings.[132]

In **Scotland**, the LTC normally holds remote hearings. It will only consider holding an in-person hearing if satisfied that it would be impossible for it to dispense justice remotely.

Do you have concerns about a remote hearing?

If you are worried about taking part in a remote hearing, raise your concerns as early as possible with the tribunal. You may wish to explain if:[133]

- you lack access to suitable technology or internet connection;
- you have a disability or health issue affecting your ability to participate remotely;
- confidentiality, data protection or fairness may be compromised;
- the case involves live evidence, complex documents or cross-examination that would be difficult to handle online.

Public hearing

Tribunal appeals are classed as public hearings. That means you can attend other hearings (including remote ones) to see how the tribunal functions before your own hearing.

However, a tribunal can decide to hold the hearing in private if any party requests it and the tribunal considers that the interests of that party would be prejudiced if the hearing were held in public.[134] In this case, the panel decides who should be present. For example, someone who might disrupt or interfere with a hearing or who is likely to prevent another person giving evidence may be excluded.

The tribunal can allow specific individuals to observe remotely. You must give advance notice if you want to observe a hearing. Observers are typically shown as a circular icon with their initials on the screen. In practice, very few hearings are observed by members of the public.

Failure to appear and striking out of appeals

In England and Wales, if you (or in Scotland, you or your representative) fail to attend the hearing, the appeal may be dismissed or struck out.[135] In England and Wales, an appeal on a valuation matter may also be struck out if any party other than the listing officer fails to attend. The VTW may also strike out an appeal or part of an appeal related to CTR if the reduction already awarded is the maximum possible under the local scheme. If the appeal covers more than one issue, only that part which relates to the reduction can be struck out, although the tribunal must give you an opportunity to be heard.

In England and Wales, if you missed the hearing for good reason, you can ask the tribunal to review its decision (see p290). The request must be made within four weeks of the notice of the decision being given.[136]

In Scotland, if you have a reasonable excuse for your absence, the LTC may set a new hearing date.[137] It must give all parties at least seven days' notice. For a hearing to be recalled in this manner, you must write to the LTC (normally within 14 days of being notified of the dismissal), requesting a new date and explaining the reason for your absence. In special circumstances, the LTC may accept an out-of-time request.

Absence of a party to the appeal

If any party does not attend at the hearing, the tribunal can still proceed in their absence.[138]

The tribunal can proceed if it is satisfied that the party has been properly notified of the hearing (or that reasonable steps were taken to notify them) and it considers that it is in the interests of justice to proceed.[139]

Local authorities do not always send an officer to the hearing. Regardless of its attendance, always send the local authority a copy of the documents you plan to use in an appeal well before the hearing.

Order of the hearing

The tribunal generally decides the order of the hearing – ie, which party puts its case first. The 'model procedure' practice statement in England provides that you are usually to open your case first.[140] However, sometimes the billing authority is invited to present its case first. If you are unrepresented, the panel is entitled to invite the local authority or listing officer to go first, where it thinks this may result in a fairer hearing.

The panel must ensure that the local authority or listing officer is given the opportunity to respond to your case. You must always be given the final opportunity to address the panel.[141]

Both parties have the opportunity to question each other during the hearing. This is known as cross-examination. You have the right to ask questions of the local authority or any witnesses it calls. Evidence can be given in written submissions, including in witness statements.[142] Witness statements are often the best way to provide evidence at hearings, with the person reading from their statement and answering any questions which the other side may have about the information it contains. Where you are unrepresented and are having difficulty in formulating questions, the clerk (or the chair) may assist you, but not to the point where they become your advocate.[143]

The statement of a witness who does not attend remains, in principle, admissible evidence. It has the status of hearsay. It is up to the tribunal to decide what weight it gives to an unsigned witness statement. Where there is a dispute, the tribunal is expected to do the best it can, even with less than perfect evidence.

Wherever there are two versions of the facts, it is necessary to resolve the conflict.[144]

Summing up at the end of a hearing

At the end of the hearing, each side is invited to make a closing submission. The aim of the summing up is to succinctly review the case and explain why your case should be preferred. You should not repeat the evidence that the tribunal has already heard nor seek to introduce any new material to the panel. The best advice is to keep the summing up short, emphasising only the most important point(s). You could bullet point the main points in your case and read them out. You are not expected to give a full speech like a barrister in a criminal trial.

At the end of the hearing, the tribunal normally retires to consider its verdict. Sometimes the tribunal, via the clerk, will request further information or clarification.

During a remote hearing, you are asked to wait online while the panel checks that it has all the information it requires. The clerk confirms within five or 10 minutes whether the panel has the information it needs or that proceedings will continue on Teams.

The clerk can advise the tribunal, but no other person should be present while it is deliberating. Unfortunately, a problem with online procedures is that one cannot be certain that these elementary safeguards are being observed. If any other person is present, the decision may be challengeable on grounds of breach of natural justice.

Adjournment and dismissal

A hearing may be adjourned (postponed) to another time or place, and on such terms as the tribunal considers appropriate. Every party must be given reasonable notice of the new time and place of the adjourned hearing.[145]

In **England**, you must apply in writing to the clerk for an adjournment. The clerk takes into account relevant factors, including:

- the reasons for your request;
- the other parties' comments on the request;
- the length of notice that was given for the hearing;
- the preparation already undertaken by all parties;
- the time remaining before the scheduled hearing;
- whether the appeal has been listed before.

If the clerk refuses the adjournment, you can apply to a member or to the VTE itself on the hearing day. Adjournments at this stage are rarely granted, as parties are expected to be prepared.

In **Scotland**, the LTC may request representations from both parties before deciding whether to adjourn.[146]

In some cases, an appeal may be dismissed if the listing officer or assessor fails to show that you have been properly served with notices and documents.

Witnesses

A person may be summonsed to attend as a witness and to produce any documents or answer any questions relating to the proceedings.[147] A summons must normally be given with 14 days' notice (or a shorter period if the tribunal directs). In England, a summons or order must state that a person may apply to vary or set aside the summons or order if they have not had the opportunity to object to it, and must state the consequences of non-compliance. There is currently no equivalent rule in Wales or Scotland.

In Scotland, a witness is required at the hearing and if it takes place more than 10 miles from their home, they do not have to appear unless their necessary expenses are paid.[148]

Evidence

Tribunals are not bound by strict court rules of evidence; rather, they are concerned with the weight of any evidence.[149] For example, what someone else has been heard to say (hearsay) would be admissible at a hearing, but given less weight than the direct evidence of a witness.

Evidence can be given orally or in written form, such as valuation reports. For in-person hearings, make sure you have multiple copies of all documents so each tribunal member and the other party have one.

For valuation appeals, evidence could include photographs or a video. Occasionally, physical evidence may even be produced.[150]

You should expect to be asked questions by the tribunal and by the listing officer or local authority's representative. For example, if you allege that your property value is affected by blighting or a nuisance of some kind, you may be asked what steps you have taken to remedy the problem. If you have taken no action, the tribunal may conclude that the problem is not serious enough to affect value.

In appeals that do not relate to valuation matters, the local authority must give the other parties two weeks' notice if it intends to produce evidence of information related to a disability reduction or liability issue. This information may be inspected and copies taken if at least 24 hours' notice is given to the local authority.[151] In a valuation appeal, the listing officer must give at least two weeks' notice of the information they propose to use at the hearing. Again, you and any other party to the appeal may, having given 24 hours' notice, inspect the documents and make a copy of all of them, or an extract, if you wish.[152]

You may request information about up to four comparable dwellings (or more, if the listing officer allows). The listing officer has a duty to produce both your documents and theirs at the hearing.[153]

Site inspections

In England and Wales, a tribunal may conduct a site inspection of the appeal property as part of the evidence. Only the tribunal can enter the appeal property. The tribunal members who hear your case will also attend the site inspection. It is important to remember that the site inspection is an extension of the hearing and a formal step. No new evidence may be introduced at this stage unless the tribunal requests it. There is no specific power for inspection in Scotland.

Caselaw

The tribunal can determine both points of fact and points of law in an appeal. While it can decide legal questions, it is not bound by its own previous decisions, though past decisions may be highly persuasive. Decisions of the Upper Tribunal, High Court, Court of Appeal and Supreme Court are binding on the tribunal.

You can raise points of law, including those based on court judgments. If citing a case, you must provide a copy of the judgment to the clerk and all other parties.

Case references should normally be provided in advance so that the tribunal and parties can study them. Bring multiple copies for the hearing, especially if the case is not well-known. For widely known cases in non-contentious matters, one copy may suffice.

Failure to agree

In **England and Wales**, where an appeal has been heard by a panel with an even number of members who cannot agree on a decision, the appeal is reheard by a completely new panel.[154]

In **Scotland**, the decision must be made by majority. In the event of a tie, the chairing member has a casting vote.[155]

Decisions and orders

Following a hearing, tribunals may give oral decisions, but written decisions with reasons are always provided.[156] A written decision, together with a statement of reasons, must be supplied to the parties. This should be done as soon as reasonably practicable after the decision has been made, and normally within 28 days. Records are normally kept for six years.[157] If a tribunal fails to give adequate reasons, the decision is invalid.

If the tribunal does not give written reasons, you may request reasons in writing. In **England and Wales**, you must request this within two weeks of receiving the final decision notice.[158] In **Scotland**, written reasons are issued to all parties as soon as possible after the decision, including a statement of facts.[159]

Reasons must be adequately expressed though not necessarily to the standard expected in court.[160]

The decision may include an order that the tribunal considers just arising from its decision. You need to think about what order you want the tribunal to make. It is a good idea to draft this and supply it to the tribunal.

If you are seeking a refund on overpaid council tax, the ruling of the valuation tribunal has become a procedural requirement following *Lone v London Borough of Hounslow*.[161]

However, the valuation tribunal president has ruled that it cannot determine other debt disputes in council tax (eg, whether a set off should be allowed on a sum) with the result that some issues have to be argued in the magistrates' or county court.

Where the alleged refund stretches more than six years, any sum recoverable is limited to within six years of the date of service of a repayment notice.[162] After the tribunal has made a decision, it has the power to make additional orders to give effect to it, such as ordering the billing authority to reverse its decision.[163] These are sometimes called 'ancillary orders'. An order may include a direction for the local authority to repay you any council tax owing or any bailiffs' fees or other charges, with interest from the date(s) of payment.

The VTE has ruled that it has no power to award interest as part of an order for repayment.[164]

An order may relate to specific time periods of liability or (in the case of an appeal against a decision by the listing officer) may require any alteration to be made in respect of such period as appears to the VTE to reflect the duration of those circumstances.[165]

In **Scotland**, the LTC may require:[166]

- the reversal of a decision of a billing authority;
- the quashing of any sum in council tax (or council water charge);
- the recalculation of any amount;
- the quashing of a penalty;
- the alteration of a list (in the future or retrospectively).

Any alteration of a list must be carried out within six weeks beginning on the day on which the order is made.[167]

In **Scotland and Wales**, an additional order can be obtained that 'may require any matter ancillary to its subject-matter to be attended to'.[168] A further order is at the discretion of the tribunal and must be exercised reasonably.

The LTC has no power to direct that the assessor revalue properties that are subject to an appeal where the decision is quashed. This remains a statutory function that can only be exercised by the assessor.[169]

Decisions become public documents and are published online. For council tax liability cases, personal identifiers are removed in the interests of privacy.[170] You can request redaction of names or other identifying details.[171] It is up to you to satisfy the tribunal that information should not be published.

Previous tribunal decisions

You may be told at some stage of the appeal process that a tribunal has already decided a particular matter and that your attempt to appeal on the same grounds will fail. You should not accept this as a reason for abandoning an appeal. Although local authorities and listing officers have tended to treat previous decisions involving points of law as binding, it should not be assumed that a tribunal will automatically find against you. Just because one appeal has been decided in a particular way does not necessarily mean that the same approach will be taken with a different appeal. Tribunals are not precedent-making bodies that are expected to follow decisions of earlier tribunals. Your case should be looked at on its merits.[172]

Records of decisions

In **England and Wales**, the clerk has a duty to make arrangements to record the tribunal's decisions. The record may be kept in various formats, such as documents or electronic records. For appeals about proposals, the record should contain:[173]

- your name and address;
- the matter appealed;
- the date of the hearing or determination;
- the names of the parties who appeared (if any);
- the decision and its date;
- the reasons for the decision;
- any orders made in consequence of the decision, including their date;
- any certificate setting aside the decision;
- any revocation.

For other appeals, the record must also contain:[174]

- the date of the appeal; *and*
- the name of the billing authority whose decision was appealed against.

A copy of the relevant entry in the record must, as soon as is reasonably practicable, be sent to each party to the appeal. Each record must be retained for six years.[175] Records of VTE and VTW decisions are published at info.valuation-tribunals.gov.uk.

Anyone may inspect the records free of charge. If a person intentionally obstructs access to the records without a reasonable excuse, they may be fined.[176]

The member who presided at the hearing can authorise corrections of any clerical errors. A corrected copy must be sent to the parties who received a copy of the original entry.[177]

The production of a document certified by the clerk or the president is evidence of the decision and the facts it records in any proceedings in any court of law.[178]

In **Scotland**, the LTC must publish its decision in writing, except for CTR decisions.[179] If evidence was heard in private, references to this evidence will be omitted from the published decision. The decision can be published in an edited form, with sensitive information redacted or removed. Scotland's tribunal decisions are available at localtaxationchamber.scot/decisions.

6. Reviews of tribunal decisions

While tribunal decisions are usually final, there are limited circumstances in which a decision can be reviewed.

England and Wales

A tribunal may review or set it aside its decision, except when the decision has been appealed to the igh Court.[180] A review can be requested through a written application from any party, provided it is in the interests of justice. It must be on one of the following grounds.

- Failure to send or receive documents on time by a party.
- A document was not sent to the Valuation Tribunal for England (VTE) or the Valuation Tribunal for Wales (VTW).
- A party did not appear and can show reasonable cause for this.
- The decision is affected by a High Court or Upper Tribunal decision.
- There has been procedural irregularity – eg, failure to provide information or allow rebuttal.[181] The 'irregularity' has been considered wide enough to cover issuing judgments and making orders.[182]
- In cases of completion notices, new evidence has become available (unless it could have been reasonably foreseen or discovered earlier).

You can request reasons for the tribunal's decision. Normally, only a summary of reasons is given, but you can request a full statement of reasons within two weeks of the decision notice.

You must usually apply for a review (or set-aside) within 28 days of the written decision being sent. In exceptional cases where there is a good reason, you may make an application outside the 28 days. The form for England can you downloaded from valuationtribunal.gov.uk/forms/review-application.

There are three stages to the review process.[183]

- The application for a review is considered by the tribunal president, who will decide if the grounds are met.[184]
- If granted, the review will assess whether the decision should be set aside.
- If the decision is set aside, the appeal will be reconsidered by the same or a differently constituted tribunal (in England, this may be treated as an appeal).[185]

If a hearing is necessary, it must take place within 28 days, though the process is usually conducted without one.

In **Wales**, an application for a review must be made in writing within four weeks. The tribunal will decide to:[186]

- not review the decision; *or*
- review and not set aside the decision; *or*

- review and set aside the decision, in which case any prior order will be revoked, and a rehearing will be scheduled.

In cases of clear errors, the tribunal may correct its own decisions without needing an appeal.

Appeals to the High Court

If you are unsuccessful at the valuation tribunal, there is no further right of appeal except on a point of law. This means you must show that the tribunal misapplied or misinterpreted the law, not simply that it reached a conclusion you disagree with. In England and Wales, this is made to the High Court.

The High Court may be cautious to interfere with decisions on valuation tribunals which are considered specialist tribunals.[187] However, a distinction has been made between decisions on valuation matters and other council tax matters. In *Marshall v Bath and North East Somerset Council*, a case about sole or main residence and exempt dwellings, the High Court stated that although the tribunal has expertise in valuation, it has no special expertise in factual findings such as residence or liability. Therefore, the court will not hesitate to scrutinise such findings as it would those of any other tribunal.[188]

A tribunal's decision may amount to an error of law if:[189]

- if applied the wrong legal test; *or*
- if reached a perverse conclusion – ie, one no reasonable tribunal could have reached; *or*
- it considered irrelevant matters or ignored relevant ones;[190] *or*
- it made a finding of fact without evidence.[191]

Disagreement with the tribunal's conclusions is not sufficient; you must show that its decision was irrational or legally flawed.[192]

The appropriate test as to whether the High Court should interfere with a decision on a point of law has been expressed as where a decision is based on several reasons and at least one is legally wrong:[193]

- if the error sgnificantly affected the outcome, the court will interfere;
- if it was insignificant, and the tribunal would have reached the same result anyway, the decision stands.

To show that a factual error amounts to a legal one, it is necessary to:[194]

- identify the challenged finding;
- show it was significant n to the conclusion;
- identify the relevant evidence (if any);
- show the tribunal was not entitled to make the finding based on the evidence.

You may also appeal if the tribunal fails to observe the rules of natural justice – eg, bias, involvement of ineligible people, refusing cross-examination or denying access to the other party's evidence. A valuation tribunal which introduces legal points of its own volition does not breach natural justice.[195]

Remote hearings can risk breaches – eg, if parties struggle with technology, cannot see the same documents or experience audio problems. It is advisable to provide paper copies of all evidence and request that these are used in any virtual hearing. See the *Consolidated Practice Statement* for best practice guidance.

The appeal proceeds by way of review unless the court considers that it would be in the interests of justice to hold a rehearing by the tribunal.[196] The scope of the court's powers on a review in most cases renders it unnecessary to hold a rehearing.[197]

Costs and risks

Seek legal advice before starting this course of action, as costs are typically over £3,000, potentially higher if contested. The High Court has discretion whether to award costs against an appellant, but the normal rule is that the loser pays the winner's costs. The court's decision depends on the facts and the conduct of the parties, whether they choose to appear and whether the matter could have been settled otherwise.[198]

Listing officers do not face cost orders, and if a local authority appeals, the tribunal (not you) bears the costs.

If a local authority agrees to grant or revise a CTR award before a judicial review application is heard, this provides grounds for the challenge to be dismissed.[199]

An appeal on a point of law to the High Court must be made within four weeks of:

- the date on which notice is given of the decision or order; *or*
- the date of a decision following review; *or*
- a determination by a tribunal that it will not review its decision where the application for review was made within four weeks of the original decision.

Time limits are expected to be strictly followed.[200] Some council tax liability appeals must be filed within two weeks of receiving written reasons.

The High Court can hear appeals which are out of time (by judicial review), but you should not rely on this, as the right is purely discretionary.[201]

Details of how to appeal to the High Court are found in the *Civil Procedure Rules Practice Directions*.[202]

Judicial reviews are mainly based on written evidence and generally do not re-examine factual disputes.[203] However, the procedures for judicial review are sufficiently flexible for dealing with such disputes. These include orders for disclosure, for the cross-examination of witnesses and the court's ability, in appropriate cases, to draw inferences from the evidence presented.[204]

If the tribunal has acted in breach of natural justice, you may make an application for judicial review (see p318). Strict compliance with the time limits is expected.[205] You are required to complete and submit a form for a statutory appeal together with a skeleton argument. The High Court may place a stay on an application for a liability or any order until the appeal is determined.

The High Court may confirm, vary, set aside, revoke or remit the decision or order, and may make any order the tribunal could have made. Where a claimant succeeds in demonstrating that the council has acted unlawfully, relief may still be refused because the claimant failed to pursue alternative remedies.[206]

Scotland

The LTC can review its own decision, either on request from a party or on its own initiative.[207] It may review a decision on the grounds that:

- the decision has been wrongly made due to an internal administrative error; *or*
- a party who failed to appear or be represented at a hearing had good and sufficient reason for doing so; *or*
- new evidence has become available which could not have been reasonably known about or foreseen when the decision was made; *or*
- the interests of justice require a review.

The request must be made in writing within 14 days of the date of the decision or the date the written reasons (if any) were sent.[208] You must set out why a review is necessary. On receipt of the request, the LTC must notify all parties of the request, set a time limit for any responses and seek views on whether the request should be decided with or without a hearing.

Where the LTC considers a request for review is wholly without merit, it must refuse it and provide written reasons for refusal.

Where the LTC proposes to review a decision at its own initiative, it must:[209]

- inform the parties in writing within 14 days of the decision (or of sending written reasons), explaining why it is being; *and*
- conduct the review as if it were a valid request from a party.

Where possible, the review should be carried out by a different tribunal member from the one who made the original decision.

Appeals to the Upper Tribunal and Court of Session

If you disagree with an LTC decision, you can apply for permission to appeal to the Upper Tribunal for Scotland. Your application must be in writing to the tribunal that made the original decision and must include the decision you are appealing, the point(s) of law you are challenging and the outcome you are seeking.

You must apply for permission to appeal within 30 days of the date the decision or statement of reasons was sent or the date of the hearing if the decision was given orally – unless written reasons were requested (within 14 days of the hearing), in which case the 30-day period runs from the date the written reasons were sent. The LTC may extend this time limit if you can show good cause ('on cause shown').

If permission is refused, you can then apply directly to the Upper Tribunal for Scotland. You, the listing officer, assessor and local authority all have an equal right of appeal.

The Court of Session may intervene where the LTC adopts the wrong procedure, reaches illogical or legally erroneous conclusions, or bases its decision on inadequate findings of fact.[210]

Notes

1. **Valuation tribunals**

1 **E** Regs 3, 4 and 5 The Valuation Tribunal for England (Membership and Transitional Provisions) Regulations 2009 No.2267 as amended by The Valuation Tribunal for England (Membership and Transitional Provisions) (Amendment) Regulations 2025 No.112; VTE(CTRA)(P) Regs
W Regs 4-14 VTW Regs
2 Sch 11 para A18A LGFA 1988
3 Statement in letter from Elena Whitham, former Minister for Community Safety, to Equalities, Human Rights and Civil Justice Committee, Scottish Parliament, 9 February 2023
4 **E** VTE CPS 2024, Part 1, para 1
S r2 FTTSLTC(RP) Regs
5 VTE CPS 2024, Part 1, para 2 citing Supreme Court in *BPP Holdings v HMRC* [2017] UKSC 551
6 *App v LB Hammersmith and Fulham* [2019] VTE Appeal No.M0247401; *Okon v LB Lewisham* [2016] EWHC 864 (Ch), reported as All ER (D) 123 (Apr)

2. **Matters that can be appealed**

7 Reg 10(2) VTE(CTRA)(P) Regs
8 *Okon v Lewisham LB* [2016] EWHC 864 (Ch), reported as All ER (D) 123 (Apr)
9 **E** Reg 10(2) CT(ALA)(E) Regs
W Reg 10(2) CT(ALA) Regs, as amended by CT(ALA)(A)(W) Regs
10 **E** Reg 10(3) CT(ALA)(E) Regs
W Reg 36(5) The Valuation Tribunals (Wales) Regulations 1995 No.3056
11 **E** Reg 7(6) CT(ALA) Regs
W Reg 8(6) CT(ALA) Regs
12 **E** Reg 7(7) CT(ALA)(E) Regs
W Reg 8(7) CT(ALA) Regs
13 **E** Reg 9(3) CT(ALA)(E) Regs
W Reg 10(3) CT(ALA) Regs
14 s81(1) LGFA 1992
15 r35(3)(f) FTTSLTC(RP) Regs
16 r11(3) FTTSLTC(RP) Regs
17 r10 FTTSLTC(RP) Regs
18 r13 FTTSLTC(RP) Regs
19 *Coll (LO) v Brannan* CO/5268/2014; *Coll (LO) v Kozak and Tsurumaki* [2015] EWHC 920 (Admin) CO/5270/2014
20 s16 LGFA 1992
21 *Arsenal Football Club Ltd and another v Ende* [1977] QB 100
22 **EW** s16 LGFA 1992
S s81 LGFA 1992
23 **S** s81 LGFA 1992
24 **EW** s16 LGFA 1992
E Reg 21 VTE(CTRA)(P) Regs
W Reg 29 VTW Regs
25 *Staines v Scarborough BC* [2021] VTE Appeal No.VT00006778
26 **E** Reg 21(6) VTE(CTRA)(P) Regs
W Reg 29(5) VTW Regs
27 s81 LGFA 1992
28 r35(2) FTTSLTC(RP) Regs
29 Reg 93 CTR(S) Regs
30 Reg 94(1) CTR(S) Regs
31 Reg 94(2) CTR(S) Regs

32 s4A(1) LGFA 1988
33 **E** Reg 21(5) VTE(CTRA)(P) Regs
W Reg 29(4) VTW Regs
34 **E** Reg 21(5) VTE(CTRA)(P) Regs
W Reg 29(5) VTW Regs
35 **E** Reg 21(6) VTE(CTRA)(P) Regs
36 **E** Regs 25 and 28(2) VTE(CTRA)(P) Regs
W Reg 40(5) VTW Regs
37 *MA v Leeds City Council* [2022] VT 00010917 and others, 14 September 2022, para 26
38 *MA v Leeds City Council* [2022] VT 00010917 and others, 14 September 2022, para 26
39 r35(3)(c) FTTSLTC(RP) Regs
40 r35(2)(h) FTTSLTC(RP) Regs
41 **E** Reg 21(4) VTE(CTRA)(P) Regs
W Reg 29(3) VTW Regs
42 **E** Reg 21(6) VTE(CTRA)(P) Regs
W Reg 29(5) VTW Regs
43 Reg 30 VTW Regs
44 **E** Reg 28 VTE(CTRA)(P) Regs
W Reg 30(5) VTW Regs
45 r52(3) FTTSLTC(RP) Regs
46 r52(4) FTTSLTC(RP) Regs
47 r52(3) FTTSLTC(RP) Regs
48 s13A(1)(c) LGFA 1992
49 See the judgment in *Morgan v Warwick DC* [2015] RVR 224
50 *S and CW v East Riding of Yorkshire Council* [2014] VTE Appeal Nos.2001M113393 and 2001M11750327
51 *British Oxygen Ltd v Minister of Technology* [1971] AC 610
52 *Associated Provincial Picture Houses v The Wednesbury Corporation* [1948] 1 KB 223
53 *R v Forest Heath* DC [1991] ex parte Lucas and West [1991] RVR 216]
54 VTE CPS 2024, PS10, para 3

3. **How to appeal**

55 **EW** Reg 37 VCCT(A) Regs
E Reg 20A VTE(CTRA)(P) Regs
W Reg 30(1) VTW Regs
56 s16(7)(b) LGFA 1992
57 **E** Reg 20A VTE(CTRA)(P) Regs
W Reg 30 VTW Regs
58 Reg 17(2)(b)(i) VTE(CTRA)(P) Regs
59 VTE CPS 2024 PS10, pp 28-31
60 Reg 17(2)(b)(i) VTE(CTRA)(P) Regs; VTE CPS 2024 PS10, pp 28-31
61 Regs 10(1) and 17(2)(b) VTE(CTRA)(P) Regs; Council Tax Reduction Appeals Practice Statement, VTE/PS/A11, President's Note, para 13
62 rr35 and 41 FTTSLTC(RP) Regs
63 rr35(3) and 41(5) FTTSLTC(RP) Regs
64 rr35(2) and 41(3) FTTSLTC(RP) Regs
65 Reg 20A VTE(CTRA)(P) Regs, as amended by reg 2 VTE(CTRA)(P)(A) Regs
66 rr36 and 42 FTTSLTC(RP) Regs
67 r9(3) FTTSLTC(RP) Regs
68 r11 FTTSLTC(RP) Regs

4. **How appeals are dealt with**

69 **EW** Reg 20 CT(ALA) Regs
E Reg 29(1) VTE(CTRA)(P) Regs
W Reg 33 VTW Regs
S r46(6) and (8) FTTSLTC(RP) Regs
70 Reg 6 VTE(CTRA)(P) Regs; a Consolidated Practice Direction issued in 2024 indicates how these powers may be exercised
71 Reg 31(6) VTW Regs, as inserted by reg 8 The Valuation Tribunal for Wales (Amendment) Regulations 2023 No.775
72 r4(1) and (2) FTTSLTC(RP) Regs
73 r4(3)(a)-(e) FTTSLTC(RP) Regs
74 Reg 33(1) VTW Regs
75 r9(1) FTTSLTC(RP) Regs
76 VTE CPS 2024, PS16, paras 4 and 5
77 **E** Reg 29(1) VTE(CTRA)(P) Regs
W Reg 20 CT(ALA) Regs; reg 33(1) VTW Regs
S rr9 and 46 FTTSLTC(PR) Regs
78 **S** r46(6) and (8) FTTSLTC(RP) Regs
79 r46(9) FTTSLTC(RP) Regs
80 r46(12) FTTSLTC(RP) Regs
81 r46(10) FTTSLTC(RP) Regs
82 rr9(8) and (9) and 46(13) FTTSLTC(PR) Regs
83 **E** Reg 6(3) VTE(CTRA)(P) Regs
W Reg 21 CT(ALA) Regs
S r4(3) FTTSLTC(PR) Regs
84 **E** Reg 21(3) VTE(CTRA)(P) Regs
W Reg 29 VTW Regs
S r4(3) FTTSLTC(PR) Regs
85 **E** VTE CPS 2024, PS1, para 7
W Reg 29(5) VTW Regs
S rr4(1) and 35 (4) FTTSLTC(RP) Regs
86 *Malt Ltd & Others v Mr C Jones & Others (VOS)* [2017] UKUT 460 (LC), UTLC Case Nos: RA/7-10 et al; *Denton v TH White Ltd and another* [2014] EWCA Civ1537
87 **E** VTE CPS 2024, PS1, para 9
S r4(1) FTTSLTC(RP) Regs
88 *Giraffe Concepts Ltd v Jackson (VO)* [2018] UKUT 344 (LC)
89 **E** Reg 7(3) VTE(CTRA)(P) Regs
S r4(3)(b) FTTSLTC(RP) Regs
90 Reg 7(4) VTE(CTRA)(P) Regs

91 r30 FTTSLTC(RP) Regs
92 *Cselko v Listing Officer Camden and LB Camden* [1997] CO/995/95
93 **E** Reg 19 VTE(CTRA)(P) Regs
W Reg 32(1) VTW Regs
94 Reg 32(1) VTW Regs
95 r37 FTTSLTC(RP) Regs
96 Reg 19(4) and (5) VTE(CTRA)(P) Regs
97 Reg 29(5) VTW Regs
98 r37(5) FTTSLTC(RP) Regs
99 *Wiltshire Council v Piggin* [2014] EWHC 4386 (Admin)
100 **E** Reg 19(8) VTE(CTRA)(P) Regs
S r55(3) FTTSLTC(PR) Regs
101 Reg 2 VTE(CTRA)(P) Regs

5. **Appeal hearings**
102 **E** VTE CPS 2024, PS4
W VTW Best Practice Protocol 1D, para 2
S r4(3)(i) FTTSLTC(PR) Regs
103 **W** Reg 31(3) and (5) VTW Regs
S r4 FTTSLTC(RP) Regs
104 VTE CPS 2024, PS4, para 4
105 *The Governor and Company of the Bank of Ireland v Jaffery* [2012] EWHC 734
106 VTE CPS 2024, PS4, para 6
107 VTE CPS 2024, PS4, para 7
108 Reg 30 VTE(CTRA)(P) Regs. The president, vice presidents and nominated senior members may sit alone as the tribunal.
109 Reg 34 (2) VTW Regs
110 r11(3) FTTSLTC(RP) Regs
111 **E** Reg 13 VTE(CTRA)(P) Regs
W Reg 36 VTW Regs
S r13 FTTSLTC(RP) Regs
112 **E** Reg 13 VTE(CTRA)(P) Regs
W Reg 36 VTW Regs
S r15 FTTSLTC(RP) Regs
113 r13(3) FTTSLTC(RP) Regs
114 **EW** Reg 25 CT(ALA) Regs
E Reg 32 VTE(CTRA)(P) Regs
W Reg 37(2) VTW Regs
115 Council Tax Reduction Appeals Practice Statement, VTE/PS/A11, 1 November 2015, para 34
116 r3 FTTSLTC(RP) Regs
117 r3(2) FTTSLTC(RP) Regs
118 VTE CPS 2024, PS11 B pp 33-34
119 Reg 14(1) VTE(CTRA)(P) Regs
120 Reg 14(2) VTE(CTRA)(P) Regs
121 s1 Bank and Financial Dealings Act 1971
122 VTE CPS 2024, PS 11, A, paras 1-2
123 VTE CPS 2024 PS 11B; reg 17(5)(b) VTE CTRA(P) Regs
124 VTW, Best Practice Protocol 1F, para 3
125 VTW, Best Practice Protocol 1F, para 4
126 Reg 38(3) VTW Regs; VTW, Best Practice Protocol 1F, paras 3 and 4
127 rr10 and 16 FTTSLTC(RP) Regs
128 **EW** Reg 17(2)(b)(i) VTE(CTRA)(P) Regs
S rr4 and 11 FTTSLTC(RP) Regs
129 Reg 17(2) VTE(CTRA)(P) Regs
130 Reg 9(1) VTE(CTRA)(P) Regs
131 VTW, Best Practice Protocol 2A(a), para 9
132 VTW, Best Practice Protocol 2A(a)
133 *Muncipio de Mariana & Others v BHP Group plc* [2020] EWHC 928
134 **EW** Reg 25(3) CT(ALA) Regs
E Reg 31 VTE(CTRA)(P) Regs
W Reg 37 VTW Regs
S r12 FTTSLTC(RP) Regs
135 **EW** Reg 25 CT(ALA) Regs
E Reg 10 VTE(CTRA)(P) Regs
W Reg 32A(1)-(3) VTW Regs
S r6(2)(b) FTTSLTC(RP) Regs
136 **E** r40 VTE(CTRA)(P) Regs
W Reg 42(5)(b) VTW Regs
137 r19(3)(e) FTTSLTC(RP) Regs
138 **E** Reg 32 VTE(CTRA)(P) Regs
W Reg 25(5) CT(ALA) Regs
139 VTE Standard Directions:
All Council Tax and Completion Notice Appeals
E PS 11 generally
S rr4(3)(i) and 11 FTTSLTC(PR) Regs
140 VTE CPS 2024, PS8, para 12
141 VTE CPS 2024, PS8, para 15
142 **E** Reg 17(1)(e) VTE(CTRA) Regs
S r16 FTTSLTC(PR) Regs
143 VTE CPS 2024, PS8, para 13
144 *Broderick v Coventry City Council* [2020] EWHC 2083 (Admin); *Shah v Luton BC* [2022] EWHC 3061
145 **E** Regs 6 and 30 VTE(CTRA)(P) Regs; VTE CPS 2024, PS4, para 11
W Reg 34(4) VTW Regs
S rr4 and 11 FTTSLTC(PR) Regs
146 r4(3)(i) and (k) FTTSLTC(PR) Regs
147 **E** Reg 18 VTE(CTRA)(P) Regs
W Reg 37(5) VTW Regs
S r8 FTTSLTC(PR) Regs
148 r8(2)(b) FTTSLTC(RP) Regs
149 **EW** *Garton v Hunter (Valuation Officer)* [1969] 2 QBD 37
E Reg 17 VTE(CTRA)(P) Regs
W Reg 37(9) VTW Regs
S r16 FTTSLTC(RP) Regs
150 *Morgan v Dew* [1964] RA 294
151 **E** Reg 17 VTE(CTRA)(P) Regs
W Reg 38 VTW Regs
152 Reg 17 VTE(CTRA)(P) Regs
153 Reg 17 VTE(CTRA)(P) Regs

154 **E** VTE CPS 2024, Part 1, para 15
W Reg 40 VTW Regs
155 r17(1) FTTSLTC(PR) Regs
156 **E** Reg 36 VTE(CTRA) Regs
W Reg 40(2) VTW Regs
S r17(2) FTTSLTC(PR) Regs
157 Reg 41(3) VTE(CTRA)(P) Regs
158 **E** Reg 37 VTE(CTRA)(P) Regs
W Reg 40(3) VTW Regs
159 r17(4) FTTSLTC(RP) Regs
160 *R v Housing Benefit Review Board of South Tynside MBC ex parte Tooley* [1995] QBD, CO/3893/94, Ognall, J
161 *Lone v LB Hounslow* [2019] EWCA Civ 2206
162 Opinion of the Deputy Registrar in *Berry and Smithwood Developments Ltd v Bolton Council* [2020] VTE Appeal No.M0258114, para 11
163 **E** Reg 38(1) VTE(CTRA)(P) Regs
W Reg 41 VTW Regs
S r38 FTTSLTC(PR) Regs
164 *Espressa Management Limited v LB Croydon* [2025] VTE reference VT00016268, 24 March 2025, per President Gary Garland
165 Reg 38(7) VTE(CTRA) Regs
166 r38(1) FTTSLTC(RP) Regs
167 r38(3) FTTSLTC(RP) Regs
168 **S** r38(4) FTTSLTC(RP) Regs
W Reg 41(2) VTW Regs
169 *Assessor for Lothian Valuation Joint Board v McLaughlin* [2020] CSIH 16 Scot (D) 11/4
170 VTE CPS 2024, PS15, para 1(ii)
171 VTE CPS 2024, PS15
172 **E** *West Midlands Baptist (Trust) Association (Incorporated) v Birmingham City Council* [1967] RVR 780 (CA)
S *Assessor for Highland and Western Isles Valuation Joint Board v Fraser* [2001] SC 473
173 **E** Reg 41 VTE(CTRA)(P) Regs
W Reg 31 and Sch 4 CT(ALA) Regs
174 **E** Reg 41 VTE(CTRA)(P) Regs
175 **E** Reg 41 VTE(CTRA)(P) Regs
W Reg 43 VTW Regs
176 **E** Reg 41 VTE(CTRA)(P) Regs
W Reg 50 VTW Regs
177 **E** Reg 39 VTE(CTRA)(P) Regs
W Reg 43(7) VTW Reg
178 **E** Reg 41(6) VTE(CTRA)(P) Regs
W Reg 42(1) VTW Regs
179 r18 FTTSLTC(RP) Regs

6. **Reviews of tribunal decisions**

180 **E** Reg 40 VTE(CTRA)(P) Regs
W Reg 42(1) VTW Regs
181 *Taskin Izzet v LB Haringey* [2025] VTE Ref 000281/2, 13 May 2025
182 *R (on the application of Reeves (Valuation Officer)) v VTE* (2015) [2015] EWHC 973 (Admin)
183 VTE CPS 2024, PS13, para 1
184 **E** Reg 40 VTE(CTRA)(P) Regs
W Reg 49 VTW Regs
185 **E** Reg 40(7) VTE(CTRA)(P) Regs
W Reg 44(2) VTW Regs
186 VTW Best Practice Protocol 3A; reg 42 VTW Regs, para 10
187 *Bracegirdle v Oxley* [1947] 1 KB 349; *Edwards v Bairstow and another* [1956] AC 14; *Hayes v Humberside Valuation Tribunal and Kingston Upon Hull City Council* [1998] RA 37
188 *Marshall v Bath and North East Somerset Council* [2024] EWHC 2551 (Admin), para 19
189 *Humphrey v Fenland DC* [2018] EWHC 2195
190 *Pengelly v The Listing Officer* [2014] EWHC 4142 (Admin)
191 *Clark v Bunyan (Listing Officer)* [2024] EWHC 486; *Ramsay v Commissioners of HMRC* [2013] UKUT 0226 (TCC), at [48]: *Edwards v Bairstow* [1956] AC 14, per Viscount Simonds
192 *Vaughan v Valuation Tribunal* [2013] EWHC 1885 (Admin)
193 *Batty v Burfoot and others; Batty v Merriman; Gilbert v Childs; Rodd v Ritchings* [1995] 2 EGLR 142; *Simplex (GE) Holdings Ltd v Secretary of State for the Environment* (1988) 57 P&CR 306
194 *Georgiou v Customs and Excise Commissioners* [1996] STC 463, per Evans LJ at 476; *Ramdhun v The Valuation Tribunal of England* [2014] EWHC 946 (Admin)
195 *Macattram v LB Camden* [2012] RA 369
196 Civil Procedure Rules 52.21(1); *Salsbury v Law Society* [2008] EWCA Civ 1285, reported as [2009] 1 WLR 1286
197 *Adesemowo v Solicitors Regulation Authority* [2013] EWHC 2020 (Admin)
198 See *Wiltshire Council v Piggin* [2014] EWHC 4386 (Admin)
199 *Kasperowicz v Plymouth City Council* [2021] EWHC 1208 (Admin)
200 *Tarbuc v Bunyan (Listing Officer)* [2024] EWHC 897 (Admin)

201 *R v London South Eastern Valuation Tribunal and Neale (LO), ex parte Moore* [2001] RVR 94
202 Ministry of Justice, *Civil Procedure Rules*, Part 52, *Practice Direction 52D – statutory appeals and appeals subject to special provision*
203 *R (St Helens BC) v Manchester Primary Care Trust* [2008] EWCA Civ 931
204 *R (on the application of British Gas Trading Ltd) v Secretary of State for Energy Security and Net Zero and others and other cases* [2023] EWHC 737; *R (Olabinjo) v Westminster Magistrates' Court* [2020] EWHC 1093 (Admin) at Holroyde LJ and William Davis, J
205 *R v London South West Valuation Tribunal ex parte de Melo* [2000] RVR 73
206 *R (on the application of John Morley) v Surrey Heath DC and Guildford Magistrates' Court* [2025] EWHC 1678
207 r19 FTTSLTC(PR) Regs
208 r19(4) FTTSLTC(PR) Regs
209 r19(7) FTTSLTC(PR) Regs
210 s82(4) LGFA 1992; *Dundee City Council v Dundee Valuation Appeal Committee and another* [2011] CSIH 73

Chapter 12

Complaints about council tax administration

This chapter covers:

1. Complaining to the local authority

If you disagree with your council tax bill or feel you have been treated badly by a local authority, or someone providing services on its behalf, you can complain. This includes issues such as delays, discourtesy, poor administration, inaccurate advice, or the impact of a department's policies on you. Every local authority has a formal complaints procedure and you must use it in the first instance to try to resolve your complaint.

The first stage is to take your complaint to the council department concerned. You should follow the council's published complaints procedure. This is usually available on its website or can be requested directly. If you are unable to access it, this in itself can form part of your complaint.

In your initial complaint, clearly explain what has happened and how it has affected you. Be polite and factual – avoid emotional or accusatory language, which may weaken your case. Keep copies of all correspondence.

Getting supporting information

To support your complaint, you can request relevant information:

– under the Freedom of Information Act 2000, for general council data;

– under the Data Protection Act 2018, for personal data via a subject access request.

If the council refuses to provide information, or if you are unhappy with the outcome of a request, you can escalate your request to the Information Commissioner or the Scottish Information Commissioner.[1]

If you are dissatisfied with the council's final response, or if it takes too long to respond (12 weeks is considered reasonable), you can complain to the Ombudsman. You should usually make your complaint within 12 months of the issue you are complaining about.

2. Complaining to the Ombudsman

The local government/public services Ombudsman

The local government/public services Ombudsman investigates complaints of maladministration by local government departments. This can include avoidable delays, failure to advise about appeal rights, refusal to respond to reasonable questions or correspondence, discourtesy, racism or sexism. The Ombudsman may recommend a proportionate, appropriate and reasonable remedy based on the facts. It is a free service and you can submit a complaint online. Before contacting the Ombudsman, you must first try to complete the local authority's complaints procedure. However, if 12 weeks have passed since you submitted your complaint and the local authority has not responded, you may go directly to the Ombudsman.

Complaints against councils and other local government bodies are investigated by:[2]

- the Local Government and Social Care Ombudsman in England (LGSCO);
- the Public Services Ombudsman for Wales;
- the Scottish Public Services Ombudsman (SPSO).

Each Ombudsman has the power to investigate errors which do not generate a right to take court action but, nonetheless, give grounds for complaint.

The Ombudsman may investigate maladministration by any district, borough, city or county council and therefore can deal with mistakes by billing authorities in administering council tax.

In 2023/24, the LGSCO made 1,141 decisions on local taxation and benefit cases. 86 per cent of those about local tax were upheld.[3]

The Ombudsman has statutory powers to commence investigations into complaints within its jurisdiction and stop them when appropriate.[4]

The Ombudsman has powers equivalent to a court in that it may call witnesses from the local authority and require the production of documents during the investigation.[5]

The Parliamentary and Health Service Ombudsman

The Parliamentary and Health Service Ombudsman (PHSO) deals with complaints about UK government departments and the NHS in England. It makes final decisions on complaints that have not been resolved through those bodies' own procedures.[6] For council tax, you can complain to the PHSO about:

- Valuation Office Agency decisions about valuation and listing matters; *and*
- DWP benefit decisions and information that may affect entitlement to council tax reduction (CTR) or deductions from benefits under a liability order.

Example

A failure by the DWP and Jobcentre Plus to tell someone that benefit entitlement would be reviewed after 26 weeks if they moved house or failed to sell their property was identified as causing council tax arrears and amounted to maladministration.[7]

A complaint must normally be made by the person directly affected. However, if that person has died or cannot act for any reason, the complaint may be made by their personal representative, a family member or another suitable person acting on their behalf.

Council tax complaints involving social services or NHS services (eg, cases involving people with severe mental impairment or individuals receiving care arranged jointly by the council and the NHS) are governed by specific regulations.[8] These cases may require additional complaint procedures.

The PHSO publishes the *Principles of Good Administration,* which outlines the standards expected from public bodies.[9] When making discretionary decisions, the PHSO stresses the importance of considering all relevant facts and disregarding those that are irrelevant.

A complaint can only be taken to the PHSO through an MP, so you must first write to your MP explaining the issue. Guidance and the complaint forms are available on the PHSO website.

Maladministration the Ombudsman can investigate

'Maladministration' is an open-ended term covering a wide range of bureaucratic errors, failures and abuses. It is not defined in law. When the term was first introduced into parliament, it was considered to include 'bias, neglect, delay, incompetence and inaptitude, arbitrariness and so on' on the part of public authorities.[10] The courts have held that maladministration 'in the context of the work of a local authority, is concerned with the *manner* in which decisions by the authority are reached and the *manner* in which they are or are not implemented'.[11]

Maladministration often involves procedural errors or poor service, which may not justify legal action but can still cause injustice or hardship. Examples include losing documents, failing to respond to correspondence, or repeated technical failures (eg, broken web portals).

Examples of maladministration relating to council tax include instances where an authority:

- fails to give you information about reductions you are entitled to or your right of appeal;
- fails to tell you about or consider an application for a discretionary CTR;
- ignores information provided which affects liability to council tax or entitlement to discounts or exemptions;
- delays dealing with disputes;
- makes payment errors – eg, misallocating payments, not crediting your account or failing to credit council tax support you have been awarded;
- seeks a liability order after promising not to obtain one or obtains an order against a person who has offered to pay the sum in full;
- continues recovery action after any debt is paid or where an agreement to pay a debt is kept;
- fails to follow paragraphs 70–78 of *Taking Control of Goods: national standards* regarding vulnerable people (see Appendix 2).

The Ombudsman cannot challenge council policy but will consider whether its stated policy is being carried out reasonably and correctly.

In Scotland, the SPSO can investigate actions taken by or on behalf of a local authority. This includes maladministration and service failure, but only where these have allegedly caused injustice or hardship.[12]

The LGSCO must allow the council to comment if it proposes to investigate a matter.[13] All investigations must be in private, but the Ombudsman has broad general and case-specific discretion over the procedures followed during an investigation.[14] An ongoing investigation does not prevent the local authority or another person from acting on any of the matters under investigation.[15]

Injustice

The Ombudsman intervenes in cases where a local authority has caused an injustice through maladministration and has failed to provide an adequate remedy. The concept of injustice is wide and open to interpretation, but it typically involves more than a trivial problem or minor inconvenience. The impact on the individual taxpayer is the key factor in determining whether injustice has occurred.

Maladministration causing you nuisance, embarrassment, financial loss or serious inconvenience and distress falls within the remit of injustice. For example, a delay in replying to correspondence which results in extra charges or fees could amount to injustice,[16] as can billing mistakes where you are wrongly informed that a bill has been paid in full.[17]

However, the Ombudsman is not a tool for retaliating against the council or targeting individual officers. Nor is it appropriate to complain simply because the council is taking steps to legitimately recover money owed. Similarly, if a local authority has taken steps to correct an injustice and you are satisfied, you cannot expect the Ombudsman to take the matter any further.

Council tax administration is often prone to errors which, if uncorrected, can cause stress, inconvenience and embarrassment for taxpayers. While these issues may not warrant court or tribunal action, they can still be difficult to resolve through the Ombudsman.

For example, a local authority may fail to record a discount, repeatedly list the wrong person on a bill or misapply payments. This can lead to reminder notices or summonses being issued to someone who has already paid or is exempt. Delays in sending information or bills may cause prejudice to the taxpayer (see p191) and trigger unnecessary enforcement. Issues may also arise if demands are sent to deceased individuals or if severely mentally impairment is not properly recorded.

Flexibility to meet service user needs

The Ombudsman expects that everyone should be able to access services easily, including those who need reasonable adjustments. Local authorities are expected to act consistently in line with published service standards and the Equality Act 2010. Councils are expected to:[18]

- tell service users what they can expect and what is expected of them;
- deal with people helpfully, promptly and sensitively, taking account of their individual circumstances;
- respond flexibly to service users' needs and, where appropriate, co-ordinate a response with other service providers;
- recognise and respect the diversity of service users by adopting an inclusive approach – eg, recognising that not everyone can digitally communicate.

If the maladministration has affected your health, this should be explained in your complaint.[19]

Outsourced services

When a council outsources its services, making a complaint can be more complex. Responsibility for errors may lie both with:

- the outsourced company for failing to deliver the service;
- the local authority for selecting an unsuitable or negligent subcontractor, or failing to properly oversee and manage the subcontractor's performance.

Ultimately, the council remains accountable for the delivery of its statutory functions, even when delivered by others on its behalf.

Interdepartmental inefficiency

Inadequate liaison between accounts, enforcement and the reduction sections in a local authority may generate problems – eg, automated enforcement letters being sent after an issue has been resolved. Local authorities cannot hide behind a 'computer error' or automated system failure as a defence.

Council tax reduction issues

Maladministration can occur when a local authority does not follow its CTR policy correctly or does not have clear, accessible information on its website.[20] In particular, the LGSCO found that it can be difficult to find 'clear explanations in council policies of what CTR reversals are, and how councils deal with them'.[21] Maladministration can occur where the local authority does not explain how to challenge a decision to recover CTR.

Maladministration also includes unreasonable delays in processing CTR applications, which can lead to financial difficulty, inconvenience, embarrassment and stress. The Ombudsman has made it clear that it is not 'fair or reasonable' for a local authority to automatically issue a summons while a CTR application is pending; instead, authorities are exected to consider individual circumstances before taking enforcement action.[22]

Refusal to accept evidence

Maladministration can occur when the authority refuses to accept evidence submitted in an application for CTR or makes repeated requests for information that has already been supplied.

You may serve a witness statement setting out the truth of what you are saying, and also give notice of an intention to escalate the complaint to the civil courts or tribunal if the issue is not resolved in your favour. Shelter has a resource on writing witness statements.[23]

A witness statement should set out the facts and any calculations, addressing issues the local authority has not accepted. It can include supporting documents as exhibits and must contain a signed statement of truth.[24]

A sworn witness statement is considered the strongest form of written evidence, second only to sworn oral testimony. It carries more weight than any unsworn information from a local authority and must be accepted by a court or tribunal as truthful unless it is contradicted by other evidence or the witness is discredited under cross-examination.

The local authority may err in law if it refuses to act upon the information in a witness statement. Ignoring such evidence can breach the local authority's statutory duties and may justify a formal complaint or legal challenge against the authority or officials concerned.

Councils should ensure that complaint investigations carried out on their behalf by contractors are thorough. This includes accepting body camera evidence used by bailiffs.

Late billing and enforcement

A growing issue of maladministration is the late initiation of enforcement action, sometimes years after the alleged liability arose (see p218).

Complaints often also involve the conduct of enforcement agents once instructed by the local authority. While the Taking Control of Goods (Fees)

Regulations 2014 provide legal remedies for excessive charging, the LGSCO is still willing to investigate the billing authority's role in appointing those agents.[25]

In many cases, submitting a complaint is more effective than a tribunal appeal for challenging delayed enforcement. The complaints process allows for broader scrutiny of delays, including record-keeping, and the reasonableness of pursuing old debts.

Offsetting against existing debt

The Ombudsman can investigate complaints even if you owe the council money. If maladministration is found, it may recommend a remedy such as financial compensation. This compensation can be used to reduce the outstanding debt, or awarded separately for issues like stress and anxiety caused by the council's actions.[26]

Disproportionate and unjust enforcement

The Ombudsman can assess whether enforcement action was excessive, disproportionate or unjustified. In a 2014 case, the Ombudsman found injustice where a council ignored a man's genuine offers to pay, failed to consider his financial situation, and instead issued a summons and instructed bailiffs.[27]

Matters the Ombudsman cannot investigate

Matters that the Ombudsman cannot investigate include:

- the amount of tax set by the local authority;
- decisions of courts or the Valuation Tribunal for England (VTE), Valuation Tribunal for Wales (VTW) and the Local Taxation Chamber (LTC) in Scotland;
- who is liable for council tax;
- decisions about banding;
- the conduct of court proceedings. These matters can only be challenged through the High Court or the VTE/VTW/LTC when they are within the specific jurisdiction of these bodies – eg, whether you should be liable for council tax. The Ombudsman expects councils to signpost to the correct place to go where the complaint should be pursued as an appeal, unless it would be unreasonable to expect you to be able to do this – eg, due to disability;[28]
- cases where the remedy is a proceeding in a court of law, a valuation tribunal or where an appeal lies to a Minister of the Crown.[29]

Matters outside the Ombudsman's jurisdiction, such as alleged breaches of the Data Protection Act and General Data Protection Regulation (GDPR), generally cannot be investigated, as these fall within the remit of the Information Commissioner.[30] However, overlap can arise in cases involving body camera footage used by bailiffs enforcing council tax debt (see Chapter 10). In May 2025, the Ombudsman entered into a memorandum of understanding with the

Enforcement Conduct Board to facilitate data-sharing in complaints about enforcement practices.[31]

The Ombudsman cannot investigate other bodies involved in council tax recovery – eg, the DWP making deductions from benefits.[32] Complaints about the DWP must be raised via its complaints procedure and, if necessary, the Parliamentary Ombudsman.

While the Ombudsman does not usually intervene in a correctly made decision to pursue enforcement, it may order redress where the service has been poor. For example, in a 2016 complaint, the Ombudsman criticised the council's failure to keep a proper record of payments made by an employer after an attachment of earnings order was obtained against a debtor, but credited to the wrong account.[33] The debtor spent nine months trying to resolve the matter. The council failed to respond adequately to her complaint, gave incorrect advice and delayed in tracing the money and resolving the situation. Following the Ombudsman investigation, the council apologised and paid compensation.

The Ombudsman must provide a report on any investigation and give reasons if it decides not to investigate or discontinue an investigation.[34] If only part of a complaint is investigated, the Ombudsman must justify why only some aspects were investigated.[35] Limited resources may be a valid reason for not proceeding with some investigations.[36]

The Ombudsman might decline to investigate a complaint if you have a right of appeal or have already appealed to a tribunal.[37] However, it can still investigate if it considers it considers an appeal would be unreasonable, or if the complaint raises issues beyond the tribunal's remit.[38] It may also decide not to investigate if the local authority has already taken steps to resolve the matter, such as offering compensation.[39]

Making a complaint to the Ombudsman

The Ombudsman investigates complaints from individuals, their families or advice agencies acting on their behalf.

You must first fully complete the local authority's complaints process before contacting the Ombudsman (see p299).

Guidance is at lgo.org.uk (England), ombudsman.wales (Wales) and spso.org.uk (Scotland). Most complaints are submitted via an online form. If you cannot access the internet, call the Ombudsman helpline (see Appendix 1).

Make sure your complaint includes:

- a short chronology of events with accurate dates;
- a summary of the issue (especially for complex cases);
- copies of all relevant correspondence.

A caseworker is assigned to handle your case. They will contact you (or your adviser) and the local authority.

The Ombudsman may decide not to begin or continue an investigation if:

- there is little chance of finding fault;
- the injustice is too minor to justify the cost;
- the issue has already been fully investigated by the council;
- the desired outcome cannot be achieved;
- a better legal remedy exists (like an appeal or legal action).

If the Ombudsman is satisfied with the council's actions or proposed actions, it can close the case and issue a decision statement.[40]

Action the Ombudsman can take

Where the Ombudsman finds that the local authority is at fault, it can recommend that the council:

- put the matter right – eg, issue the correct bill; *or*
- apply payments or CTR properly; *or*
- respond appropriately to your correspondence or appeal; *or*
- stop enforcement action and waive fees if appropriate; *or*
- pay compensation.

While compensation is not legally enforceable, councils almost always follow the Ombudsman's recommendations. In England, councils and the London Assembly also have specific powers to pay compensation.[41] However, compensation amounts tend to be low and have not kept up with inflation. This may lead some people to consider civil legal action instead, where larger damages might be awarded.

The Ombudsman can also direct councils to change their procedures to help prevent similar issues in future.

If the LGSCO issues a report finding maladministration, injustice and loss suffered, the findings are binding on the authority, unless overturned by judicial review.[42]

Ombudsman recommendations for remedies are not legally binding. However, councils must respond reasonably in line with public law.

Has the council refused to follow a recommendation?

The refusal may be challenged by judicial review. A challenge may succeed if the council's decision ignored relevant factors, relied on irrelevant reasonings, was clearly disproportionate or lacked the rationality required by law.[43]

However, the High Court may refuse to allow a judicial review if it believes the issue could have been raised earlier and the Ombudsman complaint process has caused unnecessary delay.[44] Acting promptly is therefore crucial when considering legal action.

Examples of Ombudsman complaints and settlements

Ombudsman's decisions offer valuable insight into how complaints are assessed and resolved. There is an expectation that the Ombudsman will build upon a cumulative body of decisions and exercise discretion consistently, in line with how similar cases have been handled in the past.[45] The following provides a guide to situations where the Ombudsman has found in favour of the taxpayer. See also previous editions of this *Handbook*.

Pursuing a dead taxpayer

Norfolk County Council (19 011 895) 23 March 2020

Mrs D was discharged from hospital and stayed in a care home while awaiting a longer-term placement. The council delayed assessing her needs during this transitional period. It later delayed pursuing a council tax debt until 18 months after her death. Mr C, her son, complained that his mother should not have been charged for the time in the care home and that the council failed to chase the debt for 18 months after her death.

Outcome: the reduction of the outstanding debt from £3,100 to £1,777 was ruled an appropriate remedy by the Ombudsman.

Unnecessary recovery action

Hackney Borough Council (03/A/09613) 7 October 2004

Ms Murray (pseudonym) set up a standing order to pay council tax in April 1998, but no council tax reference number was included. As a result, the council failed to allocate the payments to her account. Although the council discovered the issue in July 1998, it failed to rectify it until January 2004, despite giving repeated assurances that it would fix the problem. Arrears for 1998/99 were wrongly carried forward each year, and it began unnecessary recovery actions, including summonses, liability orders and letters from bailiffs.

Outcome: the Ombudsman found maladministration and recommended that the council pay £1,800 compensation and make changes to its accounting systems.

Failure to record a verbal agreement

Aberdeen City Council (Scottish Public Services Ombudsman Decision 200502645) 30 November 2006

Mrs C alleged that a verbal payment agreement for council tax was not recorded or honoured by the council. A verbal agreement reached between Mrs C and a member of staff about her payment schedule for council tax was not recorded, with the result that a summary warrant was issued.

Outcome: the Ombudsman recommended that the council devise and pilot a clear procedure for recording customer agreements made in face-to-face discussions. Ideally, this would include a signed agreement that both parties could keep as a record. The council was directed to apologise to Mrs C for the inconvenience and distress caused by the unnecessary summary warrant.

Wrongful seizure of a car

Merton London Borough Council (18 010 732) 2 July 2020

A taxpayer's car was seized by enforcement agents seeking to enforce a council tax debt and road traffic penalties. The taxpayer claimed the car was an essential 'tool of the trade' for her employment. The council failed to properly consider these representations and the car was sent to auction. The complainant was able to raise funds and recover her car. However, due to further debts and failure to stick to a repayment schedule, the car was seized again and sold at auction.

Outcome: the council did not follow the statutory procedure under the Taking Control of Goods Regulations 2013. The investigation uncovered 20 faults in how the council and its agents handled the debts. The council agreed to pay £1,050 for distress, time and the car's value when sold at auction. It agreed to provide a clear breakdown of one of the woman's debts to help her propose a payment plan.

Applying a blanket policy

Redcar and Cleveland Borough Council (05/C/03367) 27 September 2006

In December 2004, the council decided that all empty homes in its area should pay the maximum 90 per cent council tax. Mr and Mrs Weaver (pseudonyms) bought a bungalow, renovated it, but chose not to move in due to hostility from local residents. When they received a bill, Mrs Weaver wrote to explain their circumstances. The council refused the reduction, stating that it had set the maximum discount and that the scheme 'does not allow for any individual discretion'.

Outcome: the blanket policy adopted by the council was unlawful. The council incorrectly claimed it had no discretion when, in fact, parliament had granted local authorities discretion to consider cases on an individual basis. The failure to do so amounted to maladministration, and the Ombudsman directed the authority to properly consider Mrs Weaver's request and invite her to state her reasons for seeking the reduction. Having considered her reasons, the council was directed to give its reasons for accepting or rejecting the application, and establish a proper process for considering such cases in future.

Failure to advise properly on discount

Rochdale Metropolitan Borough Council (19 004 521) 5 February 2020

Mr X complained the council went back on an agreement to grant a 100 per cent council tax discount while his property was being refurbished.

Outcome: the Ombudsman found the council had not clearly explained the terms of the discount. The council should have told Mr X that he had a right of appeal to the valuation tribunal. The council was directed to pay Mr X £150 and to review its policy on discounts for empty properties, ensuring that service users are signposted to the tribunal if a decision on a council tax discount is disputed.

Bankruptcy as a disproportionate method of enforcement

Wolverhampton City Council (06B16600) 31 March 2008

The debtor owed less than £2,000 in disputed council tax. The local authority chose to pursue bankruptcy proceedings. This increased the debt to £38,000.

Outcome: the Ombudsman recommended that the council meet the costs of annulling the bankruptcy order. The Ombudsman's report states that a charging order should have been considered.

Failure to make proper checks about vulnerability

London Borough of Camden (07A12661) 10 July 2008

The council's revenue team began bankruptcy proceedings for council tax arrears against a woman with mental health problems who was unable to manage her own affairs. Before doing so, it did not adequately record the checks it had made and did not check with the social care department, which would have shown that bankruptcy was not appropriate.

Outcome: the Ombudsman found clear maladministration causing injustice. One part of the council (social care) knew of the woman's vulnerability, but the revenue department failed to find out, due to poor internal communication and inadequate checking procedures. The Ombudsman ruled: 'I do not think it unreasonable for revenue officers to look beyond their own departmental information and consider a council's records as a whole.' This was in line with data protection guidance issued by the Information Commissioner.

The council agreed to apply to the court to annul the bankruptcy. On annulment, the Ombudsman recommended that the council contact credit rating agencies to advise them of the position and change its procedures to make stringent checks for potential vulnerability before taking action leading to bankruptcy, a charging order or committal.

Wrongful instigation of bankruptcy proceedings

Report on an Investigation into Complaint No 08 019 113 against the London Borough of Newham [2010] BPIR 464

Ms Scott's mental illness affected her ability to manage her finances. Over several years, council tax debts accumulated, and despite the council's awareness of her illness, it made her bankrupt to recover the debt. The council correctly exercised its discretion to award Ms Scott an exemption due to her mental health for the post-bankruptcy debts, even though she did not fully qualify for the whole period. Ms Scott's solicitor applied to the court to have the bankruptcy annulled, on the grounds that she did not owe the debt as she was entitled to an exemption, but the courts rejected this application.

Outcome: the Ombudsman found maladministration. The council failed to properly consider whether bankruptcy was an appropriate enforcement method.The council agreed to apply to the court to annul the bankruptcy. The Ombudsman recommended that the council exercise its discretion in deciding whether to backdate any mental health exemption, even if Ms Scott did not technically qualify.

Wrongful pursuit of council tax debt after liability ceased

(Case reference confidential)

Mr J was involved in a long-running dispute with the council over liability for council tax on a property. He received a summons for two years' worth of arrears. Shortly before the hearing, the council issued a letter accepting that he did not have sole or main residence and that liability was with a Mrs K. The council requested details of when Mrs K left the property and a forwarding address. Despite this, the council pursued a liability order against Mr J and threatened bailiffs. Mr J made a complaint, but received no reply for three months. The council still served four demand notices covering the previous three years.

Outcome: the Ombudsman discovered that the council had continued to pursue Mr J because he failed to provide the information on Mrs K. The council acted improperly by continuing to pursue Mr J after accepting he was not liable. While it was reasonable to request information about Mrs K, liability is not conditional on a third party providing such details. The council had no legal basis to pursue Mr J for arrears after the date it had decided he was not the liable person. The council should not have proceeded with the court action. The council agreed to apologise to Mr J and pay him £350 compensation.

Council tax recovery action against a vulnerable woman with no income

Slough Borough Council (08 009 315) 4 April 2009

The council tax department failed to suspend bailiff action against a woman after being advised she was totally dependent on its own social services and had no means to pay. Mrs Carter (pseudonym) had entered the UK as a student in 2002 but was prevented from studying after developing cancer and was prohibited from working or claiming benefits. She was totally reliant on the council's social services department, who provided accommodation and a subsistence allowance, and she had no income or belongings other than those they provided. She built up council tax arrears. The council instructed bailiffs to recover the arrears, even though it had evidence that she was vulnerable, had no income and was being supported by a different council department.

Outcome: the Ombudsman found multiple failures amounting to maladministration. If the department had acted on the information provided, it is unlikely that bailiffs would have been involved and distress caused would have been avoided. The council was also criticised for the lack of interdepartmental communications and for not having a written policy for dealing with vulnerable people.

The Ombudsman recommended that the council should write off Mrs Carter's council tax arrears; pay her £250; implement a written policy on dealing with vulnerable people, and a policy on how to deal with people who are reliant on support from social services; and establish a formal link between the council tax welfare team and social services.

Instigation of bankruptcy proceedings by billing authority

Manchester City Council (O07B10432) 22 September 2009

Mr Joseph complained that the council wrongfully pursued bankruptcy proceedings against him over alleged council tax arrears. He argued that he did not owe the debt and was not made aware of the bankruptcy process. The Ombudsman could not consider whether the debt was actually owed (as it was outside its jurisdiction) and found no evidence to support Mr Joseph's claim that he was unaware of the bankruptcy proceedings. However, the Ombudsman found serious administrative failings by the council in its decision to pursue bankruptcy. It had no written procedure for determining whether bankruptcy was an appropriate recovery method and it failed to consider alternatives such as an attachment of earnings. The council also gave inadequate warning about the intention to begin bankruptcy proceedings.

Outcome: the Ombudsman found maladministration causing injustice and recommended that the council pay £1,000 compensation.

Delay in reaching decision on backdating CTR

South Ribble Borough Council (17 002 063) 31 January 2017

Mr X, who was getting universal credit, applied for backdated CTR. The council's CTR scheme required decisions to be made within 14 days. Instead, the council took an additional 10 weeks (ie, approximately 12 weeks in total) to reach a decision. The council also applied for an attachment of earnings order despite an agreement to pay £30 a month being in place when Mr X obtained paid employment.

Outcome: the Ombudsman found fault causing an injustice. It recommended the council apologise to Mr X and pay £100 for the stress and delay in processing the claim and a further £100 for seeking a second attachment of earnings order.

Failure to explain changes on council tax account

Case ref: 201602871 The City of Edinburgh Council Case ref: 201602871 May 2017

Miss C complained that the council failed to clearly explain changes made to her council tax account over a five-month period, and did not adequately communicate with her during the 10 months following her attempts to seek clarification.

The Ombudsman found the council had failed to provide an explanation for reassessing her council tax on one specific occasion. Once it became apparent that Miss C did not understand the information being provided, the council should have considered alternative communication methods, such as offering a face-to-face meeting.

Outcome: the council was directed to clearly explain Miss C's council tax reassessment. It was told to remind complaints handling staff to consider all appropriate methods of communication, including in-person discussions when necessary. It was directed to issue an apology and identify steps to prevent similar communication failures in future.

Ombudsman not satisfied by council's response after further report

Torbay Council (10 002 564) 12 May 2011

Mr Castle (pseudonym) owed £2,248 in council tax. He had mental health problems and was known to be vulnerable. The council commenced bankruptcy proceedings against him. He complained to the Ombudsman that the council had failed to have regard to his mental health issues.

The Ombudsman established the council had difficulties engaging with Mr Castle. It was known that he did not open his post and left it to accumulate. The council never conducted a home visit, despite knowing of engagement difficulties. The council ignored the findings of a bailiff which indicated illness and vulerability. The bailiff advised the council's solicitor that Mr Castle was suicidal.

Outcome: the Ombudsman found maladministration. The council had not followed proper processes or kept accurate records. It had not reviewed its decision to commence bankruptcy proceedings when information came to light that Mr Castle might be considered suicidal. The Ombudsman considered that, had such failings not occurred, the council would not have continued bankruptcy proceedings, and Mr Castle would not have incurred the costs of some £24,000. The Ombudsman recommended that the council pay Mr Castle £25,000 and issue a formal apology.

Note: the bailiff appears to have complied with principles laid down in national standards. This requires an enforcement agent who discovers a vulnerable household to report it to the creditor for reconsideration. In this case, the bailiff did, but the authority failed to act properly on receipt of the information.

Excessive and unjustified bailiff fees

Blaby District Council (11007684) 18 July 2012

Mrs S had council tax arrears relating to eight years, resulting in eight separate accounts. Bailiffs employed by the council attempted to enforce these debts. She complained that the bailiffs had not acted within the law and had overcharged her. She also complained that the council failed to properly respond to queries and complaints about these issues, including a serious allegation that four bailiffs tried to break into Mrs S's property and obtained money from her partner by clamping and taking occupation of a car that was not his.

Outcome: the Ombudsman found that the council failed to exercise proper control over the bailiffs' actions and the fees it charged. On two occasions, the bailiffs had charged eight visit fees (one for each account), even though there was one visit by one bailiff. It also failed to verify vehicle ownership and to properly investigate Mrs S's complaints until she complained to the Ombudsman. Once the Ombudsman became involved, the council reduced the fees charged by £630.50; carried out DVLA checks, which confirmed the vehicle did not belong either to Mrs S or her partner, so removed the remaining levies and associated fees; and set out a new contract under which bailiffs could only charge one fee per levy. The council agreed to pay £300 for distress and inconvenience, which it offset against the outstanding council tax arrears. The Ombudsman also advised Mrs S to enter into a reliable, regular payment plan with the council to avoid future action, such as an attachment of earnings order.

Charging of fees not permitted by law

Thurrock Council (09 006 694) 3 February 2010

The complainant owed £1,367.57 in council tax arrears. The council served a statutory demand and added a £400 administration fee. The complainant disputed the £400 fee. The Ombudsman ruled that the council had no power to charge a £400 fee since neither the Insolvency Rules nor any other legislation permitted recovery of fees for a statutory demand or an arrangement unless a bankruptcy order was made.

Outcome: the Ombudsman found maladministration. The council accepted it was not entitled to charge the fee and it ceased to do so in similar cases. It refunded the £400 to the complainant, restored the right to pay in instalments, waived an additional £42.50 in bailiff fees incurred and made a £40 goodwill payment.

Conduct of council resulting in illness

Calderdale Metropolitan Borough Council (19 005 195) 10 September 2020

Mrs X and her partner were eligible for student council tax exemptions. The council wrongly removed these exemptions and failed to correct the mistake in a timely way. As a result, Mrs X (who has autism) overpaid £240.36. She repeatedly provided information that the council already had or should have accessed. The council issued multiple incorrect demands, and its failure to act on supplied information caused distress. The constant demands from the council and the wrong information it supplied to her increased her anxiety and made her ill.

Outcome: the council was directed to apologise to Mrs X, refund her the £240.36 and pay her an additional £500 for the distress and inconvenience. The council was also advised to review its complaints procedure to ensure a senior manager unconnected with the case reviewed complaints at the first stage.

Council failure to respect payment agreement

Cotswold Council (20 008 553) 5 August 2021

Mr X complained it was wrong of the council to send him reminders to pay council tax bills when he was already making agreed payments and that it did not properly consider his request to write off arrears. The council also failed to promptly process his request for council tax support. He complained that the actions of the council caused him financial hardship and poor health.

Outcome: the Ombudsman directed the council to apologise and pay Mr X £300 for distress and uncertainty; reconsider the write-off application and invite him to apply for discretionary relief; publish a discretionary relief policy on its website and provide training and guidance for staff.

Old address used for enforcement

London Borough of Croydon Council (21 009 512) 29 March 2022

Mrs X complained that the council used her old address for recovering unpaid council tax. Despite the fact that the council tax correspondence was returned to sender, the council continued to pursue recovery action using the outdated address. This led to added recovery costs being incurred.

Outcome: the council agreed to refund the recovery costs of £495.50.

Confusion over accounts and delay

London Borough of Barnet [2023] (21 017 371) 23 March 2023

The council wrongly closed a taxpayer's council tax account and opened a new one. The taxpayer was repeatedly assured her account was in credit and she was promised a refund. After 10 months, the council realised its error, issued a demand, obtained a liability order and instructed debt collectors, who went to the wrong address. When the taxpayer complained, the council responded by email rather than post, and failed to address all her points.

Outcome: the Ombudsman found the situation caused significant confusion and distress. It found the council at fault for how it handled the matter and directed that the situation be considered by the full council, its cabinet or the appropriate committee. The council was directed to pay £334 to clear the taxpayer's council tax arrears and contact her by post in future.

Delay in processing a discretionary reduction under section 13A of the Local Government Finance Act 1992

Vale of Glamorgan Council (20 220 3385) 30 November 2022

Mrs H submitted a CTR application in January 2021, but received no response. She also submitted a section 13A discretionary reduction application, which went unanswered for over a year, and only then after she complained in May 2022.

Outcome: had the council processed the claim within its policy timescales, it would have identified earlier that no application had been received and notified Mrs H. Mrs H would likely have resubmitted the application by June 2021, making her eligible for backdating from 1 April 2021. The council agreed to apologise for the delay in processing the discretionary CTR claim and to process Mrs H's CTR as though it had been received in June 2021, thereby backdating the reduction for 1 April 2021 to 28 September 2021.

Failure to communicate and provide help

Caerphilly County Council (20 220 6541) 1 February 2023

Ms L reported ongoing difficulties understanding her council tax payments and the amounts the council presented. She also complained that the council failed to provide help and support in resolving her concerns.

Outcome: the Ombudsman concluded the council failed to clearly communicate the breakdown of Ms L's council tax payments and the lack of clarity caused her confusion and frustration. As an alternative to investigation, the council agreed to provide Ms L with a detailed summary of the current outstanding council tax balance and the amounts within 30 working days.

Retaining body-worn video footage

Merton London Borough Council (23 001 234) 24 March 2024

Ms X complained about how the council dealt with her council tax account and the enforcement action taken to recover unpaid amounts. She also complained about the enforcement agent's conduct. The Ombudsman found no fault in how the council handled or recovered the council tax debt. However, there was fault in the council's failure to follow its own policy on retaining body-worn video footage from enforcement agents. The policy requires footage to be kept for three months, but this was not done in Ms X's case.

Outcome: although the failure did not cause a personal injustice to Ms X, the Ombudsman agreed it was appropriate for the council to remind staff about the importance of adhering to the body-worn video retention policy. The council was ordered to provide evidence that this action had been completed.

Failure to respond to a freedom of information request

Hackney London Borough Council (23 019 914) 14 March 2024

Miss X argued that the council mistakenly pursued enforcement action on her council tax account. She also complained that the council did not respond to her freedom of information (FOI) request, which violated her right to access information under the Freedom of Information Act 2000.

Outcome: the council apologised for its handling of Miss X's account and the mistaken enforcement action. It offered Miss X £100 for the error, plus £150 for time, trouble and distress. The Ombudsman considered this to be a suitable and proportionate remedy. Regarding the FOI issue, the Ombudsman concluded that this issue was better dealt with by the Information Commissioner. No further investigation was deemed necessary, as it would not lead to a different outcome.

3. Complaining to the local auditor

You can complain about the local authority's financial coduct to the local auditor. Local authorities – including county, district, borough and parish councils – have a duty to:

- properly account for public money; *and*
- operate in line with the law and proper standards; *and*
- use resources economically, efficiently and effectively.

To fulfil these responsibilities, local authorities must:

- maintain robust governance arrangements for managing financial affairs and resources;
- report on these arrangements in their annual governance statements and published accounts.

The audit process is considered a key part of democratic accountability, giving taxpayers a role in holding local authorities to account.[46]

The local auditor is required to act independently, impartially and without bias or the appearance of bias.[47] Although the local authority pays the auditor, the investigation process must remain wholly independent. Following the case of *Nicolson v Tottenham Magistrates' Court* (see p220), members of the public may make referrals to the auditor about the costs of seeking liability orders.

When to report to the local auditor

You can contact the auditor if you believe the authority is failing in its financial duties. Common examples related to council tax include:

- excessive or unlawful liability order costs;
- improper accounting of payments received or recovered;
- refusal to accept payment which leads to extra costs for the taxpayer;
- unjustifiable charges or other irregularities in local tax collection.

The auditor has a range of powers including:

- issuing a public interest report to highlight issues of concern;[48]
- issuing an advisory notice;
- applying to the court for a declaration that an item of account is unlawful, or to prevent unlawful expenditure.[49]

When the auditor conducts an investigation or issues a public interest report, the reasonable costs of preparing and publishing the report must be covered by the local authority.[50]

In England, the law on the auditing of local authorities is governed by the Local Audit and Accountability Act 2014 and by the Code of Audit Practice issued by the National Audit Office (available at nao.org.uk). In April 2025, the government published a commitment to local audit reform and establishing a statutory and independent Local Audit Office in England.[51]

In Wales, the Wales Audit Office is responsible for auditing local authorities. Its code of practice is available at audit.wales/publication/code-audit-practice.

In Scotland, local authority auditing is carried out by Audit Scotland, which provides the Auditor General and the Accounts Commission with services for checking financial conduct on the part of local government.[52]

4. **Action through the courts**

The Ombudsman exists to supplement, not replace, the courts.[53] The use of the civil courts is the ultimate recourse of the citizen who is a victim of bureaucratic wrongdoing.[54]

In some cases, such as the recovery of overpaid council tax, the regulations give a direct legal right to reclaim sums. More generally, individuals can use the county court to challenge wrongful acts or omissions by a local authority, including through arbitration procedures. Local authorities may be held liable in civil law for the actions of their officers and employees (just as private individuals or companies can be). Civil claims may include negligence, breach of statutory duty (eg, failing to process a council tax reduction application) or misfeasance in a public office (ie, where officials knowingly act unlawfully, with malice or bad faith).[55] Misfeasance in a public office is recognised in Scotland, supported by English law authorities.[56]

Authorities may also be sued for personal injury, distress, loss of liberty or wrongful imprisonment, including claims for aggravated and exemplary damages in serious cases.

The authority is liable for the costs of its servants' acts and defaults, as are individual officers if sued personally, or possibly even on a third-party costs basis in exceptional circumstances.[57] Seek legal advice before commencing such civil claims.

The small claims jurisdiction of the county court may be used for acts and omissions by local authorities. The small claims track (for claims under £10,000) is particularly accessible as it is relatively cheap to use, and people on low incomes or benefits may be entitled to a fee waiver.[58] Neither side can typically claim legal costs, which limits financial risk. If the council ignores court proceedings, a default judgment may be entered against the authority and, if listed as a defendant, against named officers.

In rare and serious cases, maladministration may amount to criminal conduct – eg, corruption or fraud. Officers of the council, outsourced agents or trustees in bankruptcy may face criminal proceedings, although in some cases, liability may be limited by statute. For example, actions against trustees in bankruptcy may be limited to cases where a trustee of a bankrupt's estate has misapplied or retained money or property or where a bankrupt taxpayer's estate has suffered any loss in consequence of any misfeasance or breach of fiduciary or other duty.[59]

Where maladministration is potentially criminal liability, the matter can be reported to the police, who are obliged to investigate. If the police fail to act, you can start a private prosecution.[60]

Judicial review in the High Court or Court of Session

Judicial review is a legal process used to challenge decisions, actions or failures by public bodies, including local authorities, in the High Court (England and Wales) or the Court of Session (Scotland). Judicial review should only be used as a last resort, after all other complaints or appeal routes have been exhausted or are unavailable.

Get legal advice, as this type of action can be costly. Visit cpag.org.uk/jr for a useful guide to the judicial review process.

Judicial review is a three-stage process which requires action within three months of the wrongful decision.

In England and Wales, judicial review procedure is governed by Part 54 of the Civil Procedure Rules. You can find details in *The Supreme Court Practice,* known as 'The White Book', and online at justice.gov.uk/courts/procedure-rules/civil. In Scotland, the procedure is governed by Chapter 58 of the Rules of Court – see scotcourts.gov.uk/rules-and-practice/rules-of-court/court-of-session-rules.

In England and Wales, the first step (the pre-action protocol) involves serving a 'letter before claim' on the authority, warning it of your intention to seek judicial review and providing 14 days for it to respond (the 14-day period must not overrun the three-month time limit for an application to the High Court). There are no costs and no risk of paying the other side's costs during the pre-action stage. Failure to comply with the pre-action protocol can result in sanctions against the local authority if the matter reaches the High Court, potentially incurring high costs. If the local authority's response is unsatisfactory, you can start an application for leave for judicial review in the Administrative Court, part of the High Court. If your issue is not resolved at the pre-action stage, you are not required to pursue the matter to the next stage (ie, actual litigation) if you do not want to go to court.

The pre-action protocol does not apply in Scotland, but it is good practice to avoid litigation and sending a letter before claim can provide a way of doing so.

Letter before claim

Use the following structure when drafting your letter before claim to ensure you include all the information required by the pre-action protocol.

Background facts

What are your circumstances? Give relevant details of your family, your health and housing.

What has happened? Include relevant dates.

What actions have already been taken to try to resolve the dispute?

What has been the effect on you of the decision or action being challenged?

Legal background

What does the legislation say should have happened?

What does any caselaw say should have happened?

What does guidance suggest should have happened?

How is this different to what, in fact, has happened – ie, to the decision/action you are challenging?

Grounds for judicial review

What are your reasons for requesting judicial review? These are your 'grounds for judicial review'.

Alternative remedies

If there is an alternative remedy, explain how you have exhausted it, or justify why you are not using it.

Details of the action you expect the local authority to take

Explain what you are asking for. This will depend on the grounds for your judicial review. If you have challenged the local authority's failure to do something, your request will be for it to do that thing and might also include a request to improve future decision making.

In England and Wales, the court can cancel the wrongful decision (a 'quashing order') or require the authority to do or cease doing something unlawful (known as a 'mandatory order' or 'prohibitory order'). In Scotland, a decision can be quashed by 'reduction' and a 'declarator' (known as a 'declaration' in England and Wales) can be established to ascertain the legal position.

In England and Wales, judicial review requires permission (leave) from the High Court. A judge will first assess whether the case has sufficient merit. If permission is granted, the court issues directions to you, the local authority, and any magistrates' court involved (such as in liability order or committal proceedings). If the case is not resolved at this stage, it may proceed to a full judicial review hearing in the Administrative Court, where a judge (or judges) will review the legality of the original decision. The court may grant a remedy and determine who should pay costs. Costs are at the court's discretion. Any party to an appeal may be subject to a costs order if the case is contested. However, when a local authority or public body has acted badly, costs may be refused.[61] In rare cases, costs may be made against magistrates, clerks or tribunals where bad faith is proven.[62]

In Scotland, the procedure is similar, except no pre-action protocol is required. Judicial review starts by lodging a petition with the Court of Session. Permission to proceed will be granted if the application shows sufficient interest and a real prospect of success. If permission is refused, you have a right to an oral hearing before a different judge and, if necessary, a further appeal to the Inner House of the Court of Session.[63]

Notes

1. **Complaining to the local authority**

1 ss50 and 76A FOIA 2000

2. **Complaining to the Ombudsman**

2 **E** s23 LGA 1974
W PSO(W)A 2019; Public Services Ombudsman (Wales) Act 2005
S SPSA 2002

3 Local Government and Social Care Ombudsman, *Annual Report and Accounts 2023-2024*, 7 January 2025

4 ss24A(6) and 34B(8) LGA 1974
5 **E** s29(2) LGA 1974
W s19(3) PSO(W)A 2019
S s13(4) SPSA 2002
6 s1 Parliamentary and Health Service Commissioners Act 1987
7 PHSO, Summary 464, October 2014
8 Reg 5 The Local Authority Social Services and National Health Service Complaints (England) Regulations 2009 No.309
9 Available at ombudsman.org.uk/about-us/our-principles/principles-good-administration
10 House of Commons debates; Parliamentary Commissioner Act 1967
11 *R v Commissioner for Local Administration, ex parte Eastleigh BC* [1988] 3 All ER 151, per Lord Donaldson MR
12 ss2-5 SPSA 2002; see *Terri McCue as guardian of Andrew McCue Petitioner and Reclaimer for Judicial Review Against A Decision of Glasgow City Council* [2020] CSIH 51
13 s28(1) LGA 1974
14 s28(2) LGA 1974
15 s28(4) LGA 1974; *R (on the application of Piffs Elm Ltd) v Commission of Local Administration for England and Tewkesbury BC* [2023] EWCA Civ 486
16 Ombudsman Report 14 001 797, Adur DC, 11 February 2015, para 37
17 Ombudsman Report 19 0008 828, LB Haringey, 15 January 2020
18 LGSCO, *Equal Access: getting it right for people with disabilities*, May 2022; Calderdale MBC 19 005 195, 10 September 2020
19 For example, see LGSCO Report 1900 195 Calderdale MBC, 10 September 2020
20 The Public Sector Bodies (Websites and Mobile Applications) (No.2) Accessibility Regulations 2018 No.952
21 LGSCO, *Council Tax Reduction: guidance for practitioners*, August 2019
22 Report by Commissioner Jerry White, Complaint 03/B/12862, 29 September 2004
23 See england.shelter.org.uk/professional_resources/legal/court_action_and_complaints/court_process_and_hearings/witness_statements
24 r328 Civil Procedure Rules and Practice Direction 32
25 Complaint and decision 17 011 640, LB Merton, 4 May 2018
26 Ombudsman Report 19 010 618, LB Bexley, 11 March 2020
27 Ombudsman Report 13 016 986, Birmingham City Council, 3 June 2014
28 Ombudsman Report 13 011 879, Rochdale MBC, 21 August 2014
29 **E** s26 LGA 1974
W s13 PSO(W)A 2019
S s7(8) SPSA 2002
30 Ombudsman Report 13 007 295, Medway Council, 18 December 2014
31 'Ombudsman and Enforcement Conduct Board sign agreement', *Local Government Ombudsman and Social Care Information News*, 28 May 2025
32 See Ombudsman Report 19 013 049, LB Barnet,17 September 2020
33 Ombudsman Report 15 006 127, Birmingham City Council, 6 June 2016
34 s30 LGA 1974
35 *R (on the application of Milburn) v Local Government and Social Care Ombudsman and Oldham DC* [2022] EWHC 1777 (Admin)
36 *R (on the application of Milburn) v Local Government and Social Care Ombudsman and Oldham DC* [2022] EWHC 1777 (Admin), para 36
37 s26(6) LGA 1974
38 **EW** s26(6)(a) LGA 1974
S s7(8) SPSA 2002
39 Ombudsman Report 14 020 112, Tunbridge Wells BC, 8 March 2016
40 ss30(1B) and 34H(i) LGA 1974, as amended
41 s92 Local Government Act 2000
42 *R v Comr for Local Administration, ex p Eastleigh BC* (1988) 86 LGR 491
43 *R (on the application of Paula Gallagher and Mary McCarthy) v Basildon DC* [2010] EWHC 2824
44 *Stojak, R (on the application of) v Sheffield City Council* [2009] EWHC 3412
45 See *R (on the application of Bournemouth, Christchurch and Poole Council) v LGSCO* [2025] EWHC 224 (Admin) and *R v Local Commissioner for Administration for the North and East of England ex parte Bradford Metropolitan City Council* [1979] QB 287

3. **Complaining to the local auditor**

46 *R (Veolia ES Nottinghamshire) v Nottinghamshire* CC [2010] EWHC 2382
47 *R (on the application of Webb v LB Bromley* [2023] EWHC 2091
48 Sch 7 LAAA 2014
49 ss28 and 29 LAAA 2014

50 s24 and Sch LAAA 2014
51 MHCLG, *Local Audit Reform: a strategy for overhauling the local audit system in England*, 9 April 2025
52 audit-scotland.gov.uk

4. **Action through the courts**

53 J Auburn, J Moffatt and A Sharland, *Judicial Review: principles and procedure*, Oxford University Press, 2013, para 26.110
54 *Ferguson v British Gas Trading Ltd* [2009] EWCA Civ 46
55 *Three Rivers DC v Bank of England (No.3)* [2003] AC 1, reported as [2000] 3 All ER 1; *Coghlan v Chief Constable of Greater Manchester Police* [2018] EWHC 1784 (QB)
56 *Robert Francis Phipps (AP) Pursuer v the Royal College of Surgeons of Edinburgh Defenders* [2010] CSOH 58
57 See s51 Senior Courts Act 1981; *Dymocks Franchise Systems (NSW) Pty Ltd v Todd and others* [2004] UKPC 39; *R v LB Lambeth, ex parte Wilson* [1997] 3 FCR 437; *Flatman v Germany*; *Weddall v Barchester Healthcare Ltd* [2011] EWHC 2945 (QB)
58 Form EX160, at gov.uk/government/publications/apply-for-help-with-court-and-tribunal-fees
59 s304 IA 1986; *Oraki and another v Bramston and another* [2016] 2 All ER 1065
60 *R v Stewart* [1896] 1 QB 300
61 *Wiltshire Council v Piggin* [2014] EWHC 4386 (Admin)
62 *R v Newcastle Under Lyme Magistrates' Court ex parte Massey* [1995] 1 All ER 125; *R (on the application of Desouza) v Croydon Magistrates' Court* [2012] EWHC 1362 (Admin); see also s108 Courts Act 2003; The Justices of the Peace and Authorised Court and Tribunal Staff (Costs) Regulations 2020 No.398, amended by Courts Reform (Scotland) Act 2014 (Consequential Provisions and Modifications) Order 2015 No.700
63 ss27B-27D Court of Session Act 1988

Appendix 1

Useful addresses

Valuation Office Agency

voa.gov.uk

England
Tel: 03000 501 501

Wales
Tel 03000 505 505

Scottish Assessors Association

saa.gov.uk

Valuation Tribunal for England

valuationtribunal.gov.uk
Tel: 0303 445 8100
Email: appeals@valuationtribunal.gov.uk

Head office (and London office)
Ground Floor, Fry Building
2 Marsham Street
London SW1P 4DF

Valuation Tribunal for Wales

22 Gold Tops
Newport NP20 4PG
Tel: 01633 255 003
Email: correspondence@valuationtribunal.wales
valuationtribunal.wales

Local Taxation Chamber (Scotland only)

First Floor, Bothwell House
Hamilton Business Park

Caird Park
Hamilton ML3 0QA
Tel: 01698 390 012
Email: LTCAdmin@scotcourtstribunals.gov.uk
localtaxationchamber.scot

Local Government and Social Care Ombudsman

England

PO Box 4771
Coventry CV4 0EH
Tel: 0300 061 0614
lgo.org.uk

Public Services Ombudsman for Wales

1 Ffordd yr Hen Gae
Pencoed CF35 5LJ
Tel: 0300 790 0203
Email: ask@ombudsman.wales
ombudsman.wales

Scottish Public Services Ombudsman

Bridgeside House
99 McDonald Road
Edinburgh EH7 4NS
(Or request a Freepost envelope by phone or the online contact form)
Tel: 0800 377 7330
spso.org.uk/spso

Parliamentary and Health Service Ombudsman

Citygate
Mosley Street
Manchester M2 3HQ
Tel: 0345 015 4033
ombudsman.org.uk

The Adjudicator

The Adjudicator's Office
PO Box 11222
Nottingham NG2 9AD
Tel: 0300 057 1111
adjudicatorsoffice.gov.uk

Appendix 2

National Standards for Enforcement Agents

Taking Control of Goods: National Standards

Issued 6 April 2014 by the Ministry of Justice

Vulnerable situations

70. Enforcement agents/agencies and creditors must recognise that they each have a role in ensuring that the vulnerable and socially excluded are protected and that the recovery process includes procedures agreed between the agent/agency and creditor about how such situations should be dealt with. The appropriate use of discretion is essential in every case and no amount of guidance could cover every situation. Therefore the agent has a duty to contact the creditor and report the circumstances in situations where there is evidence of a potential cause for concern.

71. If necessary, the enforcement agent will advise the creditor if further action is appropriate. The exercise of appropriate discretion is needed, not only to protect the debtor, but also the enforcement agent who should avoid taking action which could lead to accusations of inappropriate behaviour.

72. Enforcement agents must withdraw from domestic premises if the only person present is, or appears to be, under the age of 16 or is deemed to be vulnerable by the enforcement agent; they can ask when the debtor will be home – if appropriate.

73. Enforcement agents must withdraw without making enquiries if the only persons present are children who appear to be under the age of 12.

74. A debtor may be considered vulnerable if, for reasons of age, health or disability, they are unable to safeguard their personal welfare or the personal welfare of other members of the household.

75. The enforcement agent must be sure that the debtor or the person to whom they are entering into a controlled goods agreement understands the agreement and the consequences if the agreement is not complied with.

76. Enforcement agents should be aware that vulnerability may not be immediately obvious.

77. Some groups who might be vulnerable are listed below. However, this list is not exhaustive. Care should be taken to assess each situation on a case by case basis.

- the elderly;
- people with a disability;
- the seriously ill;
- the recently bereaved;
- single parent families;
- pregnant women;
- unemployed people; *and*
- those who have obvious difficulty in understanding, speaking or reading English.

78. Wherever possible, enforcement agents should have arrangements in place for rapidly accessing interpretation services (including British Sign Language), when these are needed, and provide on request information in large print or in Braille for debtors with impaired sight.

Appendix 3

Abbreviations used in the notes

AAC	Administrative Appeals Chamber
AC	Appeal Cases
Admin	Administrative Court
All ER	All England Law Reports
Art(s)	article(s)
BPIR	Bankruptcy and Personal Insolvency Reports
CA	Court of Appeal
Ch	Chancery Division
CO	Crown Office
COD	Crown Office Digest
Cr App R	Criminal Appeal Report
CSIH	Scotland Court of Session, Inner House
CSOH	Scotland Court of Session, Outer House
E	England
EHRR	European Human Rights Reports
EWCA (Civ)	England and Wales Court of Appeal (Civil Division)
EWCA (Crim)	England and Wales Court of Appeal (Criminal Division)
EWHC	England and Wales High Court
FCR	Family Court Reports
HC	High Court
HL	House of Lords
Imm AR	Immigration Appeal Reports
JP	Justice of the Peace Reports
KB	King's Bench Reports
LC	Lands Chamber
LGR	Local Government Reports
LJ	Lord Justice
LO	listing officer
para(s)	paragraph(s)
P&CR	Property, Planning and Compensation Reports
PTSR	Public and Third Sector Law Reports
QB	Queen's Bench Reports
QBD	Queen's Bench Division
r(r)	rule(s)
RA	Rating Appeals
Reg(s)	Regulation(s)
RVR	Rating and Valuation Reports
S	Scotland
s(s)	section(s)
SC	Session Cases
Sch(s)	Schedule(s)
SCLR	Scottish Civil Law Reports
STC	Simon's Tax Cases
TCC	Tax and Chancery Chamber
UKFTT	UK First-tier Tribunal
UKHL	UK House of Lords
UKSC	UK Supreme Court
UKUT	UK Upper Tribunal (Administrative Appeals Chamber)
UTLC	Upper Tribunal (Lands Chamber)
VO	valuation officer
VOA	Valuation Office Agency
VTE	Valuation Tribunal for England
VTE CPS 2024	Valuation Tribunal for England Consolidated Practice Statement 2024, effective from 1 April 2024
VTW	Valuation Tribunal for Wales
W	Wales
WLR	Weekly Law Reports

Acts of Parliament

CSPSSA 2000	Child Support, Pensions and Social Security Act 2000
FOIA 2000	Freedom of Information Act 2000
IA 1986	Insolvency Act 1986
LA 2011	Localism Act 2011
LAAA 2014	Local Audit and Accountability Act 2014
LGA 1974	Local Government Act 1974
LGA 1992	Local Government Act 1992
LGA 2003	Local Government Act 2003
LGFA 1988	Local Government Finance Act 1988
LGFA 1992	Local Government Finance Act 1992
LGFA 2012	Local Government Finance Act 2012
LGF(W)A 2024	Local Government Finance (Wales) Act 2024
LUR Act 2023	Levelling-up and Regeneration Act 2023
PSO(W)A 2019	Public Services Ombudsman (Wales) Act 2019
SPSA 2002	Scottish Public Services Ombudsman Act 2002
SSAA 1992	Social Security Administration Act 1992
TCEA 2007	Tribunals, Courts and Enforcement Act 2007

Regulations and other statutory instruments

Each set of regulations has a statutory instrument (SI) number and date. You can find them all at legislation.gov.uk.

CCCTNR(E)(MC) Regs	The Community Charges, Council Tax and Non-Domestic Rating (Enforcement) (Magistrates' Courts) (England) Regulations 2000 No.2026
CT(AE) Regs	The Council Tax (Administration and Enforcement) Regulations 1992 No.613
CT(AE)(A)(E) Regs	The Council Tax (Administration and Enforcement) (Amendment) (England) Regulations 2004 No.927
CT(AE)(A)(No.2)(E) Regs	The Council Tax (Administration and Enforcement) (Amendment) (No.2) (England) Regulations 2012 No.3086
CT(AE)(A)(W) Regs	The Council Tax (Administration and Enforcement) (Amendment) (Wales) Regulations 2007 No.582
CT(AE)(AEO)(W) Regs	The Council Tax (Administration and Enforcement) (Attachment of Earnings Order) (Wales) Regulations 1992 No.1741
CT(AE)(S) Regs	The Council Tax (Administration and Enforcement) (Scotland) Regulations 1992 No.1332

CT(ALA) Regs	The Council Tax (Alteration of Lists and Appeals) Regulations 1993 No.290
CT(ALA)(A)(W) Regs	The Council Tax (Alteration of Lists and Appeals) (Amendment) (Wales) Regulations 2010 No.77
CT(ALA)(E) Regs	The Council Tax (Alteration of Lists and Appeals) (England) Regulations 2009 No.2270
CT(ALA)(E)(A) Regs	The Council Tax (Alteration of Lists and Appeals) (England) (Amendment) Regulations 2013 No.467
CT(ALA)(S) Regs	The Council Tax (Alteration of Lists and Appeals) (Scotland) Regulations 1993 No.355
CT(APDD) Regs	The Council Tax (Additional Provisions for Discount Disregards) Regulations 1992 No.552
CT(APDD) Amdt Regs	The Council Tax (Additional Provisions for Discount Disregards) Amendment Regulations 1996 No.637
CT(CD)O	The Council Tax (Chargeable Dwellings) Order 1992 No.549
CT(CDEDDD)(A)(E) Regs	The Council Tax (Chargeable Dwellings, Exempt Dwellings and Discount Disregards) (Amendment) (England) Order 2003 No.3121
CT(CVL) Regs	The Council Tax (Contents of Valuation Lists) Regulations 1992 No.553
CT(D)(S)(A) Regs 1993	The Council Tax (Discounts) (Scotland) Amendment Regulations 1993 No.342
CT(D)(S)(A) Regs 1995	The Council Tax (Discounts) (Scotland) Amendment Regulations 1995 No.597
CT(D)(S)(A)O	The Council Tax (Discounts) (Scotland) Amendment Order 1993 No.343
CT(D)(S)CAO	The Council Tax (Discounts) (Scotland) Consolidation and Amendment Order 2003 No.176
CT(D)(S)O	The Council Tax (Discounts) (Scotland) Order 1992 No.1408
CT(D)(S) Regs	The Council Tax (Discounts) (Scotland) Regulations 1992 No.1409
CT(DD)O	The Council Tax (Discount Disregards) Order 1992 No.548
CT(DD)(A)(E)O	The Council Tax (Discount Disregards) (Amendment) (England) Order 2006 No.3396
CT(DD)(A)(W)O	The Council Tax (Discount Disregards) (Amendment) (Wales) Order 2007 No.580
CT(DDED)(A)O	The Council Tax (Discount Disregards and Exempt Dwellings) (Amendment) Order 1995 No.619
CT(DIS) Regs	The Council Tax (Deductions from Income Support) Regulations 1993 No.494

CT(DN)(E) Regs	The Council Tax (Demand Notices) (England) Regulations 2010 No.2990
CT(DN)(E) Regs 2011	The Council Tax (Demand Notices) (England) Regulations 2011 No.3038
CT(DN)(E)(A) Regs	The Council Tax (Demand Notices) (England) (Amendment) Regulations 2012 No.3087
CT(DN)(W) Regs	The Council Tax (Demand Notices) (Wales) Regulations 1993 No.255
CT(DN)(W)(A) Regs	The Council Tax (Demand Notices) (Wales) (Amendment) Regulations 2013 No.63
CT(DPRS)(S) Regs	The Council Tax (Dwellings and Part Residential Subjects) (Scotland) Regulations 1992 No.2955
CT(DUD)(S) Regs	The Council Tax (Discount for Unoccupied Dwellings) (Scotland) Regulations 2005 No.51
CT(Dw)(E) Regs	The Council Tax (Prescribed Classes of Dwellings) (England) Regulations 2003 No.3011
CT(Dw)(S) Regs	The Council Tax (Dwellings) (Scotland) Regulations 1992 No.1334
CT(Dw)(S) Regs 2010	The Council Tax (Dwellings) (Scotland) Regulations 2010 No.35
CT(ED)O	The Council Tax (Exempt Dwellings) Order 1992 No.558
CT(ED)(A)O	The Council Tax (Exempt Dwellings) (Amendment) Order 1994 No.539
CT(ED)(A)(E)O 2005	The Council Tax (Exempt Dwellings) (Amendment) (England) Order 2005 No.2865
CT(ED)(A)(E)O 2006	The Council Tax (Exempt Dwellings) (Amendment) (England) Order 2006 No.23185
CT(ED)(A)(W)O	The Council Tax (Exempt Dwellings) (Amendment) (Wales) Order 2000 No.1025
CT(ED)(E)(A)O 2012	The Council Tax (Exempt Dwellings) (England) (Amendment) Order 2012 No.2965
CT(ED)(S)O 1992	The Council Tax (Exempt Dwellings) (Scotland) Order 1992 No.1333
CT(ED)(S)O 1997	The Council Tax (Exempt Dwellings) (Scotland) Order 1997 No.728
CT(ED)(S)O 2002	The Council Tax (Exempt Dwellings) (Scotland) Amendment Order 2002 No.101
CT(ED)(S)(A)O	The Council Tax (Exempt Dwellings) (Scotland) Amendment Order 2006 No.402
CT(ED)(S)(A)O 1995	The Council Tax (Exempt Dwellings) (Scotland) Amendment Order 1995 No.598

CT(ED)(S)(A)O 2007	The Council Tax (Exempt Dwellings) (Scotland) Amendment Order 2007 No.215
CT(ED)(S)(A)O 2012	The Council Tax (Exempt Dwellings) (Scotland) Amendment Order 2012 No.339
CT(ED)(S)(A)O 2018	The Council Tax (Exempt Dwellings) (Scotland) Amendment Order 2018 No.45
CT(ED)(S)(A)O 2022	The Council Tax (Exempt Dwellings) (Scotland) Amendment Order 2022 No.124
CT(ED)(S)(A)O 2023	The Council Tax (Exempt Dwellings) (Scotland) Amendment Order 2023 No.36
CT(ED)(S)(A)O 2025	The Council Tax (Exempt Dwellings) (Scotland) Amendment Order 2025 No.56
CT(EHA)(W) Regs	The Council Tax (Exceptions to Higher Amounts) (Wales) Regulations 2015 No.2068
CT(EDDD)(A)O	The Council Tax (Exempt Dwellings and Discount Disregards) (Amendment) Order 1998 No.291
CT(LO) Regs	The Council Tax (Liability for Owners) Regulations 1992 No.551
CT(LO)(A)(E) Regs	The Council Tax (Liability for Owners) (Amendment) (England) Regulations 2003 No.3125
CT(LO)(A)(W) Regs	The Council Tax (Liability for Owners) (Amendment) (Wales) Regulations 2004 No.2920
CT(LO)(S) Regs	The Council Tax (Liability of Owners) (Scotland) Regulations 1992 No.1331
CT(PCD)(E) Regs	The Council Tax (Prescribed Classes of Dwellings) (England) Regulations 2003 No.3011
CT(PCD)(W) Regs	The Council Tax (Prescribed Class of Dwellings) (Wales) Regulations 1992 No.3023
CT(RD) Regs	The Council Tax (Reductions for Disabilities) Regulations 1992 No.554
CT(RD)(S) Regs	The Council Tax (Reductions for Disabilities) (Scotland) Regulations 1992 No.1335
CT(RDTA)(W)(A) Regs	The Council Tax (Reductions for Disabilities and Transitional Arrangements) (Wales) (Amendment) Regulations 2005 No.702
CT(SVD) Regs	The Council Tax (Situation and Valuation of Dwellings) Regulations 1992 No.550
CT(SVD)(W)(A) Regs	The Council Tax (Situation and Valuation of Dwellings) (Wales) (Amendment) Regulations 2005 No.701
CT(TA)(W) Regs	The Council Tax (Transitional Arrangements) (Wales) Regulations 2004 No.3142

CT(VALA)(E) Regs	The Council Tax (Valuations, Alteration of Lists and Appeals) (England) Regulations 2008 No.315
CT(VD)(S) Regs	The Council Tax (Valuation of Dwellings) (Scotland) Regulations 1992 No.1329
CT(VD)(S)(A) Regs	The Council Tax (Valuation of Dwellings) (Scotland) Amendment Regulations 1993 No.354
CT(VUD)(S) Regs	The Council Tax (Variation for Unoccupied Dwellings) (Scotland) Amendment Regulations 2016 No.369
CTNDR(DN)(E) Regs	The Council Tax and Non-Domestic Rating (Demand Notices) (England) Regulations 2003 No.2613
CTR(S) Regs	The Council Tax Reduction (Scotland) Regulations 2021 No.249
CTR(S)A(No.2) Regs	The Council Tax Reduction (Scotland) Amendment (No. 2) Regulations 2013 No.218
CTR(SPC)(S) Regs	The Council Tax Reduction (State Pension Credit) (Scotland) Regulations 2012 No.319
CTRS(DFE)(E) Regs	The Council Tax Reduction Schemes (Detection of Fraud and Enforcement) (England) Regulations 2013 No.501
CTRS(DFE)(W) Regs	The Council Tax Reduction Schemes (Detection of Fraud and Enforcement) (Wales) Regulations 2013 No.588
CTRS(DS)(E) Regs	The Council Tax Reduction Schemes (Default Scheme) (England) Regulations 2012 No.2886
CTRS(DS)(W) Regs	The Council Tax Reduction Schemes (Default Scheme) (Wales) Regulations 2012 No.3145
CTRS(PR)(E) Regs	The Council Tax Reduction Schemes (Prescribed Requirements) (England) Regulations 2012 No.2885
CTRSPR(W) Regs	The Council Tax Reduction Schemes and Prescribed Requirements (Wales) Regulations 2012 No.3144
DFA Regs	The Discretionary Financial Assistance Regulations 2001 No.1167
FTTSLTC(RP) Regs	The First-tier Tribunal for Scotland Local Taxation Chamber (Rules of Procedure) Regulations 2022 No.364
LA(CR)CTI)(E) Regs	The Local Authorities (Conduct of Referendums) (Council Tax Increases) (England) Regulations 2012 No.444
LGFE(SP)O	The Local Government Finance (England) (Substitution of Penalties) Order 2008 No.981
TCG Regs	The Taking Control of Goods Regulations 2013 No.1894

TCG(F) Regs	The Taking Control of Goods (Fees) Regulations 2014 No.1
VCCT(Amdt) Regs	The Valuation and Community Charge Tribunals (Amendment) Regulations 1993 No.292
VT(A)(E) Regs	The Valuation Tribunals (Amendment) (England) Regulations 2000 No.409
VTE(CTRA)(P) Regs	The Valuation Tribunal for England (Council Tax and Rating Appeals) (Procedure) Regulations 2009 No.2269
VTE(CTRA)(P)(A) Regs	The Valuation Tribunal for England (Council Tax and Rating Appeals) (Procedure) (Amendment) Regulations 2013 No.465
VTENDRCT(E)(A) Regs	The Valuation Tribunal for England, Non-Domestic Rating and Council Tax (England) (Amendment) Regulations 2011 No.434
VTW Regs	The Valuation Tribunal for Wales Regulations 2010 No.713
VTW(W)(A) Regs	The Valuation Tribunal for Wales (Wales) (Amendment) Regulations 2013 No.547
WSSD(CUCLA)(S)O	The Water and Sewerage Services to Dwellings (Collection of Unmetered Charges by Local Authority) (Scotland) Order 2020 No.4

Other information

CTM Council Tax Manual (gov.uk/guidance/council-tax-manual)

Index

How to use this Index

Entries against the bold headings direct you to the general information on the subject, or where the subject is covered most fully. Sub-entries are listed alphabetically and direct you to specific aspects of the subject.